Reflections on Psyc Theories

Theories

Raiding the Inarticulate

Nigel Duffield

Konan University, Japan

CAMBRIDGE
UNIVERSITY PRESS

CAMBRIDGE
UNIVERSITY PRESS

University Printing House, Cambridge CB2 8BS, United Kingdom

One Liberty Plaza, 20th Floor, New York, NY 10006, USA

477 Williamstown Road, Port Melbourne, VIC 3207, Australia

314–321, 3rd Floor, Plot 3, Splendor Forum, Jasola District Centre,
New Delhi – 110025, India

79 Anson Road, #06-04/06, Singapore 079906

Cambridge University Press is part of the University of Cambridge.

It furthers the University's mission by disseminating knowledge in the pursuit of
education, learning, and research at the highest international levels of excellence.

www.cambridge.org
Information on this title: www.cambridge.org/9781108404648
DOI: 10.1017/9781108264969

First published 2018

Printed in the United Kingdom by Clays, St Ives plc

A catalogue record for this publication is available from the British Library.

ISBN 978-1-108-41715-0 Hardback
ISBN 978-1-108-40464-8 Paperback

Reflections on Psycholinguistic Theories

Raiding the Inarticulate

In a work that is part memoir, part monograph, Nigel Duffield offers a set of lyrical reflections on theories of psycholinguistics, which is concerned with how speakers use the languages they control, as well as with how such control is acquired in the first place. Written for professionals and enthusiastic amateurs alike, this book offers a 'well-tempered' examination of the conceptual and empirical foundations of the field.

In developing his ideas, the author draws on thirty years of direct professional experience of psycholinguistic theory and practice, across various sub-disciplines (including theoretical linguistics, cognitive psychology, philosophy and philology). The author's personal experience as a language learner, and as the father of three bilingual children, also plays a crucial role in shaping the discussion. Using examples from popular literature, song, poetry and comedy, the work examines many of the foundational questions that divide researchers from different intellectual traditions: these include the nature of 'linguistic competence', the arbitrariness of language and the theoretical implications of variation between speakers and across languages.

Born and raised in Belfast, Northern Ireland, Nigel Duffield received his university education in language and linguistics in England (Cambridge and London) and the USA (Los Angeles). A professor of English and Linguistics at Konan University (Kobe, Japan) since 2012, he has held previous positions in Germany, Canada, The Netherlands and England. His unique perspective on psycholinguistics is informed by his interactions with psycholinguists over a wide theoretical spectrum, and, especially, by his observations of the language development in his children, the youngest of whom was born with Down's Syndrome.

So here I am, in the middle way, having had twenty years –
Twenty years largely wasted, the years of l'entre deux guerres –
Trying to learn to use words, and every attempt
Is a wholly new start, and a different kind of failure
Because one has only learnt to get the better of words
For the thing one no longer has to say, or the way in which
One is no longer disposed to say it. And so each venture
Is a new beginning, a raid on the inarticulate,
With shabby equipment always deteriorating
In the general mess of imprecision of feeling,
Undisciplined squads of emotion.

T. S. Eliot, 'East Coker' (*Four Quartets*, 1943)

There seem to be only two kinds of people: those who think that metaphors
are facts, and those who know that they are not facts. Those who know they
are not facts are what we call 'atheists', and those who think they are facts
are 'religious'. Which group really gets the message?

Joseph Campbell, *Thou Art That: Transforming Religious Metaphor* (2013)

Contents

Part IV   A Tale of Two Cities

Figures

Tables

Introduction

In 2011, I was commissioned by a different publisher to produce an undergraduate introduction to psycholinguistics. The brief was to write a textbook that would cover the two main sub-fields of the discipline: EXPERIMENTAL PSYCHOLINGUISTICS – also known as language processing – which is concerned with how speakers understand and produce the languages they control, and DEVELOPMENTAL PSYCHOLINGUISTICS (language acquisition), which focuses on how such control is acquired in the first place. Although there are a number of excellent books available on one or other of these topics – Warren (2013), for example, provides a competent introduction to language processing, while Saxton (2010) offers a balanced and engaging discussion of many aspects of first language acquisition – there is currently no book that does dual service, so the commissioned title would have filled an awkward gap in the textbook market.

The gap remains, however, for this is not that book. It is not a conventional introduction to the field, inasmuch as it critically examines foundational issues in psycholinguistics, and sketches some (partially original) solutions to larger theoretical questions. Nor is it, especially, a survey of psycholinguistic research: I only discuss a handful of the hundreds of experimental studies that are relevant to the issues outlined here, postponing substantive discussion of experimental data to another volume.[1] It's probably not an undergraduate textbook either: whilst I hope that linguistics students will enjoy reading it, the book is unlikely to be assigned as a course text, since it's light on tested facts – an essential commodity of most undergraduate courses – and there are no graded exercises.

Even before the manuscript was halfway complete, it was clear to me (and to the original publisher) that this ugly duckling of a text was not going to walk or talk like a duck. Belatedly cut loose from my original contract, I was able to write unhampered by the need to provide an objective or comprehensive survey of contemporary psycholinguistics. What has emerged instead is a set of personal reflections on psycholinguistic theories; more generally, on the relationship between languages and the speakers who know and use them.

Several people have asked who this book is written for. The answer is simple: I wrote it for myself, in the first instance, to help me to make some sense of the theoretical issues and professional controversies that have engaged my attention for more than twenty years (*twenty years largely wasted*). To raid the inarticulate. As a reviewer of an earlier draft manuscript pointed out, everyone has their own way of making sense of their personal and professional lives: my way – like the protagonist in Nick Hornby's 1995 novel *High Fidelity* – is through popular music, also poetry, literature and verbal comedy. This book is an attempt to examine the foundations of psycholinguistics by these means.

So I didn't write it with a particular academic audience in mind. Still, I hope it will be of interest to anyone, from the lay reader to the less ideological of my professional friends and colleagues, who shares my passion for languages and love of literature, and who has some appreciation of irony.

Admittedly, some sections will be tough going for the former group. The book might be non-technical and is relatively free of jargon, but it is not 'dumbed down'; on the contrary, this is as intelligent a work as I am capable of writing. It would have been far easier to write a more difficult book. Conversely, the experts who read this will need to approach the arguments presented here in the same ecumenical spirit that I have tried to embrace, in setting them down. There are more inconsistencies and loose ends than would normally be permitted in a more conventional academic monograph: that, I suppose, is the fair price of being interesting. In the final analysis, this is a diversion, not a manifesto.

I am extremely grateful to Helen Barton, my commissioning editor at Cambridge University Press, and to the manuscript reviewers, for sharing my confidence in the feasibility of such an unlikely project. Scores of other people have helped me to bring the work this far: their contributions are acknowledged at the end of the book. See Acknowledgments, credits and permissions.

To set matters in context, I can do no better than to quote from one of the pre-eminent linguists of the modern period, Hermann Paul. In 1886, Paul published the second edition of his seminal work *Principien der Sprachgeschichte*. In the Preface (*Vorwort*), he wrote:

Auch diese zweite auflage wird vor den augen mancher fachgenossen nicht mehr gnade finden als die erste. Die einen werden sie zu allgemein, die anderen zu elementar finden. Manche werden etwas geistreicheres wünschen. Ich erkläre ein für allemal, dass ich nur für diejenigen schreibe, die mit mir der überzeugung sind, dass die wissenschaft nicht vorwärts gebracht wird durch complicerte hypothesen, mögen sie mit noch so viel geist und scharfsinn ausgeklügelt sein, sondern durch einfache grundgedanken, die an sich evident sind, die aber erst fruchtbar werden, wenn sie zu klarem bewusstsein gebracht und mit strenger consequenz durchgeführt werden.[2]

*This second edition will find no more favour in the eyes of many professional col-
leagues than did the first. Some will find it too general, others too elementary. Some
will wish for something more intellectually rigorous. I declare once and for all that
I only write for those who share my conviction: that science is not advanced by
complicated hypotheses – no matter the intellect or incisiveness of the minds that
produced them – but rather by simple basic ideas, which are rather trivial in themselves, but which yield insight once they are clearly articulated, and* consistently
followed through [original: mit strenger consequenz].

Hermann Paul, Principien der Sprachgeschichte (1880: ix)

[M]it strenger consequenz. Not being German, I might have some issues with
strenge[r] Konsequenz, but otherwise, Paul's remarks just about cover it,
130 years on. This book is written for serious amateurs – in the etymologically
faithful sense of the word – and for light-hearted professionals like myself, not
for ideologues or theoretical purists. To those, like Leon Jaworski, that 'would
rather have a competent extremist than an incompetent moderate', I'd point
out that there are other logical possibilities, that sometimes one learns more by
sitting on the fence than sniping over it.[3]

No-one likes to lose friends, however. In addition to Paul's predictions,
I well foresee that some colleagues will interpret this book as an attack on
Chomskyan linguistics; hence – given that I have been a card-carrying generativist for more than 25 years – as some kind of betrayal. If it is so construed,
then I will have failed in one of my goals in Part I, namely, to articulate the
difference between a 'Level 1 theory' of grammar on the one hand, and a viable
theory of psycholinguistics, one that appropriately captures the rich imperfec-
tions of our knowledge of languages, on the other. Any regard that I may have
as a theoretician for the austere simplicity of Minimalist theory is more than
offset by my deep suspicion and antipathy – as a parent, as a human being, as a
sentient organism – towards something as unnatural and biologically implausible as invariant perfection. We are, at every level of our being, from the genetic
to the metaphysical, confused and contradictory, full of redundancies in some
areas, gross inadequacies in others; we are shaped by our material circumstances, by our interactions with others, by our deficiencies.

> *There's a divinity that shapes our ends
> Rough-hew them how we will.*

William Shakespeare, Hamlet (5.2.10–11)

Throughout the history of philosophy and religion – those 'B-class cell-mates'
of the Library of Congress Classification (LCC) – people have found different
ways of interpreting these famous lines from *Hamlet*. To the more religious or
spiritual, divinity means just that: a divine spirit. To some atheists, especially
those unduly impressed by biological determinism, what 'shapes our ends'

more than the vagaries of experience is the genetics of our 'initial state': UG, as Chomskyans would have it. But divinity can just as profitably be understood in terms of our personal histories, the incremental sum of our prior interactions. It could even be claimed that it is the apprehension of these histories – more than general consciousness or the faculty of language – which distinguishes us from other animals. Whether or not that is the case, I am convinced that all of this rich imperfection is reflected in our knowledge and use of languages, and that an appropriate theory of psycholinguistics is one that embraces a significant chunk of that flawed estate. Echoing Hermann Paul, I write for those who share this conviction.

For what it is worth, even though I ultimately reject UG as an explanatory concept in language acquisition, and am sceptical of its relevance to theories of language processing, I subscribe to a considerably stronger and more substantive form of Universal Grammar than most current Chomskyans would be comfortable with. My theoretical research on the grammar of Modern Irish (latterly, on the syntax of Vietnamese) leads me to endorse Chomsky's early claim that:

[A]ll languages are cut to the same pattern.

Noam Chomsky, *Aspects of the Theory of Syntax* (1965: 30)

Or, as the thirteenth-century English philosopher Roger Bacon (1214–1294) had it:

Grammatica una et eadem est secundum substantiam in omnibus linguis, licet accidentaliter varietur.

Grammar is in its essence one and the same in all languages, even though it differs in superficial features.[4]

Roger Bacon, *Grammatica Graeca* 'Greek Grammar'

What we disagree on is the evidential base. My theoretical hunch about a version of the UNIVERSAL BASE HYPOTHESIS, broadly construed,[5] stems from a comparison of the surface properties of genetically and areally unrelated languages – properties that Chomsky once designated part of E-LANGUAGE when he still appeared interested enough in *languages*, in the popular understanding of the term, to dismiss them as objects of study. My intuition does not arise from any consideration of 'the child' as an idealised object, of 'discrete infinity', or of 'virtual conceptual necessity'. And since this book is about the fragments of languages in our minds, and not about generativist typology, I'll have very little to say here about the substance of any kind of Universal Grammar, abbreviated or otherwise.

I am also keenly aware of the fact that many of Chomsky's students and colleagues – some of whom I count as friends – have devoted their research careers to exploring grammatical variation within particular language families and across an extraordinarily diverse range of languages, and that the discoveries they have made in the course of these explorations have been inspired, facilitated and guided by some version of generative theory. From at least the 1980s onwards, the constant flow of MIT dissertations offering detailed analyses of the grammatical properties of almost every language family on earth gives the lie to the idea that generativist linguists (as a group) do not care about grammatical variation. However, virtually none of that work crucially depends on the deeper metatheoretical assumptions concerning innateness and the mental representation of grammar(s) that are the subject of this book, any more than the proper characterisation of String Theory depends on infants' understanding of gravity or object permanence. See Chapters 2 and 3 below.

The important thing, in science as in the law, is to respect the evidence at hand. It's no better to acquit an innocent defendant on the basis of a false alibi than it is to convict a guilty one on tainted testimony. So, even if it turned out that languages as diverse as French and Mohawk and Navajo were cut from the same grammatical cloth – see Mark Baker's excellent *Atoms of Language* (2001) for some compelling arguments in support of this idea, also Jonathan Bobaljik's *Universals of Comparative Morphology* (2012) – this wouldn't rescue UG from the charge of irrelevance when it comes to human psychology. In short, this book is not against Chomsky or Chomskyan theory, supposing it were rational to be against a theory, any more than a handbook on mediaeval architecture is against a theory of quantum mechanics. It is *for* something else.

Of course, there will also be those on the other side of the fence (and there are so many fences in linguistics) who may give this book a warmer reception, while protesting 'This is what we've been saying for years.' If your name is Joan Bybee, Peter Culicover, Hilary Putnam,[†] Stephen Levinson or Brian MacWhinney – to name only a few, on the other side of some fence or other – your complaint may be especially well-founded.[6] To those critics, my response must be that you haven't said it loudly, clearly or entertainingly enough, or with enough empirical evidence, for most generativists to pay attention. They're not a charitable bunch, on the whole, generative linguists: some of them are downright mean. In most cases, the problem lies with the fact that you haven't used their discourse or engaged with their data. With the exception of the discussions in I is for Internalism and O is for Object of Study below – which will probably be no more congenial to mainstream psychologists than to Chomskyans – I don't pretend to offer any original thesis in this book.[7] What *is* fairly unusual about the approach taken here is its critical engagement with the kinds of grammatical phenomena that generativists care about: co-reference relations, VP-ellipsis, constraints on *wh*-movement, *that*-trace

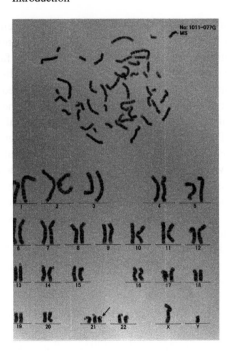

Figure 1 Austin's karyogram.

effects, discontinuous agreement, recursivity and the like. Twenty-something years of teaching generative syntax has given me a better appreciation of the empirical pressure points of grammatical argumentation than is enjoyed by many of Chomsky's opponents, and in this book, I aim to test them all – the pressure points, that is.

Before we begin properly, I need to mention the person who has taught me more about language and linguistics than I have learned in half a lifetime of research and teaching, through his *inarticulate speech of the heart*. I am not referring to my countryman Van Morrison (though several of his songs feature in this book), but to my youngest child, Austin,[8] born on 1 November 2010.

The circumstances leading up to Austin's birth were unremarkable – at least to me, as the father of two boys already – yet the events that immediately followed his arrival, from the initial reaction of the obstetrician through the downward glances of the nursing staff, intimated that Austin was not a typical baby. Although it was ten days before we received official scientific confirmation (in the form of the karyogram in Figure 1), we knew by the next morning that our third son *had* – or, as we have now learned to say, *was a child with* – Down's Syndrome (US Down Syndrome). A different book could be written about how our feelings changed in the first year: from shock, to acceptance, to something much more complex and altogether more joyful. That is not relevant here, other than to say that I will never again begin a lecture or a research paper on language acquisition with the dismissive words: 'Barring pathology, all children ...'

What is much more significant is that, six years on, Austin has grown into a more beautiful, healthy, communicative and unusually empathetic child than I ever could have wished for, who knows where he is, who his friends are, what he likes, what he did last week, what he wants to do tomorrow. A child with excellent metalinguistic skills, who says *<adyu, ada>* <'<$_{than}$>k you, dad'> in English and *<tou, mama>* <<ありが>とう、マ マ> <'thanks, mum'> in Japanese, who bows appropriately or offers his hand when he meets someone for the first time, and who just laughs at me whenever I say anything in his mother's language. My Japanese pronunciation is not so terrible – I can get by with most adults and other children of his age – but to him, it is a source of derision mingled with mild irritation.

Yet Austin *is* different from other typically developing six-year-olds in several ways, and the most striking contrasts are observable in his spoken language.

After six years of continuous language input and rich interaction, in spite of demonstrating a clear willingness to communicate, and excellent use of compensatory paralinguistic gestures, his comprehension of Japanese hardly extends beyond contexts where the utterance-meaning is obvious from the context. As for his production, this is mostly limited to proper names, a few highly frequent concrete nouns, some deictic terms, and a moderately large set of unanalysed greetings and formulaic phrases (<こんにちは、ごちそうさまでした、すみません、。。>) ... Very few utterances contain more than two or three morphemes. His production lags well behind that of a typical four-year-old Japanese child.

That's me, sadly. Given that I'm a fifty-something late learner of Japanese, it's perhaps unsurprising that my control of the language is so poor. It may be frustrating to my colleagues and is certainly personally disappointing, but it's hardly unusual. In Austin's case, on the other hand, Japanese and English are his two first languages, and his production abilities in either language (at the time of writing) are little better than is implied by the same description. This makes him special when compared to almost all children of his age, irrespective of ethnicity, gender or social experience.

It's unclear whether Austin will eventually come to understand and produce English or Japanese as his older brothers do, whether he will ever be able to express his needs and desires, aspirations and regrets – always supposing that regrets, and the counterfactual thoughts they imply, are possible without complex syntax: see F is for Functions of Language below. The range of outcomes for adults with Down's Syndrome is much wider than for typical children from similar backgrounds: a few will graduate from university, a few may become film and television actors, some will manage their own businesses. And some will remain as dependent and socially inept as typical five-year-olds, requiring constant supervision and support throughout their lives. Most, like the rest of us, fall somewhere in between: in many cases, towards the lower end of the general population in terms of lifetime income, towards the upper end in openness, empathy and likeability.

Austin's medical prognosis is equally uncertain: even though life expectancy for people with Down's Syndrome has improved dramatically over the last forty years,[9] the condition still brings with it markedly higher health risks than for typical children and adults, including – for those who make it to their forties or fifties – a significantly higher risk of early onset dementia.

Given all these imponderables, it's hard to be certain of much. What I am reasonably sure of, however, is who I should talk to to gain a better understanding of what's going on in Austin's mind, of how he represents and processes his fragments of Japanese and English, of how linguistically able he may be in five or ten years' time. First and foremost, I should talk to him: if I can learn to ask the right questions – and ask the questions right – I am certain that no-one can tell me more. After that, I should talk to other children in his class, then to his nursery teachers, then to specialist paediatricians. Then perhaps to other parents of children with Down's Syndrome, since – though children like Austin do not all show the same personality or behavioural traits – they are 'similar enough in their difference' that I can learn from their experience.

The only specialist it would be wholly pointless to talk to is the geneticist who analysed Austin's karyotype. There are no answers to be found there. I might as well consult an astrologer, or read tea leaves, as attempt to divine grammatical knowledge or specific cognitive abilities from a chromosomal pattern. For while it is incontrovertible that the ultimate cause of Austin's language difficulty lies in his genetic makeup – the chromosomal evidence is there towards the bottom of Figure 1, quite literally in black and white – it would be asinine to assume that this ultimate cause plays any significant role in understanding his language development, or indeed of any other aspect of his psychology.

Genetics is at once crucial and irrelevant in this case – the more so than with other acquired disorders – since what makes children with Down's Syndrome biologically distinct does not lie in the genes themselves, but in their disposition: as far as is known, it is that extra twenty-first chromosome (trisomy) that *makes all the difference in the world*, not a deletion or translocation of genetic material. Furthermore, even if a particular set of genes were somehow implicated in language acquisition, this wouldn't make genetics a relevant source of explanation of what we know about how languages are acquired and processed. *Pace* Chomsky, there is no reason to suppose that the genetic writ runs far beyond physiology – indeed, it only rarely extends that far. Even where phenotypical traits are relatively pure reflections of the genome, unaffected by environmental factors – as is the case, for example, for eye colour – these traits are invariably the result of polygenic interactions: see N is for Nativism below. And grammatical knowledge, on almost everyone's account, is massively affected by time and experience, especially experience of language (speech, text, discourse) itself. It makes as much sense to try to understand human language processing without considering human languages, in the ordinary sense of the word, as to explain social relationships without considering other people, or architecture without considering physical buildings and their physical and historical contexts …

… But I'm getting ahead of myself. Suffice it to say that before Austin came along, this book would have been a much more straightforward, dispassionate undertaking. It would certainly be much less worthwhile.

To understand what a child knows, or how someone acquires and processes their language(s), it can't hurt to listen to what they actually say and do. Linguistic behaviour – whether it is spontaneous or elicited – may not be a perfect clue to underlying knowledge and process, but it's the best clue available. While theories are no doubt crucial, it is my belief that, without a constant eye on behaviour, they tend to distort more than they disclose.

If that conclusion makes me a Wicked Empiricist – and it is a truism for most generativists that Empiricists, like Behaviourists, are essentially wicked – so be it. But, as Leonard Cohen said in a different context: *That Don't Make It Junk.*

Scope

The book is concerned with philosophical and empirical questions at the heart of what might be called 'classical psycholinguistics'. As implied in the opening paragraph, the field comprises two historically separate areas of enquiry: EXPERIMENTAL PSYCHOLINGUISTICS, which has mainly been concerned with theories and models of adult language processing, and DEVELOPMENTAL PSYCHOLINGUISTICS, where researchers' primary focus has been on how children come to know and use their first language(s). Previously, the boundary between these two areas was clearly demarcated by differences in the technologies applicable to each, and their associated modes of analysis. Early experimental psycholinguistics was invariably laboratory-based, employing technologies – and research assistants – that could not readily be used with young children: too many heavy monitors, too few social skills. Early developmental psycholinguistics, by contrast, tended to be based on longitudinal observations of children's language development, archetypally in the form of diary studies of researchers' children.[10] Within current psycholinguistics, the distinction is much less robust than it once was: technological advances have allowed most experimental methodologies to be adapted for much younger participants; at the same time, researchers have become more skilled at devising age-appropriate experimental paradigms (see, for example, McDaniel, McKee and Cairns 1996); they have also begun to investigate acquisition and language processing in adult second language learners and other groups of multilingual speakers (see, for example, Juffs and Rodríguez 2015) as well as the abilities of atypical language users.

More recently however, some psycholinguists have moved beyond these established behavioural paradigms to embrace more neuro-physiological measures of brain activity that are associated with language processing: the use of ERP and fMRI measures, for instance; see Morgan-Short and Tanner (2014) and Newman (2014) (same volume) for useful overviews of these techniques. Although I will occasionally refer directly to some key studies in neurophysiology – work by Michael Ullman, Angela Friederici and David Poeppel, for example – I will generally limit attention to more traditional kinds of behavioural data.

One practical reason for this restriction is precisely that most classical psycholinguistics is not 'rocket science':[11] standard behavioural tasks can be carried out by anyone equipped with a personal computer, a reasonable degree of motivation, ethics clearance and some basic instruction in experimental design. Neuroscience, by contrast, makes literal rocket science look like a facile exercise in trial-and-error ballistics; its experimental paradigms are correspondingly complex and intricate.[12] Neurolinguistic experiments currently require extremely expensive equipment and laboratory time, trained and skilled technicians to run the experiments and analyse the raw data, and – not infrequently – fairly elaborate ethics procedures. It is also much harder to recruit participants for neurolinguistic studies without access to a pre-registered pool of volunteers; only very fortunate, well-placed students able to run their own neurolinguistic experiment. For all of these reasons, and thanks in large part to advances in software development, classical psycholinguistics wins hands down over neurolinguistic research in any cost–benefit analysis of the best way to spend research time.

However, even if all the necessary technical and human resources were freely available, I remain to be convinced that it would be worthwhile carrying out neurolinguistic experiments, given our current ignorance of the applicable 'bridging theories' to connect neurolinguistic results to psycholinguistic theories. This concern echoes remarks by the cognitive scientist Gary Marcus, in a 2014 *New York Times* opinion piece:

What we are really looking for is a bridge, some way of connecting two separate scientific languages – those of neuroscience and psychology. Such bridges don't come easily or often, maybe once in a generation, but when they do arrive, they can change everything. An example is the discovery of DNA ... Neuroscience awaits a similar breakthrough. We know that there must be some lawful relation between assemblies of neurons and the elements of thought, but we are currently at a loss to describe those laws. We don't know, for example, whether our memories for individual words inhere in individual neurons or in sets of neurons, or in what way sets of neurons might underwrite our memories for words, if in fact they do.

Gary Marcus, 'The trouble with brain science'
(*New York Times* opinion, 11 July 2014)

The problem of bridging theories is examined further in Part I below; see also Coltheart (2013).

Other languages, other language learners

I think it is broadening to the mind to study a language that is so altogether different from all past experiences in that line. Imagine a language that contains only three parts of speech, the noun, the verb, and the adjective, and in which any one word may be all three, so that if you hear a word that you happen to be familiar with as a noun, you cannot tell whether it is behaving like a noun on this particular occasion, or whether it is not doing the work of a verb or an adjective. I am beginning to understand a great many of the apparently stupid mistakes that my pupils make in English, as I see what an absolutely fluid thing their native tongue is.

Alice M. Bacon, *A Japanese Interior* (1893: 125)

One distinctive feature of this book is a focus on data from language varieties other than (Standard) English.[13] The main purpose of presenting such examples is to draw attention to the ways in which alternative forms of construal and different patterns of phonological, lexical and grammatical organisation shape models of language processing, and force a reconsideration of overly narrow constraints on theories of language acquisition. If our native language appears to us to be the most intuitive, logical, reasonable and economical way of verbalising our thoughts – of moving from 'intention to articulation', as Levelt (1989) expresses it – that is only because it is precisely that: our own.

A discussion of one phenomenon, in the domain of speech segmentation, should suffice to illustrate this point. Take the nonce word <kaitch>. To a native speaker of Standard British or American English, it seems self-evident that the string of letters comprises three 'speech sounds' (phonemes) contained within one syllable [kaɪtʃ]. By contrast, it is just as obvious to a native speaker of most varieties of Japanese[14] that the same string should be analysed as three (different) 'speech sounds': three MORAE [ka.i.tʃi], represented as カ イ チ in *katakana*, the syllabary used by literate Japanese speakers to represent most non-native Japanese words, including nonce words. Two radically different analyses, therefore: what counts intuitively as a discrete phonetic constituent in one language has no readily accessible correlate in the other. It is certainly possible for a Japanese listener to analyse a word like *tako* (たこ 'octopus') as

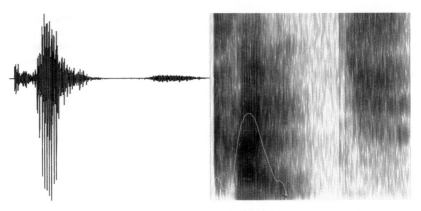

Figure 2 Two visual representations of <kaitch>.

containing four phonemes (/t/-/a/-/k/-/o/), but this is as unintuitive for him or her as it is for an English listener to treat the Japanese word *fukurō* 'owl' as containing four morae (ふくろう, /ɸu/-/ku/-/ro/-/u/), as opposed to three syllables, which is the more natural English analysis. For more detailed technical discussion, see Otake et al. (1993), Cutler and Otake (1994).

As an aside, notice that [kaɪtʃ] is a possible pronunciation of a real word in some varieties of Northern Irish English; it is, at least, a near-homophone of the word <couch>, as in <sittin' on the couch> (which means precisely what it does in many other varieties of English). See H is for Homogeneity below.[15]

The main point of presenting this non-word is to make clear that none of these analyses is 'out there', in the acoustic signal: Northern Irish, Southern British English and Japanese speakers each assign their own internal analyses to the same continuous acoustic–phonetic stimulus, visualised in Figure 2. Whatever corresponds to phonetic or phonological segments, or to timing units, like many of the more interesting concepts discussed in this book, pertains to a level of psychological – rather than external, acoustic – reality. Except, I will suggest, for language itself.

This internal property is not exclusive to linguistic analysis. Devlin (1998: 96) makes a similar observation regarding the calculus:

[The] methods of the calculus say as much about ourselves as they do about the physical world to which they can be applied with such effect. The patterns of motion and change we capture using the calculus certainly correspond to the motion and change we observe in the world, but, as patterns of infinity, their existence is inside our minds. They are patterns we humans develop to help us comprehend our world.[16]

Keith Devlin, *The Language of Mathematics: Making the Invisible Visible* (1998: 96)

The distinction between syllables and MORAE – the Japanese term is *haku* 拍 – is brought out particularly sharply when we consider the Japanese verse-form known as *haiku*. As a child, this verse-form was unknown to me; Wordsworth and Tennyson were *de rigueur* in school, with Hilaire Belloc or Ogden Nash thrown in for light relief. These days, however, it seems that every primary school class involves at least one annual stab at *haiku*, as though brevity was the guarantor of poetic accomplishment. (Or perhaps brevity is its own reward: it must be easier to mark third-grade attempts at 17-syllable completeness than to trundle through re-hashes of 'The Charge of the Light Brigade'.)

The only problem with the assignment is that traditional Japanese *haiku* doesn't involve seventeen syllables, as is commonly supposed, but instead calls for seventeen morae, arranged in a five-seven-five configuration. To appreciate the difference, have a look at the following two *haiku* – presented together with their transliterations and free English translations – and try to decide which best conforms to the classical metre:

ISSA: 江戸の雨何石呑んだ゛ 時鳥
Edo no ame/Nan goku nonda/Hototogisu

'Of Edo's rain/How many gallons did you drink/Cuckoo?'

BASHŌ: 富士の風や扇にのせて江戸土産
Fuji no kaze ya/Ōgi ni nosete/Edo miyage

'The wind of Mt. Fuji/I've brought on my fan!/A gift from Edo.'

If you read the transliterations of these *haiku* as though they were English words, you might well have concluded that neither of these poems is very well behaved: the first poem apparently consists of only 15 syllables (5-5-5), whereas the second seems to contain the correct total number of syllables, but in the wrong configuration (6-6-5). In (Japanese) fact, the Issa poem conforms strictly to the traditional verse-scheme, whereas that by Bashō breaks the classical rule by containing an extra mora in the first line, but is otherwise complete. Most significantly, the second line of both poems contains exactly seven morae: na_1-n_2 go_3-ku_4 no_5-n_6-da_7 and o_1-o_2-gi_3 ni_4 no_5-se_6-te_7, respectively. This 'fact of analysis' is as transparent to a native speaker of Japanese as end-rhyme is to a four-year-old English child.

This brief discussion of the syllable vs. mora distinction shows that by examining data from languages other than our own we discover that a lot of what seems to be reflexive cannot be innate: typically developing children may be born with the capacity to acquire and to process any language, but the particular systems of categorisation and analysis they end up regarding as intuitive arise through rich experience and extensive interaction with other language users, as well with discourse and text (ambient language).[17]

By recognising these cross-linguistic differences in representation and processing, we gain some greater insight into our own language. Goethe asserted that 'Those who know nothing of foreign languages know nothing of their own' – or better, *Wer fremde Sprachen nicht kennt, weiß nichts von seiner eigenen* (Goethe [1821] 1907). *Nichts* is doubtless an exaggeration, but the aphorism still holds an important truth.

Finally, it may have been noticed that the title of this section is 'Other languag*es*, other language learner*s*'. The plural affix is significant: real children do not acquire 'Language', they acquire (varieties of) English, Irish, Hindi, Thai, Fijian, Malayalam, and so on. Nor do real speakers process 'Language'; rather, they process varieties of these different languages. This subtle distinction implies a crucial shift of perspective from philosophical (Platonic) abstraction to empirical investigation. I'll suggest that this shift is indispensable if we want to understand what is in the minds of language users. The reification of Language, as conventionally indicated by the capital letter, is anything but harmless – especially since there may be no such thing: *A grin without a cat*, as Alice once remarked.

The songs, poems and sketches

Just where it now lies I can no longer say
I found it on a cold and November day
In the roots of a sycamore tree where it had hid so long:
In a box made out of myrtle lay the bone of song.

The bone of song was a jawbone old and bruised
And worn out in the service of the muse.
And along its sides and teeth were written words
I ran my palm along them and I heard:

    'Lucky are you who finds me in the wilderness
    I am the only unquiet ghost that does not seek rest …'

          ♫ Josh Ritter, *Bone of Song* (2003)

Many parts of this book – *my treasure[s], you [could] say* – have been written by other people: the lines set in italics were all originally composed or first incorporated by poets, authors, singer-songwriters, comedians and satirists, most of whom were active a generation or more ago. These extracts have been chosen to illustrate a particular linguistic point, or as musical or lyrical scene-setting to the different themes and topics discussed. A few are included simply to keep the reader entertained through especially difficult sections. *A spoonful of sugar*. Whatever the intended function of any particular example, they all serve to show that linguistic theories need not be viewed as something arcane or esoteric, that they are immediately relevant to the analysis of the most affective forms of language use: popular music, poetry and comedy. Just as importantly, many of the quotations provide easily verifiable, independent evidence of the violability of grammatical rules: people who are sceptical of the value of linguists' constructed examples – *Colourless green ideas raced past the barn slept furiously,* and its/their ilk – may be more convinced by language that is actually used by real authors and artists.

Very little of the quoted material is likely to be found in any canonical survey of British, Irish or North American literature; indeed, some of it isn't even in English. With the obvious exceptions of Shakespeare, T. S. Eliot, Joyce and Flaubert, the majority of the other extracts are drawn from songs and comedy sketches of the last fifty years; in particular, from those that were popular in the UK in the 1970s and 1980s. The autobiographical basis of this selection will be obvious: most of us invest in our treasury of songs, writing, music and language as teenagers and young adults, and live off the dividends thereafter (though see Bonneville-Roussy, Rentfrow et al. 2013).[18] It is true that I cite a few younger singer-songwriters, including the marvellous Swedish singer Anna Ternheim, and most especially, the *génial* Josh Ritter, one of the most thoughtful and intelligent songwriters of his generation. For the most part, though, the songs, poems and sketches are more than thirty years old: my appreciation of popular music fossilised around 1990, and since then I have moved backwards rather than forwards – into the 1960s and 1950s – for inspiration. The advice to write about what you know seems just as valuable in academic as in creative writing, and the cited or quoted material is simply what comes most easily to mind.[19]

A route-map

Pour l'enfant, amoureux de cartes et d'estampes,
L'univers est égal à son vaste appétit.
Ah! que le monde est grand à la clarté des lampes!
Aux yeux du souvenir que le monde est petit!

> *To a child, enamoured of prints and maps*
> *The universe has the size of his vast appetite.*
> *How large the world seems by the light of a lamp!*
> *How small it is, yet, in memory's eyes!*

Charles Baudelaire, 'Le Voyage' (*Les Fleurs du Mal,* 1861)

From the outset I have insisted that this book is intended as an informal conversation about psycholinguistic theory, rather than as a treatise or manifesto. Yet I'd be lying if I claimed to have no higher agenda. I care deeply about our knowledge and use of languages and the intellectual value of linguistic analysis, and want to convey that passion to as broad an audience as possible. Theoretical linguistics offers us a framework and a set of tools with which to explore one of the most inherently fascinating and complex aspects of human experience. The enquiry should be enjoyable, and it should be accessible to any intelligent reader who is prepared to make some effort. Too often, though, linguistics comes across as leaden and irrelevant, and a good deal of this impression is due to its being too abstract and unnecessarily technical. Of course, some abstraction is essential, otherwise we can't say anything interesting; some technical terminology is unavoidable if we are going to draw the right distinctions. Still, it is easy to get carried away by jargon or theoretical aesthetics, and so to 'lose the plot'. And when this happens, the search for the simplest, most elegant theory may result in a dismissal of the very phenomena it was intended to account for: in the limit, it may lead to a preference for a theory with zero empirical coverage over one with partial coverage; see Epstein and Seely (2006: 1–3). In this connection, the second part of Einstein's famous dictum (below) is as important as the first:

The supreme goal of all theory is to make the irreducible basic elements as simple and as few as possible ... without having to surrender the adequate representation of a single datum of experience.

Albert Einstein, 'On the method of theoretical physics:
The Herbert Spencer lecture' (1934)[20]

Thus, to the extent that this work has a serious purpose, it is to try to get to grips with the stuff of languages (that plural -*s*, again), to impress upon the reader what it is exactly that must not be surrendered.

For all that, the book is mostly intended as the academic equivalent of taking the dog for a weekend ramble. We'll get there eventually, but the value of such a trek is in the scenery along the way, not in the shortest distance between two points. If what you were looking for was a quick and dirty guide to (psycho) linguistic theory, you're in the wrong place. But surely you must have worked that out already. That said, there may be readers who are prepared to follow me up and down the many 'rabbit holes' in the text – to use a prospective publisher's analogy – but who'd still like to know where the conversation is leading and (roughly) how we are going to get there. If you are one of those people, here is a brief route-map of the next 400-odd pages.

 – The book consists of four principal parts. Part I offers a brief introduction to the intellectually fragmented world of classical psycholinguistics, in which I outline some of the key research questions in language acquisition and processing. I begin as I mean to continue, with Noam Chomsky, whose views on language and mind have galvanised supporters and detractors in almost equal measure. Following a brief historical overview, I first consider *how* Chomsky's framing of the big questions led to a major rift in the

theory and practice of psycholinguistic research. A proper understanding of *why* this rift came about requires a consideration of
Chomsky's ideas from a wider intellectual perspective. In pursuit of
this latter question, I spend some time considering the relationship
between elementary-school knowledge of 'times tables' (declarative knowledge) and the more abstract, algorithmic properties of
arithmetic, an analogy that I'll return to several times in the course
of the book. This is the first major rabbit hole.

Which then leads on (in Chapters 2 and 3) to a discussion of the
interplay between the ideas of Chomsky and those of the neuroscientist and psychologist David Marr, a leading proponent of what
has become known as the COMPUTATIONAL THEORY OF MIND (CTM).[21]
Emerging from this discussion – and equipped with a slightly better
knowledge of the algorithmic differences between humming birds
and eagles in flight – we return to the main path. And to an interim
conclusion, namely, that whatever position one takes on 'Level 1
questions', it is vital to be able to distinguish (within a 'Level 2
theory') between linguistic representation and process, between
declarative and procedural knowledge.

– Deciding this question in practice turns out to be a really difficult
problem. In Part II (Chapters 4–9), I consider six different grammatical phenomena, any of which might be determined to be essentially declarative or procedural in nature. *Six Different Ways*. In each
case, there is presumably a fact of the matter, though with scope for
individual as well as cross-linguistic variation. My purpose here is
less to persuade the reader of one or other position than to use the
test cases to explore the intricate nature, and tremendous variability,
of our knowledge of languages. Each case can be seen as a separate
rabbit hole – though *warren* might be a more appropriate allusion.
Indeed, the whole of Part II could be skipped by readers who don't
need to be persuaded of the difficulty of the task. But those same
readers would be missing out on a more entertaining diversion than
this summary implies.

– Part III presents a glossary of idealisations. Psycholinguistics,
like every domain of academic research, is chock-full of *a priori*
assumptions and idealisations. Most of these appear innocuous
when considered in isolation. In interaction, however, they can
produce significant distortions; in some cases, idealisations can
lead to absurd conclusions that threaten to undermine the value
of the empirical research on which they are based. (There's a
nice Escherian sentence to be getting on with.) So, in this section,
through a set of largely self-contained essays, I offer a critical

examination of some of the key notions that have underpinned classical psycholinguistic research over the last fifty years. Once more,
the intention is not to reject the idealisations outright, but rather
to give the reader a clearer appreciation of their effects, and unintended consequences. An extended *caveat lector* to work in linguistics more generally.

- Part IV focuses attention on two case studies in language acquisition, taking the second language first. The 'French Class' sketch, by
the English comic writers Catherine Tate and Aschlin Ditta, is not
only a brilliant example of comedic writing: I argue that it is also an
object lesson in second language learning, with significant implications for psycholinguistic theories of acquisition and processing. Another rabbit hole, based on a comic fiction – or worthwhile
diversion, depending upon your frame of mind. Following discussion of (Catherine Tate's character) Lauren, I consider another language learner – less hilarious, perhaps, but no less captivating, to
me at least: my middle son, Adrian. 'Adrianish' (Adrian's language
between the ages of five and ten years) offers a different kind of
lesson, namely, how perfect generalisations can lead to 'imperfect
competence'. Here, as throughout, I will suggest that the search for
grammatical perfection is as Quixotic and vain as the search for
perfection in any other area of human experience.

So, there you have it, a three-page route-map. I make no guarantees (as) to its
accuracy, but warrant that the journey is more interesting, and the terrain more
challenging, than this preview suggests. Yet, as was observed at the beginning,
you really shouldn't need a map. Baudelaire said it much better ...

> *Mais les vrais voyageurs sont ceux-là seuls qui partent*
> *Pour partir; coeurs légers, semblables aux ballons,*
> *De leur fatalité jamais ils ne s'écartent,*
> *Et, sans savoir pourquoi, disent toujours: Allons!*

> *But real travellers are just those for whom departure*
> *Is its own reward; [who leave], hearts light as air*
> *Not to evade their fate/[but] always declaring*
> *– without knowing why – 'Let's go there!'*

Charles Baudelaire, 'Le Voyage' (*Les Fleurs du Mal*, 1861)

Notes

1 That volume may not be forthcoming. Life is short, and in the meantime others may
well have done a better job in covering some or all of the bases. Anne Cutler's recent
book *Native Listening* (2015), for example, offers a brilliant summary of spoken

word recognition research from a cross-linguistic perspective, written with a deep professionalism that I could not hope to emulate.

2 It is interesting to observe that the second edition, published in Halle by Max Niemeyer, uses more English-like spelling: no capitalisation of common nouns, plus the use of <c> in lexical borrowings (*complicerte*, consequenz). Although *Duden* had been declared the official orthography throughout Prussia six years earlier in 1880, it still took time for these changes to be reflected in all printed works.

3 According to *Wikipedia*, Leon Jaworski was a Texan lawyer, a war crimes prosecutor in World War II, and second special prosecutor during the Watergate Scandal. In that role, he presumably had to deal with extremists of varying levels of competence. Perhaps the methodical ones were easier to convict.

4 See Hovdhaugen (1990). Goddard and Wierzbicka (2002) take the view that Chomsky's notion of universal grammar is fundamentally different from Roger Bacon's:

> Why did Bacon believe this? Essentially, it is because he believed that the fundamentals of grammar arise from fundamentals of human thought, which are shared by all people and all languages. This is the time-honoured tradition of universal grammar, now largely displaced by Chomsky's structure-based conception of UG in which meaning plays no real part.
>
> (Goddard and Wierzbicka 2002: 41)

5 The more traditional generativist notion that I endorse receives short shrift from recent commentators. See the following quote from David Adger (responding to the challenge of Construction Grammar):

> I don't think that anyone has said that all languages are 'underlyingly the same' since people were discussing the Universal Base Hypothesis [UBH] in the '70s. When Chomsky says that there is only one human language, he's saying that there is one set of principles that govern all human languages, not that all languages are underlyingly the same. Generativists argue that all languages obey a certain set of principles (and indeed make proposals as to what those principles are), and that individual languages vary from those principles in constrained ways. It's important, when one is criticizing a framework of ideas, not to criticize proposals that have been abandoned for 40-odd years.
>
> (Adger 2013: 3)

Pace Adger, I'm fairly sure that I am not the only one to hold on to a version of the UBH (that is to say, to the idea of a universal hierarchy of functional categories – rather than a base, in a very literal sense). The syntactic cartography movement – see for example Cinque (1999, 2002, 2005) – may also be viewed as advocating such an approach, with a new proof of concept. Kayne's *Antisymmetry* proposals (Kayne 1994), and subsequent work, also explicitly advocate an underlying SVO (Specifier-Head-Complement) order for all constituent phrases, across all languages. It hardly seems, then, that these ideas have been abandoned.

6 To steal from the acknowledgments section of Simon Conway Morris's book *Life's Solution* (Conway Morris 2003), who himself borrowed the phrase: 'To copy one paper is plagiarism, to copy many is scholarship.' I haven't knowingly stolen any unacknowledged proposal, though I freely acknowledge not knowing about everything I may have stumbled upon.

7 It has been suggested to me recently that the ideas advanced in those chapters are derivative of the work of Lev Vygotsky (1896–1934). Unfortunately, Vygotsky's work did not feature in my linguistic education; so while the charge may be valid – or perhaps not, given that Vygotskian research seems to be as much a question of exegesis as of canonical doctrine – I can only declare that the ideas presented there were 'independently arrived at'.

8 Children's names have been modified to respect privacy.

9 Average life expectancy for people with Down's Syndrome has increased dramatically from 25 years in 1983, 49 years in 1997 to 60 years in 2010, according to Weijerman and de Winter (2010); this is largely due to radical improvements in post-natal and early infant care. Frankie Boyle, listen up! (www.theguardian.com/society/2010/apr/08/frankie-boyle-downs-syndrome).

10 Often cited works include Stern and Stern (1907) and Leopold (1949). Observational research on early language development has been going on for millennia, however: Campbell (2006) provides a survey of these pre-modern studies. This tradition continues up to the present, notable studies including Smith (1973), Bowerman (1982), Clark (1993), Dromi (1987), Tomasello (1992) and Lieven, Tomasello, Behrens and Speares (2003).

11 Aside from the fact that one has to draw a line somewhere. Since almost every aspect of language has some psychological correlate, any restriction on subject matter will necessarily be *ad hoc*. It will also become clear that I have little to say, except in passing, about computational psycholinguistics, that is to say, about work that focuses on the results of computer simulations of language processing and acquisition: as interesting as this topic seems to be, my lack of knowledge and experience of the field leaves me unqualified to assess its relevance.

12 As is well known, the computing power of the Apollo 11 guidance computer is dwarfed by that of the average smartphone (*iPhone 5s*): viz. 1 MHz vs. 1.3 GHz (processing speed); 4 kb vs. 64 Gb (memory). Source: www.thedailycrate.com/geek-tech-apollo-guidance-computer-vs-iphone-5s/.

13 I assume no familiarity on the part of the reader with languages other than Standard English – something that I could have done a generation ago. George Steiner, for example, is able to rely on readers' knowledge of Latin, Greek and most 'Standard Average European' varieties, including Russian: see, for instance, Steiner (1976, 1978). These days, there aren't many monolingual native speakers of British or American English whose reading knowledge of other languages extends beyond Lauren's grasp of French; see Part IV.

14 Kagoshima Japanese is an exception, according to Kabuzono (2006).

15 An example of Northern Irish speech can be found at www.bl.uk/learning/langlit/sounds/text-only/ni/ballymoney (British Library); see also H is for Homogeneity. Here, and in what follows, I will distinguish among three types of conventional bracketing: angle brackets <x> indicate the standard orthographic representations of a word or morpheme in roman script (i.e. its usual British English spelling); square brackets [x] indicate the pronunciation of a word in IPA phonetic transcription – usually 'broad' (more approximate) transcription; slash bracketing /x/ points to the more abstract representation of the pronunciation of particular speech sounds in our heads. I do not take a stand here on whether segmental phonology is as discrete from phonetic implementation as has traditionally been supposed; I do assume, however – as a matter of 'empirical necessity' – that a fair measure of phonological

abstraction is involved in spoken language comprehension and production. See also A is for Abstraction. No two speakers share exactly the same pronunciation of any word; even the same speaker will pronounce a word quite differently depending on its immediate phonetic context (co-articulation effects). Yet there is a clear sense that something is shared by all those who know a word in a particular language variety: the segmental properties of that something belongs inside slash brackets.

16 Some would maintain that there is a crucial difference between the putatively universal notions of mathematics and the language-particular patterns of categorisation that distinguish English from Japanese, French from Fula, Chinese from Korean, etc. Others object to any form of linguistic relativity. See Pinker (2007) for useful discussion. Still others might maintain that mathematics also exhibits cultural relativity (although this is, I'd suppose, more of a fringe position). There's no obvious limit to our capacity for disagreement on this point.

17 A note to the more trigger-happy of (generativist) critics: read the previous sentence carefully. I might be brandishing the can-opener, but the worms are still secure. If you are looking for controversy, the place to C is for Competence~Performance, I is for Internalism, N is for Nativism, and beyond.

18 I am grateful to Heidi Harley for referring me to this work.

19 Most of the songs that I would have liked to have cited from turned out to be unaffordable. In general – as I found out the hard way, and in spite of the fact that almost all lyrics are freely available on dedicated websites such as www.azlyrics.com – republishing song lyrics is an expensive and vexatious business. See *Acknowledgments, Credits and Permissions* below. The largely demoralising experience of dealing with mainstream music publishers, and the scandalously anti-competitive practice of 'MFN' (= most favoured nation), makes me particularly grateful to those songwriters and their publishers and agents who allowed use of their lyrics *gratis* or for a nominal fee. Erik Gilbert (Duchamp, Inc.) deserves particular credit, up front, for issuing the most generous licence I could have hoped for in respect of Josh Ritter's songs. I came to Erik at the very beginning of the process, for five songs, and three months later for another five (including what was, for a time, the 'title track' to this book – *Lark*: see v is for von Humboldt); on both occasions, he was prompt and magnanimous to a fault.

20 Albert Einstein: 'On the method of theoretical physics', the Herbert Spencer lecture, delivered at Oxford, 10 June 1933, published in *Philosophy of Science*, vol. 1, no. 2 (April 1934), pp. 163–9. The shorter variant *Make things as simple as possible, but no simpler* may be pithier, but it is less apposite.

21 This book assumes the basic correctness of the CTM approach; indeed, it can be viewed as providing additional support for it. Not everyone accepts that language or indeed any other aspect of our cognitive faculties can be dissociated from our physiology or even from our environment: more radical variants of the theory of 'embodied cognition' explicitly reject this assumption.

Part I

Both Sides, Now

1   Breaking us in two

Cracks in the canvas

There's craic *in everything;*
To let the light get in.

Had Leonard Cohen come from Belfast, and if he had been more cheerful, the
lines above might form part of the refrain to his elegiac song 'Anthem'; they
would scan just as well. But he didn't, and since I can't afford to republish even
two lines from the original, they will have to serve as a placeholder.[1]

♫ Leonard Cohen, *Anthem* (1992)

When teaching a course on language and mind – whether it is on language
processing, language acquisition or language disorders – the first thing I have
students do is watch a BBC *Horizon* documentary, originally broadcast in
2009, with the title 'Why Do We Talk?' As it turns out, this 50-minute programme offers no clear answers at all to *why* we talk, probably because this is
an unanswerable question: philosophers, theologians, poets and other think-
ers have been trying for millennia to come up with a viable theory of human
action – why we do anything – and the results so far have been less than
encouraging. Free will is a troublesome concept, for one thing. What the programme provides instead is an articulate introduction to some core research
questions in the area of language and cognition, many of which I aim to re-
examine in this book. These include, in some particular order: the question of
whether the ability to acquire and use languages appropriately depends on a
special kind of mentally represented knowledge – a 'language faculty' – or
whether this ability rests on more general cognitive capacities; supposing we
all possess such a language faculty, where the knowledge it instantiates comes
from; the extent to which the environment – more specifically, naturalistic linguistic input – shapes grammatical development; the extent to which language
comprehension and language production skills are dissociable; the evidence
for a genetic basis to language; the problems of learning artificial languages;
and the possible mechanisms of human language evolution. A slew of fascinating topics, then. The broadcast also introduces viewers to some of the

key figures in research on language and cognition, and provides a passing glimpse of the experimental methodologies that have been employed to elicit data from language users. All things considered, it is a remarkably useful, engaging and compact piece of television, which is why I have students watch it. You should too, if you can obtain a copy of the programme.

However, to someone who has worked in the field for over twenty years, it is not the information that emerges from the interviews with language researchers that is particularly surprising. If I wasn't reasonably familiar with the general research questions and the results that have so far been obtained, I shouldn't be the one writing this book. Instead, the most astonishing feature of the programme is the implied consensus among researchers concerning the answers to these key questions: through careful narration and skilful editing, the programme-makers create the impression that linguists and psycholinguists broadly agree on all the answers to the core issues in language and mind. This is airbrushing on a massive scale, and about as far from the truth as one can get without actually misrepresenting any of the individual contributors to the programme. In the 'real world' – that is to say, the *academic* real world of psycholinguistics – what is mostly observed is not consensus, but ambivalence, controversy, dissent and energetic disagreement about nearly all of these questions, not to mention a fair degree of bitter antagonism and hair pulling. It is often one's own hair that is pulled, but still: in terms of social and political discourse, linguistics is more saloon than *salon*, more gladiatorial arena than forum.

There is a positive thing in some respects. A useful analogy here is to seismology. If you want to study earthquakes, two good places are Los Angeles, California, where I attended graduate school, and Kōbe, Japan, the city where I now live. Seismologists don't spend a lot of time in Belfast, the city where I grew up. In both regions, only just beneath the surface, the ground is fragmented by myriad fissures and thousands of minor fault-lines; it is also more obviously fractured along major fault lines, immediately visible to the naked eye. In California, the most significant seismic fault is named after a Catholic saint, San Andreas, whilst in this part of Japan, it is the more prosaically named Japan Median Tectonic Line (中央構造線 *Chūō Kōzō Sen*), a branch of which – the Nojima fault – was responsible for the Kōbe (Great Hanshin) earthquake in January 1995, which resulted in more than 6,000 deaths and caused over 10 trillion yen in damages.

In psycholinguistics the most significant fault line is anonymous, but if one were to name it, it should rightfully be called the *Noam Chomsky* fault. Though he is not himself a psycholinguist, still less a saint, Chomsky has had a more profound, and divisive, impact on the field than any other academic researcher. To gloss over the major and minor fault lines in language and mind, as the *Horizon* programme does, is to ignore much of the volatility and friction that makes the subject as treacherous – but also as vital – as it is.

The impression of consensus that the programme conveys also seems to pre-empt further research, which is precisely the opposite of what I want to achieve with this book. By clearly exposing some of the fault-lines of psycholinguistic research – especially some of the smaller cracks, where it is easier to make progress – I hope to encourage readers to develop new experiments of their own. To let the light get in.

Of course *this* truth, that the field is fractured, should hardly come as a bolt from the blue. Issues in language and mind are probably no more contentious than those in any other area of theoretical or empirical enquiry. Nor is it the case that psycholinguists in general are more vituperative than any other group of academics.[2] What's more, if the issues were as done and dusted as the pro-gramme's narration implies, the field would be intellectually moribund, and researchers with any talent would long since have moved on to something more challenging. As in all the other sciences, progress in psycholinguistics – the development of better theories and models – generally comes about through strong competition between alternative sets of hypotheses and interpretations. In principle, this competition could be dialectical in nature, the opposition of thesis and antithesis leading to a *synthesis* – a resolution – of the two opposed views. In practice, psycholinguistic arguments too often end in 'winner takes all' outcomes, which may better satisfy a journal reviewer or a funding agency but which do less to uncover the truth of the matter.

A direct consequence of the intellectual fragmentation of psycholinguistics is that many textbooks offer a partisan view, variously downplaying or dis-missing – more often than not, completely ignoring – relevant research from the other side(s). These biases are particularly stark in discussions of language acquisition, but the problem of bias also extends to books on adult language processing and language disorders. One only need contrast introductory works by Guasti (2004) or Crain and Thornton (1998), for example, with those of Harris and Coltheart (1986) or Tomasello (1992), to observe systematic biases of reporting more typically associated with ministries of propaganda than with reasoned academic discourse.

My aim here is to provide a more balanced, 'well-tempered' treatment,[3] considering the research questions from several different angles, giving credit to researchers operating from different theoretical viewpoints, and drawing together some of the key experiments that have brought us to present-day con-clusions. This approach closely reflects my own education and training. Over the past thirty years I have been fortunate enough to learn from a wide range of teachers, colleagues and students, some committed generativists, others equally passionate functionalists, still others 'pure psychologists' with no particular view of linguistic theory. See Acknowledgments, credits and permissions for details. Almost without exception, I have found these people to be intelligent and intellectually honest researchers, academics who respect empirical results whilst nevertheless disagreeing sharply on what counts as empirical, or even on what they consider to be legitimate research questions. What I have not observed is any obvious correlation between deep understanding and ideological commitment: theoretical zeal can occasionally lead to significant insights, but just as often to remarkable blind spots and arrogant bloody-mindedness. The truth is a grey area: only children, zealots – and some formal semanticists[4] – believe otherwise.

A core distinction is drawn here between two highly contrastive research perspectives, between what might be called the 'two souls' of classical psycholinguistics (to borrow an expression from Gennaro Chierchia 1995):

> On one side we find a COMPETENCE-BASED perspective, inspired and often directly informed by theoretical developments in Chomskyan grammar; the primary concern of competence-based researchers is with the mental representation of linguistic – especially grammatical, and most especially *syntactic* – knowledge, as well as with the question of how such knowledge comes to be in the mind of adult native speakers;
>
> On the opposite side of the intellectual fault line lies a PROCESS-ORIENTED ('information processing') approach, which lays emphasis on how speakers comprehend and produce spoken language in real time, in real situations, how children and adult language learners come to acquire the full array of language processing skills that are necessary for the fluent use of particular languages, and on the ways in which these abilities change throughout our lifespan.

These two souls of psycholinguistics are distinguished in the following quote, from Seidenberg and MacDonald (1999: 570):

> *Instead of asking how the child acquires competence grammar, we view acquisition in terms of how the child converges on adult-like performance in comprehending and producing utterances. This performance orientation changes the picture considerably with respect to classic issues about language learnability, and provides a unified approach to studying acquisition and processing.*
>
> Mark Seidenberg and Maryellen MacDonald, 'A probabilistic
> constraints approach to language acquisition and processing'
> (*Cognitive Science*, 1999: 570)

This book is written largely in the spirit of that quotation, while still trying to do justice to the issues that competence-based theorists consider important. It must be for the reader to decide whether I manage to square that particular circle. I also discuss research questions relating to the MENTAL LEXICON, where issues of abstract representation and information processing are more intimately linked than in the syntactic or phonological domains, and where ideological commitments are less in evidence. Finally, at various points in the discussion I will touch on experimental research at the interface between psycholinguistics and other aspects of human cognition and brain function, as well as on language typology, change and language evolution.

A(n) historical overview: dividing the soul of psycholinguistic theory

Before setting out these parallel tracks, it is worth noting that the field of psycholinguistics was not always so riven. Interest in psychological aspects of language and/or linguistic aspects of psychology predates the latter half of the twentieth century,[5] but it was only in the 1930s and 1940s in Europe, and the 1950s in the United States, that experimental psycholinguistics emerged as a discipline in its own right.[6] In the immediately preceding decades, the predominance of Behaviourism in psychology, in alliance with the strict empiricism of contemporaneous philosophy (LOGICAL POSITIVISM) and linguistics, had produced a virtual neglect of language in experimental psychology, as well as of psychology within linguistics (especially mainstream North American linguistics). Prior to the 1950s, language was mostly thought of as something 'out there', sometimes exotic, often chaotic and mysterious: linguistic behaviour was regarded as unpredictable as it was unstructured. Most American linguists of the period were concerned with the description of the indigenous languages of North America and elsewhere: many of those who worked in this anthropological tradition proceeded from a theoretical assumption that languages '... [could] differ from each other without limit and in unpredictable ways' (a much-cited, now infamous, quote from Martin Joos (1957: 29). Scholars at the time also generally adopted the methodological position that native speakers' metalinguistic judgments about their own languages were inherently untrustworthy: as Sampson (1980: 64) reports, linguists were minded to 'Accept everything a native speaker says in his language, and nothing he says about it.'

The conceptual impetus for a radically different, universalist and exclusively internalist approach to language in linguistics and psychology was provided by Noam Chomsky, whose early proposals for transformational generative grammar – see especially Chomsky (1957, 1965) – revolutionised thinking about language in many parts of the academic world, and who retains a preeminent influence in the general area of language and mind. McGilvray ([1999] 2014), offers a clear, if partisan, overview.[7]

The 'Chomskyan Revolution' in linguistics came to the attention of psychologists through Chomsky's (1959) critical review of B. F. Skinner's *Verbal Behavior*, which had been published two years earlier, and which had outlined a strictly externalist account of linguistic behaviour, centred around the notion of OPERANT CONDITIONING. In more hagiographical discussions of Chomsky's work, it is standard to assert that this review article provided clinching arguments that signalled the death-knell of Behaviourism as a viable psychological theory for the study of language (or, indeed, for much else).[8] A case of David vs. Goliath – at least before Malcolm Gladwell's anti-heroic re-interpretation of the Biblical story (Gladwell 2013).

On closer consideration, the issues are considerably less clear-cut, as Palmer (2006) discusses: strip away the polemic, and the arguments against any reasonably nuanced interpretation of Skinner's proposals are less persuasive than they are often held to be; see also Schlinger (2008). Indeed, as Matthew Saxton (2010) makes clear, Chomsky's position at the time was in some respects 'more Behaviourist' than that of Skinner himself: see also Radick (2016). With respect to the role of imitation, for example, Saxton reminds us that it was Chomsky, not Skinner, who claimed that 'children acquire a good deal of their verbal and non-verbal behaviour by casual conversation and imitation of adults and other children' (1959: 42), and who later observed, with regard to grammatical intuitions, that 'a child may pick up a large part of his vocabulary and "feel" for sentence structure from television' (1959: 42). This latter assertion is highly questionable, as subsequent research has shown; see, for example, Kuhl, Tsao and Liu (2003). Yet such remarks have been lost to revisionist history.

Even supposing that Chomsky's critique had delivered a fatal blow, Behaviourism was not killed off overnight. Paradigm shifts in science, like historical grammatical changes, can take several decades at least to work through – centuries, in the case of some syntactic changes. This is the case even though they might appear abrupt in retrospect, and even where they have a clearly pinpointable year of origin; 1066, say, in the history of English. See I is for Internalism below. Moreover, whereas Behaviourism in its classic form might have died as a theory, it has survived well as a methodology: contemporary cognitive psychology inherited from the Behaviourists a concern with rigorously controlled experiments, careful quantitative analysis of elicited data, and replicability as essential aspects of good research practice. (It is another matter, of course, whether such concerns are justified: see Bauer 1994.)

I've learned from my mistakes and I'm sure I could repeat them exactly.

> Peter Cook, 'Frog & Peach' (*Behind the Fridge*, 1973,
> republished in *Tragically I was an Only Twin*, Peter Cook 2002)

Viewed in the round, it seems likely that Chomsky's critique simply nudged Behaviourist psychology in a more internalist direction rather than dislodging it entirely; see also I is for Internalism. Psychologists of language also generally retained the idea that linguistic behaviour was a worthwhile object of study in its own right, something that Chomsky soundly rejected: whereas generative linguistics abstracts away from 'performance-related' issues and focuses rigidly on static grammatical competence, cognitive psychology is still fundamentally concerned with the contingencies of language performance, and especially, with the constraints imposed by time. See Eysenck (1984), also C is for Competence~Performance, for discussion.

An awareness of temporal constraints on language is by no means restricted to cognitive psychology. As C. S. Lewis, another Belfast native, observed:

[A] grave limitation of [spoken: NGD] language is that it cannot, like music or gesture, do more than one thing at once. However the words in a great poet's phrase interinanimate one another and strike the mind as a quasi-instantaneous chord, yet, strictly speaking, each word must be read or heard before the next. That way, language is as unilinear as time. Hence, in narrative, the great difficulty of presenting a very complicated change which happens suddenly. If we do justice to the complexity, the time the reader must take over the passage will destroy the feeling of suddenness. If we get the suddenness we shall not be able to get in the complexity. I am not saying that genius will not find its own way of palliating this defect in the instrument; only that the instrument is in this way defective.

C. S. Lewis, *Studies in Words* ([1960] 2013: 313–14)

Yet much of what seems crucial about language to other writers, philosophers or/and psychologists is largely ignored by most theoretical linguists, not only generativists.[9] See A is for Abstraction, H is for Homogeneity, I is for Internalism, O is for Object of Study (in Part III), for further discussion; cf. Poeppel (2014), amongst others.

Whatever was the true impact of his review of Skinner's work, Chomsky's own theoretical proposals (Chomsky 1957, 1965) did much to kick-start the field of competence-based psycholinguistics as a separate discipline, shifting general scientific attention from the more directly observable aspects of linguistic behaviour – spoken and written utterances, and the corpora derived from them – to the (putative) set of implicit grammatical rules that allow native speakers to acquire and use language productively. More generally, Chomsky redirected psychologists' attention to the 'tacit knowledge' that underlies LINGUISTIC CREATIVITY, which enables speakers to use language in ways that project beyond the primary linguistic data which they are exposed to as children; cf. Sampson (2015). Within generative grammar, the theory of this implicit grammatical knowledge has come to be referred to as UNIVERSAL GRAMMAR (or UG, for short); for clear discussion, see especially Crain and Pietroski (2001). Although the precise characterisation of UG has been revised continuously since Chomsky's early work, claims about its fundamental nature have remained largely unchanged: by hypothesis, UG is internal, implicit (inaccessible to consciousness), INTENSIONAL [with an 's', see below] and domain-specific. Most crucially, perhaps, for many researchers in this tradition, UG is also innate:[10,11]

UG is used in this sense … the theory of the genetic component of the language faculty … that's what it is.

Noam Chomsky, *Poverty of Stimulus: Some Unfinished Business* (2010)

Consequently, for psychologists and philosophers persuaded by Chomsky's approach, theoretical interest in language resides not in linguistic behaviour *per se*, nor in the study of different languages (in any ordinary person's understanding of that term), but rather in a hypothesised mental organ – the innate LANGUAGE FACULTY – that is supposed to make linguistic behaviour possible, and whose epistemic content is assumed to set strict formal limits on grammatical variation.

Initially, psychology appears to have greeted Chomsky's proposals enthusiastically, with many experimentalists of the period setting out to test the 'psycholinguistic reality' of the theoretical constructs of TRANSFORMATIONAL GENERATIVE GRAMMAR (TGG). A key construct of early TGG, which received a good deal of attention from psychologists, was the distinction between the 'surface structure' of a sentence and its 'deep structure', these two levels of representation being related by a set of TRANSFORMATIONAL RULES, which moved, inserted or deleted phrasal constituents.

This model can be illustrated by considering the English passive construction. In TGG it was proposed that active and passive paraphrases of a given proposition such as 'Alice drank the potion/The potion was drunk by Alice' shared a common deep structure, but differed in the number of transformational rules necessary to derive the two surface variants, with more transformations applying to the (ostensibly more complex) passive structure.[12] Early psycholinguists reasoned that if these theoretical constructs were psychologically real, and if they were isomorphic with the processes of language comprehension and production, then grammatically more complex sentences – for instance, those involving more transformations in their derivation – should incur greater processing costs relative to derivationally simpler sentences. An additional premise was that these costs should be directly measurable in terms of increased RESPONSE LATENCIES – informally known as 'reaction times' – and/ or higher error rates. This reasoning formed the basis of what became known as the DERIVATIONAL THEORY OF COMPLEXITY (DTC).

In spite of some early apparent successes, e.g. Miller and Chomsky (1963), Miller and McKean (1964), the DTC foundered rather quickly, as further empirical work failed to show any transparent relationship between derivational complexity and processing costs.[13] A much-cited quote from Fodor, Bever and Garrett (1974: 368) summarises the state of play by the mid-1970s:

Investigations of DTC ... have generally proved equivocal. This argues against the occurrence of grammatical derivations in the computations involved in sentence recognition.

Jerry Fodor, Thomas Bever and Merrill Garrett,
The Psychology of Language (1974: 368)

With hindsight – and especially given the crucial distinction between levels of explanation outlined in Marr ([1982] 2010), which I'll come to in a moment – the absence of any direct correspondence between transformational depth and reaction times or error rates is unsurprising. It's easy to be clever after the fact. Nevertheless, the alleged failure of the DTC was one of the factors that led many psychologists interested in language to turn away from the grammatical theories offered by formal linguists. Many never turned back.

There were several other reasons. For one thing, generative research was – and generally remains – restricted to the level of the canonical sentence, that which begins with a capital letter and ends with a full stop; see T is for Sentence, v is for von Humboldt. By contrast, experimental psychologists were typically more interested in smaller or larger units of speech: for example, in the problems of real-time word recognition, the role of lexical frequency in acquisition and processing, or the interplay of grammatical and pragmatic information in the interpretation of spoken and written discourse, to cite just a few relevant issues. Two key findings of the period were those of Sachs (1967), whose results suggested that listeners do not retain any conscious memory of the surface syntactic form of an utterance, though they do retain its meaning, and slightly later, the work of Bransford and Franks (1971), whose experiments implied that the final interpretations that listeners derive from sentences involve (inextricable) inferential content that is not represented anywhere in the deep structure of the sentence; in other words, listeners are unable to disentangle assertions from inferences.[14] Many psycholinguists came to interpret findings such as these as suggesting that transformational grammar had little empirical – or even heuristic – value.

One final consideration was as much sociological as it was empirical: psychologists turned away from theoretical linguistics because generativist theory was almost wholly unresponsive to their results, supportive or otherwise; see Cutler (2005). *Plus ça change.* Formal linguistic theory (generative theory, at any rate) has developed considerably since the 1960s, and especially since the mid-1990s, but this has invariably been in reaction to internal theoretical arguments – to a lesser extent, to new intuitional data – rather than to the empirical results from the types of group studies favoured by psychologists. The University of Massachusetts linguist and acquisitionist Tom Roeper summed it up nicely back in 1982 (in a quotation cited by Newmeyer 1983):

When psychological evidence has failed to conform to linguistic theory, psychologists have concluded that linguistic theory was wrong, while linguists have concluded that psychological theory was irrelevant.

> Tom Roeper, 'Review of *Linguistic Theory and Psycholinguistic Reality* (1981), edited by Halle, Bresnan and Miller' (1982)

It could be argued that generativists' dismissal of relevant data is a near-inevitable consequence of strictly deductive modes of reasoning. By definition, the inductive mode of enquiry favoured by most psychologists is more responsive to new data than the deductive approach pursued, in its purest form, by Chomsky and others at the vanguard of generative research. This Galilean (hypothetico-deductive) style can be clearly appreciated by watching a recent lecture, recorded at CNRS in Paris in 2010.[15] See Box A below for an excerpt from the transcript; for a detailed critique, see Appendix B (website). Over 120 or so minutes, Chomsky develops a logically compelling discussion of I-LANGUAGE and UG – compelling, as long as one grants all of the segues from description to theory, and all of the necessary auxiliary assumptions, very few of which are presented with supporting evidence. More generally, Chomsky is often dismissive of the use of certain kinds of empirical data – particularly quantitative data – in counter-arguments to his theoretical positions. The following comment from another article is typical of his response to evidence-based challenges from non-generativists:

[Galileo] dismissed a lot of data; he was willing to say: 'Look, if the data refute the theory, the data are probably wrong.' And the data that he threw out were not minor.

> Chomsky, Belletti and Rizzi, *On Nature and Language* (2002: 98, cited in Behme 2013)

It is hard to see that such a stridently anti-empiricist position is defensible, let alone commendable: see Yngve (1986) for a diametrically opposed view.

Whatever the relative weighting of these various factors may have been, the psycholinguistic paradigms of generative linguists and those of psychologists had largely drifted apart by the mid-1970s, giving rise to the 'two souls' situation that persists to the present, and which is reflected in the partisan publications mentioned above.

♫ Leonard Cohen (words), Sharon Robinson, *Alexandra Leaving* (2001)

Box A: On I-language

Excerpt from Noam Chomsky, *Poverty of Stimulus: Some Unfinished Business*, lecture delivered at CNRS Paris, 2010. See Appendix B (website) for a critique.

The direct study of the internal capacity of a person is the study of what is sometimes called 'internal language' – (ii)whatever you have in your head – I-language, for short ... (iii)So, that concept ... the study of I-language is somehow logically prior ... presupposed by everything. (iv)And if we investigate that topic, we enter into an enquiry, into language as essentially part of biology ... (v)Whatever the linguistic capacity of a person is, it's something internal to them, (vi)it's essentially a kind of an organ of the body on a par with the visual system, or the immune system, (vii)or some other sub-system, sometimes called subsystems, or organs of the body ... (viii)So, I-language is such a system ... (ix)What is it? Well, its most elementary property is the property of what is called discrete infinity. (x)So, take sentences: you can have a five word sentence, you can have a six word sentence, but you can't have a five-and-a-half word sentence. (xi)*And it goes on indefinitely ... You can have a hundred-word sentence, a 10,000-word sentence, and so on.* (xii)*It's like the numbers, the natural numbers.* (xiii)*That property of discrete infinity is important, and from a biological point of view it's quite unusual ...* (xiv)You don't find it in the biological world, above the level of maybe DNA, (xv)but it seems to be a unique property of human language ... (xvi)You find it in the number system, but that's probably an offshoot of language. (xvii)There's no other system in the world that's known to have that property. (xviii)Well, the general theory of discrete infinity is pretty well understood; it has been well-understood since the 1940s, it's called the theory of algorithms, the theory of recursive function, various other names, (xix)and the theory of language is going to fit in there somewhere. (xx)That is, the core of an I-language is going to be some kind of an algorithm, some kind of a generative procedure, (xxi)that constructs an infinite array of hierarchically structured expressions ... all internal to us, (xxii)which are then transmitted to what are called interface systems, to other systems of the cognitive system, the physical system, (xxiii)and there are at least two of these: the one is the sensorimotor system – because it's externalised somehow – (xxiv)and the other is systems of thought, planning, understanding, perception, interpretation – loosely called the Semantic Interface. (xxv)So there's a Phonetic Interface and a Semantic Interface: Phonetic interface is with the sensorimotor system, semantic pragmatic interface is with systems of thought, planning, action, and so on. (xxvi)And the core properties of language are [sic] that it has such a generative system, that's the I-language, which essentially provides instructions to these other systems. (xxvii)Now we're interested in this generative procedure in what's technically called 'in intension' not 'extension' (that's intension with an 's'), (xxviii)meaning we want to know what it actually is, not just what is the class of structures that it generates, so that's a study of function in intension, (xxix)and that's what we're interested in if we want to consider language as part of the biological world, (xxx)because what's represented in the brain somehow is a particular algorithm, not a class of algorithms, which are equivalent in the sense that they have the same category of structures that they produce ...

Notes

1 Advance warning. Part I – like the foundations of most structures – is somewhat greyer and more dense than the other sections of this book, and less in keeping with the atmosphere of the work as a whole. There are limits on the extent to which one can leaven foundational material. Readers who could care less about meta-theory are advised to begin with another section, and to return here if or when they become more interested in the philosophical underpinnings.

2 That said, if my personal experience of the field is typical, generative syntacticians are a particularly hostile group, not unfamiliar with the knife drawer. This hostility is epitomised by a recent blog by Norbert Hornstein (2012), which is self-described as a 'partially a labor of hate'. The author and his supporters claim that this description is intended to be tongue-in-cheek; however, given the mordant tone and scorched-earth tactics of some of the contributions, many observers remain unconvinced; cf. Behme (2013). And Hornstein's blog is charitable when compared with some of the yet more caustic commentary in the biolinguistic Blogosphere.

3 '"Well-tempered" means that the twelve notes per octave of the standard keyboard are tuned in such a way that it is possible to play music in most major or minor keys and it will not sound perceptibly out of tune.' (https://en.wikipedia.org/wiki/Well_temperament). My ambition here is similar: to tune the discussion in such a way that psycholinguists of all theoretical persuasions will not detect too much dissonance, nor feel themselves misrepresented by it.

4 Psycholinguistics and syntax are not the only areas of linguistic enquiry that are so divided: as Kimberley (2015) discusses, a similar conflict is played out in formal semantics, between what he terms SEMANTIC MINIMALISTS (e.g. Cappelen and Lepore (2005) and CONTEXTUALISTS (e.g. Recanati 2004), the former group remaining faithful to the idea that meaning can be usefully explained with reference to truth-conditions, the latter insisting on the role of context-sensitive contingencies.

5 See, for example, Wundt (1874), Paul (1898, third edition). Hermann Paul begins Chapter 15 of *Prinzipien der Sprachgeschichte* with the sentence: 'Every grammatical category develops on the basis of a psychological one. The former is nothing more than the external realisation of the latter.' [*Jede grammatische Kategorie erzeugt sich auf Grundlage einer psychologischen. Die erstere ist nichts als das Eintreten der letzteren in die aüssere Erschienung.*' Paul (1898: 241).] A *Wikipedia* article dates the first published use of the term *psycholinguistics* to a 1936 work by J. R. Kantor. Kantor was a professor of psychology at Indiana University, where B. F. Skinner also worked for a short time.

6 Natasha Warner drew my attention to the pioneering research of Elise Richter, active during the 1930s and early 1940s at the University of Vienna. Richter became the first female Dozent (assistant professor) in Austria in 1907, having completed her *Habilitation* for her work on Romance languages; in her sixties, she took over a phonetics laboratory and began doing ground-breaking work in speech perception. Her Jewish ancestry resulted in her dismissal in 1942, and subsequent deportation to Theresienstadt concentration camp, where she died on 9 October 1942.

7 Cutler (2005) points out that the rapid development of psycholinguistics during this period was as much due to technology as to conceptual advances. Prior to the 1950s, researchers did not have access to voice-recording equipment of sufficient quality to prepare experimental stimuli, nor did they have the technical resources needed to

measure and analyse real-time language processing. As these resources improved and became more widely available, so the field progressed. Psycholinguistics saw exponential growth in the later 1980s and 1990s, as hard disk drives and affordable software packages became more available. Before that, the equipment available in the best linguistics laboratories was expensive and hard to program. The machine used to run some of the experiments reported in Marslen-Wilson et al. (1994), for example, was the size of large filing cabinet using IBM 'Winchester' disks (36 cm diameter platters with 30 MB fixed storage and 30 MB removable storage). Every minor modification in the experimental design involved extensive re-programming. (I know this from personal experience, having worked as a research assistant for part of that project.) At the time, only relatively few research facilities had access to such modern technology. Given the huge advances that have been made since, it is possible that the same thing will happen in neuroscience, so that within a decade or two any undergraduate student can run a neuro-imaging experiment. But we're not there yet.

8 The term *hagiographical* is hardly exaggerated: Chomsky's writings are frequently treated more as objects of veneration and exegesis than as objects of study. This is especially true of Chomsky (1959), which is, I suspect, vastly more cited than read. Like the Bible, or the Quran, or the Second Amendment to the US Constitution, it scarcely seems to matter what actually appears on the page; what counts is what people believe is written there. Conventional academic wisdom has it that Chomsky's review stopped Behaviourism in its tracks, so it must be true.

9 However, early work from the 1970s, reproduced in Saberi and Perrott (1999), and subsequently reported by David Poeppel, shows, rather remarkably, that listeners can understand speech that is played backwards, with no apparent loss of intelligibility, provided that the reversed temporal splices are sufficiently small (<60 ms); see Poeppel (2014). The implication of this research is that our intuitions about how the mind processes language – i.e. in close temporal sequence – may be quite mistaken.

10 See Crain and Pietroski (2001) and below for discussion of all of these 'I-predicates'. Note that the term Universal Grammar (UG) is easily confused with another construct, namely, Language Universals. As discussed in greater detail in Part II, the term LANGUAGE UNIVERSALS refers to those relatively concrete formal and substantive properties that are shared by the (end-state) grammars of the world's languages. It is controversial whether there are *any* absolute Language Universals in this sense, beyond conceptual necessity or tautological statements; see especially Evans and Levinson (2009), and commentaries to that work. For example, it is a universal that all spoken languages have at least one vowel in their phonological inventory, but this is a matter of effability. Similarly, languages generally employ egressive speech sounds: if a language had only ingressive sounds – that is, sounds made by breathing in, rather than exhaling – utterances would be too short, and speech too uncomfortable, to permit any viable spoken communication. It is also a universal of spoken language that speech must be temporarily sequenced, so that we cannot pronounce different words simultaneously. And so on. Notice, though, that many universals cannot be part of UG since they are generalisations over extant 'E-languages': as such, they are linguists' discoveries, inaccessible to lay speakers of individual languages. The role of processing in explaining Language Universals is discussed in more detail in Part II. Here, the main point to stress is that arguments for or against

UG are wholly independent of the existence or otherwise of Language Universals, and *vice versa*, in spite of what is sometimes assumed, particularly by opponents of generative grammar.

11 Another term that was used for some time to describe this internal, implicit knowledge of language was I-LANGUAGE (distinguishing this phenomenon from E-LANGUAGE, which refers to the commonly held notion of individual languages, such as the 'English Language', the 'Greek Language', etc. See below. It is now clear that I-language, though already highly abstract, cannot be identified with UG: Chomsky (2005) makes clear that UG refers to the initial state, whereas I-language is a steady-state grammar that emerges from the interaction of UG, the linguistic environment and 'third factor' properties: hence, current UG is clearly a much more rarified and circumscribed notion than was the 1980s construal of I-LANGUAGE). In I is for Internalism, I question whether the distinction between E-LANGUAGE and I-LANGUAGE is at all helpful in understanding grammatical competence.

12 The passive construction was extensively re-analysed at the height of the Government–Binding era; see especially Baker, Johnson and Roberts (1989). The improvement in descriptive adequacy, however, came at the cost of observational adequacy: after Baker et al., the lexical and pragmatic exceptions to the passive rule received even less consideration than previously. See G is for Grammar (introduction), Pullum (2010).

13 See Fodor and Garrett (1967), Bever (1970), Johnson-Laird and Stevenson (1970), Fodor, Bever and Garrett (1974), references in MacWhinney and Chang (1995).

14 More recent studies of 'syntactic priming' suggest, however, that the surface form of sentences *is* implicitly retained in short-term memory, at least for long enough to influence the form of responses produced in spoken dialogue: see Bock (1986), Potter and Lombardi (1990).

15 Source: www.youtube.com/watch?v=3VyteV_7sxI.

2   Marr's *Vision* I

There may be said to be two classes of people in the world; those who constantly divide the people of the world into two classes, and those who do not.

Robert Benchley, *Of All Things* (1921)

No representation without process, no process without representation

A proper understanding of how language is comprehended and produced requires an integrated approach that gets beyond ideology, and which combines theories of representation and process. In his seminal work on computer vision, titled (obviously enough) *Vision*, David Marr had this to say:

Vision is ... first and foremost an information-processing task, but we cannot think of it as just a process. For if we are capable of knowing what is where in the world, our brains must somehow be capable of representing this information ... The study of vision must therefore include not only the study of how to extract from images the various aspects of the world that are useful to us, but also an inquiry into the nature of the internal representations by which we capture this information and thus make it available as a basis for decisions about our thoughts and actions ...

... This duality – the representation and the processing of information – lies at the heart of most information processing tasks, and will profoundly shape our investigation of the particular problems posed by vision.

David Marr, *Vision* ([1982] 2010: 3)[1]

Replace the term *vision* with '(spoken) language comprehension and production', and *will* with 'should' in the penultimate line, and you have – in a fairly large nutshell – what classical psycholinguistics is concerned with, namely: 'the study of how to extract from [speech and text] the various aspects of the world that are useful to us, [and] an enquiry into the nature of the internal representations by which we capture this information and thus make it available as a basis for our thoughts and actions'.[2]

Marr's book contains several other highly relevant ideas concerning the nature of explanation in vision research: the first chapter is required reading

17

for anyone interested in any kind of cognitive process from a computational perspective. I'll return to these ideas directly, not only because they had a significant influence on the direction of psycholinguistic research through the latter part of the twentieth century, but also because they provide a vital clue to understanding why many theoretical linguists and psychologists so consistently *mis*understand one other when it comes to language and cognition.[3]

On the face of it, integration would seem to be a simple matter: take what competence-based approaches have determined about what is mentally represented and tack on what processing theories have discovered about how this internalised knowledge is put to use in language comprehension and production. Closer scrutiny, however, shows this to be about as practicable as splicing a gene sequence to the front half of a donkey to make a horse, or merging an architectural blueprint with the physical foundations of a house to create a palace.

The problem of incommensurability is compounded by the fact that even if the two theories were immediately compatible at a psychological level of explanation, we have no clear idea, *a priori,* of which linguistic phenomena should properly be handled in terms of stored representation, and which in terms of process, or even – as some researchers would contend – whether the distinction is a useful one. See also Stone and Davies (2012).

A fuller appreciation of the (in)commensurability problem involves a philosophical journey from Chomsky to Marr and back (to Chomsky). Though I believe this trip is worthwhile, it's not entirely necessary to appreciating the challenges of integration: if such scientific navel-gazing is not for you, you can skip ahead to Part II.

From Chomsky to Marr ...

If I could trace the lines that ran
Between your smile and your sleight of hand
I'd guess that you put something up my sleeve.
Now every time I see your face
The bells ring in a far off place
We can find each other this way, I believe.

♫ Josh Ritter, *Come and Find Me* (2002)

My main purpose in this chapter and the next is to develop the claim that Chomskyan grammar and classical psycholinguistics constitute two largely orthogonal approaches to the study of language and mind, each with their own domains of enquiry and research agendas. The answers you get invariably depend on the questions you ask, so different questions lead to different answers, not necessarily better ones:

Most generative linguists are interested in modelling the fundamental formal properties of natural language grammars, and – in some cases – understanding the limits on grammatical variation.[4] In more recent years, the emphasis has been on describing the computational properties of the 'initial state' of the language faculty, that is to say, the knowledge of language that all typically developing children are assumed to share at birth, prior to exposure to any particular language(s); see, in particular, Chomsky (2005). Such knowledge – supposing it exists as a distinct component of mind – is by definition extremely abstract, very far removed from the kinds of linguistic behaviour that psycholinguistics is mostly concerned with.

A comparison between investigations of the beginnings of the universe and the applied mathematics of downhill skiing is an extreme, but not totally far-fetched, analogy.

By contrast, researchers in (experimental) psycholinguists are primarily interested in explaining how adult language users are able to understand and produce the particular language(s) they actually speak. No-one 'speaks UG', nor does knowing UG help a native English speaker to understand spoken Hungarian, even to the same level of proficiency as a Hungarian speaker's pet Labrador. (See Andics et al. (2016), also Hoffman (2016), for some balanced commentary on the language ability of our canine companions.) The ability to use a variety of English, or Russian, or Chichewa, or Inuktitut – or any of the thousands of languages that humans speak – *may* rest in small part on innate epistemic content, but it also depends to a much larger extent on learned knowledge about those particular varieties, as well as on a diverse set of interactions with other cognitive and sensorimotor skills, most of which are not at all specific to language. It follows from this that the kinds of constructs that are postulated by some theoretical linguists as grammatical axioms are only tangentially related to the constructs recruited by psycholinguistics to explain language use. Indeed, the former concepts may not be relevant at all to explaining how we use the languages we know. See especially G is for Grammar, H is for Homogeneity, I is for Internalism below.[5]

This disconnect between linguistics and psycholinguistics would be clearer were it not for the fact that many of the terms that crop up in psycholinguistics also appear – without scare quotes or other flags – in more abstract grammatical theories. So, for example, it is easy to conflate the debate among generative linguists between representational vs. derivational approaches to (UG/I-language) syntactic analysis with the representational (declarative) vs. processing (procedural) distinction in psycholinguistics. The two may be related, but they are not ISOMORPHIC with one another: that is to say, there is no one-to-one correspondence between them. This lack of isomorphism means, for instance, that there is no fundamental incompatibility between the generative assumption that syntactic derivations proceed asynchronously, bottom-up (from 'right to left') through recursive application of *Merge*, or some similar Minimalist operation, and the psycholinguistic proposal that English utterances are parsed incrementally in real time, from 'left to right', with listeners making almost instantaneous use of all potentially relevant information to arrive at an appropriate interpretation of a sentence (in a particular context of utterance).[6] Likewise, whereas CONSTRUCTION-SPECIFIC RULES are anathema to most theoretical accounts of UG, this does not mean that different constructions are not parsed as such by the language processor.

[Take a breath, here.]

The refusal to distinguish these two levels of explanation has generated an enormous amount of heat – and precious little light – in the psycholinguistics world. It has also led to the publication of articles with titles such as 'Empty categories access their antecedents during comprehension' (Bever and McElree 1988). This is rhetorical sleight of hand – *shorthand,* at best – for: '[Whatever mental constructs or processes are correlated with the notion of] empty categories [in the version of generative theory we are currently using] access [whatever mental constructs or processes correspond to the notion of grammatically expressed] antecedents during spoken language comprehension.'

Admittedly, the expanded version of the title is hardly slick, but it's considerably less misleading. The general point here is that whatever turns out to be the best theory of grammar is not necessarily the right theory of language processing or of 'language in mind': it needn't even be close.

In order to better appreciate this argument, it is helpful to consider some very rudimentary problems in arithmetic. This initial take will be fairly quick and mostly painless. The approach taken here is also extremely rudimentary: coming from an absurdly narrow Arts and Humanities background, my last formal brush with mathematics was a mediocre pass at GCE 'O-level', *circa* 1977. For this reason, mathematicians, and the excessively numerate, should look away.

The Joys of Arithmetick

Seven Sciences fupremly excellent,
Are the chief Stars in *Wifdom*'s Firmament :
Whereof *Arithmetick* is one, whofe Worth
The Beams of Profit and Delight fhine forth;
This crowns the reft, this makes Man's Mind compleat;
This treats of Numbers, and of this we treat.

From Preface to *Cocker's Arithmetick* (1736 edition)

'Two numbers of like kind'

First, try to figure out as quickly and accurately as possible the answers to the following simple multiplication problems:

(1)   What is ...

    a. 14 times 5?
    b. 21 times 17?
    c. 10 times 7?
    d. 9 times 13?
    e. 9 times 12?
    f. 30 times 2?
    g. 8 times 7?

The recursive principle involved in each of these problems is precisely the same, namely, iterative addition: the product of any two numbers is obtained by taking one number and adding it to itself the number of times represented by the other number. Or, as Edward Cocker expressed it in his immodestly titled (albeit posthumously published) *Cocker's Arithmetick* (1736):

Multiplication is performed by two Numbers of like Kind, for the Production of a Third, which shall have Reason to the one, as the other hath to the Unit, and in Effect is a most brief and artificial Compound Addition, of many equal Numbers of like kind into one Sum. Or, Multiplication is that by which we multiply two or more Numbers, the one into the other, to the end that their product may come forth, or be delivered. Or, Multiplication is the increasing of any one Number by any other, so often as there are Units in that Number, by which the other is increased; or, by having two Numbers given to find a Third, which shall contain one of the Numbers as many times as there are Units in the other ...

Edward Cocker, *Cocker's Arithmetick* (1736)

As you might recall from some school mathematics lesson, the property of COMMUTATIVITY means that whichever number you choose to operate on, the result is identical ($mn = nm$): so, $(26 \times 378) = (378 \times 26)$, to take a specific pair of values. All of these problems can be described by the same recursive function. Computationally, they are identical kinds of function in intension.

In spite of this equivalence, some sums are markedly easier for the average human (calculator) to solve quickly – unless you are a mathematical prodigy – though the precise ranking from trivial to challenging depends in part upon your age, and where and when you went to school. For almost everyone, (1c) and (1g) are the easiest, closely followed by (1f) and (1e);[7] problems (1b) and (1d) are among the most difficult. And for most people, (1a) is significantly harder than (1c), in spite of the fact that they are instances of the 'same problem': $(14 \times 5) = (7 \times 10) = 70$.

In the simpler cases, no actual calculation is involved, assuming that you're older than nine or ten years of age. We don't *figure out* 8 times 7 (1g); instead, we *look it up*, something we are able to do in virtue of rote learning of times tables in elementary school. In many countries, times tables go to 9 (10 is assumed to come for free) – in others, to 12; it may be even higher in some educational systems. In my own case, ['twelve twelves are ...'] 144 constitutes the outer edge of my finite arithmetic universe, at least that part which is stored in declarative memory. As a result, for adults with my education, problem (1e) is trivial compared to problem (1d); indeed, it's not really a problem, since nothing is computed. For Japanese readers, on the other hand, (1d) and (1e) require approximately the same amount of additional calculation.

Having declarative knowledge of up to 12 times 12 also means that the answer to (1d) is usually derived by going to the edge of the nines and adding one more: (('twelve nines are one-hundred-and-eight), plus nine, makes one-hundred-and-seventeen'). That at least is my intuition – and intuitional judgments presumably tell us something.

> If you consider that this type of intuitional judgment might be unreliable, you are probably in good company. You are *not*, however, in the company of typical generative linguists, for whom such introspection is an unexceptionable part of data collection. Validating arguments for this position are offered by Sprouse and Almeida (2012); cf. Gibson, Piantadosi and Fedorenko (2013), also J is for Judgment below, for some opposing views.)

In the case of (1d), there are many other paths (algorithms) that might be taken to arrive at the correct answer, including adding 9 to itself 13 times in incremental steps, but – once again, intuitively – I suspect that this is the last one chosen. There is no reason to suppose that the (intensionally) simplest algorithm is the one selected. Similarly, a moment's reflection tells us that (1a) and (1c) are equivalent, and that the fastest way to calculate (1a) is to transform it to (1c); in spite of this, it seems that most people tackle problem (1a) procedurally, through a variety of different algorithms $((14 \times 5); ((14 \times 2) \times 2) + 14); (10 \times 5) + (4 \times 5)$, etc.), rather than converting it to a look-up problem.

Notice that it is possible that the preferred algorithm in a particular instance might vary according to the individual, or to the relative size of the numbers – for example, larger number times smaller number, or *vice versa* – or to the presentation order, or even, conceivably, to the time of day, or what the person had for breakfast. As long as all of these paths through numerical maze converge on the same result, they are equivalent. And no matter which path (algorithm) is chosen, it will take fractionally longer than 'reading off' the answer, which is what happens in the case of problem (1c); 'real problems' are also more prone to error.[8]

Despite the connotations of complexity, there is nothing inherently mysterious or difficult about the term ALGORITHM: an algorithm is no more than a set of steps taken to lead to some outcome; in this case, a path through arithmetic space to a particular destination (or finite range of destinations). The simplest algorithms are deterministic, which is to say, they produce the same results every time. Simple addition and multiplication involves deterministic algorithms: except in George Orwell's *1984*, 2 + 2 always makes 4. Real life, however, almost invariably involves probabilistic algorithms: boil an egg for exactly three minutes and it should be perfectly soft-boiled, but not if it's really fresh, or has been sitting around too long, or is oversized, or ... Although I adopt the metaphor of multiplication here, language processing is more like boiling an egg – making a *soufflé*, even – than it resembles simple arithmetic.

Something that is easily overlooked is that we never calculate through pure iterative addition *even in those cases where we can't look up the answer*: without applying some declarative knowledge of times tables, most people can't get off the ground at all. To appreciate this, try working out 43 times 89 using only iterative addition: simply adding 89 to itself three – let alone *forty*-three – times, is strenuous enough. Once again, Edward Cocker was clear on this point, three hundred years ago:

The Learner ought to have all the Varieties of Single Multiplitation [sic] by Heart, before he can well proceed and farther into this Art, it being of most excellent Use, and none of the following Rules in Arithmetick, but what have a principal Dependance thereupon, which may be learned by the following Table.

Edward Cocker, *Cocker's Arithmetick* (1736)

The availability of two systems of reckoning leads to the theoretically incoherent yet entirely reasonable conclusion that – in a purely declarative way – it is possible to know the answer to '9 × 6 = ?' while being mistaken about '3 × 18 = ?', or even '6 × 9 = ?'[9] Anyone who supposes that people 'reflexively know' the property of commutativity must not have spent time helping average six or seven year-olds with their mathematics homework. (This observation is routinely ignored by many of my professional linguists, who may themselves have been mathematical prodigies, and whose children may display similar talents. By contrast, arithmetic calculation has always been a challenge for me, as it is for my children. There are times when being stupid helps you to understand things more clearly.)

What's more, the general concept of abstract number appears to be a very recent cognitive attainment. Devlin (1998: 21), for example, asserts that:

[It] was not recognised, nor were behavioural rules such as those concerning addition and multiplication formulated, until the era of Greek mathematics began around 600 BC.

Keith Devlin, *The Language of Mathematics:*
Making the Invisible Visible (1998: 21)

In other words, in spite of our educated intuitions on the matter, knowledge of the principle of commutativity is more likely to be a deductively discovered fact about the world of numbers than an instinctive, biologically wired construct.

From times tables to grammatical productivity

The parallels with typical second language learning should be obvious. Thanks to rote learning, we can fairly easily learn and record the meaning of some complex grammatical expression such that we are able to use it fluently and appropriately ('phrase-book French'); see Part IV. But without some further analysis and computation, it is impossible to generalise that knowledge to produce related expressions in the way that an adult native speaker seems to be able to do.

Two examples serve to illustrate this point.

The first case comes from Japanese, a language that has been pestering me on a daily basis for several years now. Specifically, the concern is with the Japanese expression *x mitakotonai (desu)*, usually translated as '(I) haven't seen *x* (before).' The corresponding question form is *x mitakotoaru?* 'Have you seen *x* (before)?' Given this alternation, it doesn't take much effort to figure out that *nai* is the negative form of *aru* (especially if you spend time around Japanese toddlers, *nai* being heard about as often as English *No!*). But the analysis of the rest of the string eluded me for nearly a year after I first heard it: it was clear how to use the expression appropriately, and what it meant, but not how that meaning was composed. One day, however, the light went on – or at least, began to flicker fitfully. At a certain moment I understood that there were four morphemes in the string: 見/*mi*, the root, meaning 'see'; *ta*, the perfect morpheme; *koto* 'fact'; *nai/aru* 'not/is'. Following this stunning breakthrough, I was able to generalise the analysis to other predicates, such as 行ったことない/*i.tta.koto.nai* '(I) haven't been there before' (from行/*ik.u* 'go'). Significantly, however, I am still not sure some five years later how to generalise to predicates from different conjugations, or to those of lower token frequency (e.g. 読む *yom.u* 'read', 買う *ka.u* 'buy'), nor do I know whether the same syntax can be used with light verb expressions (e.g. *benkyou suru* 'study' → *furansugo-o benkyou shita koto nai* '(I) haven't studied French before'). As soon as I hear the construction used with another predicate root, I can immediately analyse it, but I have no confidence in spontaneously producing a new form. In short, I can generalise, but only partially. Hence, though the grammatical rules that linguists invoke to describe the process may have an infinite extension *in principle*, in my Japanese INTERLANGUAGE this grammatical knowledge is highly restricted. It hardly amounts to a rule at all. Instead, my knowledge in this syntactic domain consists of what the psychologist Michael Tomasello has termed 'verb islands' (Tomasello 1992) – though *islets* or *atolls* might be more appropriate metaphors. And this knowledge shows no sign of further development, five years on.

Table 1 *'Angry lions, brightly painted horses, [for] a little while': nominal inflection in German.*

Case/ Gender	Masculine 'an angry lion'	Feminine 'a little while'	Neuter 'a brightly coloured horse'	Plural
Nominative	ein bös*er*	eine klein*e*	ein bunt*es*	bunt*e*
(default)	Löwe	Weile	Pferd	Pferd*e*/Löw*en*
Accusative	einen bös*en*	eine klein*e*	ein bunt*es*	bunt*e*
	Löwen	Weile	Pferd	Pferd*e*/Löw*en*
Genitive	eines bös*en*	einer klein*en*	eines bunt*en*	bunt*er*
	Löwens	Weile	Pferdes	Pferd*e*/Löw*en*
	einem bös*em*	einer klein*en*	einem bunt*en*	bunt*en*
	Löwen	Weile	Pferd	Pferd*en*/Löw*en*
Nominative	der bös*e*	die klein*e*	das bunt*e*	die bunt*en*
(default)	Löwe	Weile	Pferd	Pferd*e*/Löw*en*
Accusative	den bös*en*	die klein*e*	das bunt*e*	die bunt*en*
	Löwen	Weile	Pferd	Pferd*e*/Löw*en*
Genitive	des bös*en*	der klein*en*	des bunt*en*	der bunt*en*
	Löwens	Weile	Pferd*es*	Pferd*e*/Löw*en*
Dative	dem bös*en*	der klein*en*	dem bunt*en*	den bunt*en*
	Löwen	Weile	Pferd	Pferd*en*/Löw*en*

Similarly, when learning German as a teenager, I struggled with the problems of nominal inflection, and in particular, with the interactions between case, number and gender across so-called 'strong' vs. 'weak' nominal paradigms. The full system of endings, no doubt familiar to readers of any standard teaching grammar (e.g. Durrell 2011), is exemplified in Table 1, which displays the inflectional paradigms for indefinite and definite noun-phrases, respectively.

The Rilke poem below ('Das Karussell') offers a much more brilliant use of a subset of these forms.

Closer inspection of these tables reveals that the inflectional system of Standard German is less horrendous than it could be, given the many neutralisations across rows and columns. For example, gender distinctions in both 'weak' and 'strong' paradigms are neutralised in the plural (e.g. *der~die~das* → *die*), gender distinctions between masculine and neuter are neutralised in the dative singular (both *einem/dem x_{adj}-en*); strong forms of inflection are only expressed once (either on the attributive adjective or on the determiner, but not both). So in some sense, it could be a lot worse: in the limit, there could be a separate exponent for each cell in the paradigm, with different phonological endings for determiners and adjectives.

In spite of these simplifications, many second language learners never achieve full control of the inflectional system: see Lardiere (2016). Some people don't even try, settling instead for a schwa or zero ending on every adjective, and a near-uniform choice of nominative determiner (either *der*, *die* or *das*, across the board). With a few tweaks, these learners could almost be speaking Dutch, which – in this regard at least – is a much simpler proposition. For learners who persevere, their knowledge of the German paradigms grows, sporadically and partially, driven by both type and token frequency:

> In terms of TYPE FREQUENCY, most learners acquire the more frequent nominative (default) and accusative singular forms of a (D)-(A)-N sequence before mastering the genitive or dative. Genitive forms (of common nouns) are hardly ever encountered in colloquial German, and so may never be fully acquired by native speakers, let alone second language learners. Indeed, several German dialects have lost their genitive declension forms, except for the possessive *-s* found with proper names; e.g. *Marias Schwester* ('Mary's sister'); what in English is sometimes termed the 'Saxon Genitive'.[10]
>
> The same holds for TOKEN FREQUENCY. Even a non-German speaker is likely to produce *Eine Kleine Nachtmusik* correctly, without recognising the case and gender of the noun *Musik*; yet, in spite of this, an intermediate L2 learner may have serious difficulty in deciding which of the *dative* alternants in (2) is grammatically appropriate (note that the preposition *mit* 'with' requires the dative case):

(2) a. Mit *Eine Kleine Nachtmusik* verabschieden wir uns für heute.
      b. Mit *Einer Kleinen Nachtmusik* verabschieden wir uns für heute.
      c. Mit *Eine Kleinen Nachtmusik* verabschieden wir uns für heute.

'With *Eine Kleine Nachtmusik* we take our leave for today.'

Bayrischer Rundfunk (Bavarian Radio) sign-off

Somewhat remarkably – remarkably to an English speaker, that is – the answer is (2b): even titles inflect for case.

The acquisition of grammatical knowledge, here and elsewhere, is intimately tied to particular lexical entries, and to usage.[11] It's vanishingly unlikely that *anyone* – native speaker or second language learner – has internalised the inflectional paradigms as a table, or as a fully autonomous set of inflectional rules, even though evidently their knowledge can be represented that way in a linguistic description. Here once more, rules may be a useful way of describing grammatical knowledge, but one can have internalised grammatical knowledge without ever knowing a rule in the classical sense. For further discussion, see G is for Grammar below, also Part IV; for an enlightening, computational analysis of German inflection, see Cahill and Gazdar (1999), also Kilbury (2001).

In Part IV, I return to the question of partial knowledge in (second and first) language acquisition, respectively. For now, these examples serve to highlight the difficulty in determining the source and generality of grammatical knowledge in the mind of any particular language learner.

Figure 3 *Und dann und wann ... [ein blaues Pferd]*: carousel at Kobe Zoo.

Mit einem Dach und seinem Schatten dreht
    with a-MASC.DAT.SG roof and its-MASC.DAT.SG. turns
sich eine kleine Weile der Bestand
    itself a-fem.acc.sg small-fem.acc.sg the-m.nom.sg stock
von bunten Pferden, alle aus dem Land,
    of brightly painted-DAT.PL horse-DAT.PL, all-NOM.PL out the-NEUTER.DAT.
    SG land
das lange zögert, eh' es untergeht.
    which-NEUTER.NOM.SG long-adv hesitates, before it-NEUTER.NOM.SG.
    disappears

Zwar manche sind an Wagen angespannt,
    though some-NOM.PL are to carriages.PL harnessed
doch alle haben Mut in ihren Mienen;
    still all-NOM.PL have courage in their-DAT.PL expression.PL
ein böser roter Löwe geht mit ihnen
    a-masc.nom.sg fierce-masc.nom.sg red-masc.nom.sg Lion-masc.nom.sg
    goes with them.dat.pl
und dann und wann ein weißer Elefant ...
    and now and then a-masc.nom.sg white-masc.nom.sg Elephant-masc.
    nom.sg.

    With its roof and its shade there turns / a brief while the collection / of
    colourful horses, all from that land / that hesitates long, before it slips
    away. / Though some are harnessed / they all display spirited expres-
    sions: / among them stalks an angry red lion / ... and now and then a
    white elephant ...

                          Rainer Maria von Rilke, 'Das Karussell', first stanza

A little more arithmetic

Before leaving arithmetic, consider the additional problems in (3) and their correspondents (4) below. Computationally, these are nearly identical to one another, but for various reasons – because of the representational format in (4a), the less common sequence of operations (division vs. multiplication (4b)), the number base involved (4c) – the latter problems demand more processing resources, and considerably more time, on the part of the ordinary reader/human calculator.

(3) a. What is 78 times 26?
      b. What is 12 times 80?
      c. What is 3 times 2?

(4) a. What is LXXVIII times XXVI?
      b. What is 960 divided by 12?
      c. What is $(11)_2$ times $(10)_2$?

In the following extract, Frank Land provides a clear explication of the contrast between (3a) and (4a):

The difficulties of using other notations for quite simple arithmetical operations may be illustrated by the simple calculation of seventy-eight multiplied by twenty-six, using Roman numerals. We must multiply by one symbol at a time, remembering that multiplying by I simply gives the original number, multiplying by V involves replacing I by V, V times V is XXV, V times X is L, V times L is CCL. The calculation would be:

$$\begin{array}{r} \mathit{LXXVIII} \\ \mathit{XXVI} \\ \hline \mathit{LXXVIII} \\ \mathit{CCLLLXXVVVV} \\ \mathit{DCCLXXX} \\ \mathit{DCCLXXX} \\ \hline \mathit{MMXXVIII} \end{array}$$

where in adding the rows together we replace two Vs by one X, five Xs by L, two Ls by C, five Cs by D, and two Ds by M. The reader can best appreciate the work which is involved by first writing seventy-six and thirty-seven in Roman numerals, and then multiplying them together. If the answer is then checked by ordinary multiplication, the labour required by the two methods may be contrasted.

If multiplication is somewhat laborious, division becomes almost impossible.

Frank Land, *The Language of Mathematics* (1974: 4)

What has this got to do with language(s)? The answer should be reasonably clear: just like mental arithmetic, language (acquisition and) processing also involves some combination of stored, rote-learned knowledge and more general procedural rules – *or whatever properties of the processing system allow for productive generalisations* (so-called 'linguistic creativity'). This is what was illustrated by the examples in (1–2) above; the contrast between the examples in (3) and (4) demonstrates, in addition, some ways in which representational format significantly impacts on processing difficulty.

There are 10 kinds of people in the world: those who understand binary, and those who don't.

Why was 6 afraid of 7? Because 7 8 9.

Why don't jokes work in base 8? Because 7 10 11.

Original authors unknown, *Binary and Other Base Jokes*

Hence, the empirical questions of adult (end-state) psycholinguistics boil down to these four: (i) What is actually stored in a speaker's mind? (ii) What, if anything, is generated 'by grammatical rule'? (iii) How does the representational format of (i) impact on (ii). Finally, (iv) to what extent do the answers to (i)–(iii) vary across languages and across individuals, and/or groups of speakers?

In addressing these questions, it is vital to distinguish between the *logical* answer to a different question – *What would an ideal computational system look like (in respect of these questions)?* – and the *empirical* answer (to the questions at hand). The first may be tantalising to the theoretical linguist, but it is almost completely irrelevant from a psycholinguistic point of view.

In the case of inflectional morphology, for example, it is clear that information about irregular or syncretic forms – irregular past-tense forms in English, for example – must be mentally represented in some way, as must some information concerning the form and meaning of lexical roots (see B is for Arbitrariness below). By contrast, predictable, readily calculable information, such as the plural or past-tense forms of regularly inflected nouns and verbs, does not *need* to be stored since in principle it can always be generated by rule. This redundancy means that stored regular plurals have no place in an elegant theory of word-formation, any more than times tables belong in a pure theory of arithmetic. But this is not to say that storing precompiled regular plurals or past-tense forms might not be very useful to the speaker or listener having to process English nouns and verbs in real time. Irrespective of what the theory minimally requires, it is a separate empirical question just how much redundancy is involved in morphological processing, specifically, whether regular inflected forms are represented, or derived by rule, or both, and how much the answer to this question varies from one individual, or subset of speakers, or one language variety to the next. (It is also possible that some kinds of irregular forms are treated as morphologically decomposable: see, for example, Fruchter, Stockall and Marantz (2013). See also Bonet and Harbour (2012) for a particularly lucid discussion of the regular vs. irregular distinction more generally, a contrast that turns out to be more nuanced, intricate and theoretically interesting than most experimentalists have typically assumed.)

Parallel considerations apply to sentence processing. Over the years, mainstream generative syntax has dispensed with a very large number of theoretical notions. The set of discarded constructs, some of which play a significant explanatory role in other grammatical theories, includes the notion of CON-STRUCTION. At least since Chomsky (1981) it has been taken for granted in generativist circles that there are no construction-specific rules of grammar, that every grammatical sentence is informed and regulated by a common set of more abstract rules and constraints. Take, for instance, the Passive Transformation of TGG, discussed earlier: this language-particular, construction-specific, rule of the Extended Standard Theory was replaced in the 1980s by a set of interacting constraints and general movement rules ('Case Filter', 'Move-alpha') that together derive the effects of the Passive Transformation without reference to any specific structural descriptions. For discussion, see Chomsky (1981), Baker, Johnson and Roberts (1989), also Kiparsky (2013); though cf. Pullum (2010), also Part II below. At a theoretical level then, references to particular constructions are generally considered redundant and therefore eliminable. Yet this theoretical modification clearly doesn't exclude the possibility that constructions are psychologically real and used by the language processor in analysing utterances. Once again, for psycholinguists, this is an empirical question to be decided by experimental evidence, rather than by considerations of formal economy or theoretical elegance. And there is no shortage of data from a wide variety of sources – from syntactic priming experiments, from production errors, from first and second language acquisition studies, from agrammatism and dementia research – all of which supports the idea that constructions, as well as fully fledged formulaic utterances, are stored as pre-compiled strings in declarative memory. (With respect to dementia research, for example, see Sidtis et al. 2012, Sidtis and Bridges 2013; see also Theakston 2004, Cornips and Corrigan 2005.)

The possibility that (at least high-frequency) constructions and schemata are stored complete, ready to use 'off the peg', has significant implications for our capacity to judge grammatical acceptability – traditionally, one of the empirical cornerstones of generative grammar. If we only have 'words and rules' in our heads, the ability to judge grammaticality must depend on syntactic computation. If, however, constructions are stored as pre-compiled templates, then it is possible that we could judge the ill-formedness of *Peter buys often books* or even of *Who did you say that left?* without any syntactic computation, given a sufficiently enriched lexical–grammatical network, just in the same way that we can judge the ill-formedness of *8 × 7 = 66 without doing any arithmetic at all; see Allen and Seidenberg (1999), MacWhinney (2000); cf. Akhtar and Tomasello (1997).[12] This issue is taken up again in Part II, Cases #5 and #6, and in various chapters in Part III, further below.

Before adjourning discussion of declarative vs. procedural knowledge, it is important to mention the seminal contribution of Michael Ullman and his colleagues, e.g. Ullman (2001b, 2001a, 2004), Ullman and Pierpont (2005), Hartshorne and Ullman (2006). Expert readers may find it remarkable that Ullman's name has not come up before now, since he is probably more closely associated with the procedural–declarative distinction than any other psychologist. Ullman's work offers extensive behavioural and neurological evidence of a clear distinction between two brain memory systems, one declarative, the other procedural, which together share responsibility for spoken language comprehension and production in normal speakers, and which have been shown to be selectively impaired in aphasic patients. See also Paradis (2009) for discussion of the declarative vs. procedural contrast in second language learners.

The reason for omitting this research from the discussion to this point is not that it is unpersuasive – though see Embick and Marantz (2005) – but because it massively complicates the picture. For what Ullman's research demonstrates is the dramatic variability that exists within different sub-populations of speakers of the same language, with respect to how particular kinds of linguistic knowledge are represented and processed: typical native speakers are shown to contrast with typical second language learners, but so do boys and girls before, during and after puberty; women's language processing has been shown to differ at different points in their menstrual cycle, and so on. Crucially, these are also dynamic continua: one can predict rough probabilities across sub-groups, but it is impossible to say for any individual, on any particular occasion of utterance, which of the two systems they will rely on more.

Interim summary

In this chapter, I have considered a crucial contrast that David Marr's work helped to highlight: the distinction between representation and (algorithmic) process. My aim has been to demonstrate that the two notions are intimately inter-related, and critically balanced: the nature of the linguistic representations in our heads, in whatever modality, affects and partially determines the class of algorithms that make use of these representations. And *vice versa*. It has also been suggested that theoretically relevant parts of the overall language processing system are subject to variation, both cross-linguistic and inter-personal. In short, processing French or Japanese or Navajo involves far more than substituting one mental lexicon for another and flipping a few parametric switches to get the word-order to come out right.

This point is elaborated in Part II. Before considering these test cases, however, it is important to examine an equally fundamental distinction, namely, that among levels of explanation. This is the concept for which Marr is probably best remembered, and that forms the basis of the COMPUTATIONAL THEORY OF MIND (CTM). By understanding how this concept works and how it applies to the study of language in mind, we may find a way to reconcile the two souls of psycholinguistic theory with which we began this section. This will be less a true conciliation of theories, than it is a 'two-state solution', but that is surely better than unresolved and fruitless conflict.

Notes

1 David Marr died in 1980, at the age of 35. *Vision* was published posthumously in 1982 (republished in 2010). Had he lived to pursue a full research career, it is almost certain that his influence on cognitive science and on psycholinguistics in particular would be vastly greater still.
2 The perceptual part, at least. Vision is distinguished from language in being an exclusively incoming process; there is no correlate of production (projection) in vision, outside science fiction – *The Matrix,* for example – or the extreme solipsism of Trent Reznor's 'Right Where It Belongs'. It is nevertheless interesting to note that the Emission Theory of Light was widely accepted for centuries from Empedocles in the fifth century BCE, and has retained some traction up to the present day: Winer, Cottrell, Gregg et al. (2002) report a study in which 50 per cent of American undergraduates still appeared to believe in the theory.
3 This is in spite of assuming widespread familiarity with Marr's work. In more philosophical discussions of cognitive theory – the Computational Theory of Mind – it is standard to read Marr's (1982) work cited as 'well-known': see, for instance, Phillips and Lewis (2013), who in their exemplary discussion of these issues, make reference to '... the *well-known* terms of Marr (1982)'; compare also Thompson, Palacios and Varela (2002: 353): 'It is *well-known* that Marr claimed that these three levels of analysis were independent.' Or see Wiggins (2013): 'It is now possible to relate the descriptive/explanatory hierarchy to Marr's (1982) levels of description, a *very well-known* attempt to address the philosophy of machine modelling of perception ...' (2013: 182). However, experience tells me that Marr's work is not well-known to many undergraduate students, or if it is, his distinctions are quite poorly understood.
4 Since Chomsky (1995), most radical Minimalists have tended to deny that there is any significant grammatical variation in UG: 'There is only a [i.e. one] computational system and one lexicon, apart from its limited kind of variety' Chomsky (1995: 170). See Boeckx (2008).
5 Just as these constructs are almost certainly irrelevant at an explicit, meta-linguistic level: no-one ever became a more fluent or proficient speaker of any language by studying Minimalism. If that is your reason for reading this book, you should stop now: you'll only become increasingly bitter. Or take quantum mechanics and

standard Newtonian physics, as they are popularly understood. Our understanding of the behaviour of medium-sized physical objects – including all of those objects with the range that humans can perceive – has not been radically changed by Quantum Theory (notwithstanding the efforts of Gary Zukav, author of *The Dancing Wu Li Masters*: Zukav 2001).

6 I don't take a view here on whether or not either of these theoretical proposals is correct: the point is merely that the two are independent of one another. See also Soames (1985), Phillips (1996).

7 Problem (1g) is easier than (1f) for children that have learned their times tables by rote, but haven't yet learned to generalise from units to tens. In hindsight, this might seem like a trivial step, but I have watched children – and some adults – closely, and it's far from automatic: typical six year-olds can know $4 \times 3 = ?$, but be mistaken about $40 \times 3 = ?$, and have no clue at all about $40 \times 30 = ?$

8 It also bears pointing out that even the simplest calculation pre-supposes control of a number of more basic mathematical skills, including fundamentally, the concepts of numerosity and of abstract number. See Siegal (2008: chapter 6) for an accessible introduction.

9 It turns out that we have other systems for calculating large numbers: in addition to procedures of look-up and deterministic calculation, we also employ a system of approximation (the kind of notional calculation used by most of us to calculate 15 per cent tips). Work by Stanislas Dehaene and his colleagues provides evidence that these latter two systems – exact vs. approximate calculation – are functionally dissociated; see, for example, Dehaene and Cohen (1991).

10 See, for example, Sick (2004). For more theoretical discussion of the first language acquisition of nominal inflection, see Eisenbeiss (2000, 2002).

11 A pertinent example comes from the names for shops, pubs and restaurants, which often have 'dative addresses'. In Cologne, for example, there is an old pharmacy called *Zum [= Zu dem] goldenen Horn* ([At the] Golden Horn). The number and case marking on the determiner and adjective tells me that *Horn* is not a feminine noun, but I'm still unsure of whether it is masculine – *der/den Horn* – or neuter *das/das Horn,* in its nominative and accusative forms.

12 Observations such as these are more readily compatible with less abstract theories, such as Role and Reference Grammar (Foley and Van Valin 1984, Van Valin and La Polla 1997), Cognitive Grammar (Lakoff 1987, Langacker 1991, Goldberg 1995), or the Simpler Syntax proposals of Culicover and Jackendoff (2005) – and especially with usage-based theories such as those developed in Barlow and Kemmer (2000), Bybee and Hopper (2001), Bybee (2010), each of which constitute different attempts to develop theories with greater psychological plausibility. Some will see this argument as the thin end of the wedge. They are probably not wrong.

3   Marr's *Vision* II

Levels of explanation: Chomsky

The claim that generative theory is only tangentially related to psycholinguistics is hardly original. In fact, it is clearly pre-figured in Chomsky's own more general writings of the 1980s, including his 1988 monograph *Language and Problems of Knowledge,* in which a broader framework for understanding the competence-based approach to psycholinguistics is articulated, one that clearly dissociates three distinct levels of explanation. At the outset, we find the questions diagrammed in Figure 4 (Chomsky 1988: 3).

As the figure shows, these three sets of theoretical questions are taken to map fairly directly to three separate domains of empirical enquiry: theoretical linguistics, psycholinguistics (especially language acquisition) and neurolinguistics, respectively.

There are several things to observe about this way of framing the problem. First, as has already been mentioned repeatedly, the primary concern of psycholinguistics from a Chomskyan perspective is with the mental representation of grammatical *knowledge* – and with the acquisition of this knowledge – rather than with developmental or processing mechanisms *per se*. It is easy to overlook the fact that Chomsky's question of how knowledge of language is put to use is *not* the broader question of how we use language. Notice further that with respect to language acquisition theory ('How does knowledge of language arise?'), many competence-based researchers believe that there is effectively no interesting grammatical development beyond a very early stage of PARAMETER-SETTING: virtually all core grammatical knowledge is taken to be innate; see below, also Wexler (1998), Chomsky (2005).

A separate point to bear in mind about this hierarchy is that Chomsky's answers to the first question have focused almost exclusively on formal syntax: most other types of putative linguistic knowledge have been given short shrift – typically, no shrift whatsoever. The set of dismissed topics includes knowledge of phonetics, supra-segmental phonology, intonation, language-particular morphology, word-level semantics, pragmatics and discourse structure, as well as structure and organisation of the entire 'mental lexicon' (except

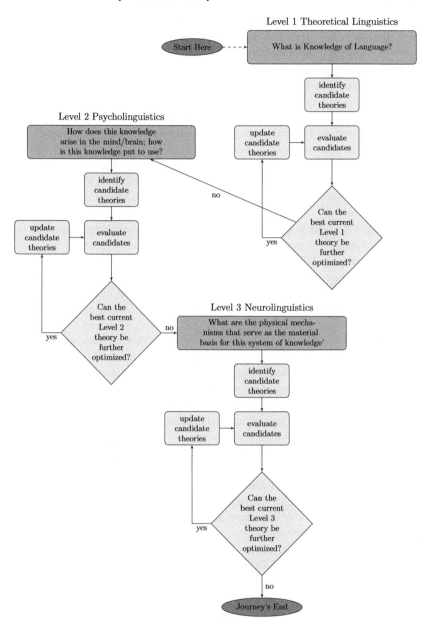

Figure 4 Chomsky's questions (1988).

for abstract formal features relating to so-called 'functional categories') . As a result, most competence-based psycholinguists have devoted the lion's share of their research efforts to questions of syntax. This has meant a preoccupation with syntactic parsing – how the human language processor assigns syntactic analyses (structural descriptions) to the incoming speech signal and/or with the psychological reality of specific theoretical constructs, especially EMPTY CATEGORIES and anaphoric dependencies, which are supposedly involved in syntactic computation. For language acquisition researchers taking their lead from Chomsky, the narrow focus on syntax has inspired work on young children's knowledge of abstract syntactic principles, such as the principles of BINDING THEORY and LOCALITY CONSTRAINTS ON MOVEMENT, as well as on the mechanisms of syntactic parameter-setting in different languages. See Cases #4–#6, in Part II below.[1]

Indeed, Chomsky's answers to the Level 1 question have restricted the domain of enquiry of psycholinguistics not just to sentence grammar, but to the 'narrow syntax' of UG. All but the most zealous generativist will concede that this type of abstract knowledge constitutes a minuscule proportion of all the grammatical knowledge that is involved in understanding and producing spoken language. Hence, even allowing for the kinds of idealisations and abstractions discussed in Part III below, most of the knowledge relevant to processing any particular language must be non-UG-related. This problem of relevance has become especially acute *post*-'Principles and Parameters' theory – that is to say, after 1995, when many generative syntacticians moved away from any serious examination of end-state grammars (I-language), preferring to concentrate on properties of the initial state. As a result, Chomsky's questions have encouraged an excessive regard for what are comparatively minor issues, when considered from a psychological perspective.

To draw a medical analogy: it may very well be the case that genetics plays a significant role in heart disease or congenital cardiac abnormalities – it undoubtedly plays a crucial role in embryology, which gives us a heart in the first place – but to the physiologist concerned with the functional modelling of cardiovascular behaviour in mature adults, as well as to the cardiac surgeon, genetics is largely irrelevant.[2]

A final point to observe about Chomsky's framing of research questions in *Language and Problems of Knowledge* is that they establish a priority of linguistic theory over questions of psychology or neurophysiology. At first glance, this appears to reflect a real logical priority: after all, there would seem to be little point in examining how something is acquired if you can't state what that something is. However, there is also the strong implication that constraints only work from the top down; conversely, that the answers to the psychological and neurophysiological questions do not also constrain what knowledge of language can look like. The latter implication is at least questionable: at all events, quite a different epistemological picture emerges if the question order is inverted:

1   What are the physical substrates and mechanisms that serve as the material basis for the processing (comprehension and production) of language; how do these constrain the set of physiologically plausible models of language use?
2   What are the logical and contingent external constraints on comprehension and production that must be incorporated into any psychologically plausible model of language processing (e.g. frequency, constraints on working memory and executive function, lexical size, fluency, etc.)? To what extent is the shape of the language processor conditioned by variation in end-state grammars? (Are all languages processed in essentially the same way?) How does the ability to comprehend and produce particular languages develop in children's minds?
3   (Given the answers to questions 1 and 2), what is in the mind/brain of the adult speaker of English? In what ways – if any – does this knowledge overlap with the knowledge of language represented in a speaker or Spanish, or Japanese or Fula?

The notion that higher-level theories are also constrained from the bottom up is developed in radically different ways by Christiansen and Chater (2008) and Phillips and Lewis (2013). Although these authors sharply disagree on most points of content, both suggest that UG is probably not what Phillips and Lewis term 'implementation independent'. That is to say, at least some researchers from both intellectual traditions are agreed that theories of grammar and of processing may well be shaped in crucial respects by the fact that they are implemented in the human brain. In the final analysis this is an empirical question, albeit an extremely complex one. See also Elman et al. (1996).

The question is also one that can only be investigated once the two levels are initially teased apart. Looking at things from *Both Sides, Now,* it becomes clear that what counts as a satisfactory explanation to researchers investigating language and/in mind depends not just on how these more general questions are framed, but also on how they are ordered.

♫ Joni Mitchell, *Both Sides, Now* (2000)

Levels of explanation: Marr

This brings us back to David Marr. About a decade before Chomsky published *Language and Problems of Knowledge*, Marr had also developed a set of theoretical maxims for understanding vision, or any other cognitive process, in computational terms.[3] These maxims, as much as the particular theory of vision he advanced, changed the way many researchers in the cognitive science community went about their business. Marr's insight was that a real understanding of cognitive processes was impossible unless one adopted a functionalist framework with at least three (intensional) levels of explanation, each with its own primitives and relational networks. He proposed the following levels:

1   The Computational Level (⇒ 'What is computed, and why?')
2   The Representational Level (⇒ 'What representations, primitive and derived, and algorithms are involved in that computation?')
3   The Implementational Level (⇒ 'How are these representations and algorithms implemented in a particular machine?')

In order to appreciate these distinctions, it is useful to consider the phenomenon of flight, Marr's most developed and familiar metaphor. Most birds, planes and (some) insects can fly, whereas rocks, jokes and insults don't, except figuratively. There is a sense in which birds and flying insects, 'know how to' fly and need to deploy this knowledge in order to succeed at the activity: comatose pigeons and dead grasshoppers fare no better than clods of earth. So, in the case of sentient animals some kind of tacit knowledge seems to be important. But what about inanimate flying objects?

Learning to fly

Although planes can fly, we don't usually consider that they *know how to* (outside of anthropomorphic CGI movies).[4] But if they are not in possession of implicit, internalised knowledge, what is it that [planes+pilots] and (conscious) birds have in common that distinguishes them from rocks, platypuses and other projectiles? Marr's answer is that, *in flight,* birds, flying insects and Airbuses are able to satisfy the same computational principles, which include the 'Level 1' principles of fluid dynamics. These abstract principles make reference to complex mathematical formulae, including the so-called *Euler equations*, named after the eighteenth-century Swiss mathematician Leonhard Euler. In differential form, or so I am told, the original Euler equations are as shown in Figure 5.[5]

The Euler equations are one form of the more general *Navier–Stokes* equations, with the viscosity and heat conduction terms deleted, and it is the 'ability' of conscious birds, planes and some insects to interact with fluids satisfying equations such as these that distinguishes them from other non-flying objects, and which enables them to get (and to remain) off the ground. In terms of a Level 1 computational theory, there is no significant difference between a Dreamliner, a model airplane and an eagle.[6]

$$\frac{\partial \rho}{\partial t} + \nabla \cdot (\rho \mathbf{u}) = 0,$$

$$\frac{\partial (\rho \mathbf{u})}{\partial t} + \nabla \cdot (\mathbf{u} \otimes (\rho \mathbf{u})) + \nabla p = \rho \mathbf{g},$$

$$\frac{\partial E}{\partial t} + \nabla \cdot (\mathbf{u} (E + p)) = \mathbf{u} \cdot (\rho \mathbf{g}),$$

$$E = \rho \left(U + \frac{1}{2} u^2 \right).$$

Figure 5 The Euler equations: ρ = fluid mass density, $\mathbf{u}$ is the flow velocity vector, E = total energy density, U = internal energy density, p = pressure, ∇ is the nabla, or gradient operator, and $\otimes$ denotes the tensor product.

But what do these flying objects *know*? Some would dispute the point, but there is no obvious sense in which either the Dreamliner or the eagle knows the Euler equations, any more than a thermostat knows what temperature it is: they may instantiate this mathematical information in their interaction with the local environment, but this is not knowledge. Even when we bring human beings into the picture, it doesn't help much. Through years of training, aeronautical engineers may have internalised the Euler equations better than trained pilots, but it's clear which group inspires more confidence at 30,000 feet. As Tom Petty observes in his song *Learning to Fly,* it's hard coming down, without wings.

♫ Tom Petty and The Heartbreakers, *Learning to Fly* (1991)

What's more, birds, planes and insects – and even different species of birds, planes and insects, satisfy these aerodynamic principles in myriad ways, involving vastly different representations and algorithms (Level 2 theories). Eagles and humming birds, for example, might be grouped together on ethological grounds as being distinct from gliders and bees, but in terms of a Level 2 theory of flight (the algorithmic–representational level), eagles have much more in common with gliders, and humming birds with bees, than either has with the other. (This is for two reasons: first, because humming birds generate lift using both upward and downward strokes of their wings – like bees, but unlike other flying birds, which only generate lift through downward movement;[7] second, because neither humming birds nor bees are capable of gliding – as soon as their wings stop beating, they drop like the proverbial stone).

Marr argued that we can really only understand flight once we have rigidly distinguished these different levels of explanation (Level 1 (Euler principles, shared)) vs. Level 2 (algorithms and representations, varying according to kinds of flying body). He also emphasised that no one level is more important than the others in understanding flight: they are all distinct but equally valuable parts of the same overall explanation. With respect to computer vision, Marr was most concerned to stress the independence of Level 2 theories (representational–algorithmic level) from issues of implementation (Level 3 explanation). His flight metaphor bears this out: whether wings are made of skin and feathers, or carbon fibre, or balsa wood, may indirectly impact on Level 2 theories, but it makes no real odds to Level 1 theories. As Marr observed:

Trying to understand perception by studying only neurons is like trying to understand flight by studying only feathers. It just cannot be done ... If having feathered wings were necessary for flight, bats could not have evolved as they did, and airplanes would look a good deal more interesting.[8]

David Marr, *Vision* ([1982] 2010: 23)

Stephen Jay Gould (1987) makes a similar point when criticising sociobiological approaches to culture:

A claim for the independence of human culture is not an argument for fundamental ineffability (like a soul), but only for the necessity of explaining culture with principles different from the laws of evolutionary biology. New levels require an addition of principles; they neither deny nor contradict the explanations appropriate for lower levels. The principles of aesthetics do not preclude a chemical analysis of pigments in the Mona Lisa, but only a fool would use chemistry to explain the essence of the lady's appeal. *In this sense, the notion of partially independent hierarchical levels of explanation strikes me as a statement of common sense, not mystery or philosophical mumbo-jumbo. I also regard hierarchy theory as an indispensable approach for the proper analysis of human culture.* [my emphases: NGD]

Stephen Jay Gould, *An Urchin in the Storm* (1987: 69)

For most people – though probably not for Chomsky – language can be substituted for culture in Gould's argument, with no loss of force.

Of course, Chomsky is no reductionist. Quite the contrary: when he says that 'UG is the theory of the genetic component of the language faculty' he is not saying that grammatical knowledge can be reduced to the principles and mechanisms of genetic theory. He does seem to be claiming, however, that there is an identity relation between grammar and genetics: the theoretical coverage of UG – a Level 1 theory – is co-extensive with that part of the human genome responsible for brain development, at a different level of explanation. This is highly questionable, since even if it were possible to relate specific kinds of grammatical knowledge to the locations and operations at a neurophysiological level, the extrapolation to genetics would still be deeply problematic. See I is for Internalism, also Elman et al. (1996), for further discussion.

Notice also that if Marr is correct that Level 2 phenomena should be explained independently of Level 3 considerations, then the argument surely works in the other direction as well: an adequate (Level 2) theory of psycholinguistics should provide an explanation of linguistic behaviour that is largely independent of the principles of a Level 1 theory of grammar.

In fact, Marr's flight analogy is telling in two different ways. It is not only that the analogy rigidly distinguishes different levels of explanation, so allowing diverse classes of Level 2 algorithms to satisfy the same Level 1 computational constraints. Just as significantly, a Level 1 (mathematical) theory of flight is *not* an internal theory, it is not a theory of mental states or processes. Adopting a strictly computationalist theory does not require that what is computed is internalised: birds may know how to fly, in some sense, but that does not mean they know the Euler equations, or any other formal property of a Level 1 theory of flight. Similarly, *contra* Chomsky, a commitment to a computational theory of grammar does not entail that language users have internalised this theory, much less that it should be part of our genetic endowment. In short, it is perfectly possible to be (partially or wholly) externalist about language, and still to 'believe in UG': it is not necessary to adopt an internalist stance. In I is for Internalism and O is for Object of Study below, I'll argue that such a position is not only more plausible than the standard alternative, it is also empirically better supported.

The quotation from Seidenberg and MacDonald (1999: 570), cited earlier, deserves repetition here:

Instead of asking how the child acquires competence grammar, we view acquisition in terms of how the child converges on adult-like performance in comprehending and producing utterances. This performance orientation changes the picture considerably with respect to classic issues about language learnability, and provides a unified approach to studying acquisition and processing.

> Mark Seidenberg and Maryellen MacDonald, 'A probabilistic
> constraints approach to language acquisition and processing'
> (*Cognitive Science*, 1999: 570)

Seidenberg and MacDonald's quote is standardly interpreted as implying a rejection of the generativist approach to psycholinguistics. That may well have been their intention: it is not for me to second-guess. Whatever is the case, Marr's distinction between levels of explanation affords us a way of reconciling the two approaches, without compromising on either. We *do* need a computational theory of language; we also need a computational theory of language users. One does not preclude the other in linguistics, any more than it does in mathematics or music, or in any other domain that involves sentient organisms, and inter-subjective realities.

Notice, finally, that Marr's conceptual system not only stipulates three distinct theories, one for each level of explanation, but it also calls for two additional 'bridging theories' to relate the three levels (or three perhaps, if one allows for the possibility that Level 1 and Level 3 constructs can be related to one another in an unmediated fashion). In the absence of bridging theories, there is no way for theoretical objects at one level to be mapped to objects at another; hence, the 'genetics to donkey'/'blueprint to foundations' analogies I suggested much earlier in this section.

This is the other reason, then, for restricting attention to classical psycholinguistics, as first outlined in the Introduction (see Scope). The principled justification for ignoring many of the results of neurolinguistic experiments on language is that we currently lack an articulated theory of the relationship between neurophysiology and language representation and process, beyond fairly crude studies of localisation. Technology may have given us high definition views of the cerebral cortex and real-time images of patterns of vascular or electrical activity, but it's far from clear how these relate to linguistic, grammatical or lexical distinctions. Only time will tell whether high expense – neurolinguistics is a hugely expensive enterprise – will ever translate into high intellectual value.

It should be acknowledged that the bridging problem has been recognised by other researchers in the cognitive science. Embick and Poeppel (2015), for instance, offers a sophisticated attempt to go beyond observing correlations between verbal performance and neurological activity. Nevertheless, it is fair to say that such proposals have yet to make inroads into the theories or practices of most researchers, whether they are linguists, psycholinguists or neuropsychologists. On one side of the fence, many competence-based researchers continue to assume that all levels of explanation are broadly isomorphic, such that all and only the theoretical constructs that are properties of one level of explanation (generative grammar) will have direct functional correlates at the other two levels. This has led, for example, to the conclusion that constructions and utterance templates cannot be psychologically real because, at Level 1, there are no construction-specific rules: see Adger (2013). Conversely, the finding that constructions have distinct behavioural signatures, or that parsing proceeds incrementally from left to right, has led many process-oriented psycholinguists to conclude that 'the theory is wrong' (at least, 'the theory' that builds every syntactic analysis from an unordered lexical array, from the bottom up, right to left via *Merge*). Neither conclusion is warranted, given a levels of explanation approach.

... and back to Chomsky

Returning to language, if Chomsky's levels corresponded to those of Marr, and if generative theory had remained a Level 1 theory throughout its development, then we could largely ignore generative theory for the purposes of developing a representational–algorithmic theory of language use. Just as ethologists are little concerned with the Euler principles in their pure form when explaining the differences between the flying abilities of eagles vs. humming birds, so the question of how humans process natural languages could be studied independently of any abstract (mathematical) principles of grammar. Level 1 principles might set absolute formal limits to the set of possible representational–algorithmic combinations, but the interest from the point of view of determining how humans understand and produce different languages – or do mental arithmetic, as touched on earlier – lies in describing and explaining the phenomena at Levels 2 and 3.

Of course, many (psycho)linguists have done exactly that: ignored pure Level 1 theories and built models from the bottom up; see Spivey, McRae and Joanisse (2012) for examples of work that adopts this perspective. Within theoretical linguistics, usage-based approaches of language can also be understood in this light; see Barlow and Kemmer (2000), also Goldberg (2006), Croft (2001). Nevertheless, the reason that we should not ignore Chomskyan grammar is that for about 25 years, from the 1970s into the 1990s, generative grammar came much closer to being a Level 2 theory than it was a pure computational theory in Marr's sense, despite the clear division of labour implied by Chomsky's questions. As Christopher Peacocke (1986) argued, generative grammar at the time offered explanation 'at Level 1.5'. See Figure 6. As a result of this literal (though not figurative) *rapprochement*, psycholinguists sympathetic to generative theory have often operated as though their theory of grammar subsumed most of the representational component and some of the processing aspects of processing theory, leaving to 'psycholinguistics proper' only a small set of preference rules for dealing with ambiguous grammatical strings, and unpredictable lexical information. This view of things is nicely summarised in the catch-phrase 'the grammar proposes, the parser disposes'.[9]

And it is because of this theoretical mission-creep that to ignore the generative research of this period is to miss out on an important set of interesting findings concerning the question we started with, namely, 'Why Do We Talk?'

Since the mid-1990s, however, there have been moves to restore generative grammar as a pure Level 1 theory. Indeed, it might be even argued that Minimalism/biolinguistics is headed for 'explanation at Level −1', in so far as it aims to go 'beyond explanatory adequacy'. Whether or not this form of

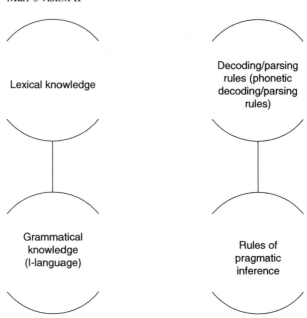

Figure 6 Components of language comprehension: language, perception and Level 1.5.

enquiry is congenial or explanatory is partly a matter of intellectual taste. Whatever view is adopted, many generative grammarians have now moved far away from any of the empirical questions that are immediately relevant to psycholinguistic research: what was once a fault-line has become an ideological chasm.

Notes

1 Note the distinction drawn here between LANGUAGE-PARTICULAR and LANGUAGE-SPECIFIC. As the terms will be used throughout this book, a language-particular property is one that is restricted to a certain language variety (or set of varieties); for example, the English morpho-phonological phenomenon of TRI-SYLLABIC LAXING which refers to alternations such as *opaque/opacity*, *serene/serenity*, *obscene/obscenity* (but which fails to apply to *obese~obesity*: see e.g. Lakoff ([1965] 1970). By contrast, a language-specific property is one that is special to language in general, having no obvious correlates in other areas of cognition: for example, the theoretical notion of C-COMMAND, which is claimed to regulate anaphoric dependencies (see Case #4 below), or the Minimalist operation *Merge* (see G is for Grammar). 'Specific' also features in the name of disorder referred to as *specific* language impairment (SLI). Whereas LANGUAGE-PARTICULAR is essentially a descriptive label, the term LANGUAGE-SPECIFIC involves a set of theoretical and empirical claims, many

of which are controversial. Specifically (!) in the case of SLI, many researchers dispute the legitimacy of the term.

2 Or even to the computationalist. For example, the editorial introduction to a recent special issue of *Computational and Mathematical Models in Medicine* devoted to Cardiovascular System Modelling makes no mention of genetics whatsoever (Xia et al. 2012).

3 There is a cycle of mutual influence here. Just as Chomsky's questions in *Language and Problems of Knowledge* are apparently derivative of Marr's questions, so Marr directly draws on Chomsky's earlier work, especially *Syntactic Structures* (1957) and *Aspects of The Theory of Syntax* (1965) in Chapter 1 of *Vision*.

4 At least, this was true for most of the history of powered flight – before onboard computer systems took over responsibility for many procedures. On a recent trip back to Japan from the UK, I flew *via* Dubai on an Emirates A380. By chance, I was seated next to the wife of a commercial pilot. We landed unusually abruptly and uncomfortably, and immediately veered sharply to the left. 'Oh, I see they turned off the Autoland tonight,' she said, 'Human pilots can't really land these things properly.' If what she said was true – though see www.askthepilot.com/questionanswers/automation-myths/ for a rebuttal – then in non-critical situations the plane (rather, the plane's operating system) is now its own best pilot. For all I know, this is true of critical situations as well. The same may soon be true of driverless cars.

5 I do not pretend to understand this piece of mathematics: in my defence, it is doubtful whether the Wright brothers did either.

6 This point is brought home dramatically in the 1965 Oscar-nominated movie *Flight of the Phoenix*, starring James Stewart, Richard Attenborough, Ernest Borgnine and Hardy Krüger. *Spoiler Alert*. If you haven't seen it, there are worse ways to spend a damp Sunday afternoon. In the movie, which is based on a 1964 novel by Elleston Trevor, a desert sandstorm forces a transport plane to crash-land in the desert, stranding the survivors miles from the nearest oasis. The survivors include a veteran pilot Frank Towns (Stewart), the plane's alcoholic navigator Lew Moran (Attenborough), and a German aeronautical engineer Heinrich Dorfmann (Krüger). After a failed attempt to walk to the oasis, and with their supplies of water running out, Dorfmann devises a plan to construct a new plane from salvaged parts, using an intact engine. As the survivors work to rebuild the plane – *The Phoenix* – it emerges that Dorfmann is in fact a designer of radio-controlled model airplanes, and has never constructed anything with a wingspan greater than two metres. When Moran and Towns find out, their hopes of escape from the desert are immediately replaced by a bitter fatalism. Dorfmann however is unconcerned, quietly insisting that the principles are the same, so it shouldn't matter ... In the movie, (it may be) needless to say, the rebuilt plane flies. However, the real plane that was constructed for the filming crashed, killing the stunt pilot (Paul Mantz, who is acknowledged in the closing credits). Even with this spoiler, the film is worth watching, and not only for the conflict between the experienced and jaded pilots (Stewart/Attenborough) and the idealistic theoretician (Krüger).

7 See e.g. www.nature.com/news/hummingbird-flight-has-a-clever-twist-1.9639

8 The word 'only' here is crucial: Marr is not saying that feathers and other physical structures are completely irrelevant to understanding avian flight, just that they are not especially relevant to Level 1 explanation.

9 The original source of this phrase (and its variants) is unknown to me.

Part II

Six Different Ways

Six case studies distinguishing representation
from process

Introduction to Part II

♫ The Cure, *Six Different Ways* (1985)

Level 2 integration means more than simply creating an ecumenical and respectful research environment, as desirable as this might be. An integrated approach is necessary primarily because it is not clear *a priori* which aspects of linguistic behaviour (performance) should best be explained in terms of a representational theory, which by a language-specific processing model, or some more general processing theory, finally, which aspects of language use are best explained in terms of extra-grammatical factors, such as memory limitations or motor skills; cf. Chomsky (2005). At every level of analysis, researchers face what Hofmeister et al. (2013b) term the SOURCE AMBIGUITY problem, namely, that of determining the underlying source of a speaker's intuition that some piece of language – be it a speech sound, a word, sentence, a fragment of discourse – is less acceptable than some other in a given context of utterance. See also Goodluck and Zweig (2013), Phillips (2013); Featherston (2001, 2007).[1] Even assuming all of the idealisations discussed in Part III below, it is often extremely difficult to tease apart the various factors that contribute to native speakers' intuitions about linguistic acceptability.

What *is* reasonably certain, however, is that the answer in any particular case cannot be determined by further introspection. Our intuitions about language may be fairly sharp inasmuch as native speakers can (usually) reliably tell that one utterance is more acceptable to them than another in a given context, or will judge one speaker's output as more native-like than another's. In most other respects, however, our intuitions are extremely imprecise: except in very crude cases such as word-scrambles,[2] we can't say *why* the less acceptable utterance in any minimal contrast is less acceptable, or put a finger on exactly what it is that makes a non-native speaker's utterance seem 'foreign'. See also J is for Judgment below. As Chomsky observed, as far back as 1977:

We may make an intuitive judgment that some linguistic expression is odd or deviant. But we cannot in general know, pre-theoretically, whether this deviance is a matter of syntax, semantics, pragmatics, belief, memory limitations, style, etc.

Noam Chomsky, *Essays on Form and Interpretation* (1977: 4)

To better appreciate the source ambiguity problem, I offer a discussion of six phenomena, each of which involves a different kind of 'unacceptable grammatical behaviour' in acquisition and processing. In each case, the aim of the exercise is to probe the sources of unacceptability, and so to begin to tease apart issues of representation and process, or, at the very least, to better appreciate the difficulties involved in separating these notions.

Notes

1 Hofmeister et al. (2013b) employ the term more narrowly to refer to the alternatives of syntax vs. sentence processing; specifically in that paper, whether so-called 'Superiority effects' have their source in grammatical constraints or are due to various kinds of processing difficulty; see Case #6 below; cf. Phillips (2013). In this section I will use the word 'sentence' loosely to refer to written utterances, as well as to their abstract analyses. Strictly speaking, sentences – like phonemes, or whatever corresponds to phonemes psychologically – are purely internal notions: what we produce and comprehend are utterances (spoken or written). See Part III, T is for Sentence, also v is for von Humboldt.
2 Perhaps even in such cases: see Moore and Carling (1982), Duffield (2015).

4   (Case #1) 'Starry, starry night': The problem of phoneme discrimination

Consider first, the specific problem of discriminating the English speech sounds [r] and [l], as evidenced (and experienced) by second language learners of English whose native languages lack this contrast at a phonemic level. For such learners, the third stanza of Don McLean's famous song *Vincent* ('Starry, Starry Night') is not so much alliterative verse as it is cruel and unusual punishment: in the space of two lines, McLean juxtaposes thirteen [C(onsonant)+r] and [C(onsonant)+l] segments in tight succession. (The relevant words are presented below, in alphabetical order for reasons of copyright):

blaze; *blue*; *brightly*; *clouds*; *flaming*; *flowers*; *reflect*; *starry*, *swirling*; *violet*

♫ Don McLean, *Vincent* (1971)

Many second language learners – most notoriously, Japanese learners of English – fail to distinguish [r] from [l] in perception, particularly whenever these sounds appear in syllable-internal position: *crowds* vs. *clouds*, for instance, presents greater difficulty than *rock* vs. *lock*. An impressive number of experimental studies have confirmed that the problem is real, persistent and pervasive: even after prolonged exposure to English, the majority of adult Japanese learners continue to have problems in reliably distinguishing the two sounds, especially in less familiar words; see, for example, Goto (1971), Miyawaki et al. (1975), Flege, Yeni-Komshian and Liu (1999), Flege, Takagi and Mann (1996). Interestingly, this difficulty remains even for speakers who are well able to distinguish the two sounds in production: high-proficiency Japanese learners of English learn to articulate *flame* and *frame* reasonably distinctly; they just can't perceive the phonetic difference. The clear implication of this is that highly proficient *speakers* need not be near-native *listeners*; see also C is for Competence~Performance below.

A theoretical question that arises here is whether this perceptual failure on the part of many L2 learners is due to a difference in representational knowledge, such that for these listeners *flame* and *frame* are mentally represented as homonyms, like English *bear* (v. 'stand, tolerate') and *bear* (n. 'animal') – they are certainly homographs in Japanese orthography (フレム, 'fu-re-mu') – or

51

(alternatively) whether the failure to perceive the phonetic contrast is due to a processing deficit triggered by the close phonetic similarity between the two sounds, and compounded by the absence of any comparable distinction in the learner's native language. In this case, the available experimental evidence tends towards a representational interpretation. In the first place, a large number of experiments on infant speech perception, especially those of Janet Werker (Werker and Tees 1984, Werker and Lalonde 1988) and Patricia Kuhl (e.g. Kuhl 2004, Kuhl, Tsao and Liu 2003) support the existence of a very early CRITICAL PERIOD in phonological discrimination. Werker and others have demonstrated that up to around six months infants readily discriminate phonetically similar speech sounds in any language, whilst after 10–12 months of age most young children can only usually discriminate contrasts that are distinctive in their native language (that is, those that make a difference to lexical meaning). These behavioural results are also backed up by neurological data: see Zhang et al. (2005).[1]

Paradoxically, this perceptual narrowing typically occurs several months – sometimes years – before children are able to produce any words at all, let alone show mastery of paradigmatic contrasts: that is to say, children appear to perceive 'lexical contrasts' before they have any lexicon to speak of. See Martin, Peperkamp and Dupoux (2014) for a possible resolution of this puzzle.

The L2 learners' situation is actually more abstract and interesting than simply being the result of perceptual failure. Work by Brown (1997, 2000), for instance, provides support for the idea that L2 learners' perceptual success is determined by the structure of the L1 phonological system (the feature geometry) rather than by the presence or absence of an /r/ vs. /l/ contrast in a language in question. In Brown's study, Chinese L2 learners of English significantly outperformed Japanese learners in a phoneme perception task (86 vs. 61 per cent accuracy), even though neither Japanese nor (Mandarin) Chinese directly contrasts /r/ and /l/. See Table 2. Brown attributes Chinese learners' relative success to the presence of an abstract phonological feature [coronal] that is abstractly represented in Chinese phonology, but not in Japanese.

However, even if experimental results such as these suggest a representational source of this behaviour, we need to investigate further to establish the exact nature of that representation: whether, for example, what is represented is an abstract formal feature, as Brown (2000) proposes – one that is autonomous of individual lexical items – or whether the distinction is instead an emergent property of patterns of lexical connections. The latter possibility is supported by the fact that advanced Japanese learners of English show LEXICAL BIASES in perception: subjectively more familiar English words are easier to discriminate (even in isolation) than less familiar ones (Flege, Takagi and Mann 1996). Other theoretical possibilities exist also: see Duffield (2016).

Table 2 *Chinese vs. Japanese differences in r/l discrimination (redrawn from Brown 2000). The main point of interest is in the third column, where the Chinese learners in the study reliably outperformed their Japanese counterparts.*

Forced-choice word–picture matching task D/V = mean accuracy in picture selection (%)		Phonological contrast	
Participant group	/p/ vs. /f/	/f/ vs. /v/	/l/ vs. /r/
L1 Japanese	94	99	61
L1 Chinese	90	96	86
English native speakers	100	98	96

NVS	What does [maus] mean?
A	Like a cat.
NVS	Yes: what else?
A	Nothing else.
NVS	It's part of you.
A	[disbelief]
NVS	It's part of your head.
A	[fascinated]
NVS	[touching A's mouth] What's this?
A	[maus]

Figure 7 A's /s/ vs. /θ/ distinction (from Smith 1973: 137).

Related to this phenomenon, we observe in child language what appears to be the inverse effect. Initially reported in Berko and Brown (1960) is the so-called *fish*-phenomenon exhibited by children who are quite able to perceive particular speech sound contrasts, but cannot yet distinguish them in production. The name of the phenomenon specifically derives from children who pronounce *fish* as [fɪs] (as opposed to [fɪʃ]) whilst nevertheless treating [fɪs] as a non-word when it is pronounced by an adult. Smith (1973), who develops this point at length, reports an exchange with his son A, in respect of a parallel contrast ([s] vs. [θ]), as shown in Figure 7.

In the same section of the book, Neil Smith reports a contrast that is still more relevant to the present discussion:

A had (completely) free variation between e.g., [l] and [r] for adult words beginning with /r/, whereas he invariably had [l] for adult words beginning with /l/.

Neil Smith, *The Acquisition of Phonology: A Case Study* (1973: 135)

These clear mismatches between perception and production in first language acquisition raise important theoretical questions. On one hand, it is clear that in spite of neutralising the contrast between *mouth* and *mouse* in his own speech, Smith's child has adult-like intuitions concerning the adult pronunciation of the two words. Given Saussurean arbitrariness (see B is for Arbitrariness below), these intuitions must be based on distinct perceptual representations. Hence, it seems reasonable to conclude that – at least with respect to perception – A's 'unacceptable behaviour' is not due to a representational deficit. It is much less clear how to account for A's systematic production error. It could be that the problem is due to a 'faulty implementation rule': for example, the production rules for pronouncing the more marked /θ/ sound have not yet been fully acquired. In other words, it could be that this is competence-based – linguists might add the word 'merely' here – a 'processing problem'. However, to many process-oriented psycholinguists such errors are better interpreted as evidence of a representational deficit (of a different kind from that observed in Japanese L2 learners): in this case, the problem lies *with* – or perhaps in the connections *to* – A's 'phonological output lexicon', rather than with his more (adult-like) 'auditory input lexicon'.

The concept of multiple lexicons (lexica) is one that most competence-based psycholinguists are loath to adopt: for the various reasons discussed below, more formally minded psycholinguists don't much like the idea of even *one* highly specified mental lexicon, let alone a proliferation of different vocabulary stores, each with their own sets of specifications. Process-oriented researchers, by contrast, can point to a range of experimental data showing asymmetric interactions across modalities, as well as certain kinds of dissociation in the behaviour of atypical and non-native language users whose data clearly support these kinds of functional models: see, for example, Patterson and Shewell (1987); see also Monsell (1987), Ellis and Young (1988), Kay, Lesser and Coltheart (1992), Coltheart et al. (2001). And models such as the one in Figure 8 comport much better with our intuitions about mismatches in receptive vs. productive (also spoken vs. written) vocabulary in first and second language acquisition, as well as in aphasia: see C is for Competence~Performance.

(As an aside, notice that such models – complex as they are already – are only concerned with the cross-modal processing of *single words*: there is no specification of the processes involved in analysing multi-word *utterances*. Furthermore, it is important not to confuse *functional* localisation, represented by the boxes and arrows in model diagrams, with *physical* localisation, how and where words are neurologically encoded. At the implementational level, boxes and arrows are no more to be found in the brain than are syntactic phrase-markers or metrical grids: see Wilshire (2008) for some useful discussion.)

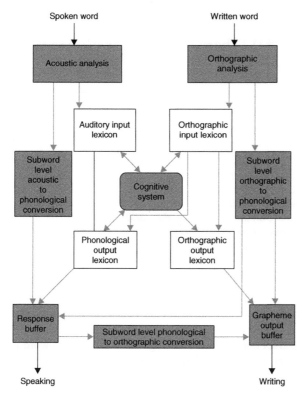

Figure 8 A 'multiple-lexicons' model of word production (redrawn after Patterson and Shewell 1987).

Note

1 On the other hand, just because two language varieties share a phonemic contrast, this doesn't guarantee that second language learners will be able to perceive it reliably. A case in point is the /d/~/t/ distinction found in many unrelated languages, including English and Japanese. In one of my own recent experiments comparing Canadian and Japanese participants – Duffield (2016, 2017b) – it was found that English monolinguals had considerable difficulty in discriminating between minimal contrasts in voicing in Japanese words (*dango* vs. *tango*) even though English manipulates the same phonemic distinction (e.g. *dank* vs. *tank*); by contrast, Japanese participants were just as reliable as English native speakers in discriminating between English minimal contrasts. Plausibly, this is due to the fact that English Voice Onset Time (VOT) for 'voiceless' plosives ({p, t, k} is markedly longer than in Japanese: as a result, Japanese /t/s are phonetically more like /d/s than are English /t/s; see Riney, Takagi, Ota and Uchida (2007), Duffield (2016).

5 (Case #2) 'There's a word for it': Are words more than labels?

> *There's a word for it,*
> *Words don't mean a thing.*
> *There's a name for it:*
> *Names make all the difference in the world.*
> *Some things can never be spoken*
> *Some things cannot be pronounced*
> *That word does not exist in any language*
> *It will never be uttered by a human mouth.*
> ♫ Talking Heads, *Give me Back my Name* (1985)

Anyone who has spent time on social media sites will occasionally have come across lists of interesting words from other (more or less exotic) languages, used to label abstract concepts ... that English doesn't have a word for. Some examples are given in (5) below.[1] Just what is involved in this labelling and matching process is an intriguing question in itself. Though some philosophers would dispute the point (see e.g. Fodor 1975, 1981, also 1998; cf. Margolis and Laurence 2011), I will assume that we don't already have the 'concept-in-waiting' – missing its label, to that point – and so it seems as if we must be able to partition or extend our pre-existing conceptual space in such a way as to accommodate the new word in our vocabulary. Even if the arrangement only remains in place for the time it takes to read the article.

In most instances, except for the labelling of new gadgets or technologies (*Google*, *zap*, *Hotchkiss* ...),[2] the foreign words are as arcane as their meanings are abstract, and adopting them will make little or no difference to our lives, other than to make us seem slightly more pretentious than before. Indeed, the fact that these words only crop up in a handful of languages, and that without social media most English speakers would have remained cheerfully ignorant of their existence, strongly suggests that they are unnecessary for our physical or spiritual well-being.

(5) a. *Fernweh*: German, 'feeling homesick for a place you've never been to'
     b. *Papakata*: Cook Islands Maori, 'to have one leg shorter than the other'
     c. *Itsuarpok*: Inuit, 'the frustration of waiting for someone to turn up'

d. *Friolero*: Spanish, 'a person who is especially sensitive to cold weathers and temperatures'
e. *Gattara*: Italian, 'a woman often old and lonely, who devotes herself to stray cats'
f. *Utepils*: Norwegian, 'to sit outside on a sunny day, enjoying a beer'
g. *Aware*: Japanese, 'the bittersweetness of a brief and fading moment of transcendent beauty'
h. *Tsundoku*: Japanese, 'the act of leaving a book unread after buying it, typically piling it up together with other such unread books'

On closer scrutiny, it turns out that most of the translations are either fanciful, or that the forms themselves are polymorphemic in their respective languages; that is to say, the words are composed of smaller – usually more banal – units of meaning. The German expression *Fernweh* in (5a) is quite obviously a compound (literally, 'distance-pain'), in syntagmatic opposition to *Heimweh* ('home-sickness'), while *friolera* and *gattara* each contain a familiar root with a productive derivational affix attached to it (Spanish *frí(o)* 'cold'; Italian *gatt-* 'cat', cf. English 'cat lady'). Similarly, the Norwegian word *utepils* is a compound that simply means 'outside beer', and Japanese *aware* only means sadness, albeit sadness of a particular kind: compare the French word *ennui* or German *Angst,* as used by educated English speakers. The additional sense suggested by the translation 'sadness at the state of things' is understood elliptically: the full expression is *mono no aware* (lit. 'thing's sadness'), a phrase that can be compared to Virgil's *lacrymae rerum*. In almost all of these cases, then, the simple morphemes that make up these words generally have immediately accessible counterparts in other languages. As for *tsundoku*, few Japanese speakers have any clear idea of the meaning of the first morpheme *tsun-*; *doku* just means reading. This inevitably raises suspicions about the veracity of translations from less familiar languages.

So perhaps there is no mystery here, after all.

Ironically, it is much more mundane words, like *bread* and *water*, and relational concepts such as *on* or *down*, that raise more serious theoretical issues. If you have only studied English – or perhaps one or two closely related European varieties such as French or Spanish – it is natural to imagine that speakers of every language have their own words to label these very basic notions, and that the concepts themselves are largely fixed (perhaps even innate, in the case of spatial terms).[3] Yet experimental and typological evidence suggests otherwise. Take *water*, for example. If I ask a native speaker of English how many containers of water they can see in Figure 9, the answer is invariably 'two': a container of (cold) water on the left, and one containing (hot) water, on the right. As suggested by the parentheses, the temperature of the water is irrelevant: between freezing and boiling point 'water is water'.

Figure 9 H_2O = (cold and hot) water?

Or is it? Posing the same question to Japanese second language learners of English – *in English* – produces some confusion: some respondents say one, others say two. And when I ask what is apparently the same question in Japanese (なんばいのみずをみえますか?) the answer is unequivocal: in Japanese, there is only one container of water in the figure above, namely, the one on the left. This is because the substance on the right is *not* 水 (*o-mizu* 'water'), it's 湯 (*o-yu* 'hot water'). To a Japanese speaker, calling the substance on the right 'hot water/*mizu*' is as unnatural as it is for an English speaker to call *steam* 'evaporated water' or *ice* 'frozen water': the expression is comprehensible, but it's a distinctly odd way of speaking. (Similarly, in English, we don't wear *clocks* – though some Japanese speakers of English say that *they* do: when *we* wear them, they're *watches*.)

The specific question that arises in this case is whether information about temperature is encoded in the concepts labelled by the Japanese words 水 (*o-mizu*) and 湯 (*o-yu*). It is theoretically possible that the contrast is an intensional one, which is to say, that the attribute COLD is semantically represented in the lexical entry for 水, perhaps in the form of a MEANING POSTULATE (see Hurford, Heasley and Smith 2007 for explication):

(6)   a. (Japanese) x 水 ➜ x WATER & x COLD
      b. (English) x water ➜ x WATER

Example (6a) translates roughly as 'something is 水(*o-mizu*) just in case it is WATER and is COLD'. This analysis seems improbable, though. For a start, it is not generally possible to say at what temperature 水 becomes 湯, or *vice versa*. The water in a swimming pool is 水 (*o-mizu*) even if it is relatively warm, whereas water of nearly the same temperature in an *onsen* (public hot bath) is 湯. Sea-water is always 潮水 (literally 'salt water'); even on a hot day it doesn't become 潮湯 ('salt hot-water'). And so on. The most satisfactory explanation I have been given – by only one student, after interrogating many classes over five years – is that 湯 refers to water above normal body temperature. This makes a lot of sense, but it is clearly not an immediately accessible definition for most Japanese speakers.

These intuitive results suggest that the difference between English and Japanese is largely determined pragmatic–contextually, rather than intensionally: Japanese learners infer that 水 is generally, rather than necessarily, cold, because 'there is a [better] word for it' whenever it's (supposed to be) hot. In other words, 湯 pre-empts 水 in certain pragmatically determined contexts of utterance – in much the same way as reflexive anaphors pre-empt anaphoric uses of pronouns; see Case #4 below. This is a problem for static theories of lexical semantics that assume discrete, intensionally determined boundaries on individual concepts. Unfortunately for such theories, that doesn't seem to be how native speaker judgments work. See also J is for Judgment below.

The example of 湯 'hot water' raises further questions about how best to characterise a given speaker's lexical knowledge. Consider, first, an English-speaking beginning learner of Japanese, someone who has learned the Japanese word 水 (*mizu*), but who does not yet know the existence of the term 湯. If this speaker uses 水 to refer to hot water on a particular occasion, we may rightly infer that there is a representational difference between this learner's declarative lexical knowledge and that of a Japanese native speaker. Consider, next, an advanced learner who knows that there are two Japanese words for water, but who can only recall – the term ACCESS is commonly used in the psycholinguistics literature – the more frequent of the two expressions. If this advanced learner uses 水 when referring to hot water in the same context of utterance, we would be inclined to conclude that this is due to a processing error (an 'access problem'), rather than to any representational deficit. Parallel issues arise with respect to many other phenomena in language learning, including children's over-generalisations; see below.

The empirical difficulty, of course, is that since we can't look into these speakers' minds directly, and since they exhibit the same 'unacceptable behaviour' in the same context of utterance, we have no principled reason to draw different inferences concerning their underlying knowledge. Of course, it may be possible to tease the two speakers apart: given the right cues and sufficient time, the advanced learner should eventually be able to access the less frequent term (湯), whereas no amount of time will help the learner who has never internalised this lexical knowledge in the first place.[4]

Things become even less clear when we consider Japanese learners' of English use of the expression 'hot water'. In this case, it is conceivable that both beginning and advanced learners would correctly use the same term to describe hot water. However, whereas the advanced learner of English may have figured out that 'hot water' is the most frequent and economical expression in this context – and by implication, has a native-like understanding of the extension of the word *water* – the beginning learner may be using the expression as a pragmatic 'gap-filler' because s/he does not yet know the English for 湯 (still being ignorant of the fact that no such word exists). The beginner is 'fa[i]ling, with style'. In between these two, one could well find an intermediate learner, who has a uneasy sense that there is something different about Japanese '水' and English 'water': not being quite sure what it is, s/he will use the term *water* in both contexts, but with less confidence in hot water situations. In this scenario, the advanced learner of English is right for the right reasons, the beginning learner is right for the wrong reasons, while the intermediate learner is wrong (or at least uncertain) for the wrong reasons.

This discussion indicates just how difficult it is to draw conclusions about representation vs. process, even with some of the most basic words in any language. It also points up the fact that performing like an adult native speaker most – or even all – of the time offers no guarantee that the same knowledge is being put to use.[5]

What's more, sometimes it may be right to be wrong, from a particular theoretical perspective. This is especially clear in studies of English inflectional morphology, where one finds professional conflicts over the correct interpretation of children's morphological productions. As discussed later in the book (Part IV), many English-speaking children pass through a developmental stage during which they produce past-tense (also plural) forms that are different from those they end up producing as adults. Some of these non-adult forms – specifically, OVER-REGULARISATIONS, e.g. *comed* for *came*, *seed* for *saw* – are grist to the mill of so-called DUAL MECHANISM models, the most well-known example being that of Pinker (1998), also Pinker and Prince (1988). Proponents of this type of model claim that over-regularisations provide evidence that regularly affixed past-tense and plural forms are not lexically stored but are instead derived by lexical rules of affixation. Hence, over-regularisations like these are deemed 'good errors', and are taken as showing that the child has (correctly) internalised a general morphological rule; see Berko (1958), and any of innumerable replications of this seminal research.

By contrast, where a child produces a non-adult form by analogy with irregular past-tense form – e.g. *brang* for *brought*, *sawn* for *saw* – this has generally been to support a model without separate rules, which generalises on the basis of local phonetic, morphological and semantic contingences; see, for example, MacWhinney and Bates (1989), MacDonald, Pearlmutter and Seidenberg (1994), MacWhinney and Leinbach (1991). (It is also consistent with models in which both regular and irregular forms are generated by rule: see Embick and Noyer 2007, Bobaljik 2015; cf. Bonet and Harbour 2012). From the point of view of a classical dual mechanism model, however, these latter productions are 'bad errors': they don't fit the representational theory, and so, if possible, are to be dismissed as imperfect performance. Yet the idea that there is a principled distinction between good and bad errors – as desirable as it might be from a certain theoretical perspective – is simply not well-supported by the available empirical data. Even if it were, it would be once again impossible to tell, for any given data point, whether it has its source in representational or processing mismatch: a child who produces *catched* for *caught* on a given occasion may or may not know the correct form, and even adults occasionally misspeak, particularly with very low-frequency stems. (What's the present perfect form of *wring*, *wreak* or *strive*, for example?).

This problem isn't restricted to child language acquisition contexts, as is nicely illustrated in Neil Diamond's song *Play Me*. The word in question is *brang*, which appears as the end-rhyme on a line preceded by *sang* and followed by *rang*. (Licensing costs prohibit the republication of song here; in its place is a phrase-structural representation of the relevant line.)

The additional issues raised by the first two lines of the verse should be clear. If either of these lines were spoken in isolation by a four-year-old child – or by a Japanese learner in accented English – most native speakers of English would judge them grammatically unacceptable. This is because there are no fewer than three anomalies in the verse: first, as everyone knows, objects should follow the verb in English (unless they are marked as topics through the use of comma intonation); second, singular count nouns require a determiner (*She sang song just now*), unless they are treated with exceptional mass-noun readings; third, the past tense of *bring* is *brought* (in most varieties of English). Innumerable hours are spent in second language classrooms rehearsing these elementary points of English grammar, especially the second, 'time after weary time'. Yet the lines are completely acceptable in this particular lyrical context. More than that: to native speakers of English it seems fairly clear that 'correcting' the lines would make the verse less acceptable – for reasons of rhyme and metre – and that a significant part of the meaning of the verse would be lost; as a result of any such changes, the third and fourth lines would have very little point. If a less proficient speaker were to alter these lines to make it them 'more grammatical', as in (7), we would hardly hail the result as an improvement:

(7) She sang me a song
     She brought a song to me …

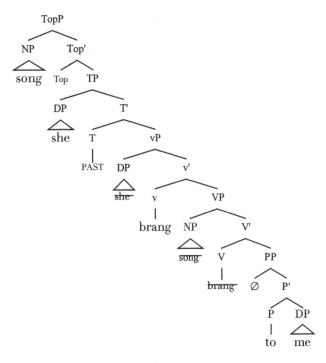

♫ Adapted from Neil Diamond, *Play Me* (1972)

Naturally, it could be claimed that the object of poetic writing is precisely to push grammatical boundaries, and that examples such as these 'prove the rule'. That is as maybe, although it does not really seem that any grammatical boundaries are being tested here: this case is not akin to a violation of Superiority or Subjacency, for example; see Case #6 below. Nor does this have the feel of a typical child's syntactic error, such as those in (8):

(8)　a.　Why did he didn't come?
　　　　　[adult form: Why didn't he come?]
　　　b.　Everyone doesn't know that.
　　　　　[adult forms: Not everyone knows that ~ No-one knows that.]

See Part IV for some further discussion of children's grammatical anomalies. Arguably, the right conclusion to draw from Neil Diamond's verse is that the sentence structures are grammatically acceptable and that, morphologically, *brang* is just perfect – in this context. But if this is true, it demonstrates that acceptability judgments can never be context-neutral: our judgments of acceptability necessarily weigh *in* – rather than abstract *away from* – a large number of contingent factors. Just as significantly, intuitions of acceptability are inextricably tied to very specific contexts of utterance: just because *brang* is the most suitable form of *bring* in this verse does not mean that *brang* is acceptable in other verses of this song, let alone in every poetic text.

> One might also consider what the use of *brang* suggests about the Neil Diamond's internal representation of the past tense of *bring*. I assume the correct answer is 'nothing at all': at least, this piece of performance does not invite the conclusion that the singer's mental representation of the past tense of *bring* is different from that of other native New Yorkers. See A is for Abstraction below.

This conclusion has consequences for any theory of lexical and grammatical representation that is based on judgments of morphological or syntactic acceptability. If such judgments are inherently context-dependent, then they must have their source in the dynamic interaction between different kinds of linguistic and non-linguistic information encountered in the course of language processing, rather than in fixed, autonomous, lexical or syntactic representations. See also G is for Grammar, J is for Judgment.

Not surprisingly, these implications have been noticed by others, even by those within the Chomskyan circle. In a footnote to the second chapter of his 1996 book *The Empirical Base of Linguistics,* Carson Schütze writes:

It is conceivable that competence in this sense of a statically represented knowledge does not exist. It could be that a given string is generated or its status computed when necessary, and that the demands of the particular situation determine how the computation is carried out, e.g., by some sort of comparison to prototypical sentence structure stored in memory. Since such a scenario would demand a major rethinking of the goals of the field of linguistics, I will not deal with it further.

Carson Schütze, The Empirical Base of Linguistics (1996)

Much of the experimental research discussed in any standard psycholinguistics textbook implies that this scenario is not only conceivable, but that it stands a very good chance of being true.

Notes

1 See, for example, www.buzzfeed.com/alanwhite/23-charming-illustrations-of-untranslatable-words-from-other
2 *Hotchkiss* ホチキス (hochikisu) is a regular Japanese word for an office stapler, named after an American office products firm E. H. Hotchkiss & Company (founded in 1897). Compare the British English use of *hoover* as the generic name for a vacuum cleaner, and by extension, the use of this appliance ('Haven't you finished the hoovering yet?').

3 Or consider the Japanese *wh*-word どちら (*dochira*)? which translates as English 'which'. Except that どちら strongly implies two alternatives, whereas English 'which' can refer to one of any number of choices: 'There are five sweets in this container: which (one) do you want?'

4 Notice, however, given the possibility of separate input and output lexicons, that evidence from *comprehension* studies may not tell us anything about whether or not a speaker has represented a word in his/her production lexicon: it is quite possible, for example, to recognise and identify the meaning of a word without knowing how to pronounce or use it on another occasion. This is often overlooked by competence-based researchers, who place disproportionate weight on comprehension data. See C is for Competence~Performance below.

5 Nearly identical issues arise in the case of young children's over-extension errors. See Saxton (2010: chapter 6).

6 (Case #3) 'Running up that hill': Mapping events to syntax

Improbable as it may seem, Kate Bush's classic song *Running Up that Hill* presents a significant challenge when it comes to translation into French, Spanish, Japanese and many other languages (though not, for example, to translation into Dutch or Swedish).

♫ Kate Bush, *Running Up that Hill (A Deal with God)* (1985)

As the samples in (9) and (10) illustrate, regular translations of the refrain are either longer and more cumbersome than the original – with the main verb, meaning *go up/ascend*, varying according to the object noun-phrase in each line (Japanese) – or else they sacrifice idiomaticity for the sake of symmetry. In Japanese, French and Spanish 'going up a road' is typically construed differently from 'going up a hill (or building)': in the latter cases, the notion of near-vertical ascent is an essential part of the meaning conveyed.[1] Notice that in all of the foreign translations the idea of running is downplayed: in fact, the manner of motion is omitted altogether in the particular French and Spanish translations given in (9) and (10), partly in order to better fit the metrical structure of the song. As for *up*, that's gone too (as a separate word), the idea of upward path or direction having been merged into the main verb.[2]

(9) a. Michi-o   (hashitte)   agatteiru,
        street-ACC   (run-INF)   climb-PROG
        'Running up (that) road'

     b. Saka-o   (hashitte)   nobotteiru,
        slope-ACC   (run-INF)   climb-PROG
        'Running up (that) hill'

     c. Ano biru-o   (hashitte)   nobotteiru.
        that[3] building-ACC   (run-INF)   climb-PROG
        'Running up (that) building'

(10) a. M'élancer sur cette route,
          M'élancer vers cette colline,
          M'élancer contre cet édifice.

      b. Venir à bout de cette rue.
          Venir à bout de cette colline
          Venir à bout de cet immeuble.

      c. Je franchirais cette route,
          Je franchirais cette colline
          Je franchirais cet immeuble.

      d. Subiendo ese camino
          Subiendo esa colina
          Subiendo ese edificio.

The translators' difficulty with these lines is compounded by uncertainty of how best to translate another apparently simple word: the demonstrative article *that*. Whereas Standard English is content with a two-way deictic contrast (*this* vs. *that*) many languages – including some varieties of non-standard English – draw a three-way distinction in spatial deixis between *this* (closer to the speaker than to the listener), *that* (closer to the listener than to the speaker), and a third term indicating some further-distant position: cf. Spanish *aquello*, Japanese あの (*ano*); Ulster-Scots *thon*. (See Harbour 2015 for more sophisticated discussion of the formal constraints on variation in deictic contrasts.) In the Japanese prose translation in (9), the distal form あの (*ano*) is selected; in the examples in (10), on the other hand, the French translator picked the proximate form *cette*, while the Spanish translation shows the intermediate pronoun *ese*. These differences may be subtle, but they nevertheless evoke distinct images in the listeners' minds.

Returning to the problem of the main verb, notice that the problem doesn't apply only to *run up*, but extends to all so-called MANNER OF MOTION predicates. In English, 'manner' information is usually encoded in the main verb, with 'path' information being expressed by a preposition; what Talmy (1985, 2000) calls a 'satellite'. The set of manner of motion verbs includes *walk down, swim through, creep over, clamber out of, skip into, flutter past*, and *swoop down on*, to cite only a few of thousands of verb–preposition combinations.

By contrast, in languages such as French and Japanese, PATH information is typically merged into the main verb of directed motion, with the MANNER component being optionally expressed as an adjunct modifier (similar to an English gerundive). As often as not, as Slobin (2003) discusses, the manner component goes unmentioned in these languages; it is literally 'lost in translation'.

This grammatical distinction – between so-called VERB-FRAMED and SATELLITE-FRAMED languages (Talmy 1985, 2000) – clearly illustrates the fact that languages vary not only in their phonologies, and in their differing

Figure 10 Wandering down that hill.

vocabularies, but also in the particular means at their disposal of construing events linguistically, that is to say, mapping lexical predicates to event representations. See Slobin (2003), Kita and Özyürek (2003); see also Kellerman and van Hoof (2003) for a discussion of L2 learners.

The distinction also implies an essential psychological distinction between a non-linguistic level of CONCEPTUAL REPRESENTATION and one of LINGUISTIC (SEMANTIC) CONSTRUAL. It may literally be true that that one cannot *say* 'They ambled up that hill' or 'They wandered along the path' in French or Japanese, but it seems absurd to suppose that French, Japanese and English speakers do not share the same non-verbal understanding of the image in Figure 10, even if they express this understanding by means of different linguistic frames: cf. Kita and Özyürek (2003).[3]

A further implication of this cross-linguistic contrast is that speakers of different languages must employ different sets of processing algorithms for encoding and verbalising events, different ways of 'THINKING FOR SPEAKING', as Slobin (2003) describes it. In other words, in language comprehension and production, different modes of lexical representation necessitate different kinds of semantic decomposition and merger.

These differences give rise to the kinds of L2 errors studied by Shunji Inagaki (2001), and illustrated in (11). In Inagaki's study, English L2 learners of Japanese failed to recognise that manner-of-motion verbs used with GOAL PPs are normally unacceptable in the target language. Notice that each of the constituent phrases is grammatically acceptable in its own right: the problem is simply that they cannot be combined to express this particular event construal.

(11) a. ?*John-ga [gakkoo-ni] [aruita].   (Inagaki 2001: ex. (4))
        John-NOM   school-LOC   walked
        'John walked to school.'

      b. ?*John-ga [ie-no   naka-ni] [hassita].
        John-NOM   house-of inside-at   ran
        'John ran into the house.'

This is a significant point, since it gives the lie to the idea that representation and processing can be studied independently of one another, or that processing mechanisms could be strictly invariant across different grammatical systems.

Words, then, are more than simply labels for pre-existing, fixed concepts; this is one reason why L2 vocabulary acquisition is so tricky, and why a bilingual dictionary often yields unintended translations. On the other hand, it is not the case that words and contexts give us concepts directly, as some strong relativists would like to believe. Instead, as Bowerman and Choi (2001) demonstrate (see below), the relationship between a word and its meaning(s) is more often than not an emergent property, one that develops through interaction with the input, and which varies in significant ways across languages.

The two examples considered thus far illustrate relatively straightforward cases of lexical adjustment inasmuch as they are both instances of what might be termed 'variable extension'. In the case of words such as *water* and *bread*, their correlates in other languages have broader or narrower application depending on the availability of other words in the same semantic field; as we have seen, where Japanese 湯 pre-empts 水, or English *toast* pre-empts *bread*. So, although there are certainly differences in the word-to-concept mapping here, the adjustment required is little more than an exercise in building a Lego™ wall using smaller or larger bricks: the presence of a short brick 湯 precludes the use of the long version of 水. Either way you build the brick wall, it looks much the same, with most of the cracks coinciding neatly. This is schematised in Figure 11.[4]

Similarly, the contrast between verb-framed and satellite-framed languages can also be seen as largely a matter of bricklaying, combining the same semantic primitives (PATH, MOTION, MANNER, etc.) in different ways: English-type languages combine MOTION and MANNER in one long brick, with an (extra) short brick for PATH, while Japanese-type languages combine MOTION and PATH into one longer brick, with an additional short brick for MANNER. Either way the concepts

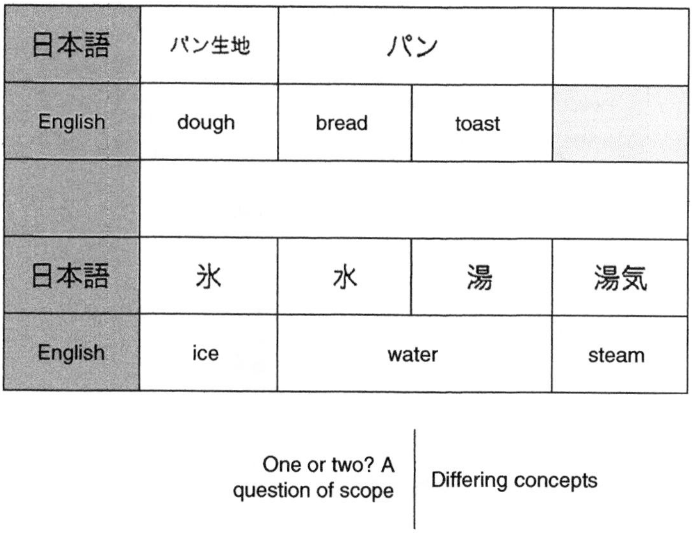

日本語	パン生地	パン		
English	dough	bread	toast	
日本語	氷	水	湯	湯気
English	ice	water		steam

One or two? A question of scope | Differing concepts

Figure 11 (Hot and cold) water revisited.

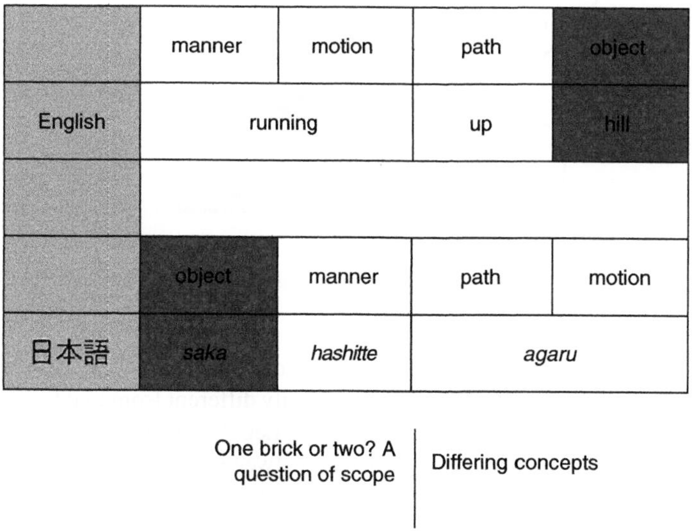

	manner	motion	path	object
English	running		up	hill
	object	manner	path	motion
日本語	saka	hashitte	agaru	

One brick or two? A question of scope | Differing concepts

Figure 12 Verb-framed vs. satellite-framed languages.

are merged the total extent of the wall – the conceptual coverage – remains the same. See Figure 12. Hence, although there may well be representational differences as a result of different mapping rules, the adjustments required are quite trivial in these cases, as is the associated learning problem.

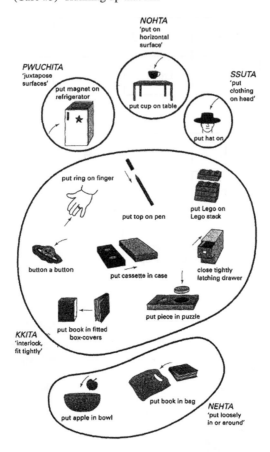

Figure 13 Construal of spatial relations in English vs. Korean (from Bowerman and Choi 2001).

In other instances, however, acquisition of lexical items leads to a system of semantic categorisation that is fundamentally different from that found in one's own language: Tetris™-shaped blocks in a Lego™ set, if you will. A paradigm example of this is given by the contrast between English *on/in* versus Korean *kkita/nehta*. As shown in Figure 13, adapted from Bowerman and Choi (2001), whereas English *in* vs. *on* delineates a two-way conceptual contrast between containment/insertion ('in') and Figure-to-Ground contact ('on') – the cup is *on* the table, but the picture is also *on* the wall, the ring is *on* the finger, the apple is *on* the tree – the Korean predicates *nehta* vs. *kkita* are distinguished by the opposed notions of 'tight-fit' vs. 'loose-fit'. This conceptual contrast, which has no natural realisation in English, gives rise to a completely different set of adult categorisation preferences, illustrated in Figure 13.

For adult Korean speakers, stacked Lego™ bricks, the action of inserting a video-cassette into its cover, tightly packed cigarettes, or a ring on someone's finger are intuitively construed as instances of the same Figure/Ground relation; these are opposed to placing a cup on the table, or an apple in a bowl, which are understood as instantiating different kinds of relation. In this way, the Korean system of classification cross-cuts the English one. There is no easy shifting of category boundaries, no inversion of subset–superset relations, no simple default inheritance: instead, for an English speaker to use these Korean predicates correctly involves a radical reconceptualisation of what counts as 'natural kinds' of events and situations.

Two aspects of this phenomenon are particularly significant, as Bowerman and Choi observe. The first is the finding that language-specific categorisation patterns are applied not just to verbal tasks but in non-linguistic contexts as well: categorisation extends 'beyond *Thinking for Speaking*'. Even without verbal cues, native Korean adults will naturally sort objects/representations of events in different ways from their English-speaking counterparts. The other notable feature of this contrast is its early emergence in language development: from the beginning of language acquisition, English and Korean infants have been shown (by means of preferential looking experiments) to display divergent preferences of semantic categorisation.

At first blush, these results challenge the idea that core properties of lexical semantics are innately given, as many competence-based theories assume; see, for example, Johnston and Slobin (1979). Instead, they seem to show that such properties must be learned – and *perfectly* learned – through 'imperfect experience': variable linguistic input plays a determining role in establishing (what appear to the adult native speaker to be) natural and discrete conceptual categories.

More recent research, however, including work by Soonja Choi herself (one of the co-authors of the Bowerman and Choi 2001 study) suggests that pre-verbal infants are sensitive to a larger set of spatial concepts than are found in their particular language: in subsequent experiments reported in Choi ([2009] 2015), pre-verbal infants raised in English-speaking and in Korean-speaking environments were found to behave no differently from one another in familiarisation experiments in which loose-fit vs. tight-fit containment scenes were contrasted. See also Spelke and Hespos (2002). Hence, these latter results support the idea that, with respect to lexical concepts, young infants may be as much 'citizens of the world' (to borrow Patricia Kuhl's expression) as they are in the case of speech perception (see Case #1 above). In other words, conceptual development, like phonological development, may involve 'pruning' and 'trimming' of pre-existent categories, as much as the creation of phonological categories based on language-particular contrasts; cf. Kuhl et al. (1992), Werker and Lalonde (1988).

The jury is still out, then, with regard to the innateness of spatial contrasts. Yet even if pre-verbal infant studies provide evidence for some innate contrast, it seems equally clear that first language acquisition – by reinforcing and reshaping selected concepts, while leaving others to atrophy – radically alters the 'natural pathways' between words, conceptual categories and syntactic frames found in different languages. As a result, THINKING FOR SPEAKING (and for listening, and reading and writing, and judging grammaticality, and for every other kind of linguistic behaviour) must give rise to a different set of processing algorithms for each language variety. Sometimes these differences will be minor (two- vs. three-place deictic contrasts, for example), sometimes they will be more pervasive (e.g. the use of morphological case and/or agreement cues in syntactic processing). Still, whatever the nature of the contrast, every representational difference has inextricable consequences for adult language processing.

In summary, we might start out, both cognitively and linguistically, as 'citizens of the world', but the experiences we have, and the words we acquire to communicate those experiences, serve to narrow our perceptual horizons and to channel our thoughts.

Notes

1 The English verb *climb*, like other more fully specified verbs, shows its own 'preference rules': *climb* entails vertical movement, but also implies that this movement is upward, rather than downward, and also suggests some measure of physical effort: (i) *The mountaineer climbed up K2*, (ii) *?The snake climbed straight up the tree*, (iii) *The mountaineer climbed back down the mountain*, (iv) *?The child climbed down the slide*, (v) *The snake??climbed/slithered down the tree* (Levin and Rappaport Hovav 2007, Geuder and Weisgerber 2006). By contrast, manner-of-motion verbs such as *run*, *crawl*, *creep*, *stumble* have no inherent directionality. And the light verb *go* has virtually no meaning whatsoever: cf. *go off* = 'turn sour/explode/start to sound/depart …'.

2 Sources: (10a) http://traductionsetparoles.over-blog.com/article-10350329.html; (10b) www.placebocity.com/paroles-et-traduction-139-running-up-that-hill.html? fb_comment_id=496542024256_32987224; (10c) www.lacoccinelle.net/246223 .html; Spanish translation from http://lyricstranslate.com/es/running-hill-subiendo-esa-colina.html.

3 English speakers are unusual in having both construals available to them, thanks to the Norman Conquest. As a result of French contact, we can *enter* or *go into* a room, *traverse* or *climb across* a crevasse, and so forth. For speakers of many languages, there is no choice: Dutch and Swedish speakers, for example, cannot *exit* a room, though they can easily *go out* of one. The reader should also be aware that the implied simple dichotomy between VERB-FRAMED and SATELLITE-FRAMED languages obscures some subtle, intermediate cases: Japanese is a case in point.

4 The notion of pre-emption here appears to be related to the idea of DEFAULT INHERITANCE in computational morphology: see, for example, Corbett and Fraser (1993), Fraser and Corbett (1997).

7 (Case #4) 'Me, myself, I': Representing and processing co-reference

A: *Dad, how tall is* myself?
N: *You mean how tall are you?*
A: *Yeah* ... [stands against the wall-measure]
N: *137 cm.*
A: *So, no change then.*
Father–son (eight years) conversation (11 September 2014)

♫ Joan Armatrading, *Me, Myself, I* (1980)

As has already been mentioned, many competence-based psycholinguists have devoted a significant chunk of their research time to trying to understand how language users handle potentially co-referential expressions, how speakers decide which linguistic expressions are actually co-referential in a given context of utterance, and which are necessarily disjoint in reference. Taken together, these relationships can be referred to as ENDOPHORIC REFERENTIAL DEPENDENCIES. One rather negative reason for this research focus is that many linguists can't seem to figure out how to explain EXOPHORIC reference – that is to say, the relationship between words and non-verbal entities beyond the text~speech stream. As a consequence, rather like the agoraphobic or the prisoner under house arrest, a disproportionate amount of time is spent examining internal relations.

Whether referentiality is really so intractable is open to question – see R is for Reference below – but for now let us assume that this is the case. To appreciate why the study of referential dependencies is worthy of anyone's passing interest, let alone their academic careers, consider how the numbered nominal expressions are understood in the following passage from Gustave Flaubert's *Madame Bovary*. (In this chapter, I'll restrict attention to the pronouns in the extract, largely postponing discussion of proper names and other referring expressions).[1]

Elle$_1$ était à Tostes. Lui$_2$, il$_2$ était à Paris$_3$, maintenant; là-bas!
Comment était ce Paris$_3$? Quel nom$_4$ démesuré! Elle$_5$ se le$_6$ répétait à demi-voix$_7$, pour se$_8$ faire plaisir; il$_9$ sonnait à ses$_{10}$ oreilles comme un bourdon$_{11}$ de cathédrale$_{12}$, il$_{13}$ flamboyait à ses$_{14}$ yeux jusque sur l'étiquette$_{14}$ de ses$_{15}$ pots$_{16}$ de pommade.

La nuit, quand les mareyeurs, dans leurs charrettes, passaient sous ses fenêtres en chantant la Marjolaine, elle s'éveillait, et écoutant le bruit des roues ferrées, qui, à la sortie du pays, s'amortissait vite sur la terre:
– Ils y seront demain! se disait-elle.

> *She$_1$ was in Tostes. And he, he$_2$ was in Paris now; way over there! What sort of a place was Paris$_3$? What a boundless name$_4$. She$_5$ whispered it$_6$ to herself$_7$, because she$_8$ loved its sound. It$_9$ resonated in her$_{10}$ ears like the great bell$_{11}$ of a cathedral$_{12}$; it$_{13}$ glowed from her$_{14}$ eyes even onto the labels$_{15}$ of her$_{16}$ pomade jars.*

> *At night, when the fish carriers passed by in their carts, beneath her windows, singing the Marjolaine, she would wake up, and hearing, as they left the village the noise of the iron-clad wheels quickly muffled by the dull earth of the country road, she said to herself:*

> *'They will be there tomorrow.'*

Gustave Flaubert, Madame Bovary, chapter 9 (1857)

It is immediately clear to the English reader that every instance of *she* and *her* must be interpreted as co-referring to the same woman (Emma Bovary), just as the two instances of *he*, as well the various instances of *it*, are co-referential with their respective discourse antecedents; that is to say, both *hes* must co-refer, all of the *its* co-refer. This might seem unremarkable but for the fact that consecutive pronouns are not required to be co-referential in other contexts, as is shown by the examples in (12) and (13). Moreover, as we shall see directly, there are cases where pronouns *must* be interpreted as disjoint in reference even in contexts where co-reference would seem to be pragmatically felicitous.

(12)   a.   She$_1$ told Marjolaine that she$_2$ was not allowed to leave, without her permission.
       b.   She$_1$ told Marjolaine that she$_2$ was not allowed to leave, without her passport.

In the sentence in (12a), it is unclear whether the two instances of *she* should be interpreted as co-referential, or whether they involve disjoint reference, with the second *she$_2$* plausibly taking *Marjolaine* as an antecedent. (Notice that in these examples *Marjolaine* is intended to refer to a person, not the name of a song, which was the case in the original passage.) What *is* clear however, given the presence of the word *permission* in (12a), is that the second *she* cannot easily be understood as co-referential with the following possessive pronoun *her*.[2] Crucially, no similar restriction applies in (12b), where *permission* is replaced by *passport*. These restrictions are schematised in Figure 14, with subscripted indices representing the possibilities of co-reference, and arrows showing the most plausible co-reference chains.

An opposing restriction is observed in the examples in (13), where *intend* replaces *allowed*: in these latter sentences, the second instance of *she* cannot naturally be construed as co-referential with *Marjolaine* (since no-one can know another person's intentions).[3]

(13) a. She₁ told Marjolaine that she₂ did not intend to leave, without her permission. [she₂ ≠ Marjolaine]
      b. She told Marjolaine that she did not intend to leave, without her passport. [she₂ ≠ Marjolaine]

What might have appeared just a moment ago to be a trivial inference emerges as a fairly interesting theoretical puzzle: how are readers (or listeners) able to process lexical, syntactic and pragmatic information so efficiently that they can decide, almost instantaneously, which pronouns should be treated as co-referential – and which must not be – in a given context? Furthermore, given that the rules of pronoun construal vary to some extent from one language variety to another, how does this processing ability arise?

Whether we are considering acquisition or processing, the issue arises as to how the transient information about disjoint reference in (12) and (13) is mentally represented. It seems very unlikely to be part of the lexical representation of the pronoun *her*, such that the lexical entry for *her* lists all of the pairs of predicates in the context of which possessive *her* may or may not be interpreted as co-referential with a preceding pronoun (*allowed~permission*, ᵒᵏallowed~passport, *intend~permission*, etc.). In any event, there are a large number of contexts, including for example those in (14), where *her* can easily be construed as co-referential with *she* in the context of *permission*:

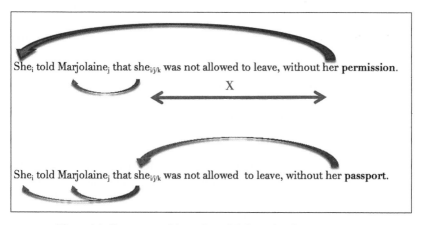

She₁ told Marjolaine_j that she_{i/j/k} was not allowed to leave, without her **permission**.

X

She₁ told Marjolaine_j that she_{i/j/k} was not allowed to leave, without her **passport**.

Figure 14 Context-sensitive referential dependencies.

(14)   a. <u>She</u> refused to give <u>her</u> permission for Marjolaine to leave.
       b. Though some dispute whether <u>she/the Queen</u>ᵢ should have such authority,
          <u>her</u>ᵢ permission (assent) is still required for the enactment of legislation.

Crucially, in spoken language comprehension, the referential possibilities of either of the examples in (12) and (13) cannot be finally determined until the last word – *permission* or *passport* – is encountered, yet resolution appears to be nearly instantaneous immediately thereafter. Of course, in deciding upon the interpretation of these pronouns, the listener must draw on some stored knowledge: specifically, it is at least necessary to know the conventional meaning of the English words *passport* and *permission*. However, the interpretive restrictions in (12) and (13) cannot reasonably be derived from stored lexical knowledge or from autonomous syntactic knowledge – most parsers (and theoretical linguists) would assign exactly the same structural representation to both strings. Instead, it seems that it must be due to contextually informed pragmatic knowledge: in the case of the examples in (12), listeners know that one normally cannot grant oneself permission to do something, whereas leaving with one's own passport is normal practice; as for the examples in (13), we are aware of the fact one cannot know another person's intentions better than they do themselves. It is in the light of this non-linguistic knowledge that disjoint reference is inferred in the former, but strongly dispreferred in the latter examples.

Having noted this, there are other situations where it seems as if the possibilities of co-reference are invariable, and where interpretation is largely insensitive to contextual or pragmatic information. These are the cases that, according to many generative linguists, fall under the purview of BINDING THEORY. Some of the technical details of this theory are spelled out in Appendix A (website). At this point, it is sufficient to consider some of the data that the theory is intended to explain.

Consider first the basic examples in (15), which continue the theme from those above:

(15)   a. Emma told George [that Marjolaine admired <u>herself</u>].
       b. Emma told George [that Marjolaine admired <u>her</u>].
       c. Emma warned her not to admire <u>Marjolaine</u>.

In (15a), there are two *prima facie* noun-phrase antecedents for the reflexive anaphor *herself* – three, if *George* is treated as referring to a woman (George Sand, for example). However, only *Marjolaine* is a grammatically licit antecedent for *herself* in this sentence. (Unlike pronouns, reflexive anaphors *must* normally be co-indexed with another linguistically represented expression, by definition). Conversely, in (16b), *her* must not be construed as referring to

Marjolaine, though it *may* be construed with Emma (or George). Hence, the possibility of using *herself* seems to pre-empt any use of *her* to signal local co-reference. Finally, the contrast between (15b) and (15c) shows that while pronouns can have antecedents outside of their own clause, the converse does not hold: the noun-phrase *Marjolaine* must not be referentially related to any other syntactically prominent expression either inside or outside its clause.

What is moderately interesting about this is that the co-reference possibilities of anaphors, pronouns and names (R-EXPRESSIONS) are not explicable in purely linear terms. This is evidenced by the examples in (16):

(16)   a. Emma told Marjolaine something very interesting about herself/??her.
       b. The dream that Emma$_i$ had about Marjolaine$_j$ surprised *herself/her$_{i/*j}$.
       c. The gift that Emma$_i$ had given to Marjolaine$_j$ had surprised *herself/her$_{?i/j}$.
       d. Once she had got herself settled, Emma told Marjolaine about her/
          *herself's dream.
       e. Emma warned her$_i$ sister$_j$ that Marjolaine$_{?i/*j}$ was not to be trusted.

Observe that sentence (16a) is acceptable with *herself*, but is broadly unacceptable with *her*, unless *her* is understood as referring to some other previously mentioned individual. What is more, the string in (16a) is ambiguous for native speakers of English: although the anaphor *herself* is most readily construed with the clausal subject *Emma*, it can also be associated with the (indirect) object *Marjolaine* given a felicitous context – for example, if the subject noun-phrase *Emma* is understood as referring to a psychotherapist, or astrologer. In (16b) and (16c), on the other hand, the alternatives with *herself* appear to be completely unacceptable, in spite of the fact that the NPs *Emma* and *Marjolaine* are as close to the reflexive anaphor in linear terms as they were in the previous examples (where co-reference was possible). In the case of pronominal construal, example (16b), where *dream* is the head noun, preferentially allows construal of *her* with *Emma*. In (16c) on the other hand, where *dream* is replaced by *gift*, the preferred construal of *her* is with *Marjolaine*: one can be surprised by one's own dream, but not by one's own gift. Finally, examples (16d) and (16e) show that proper names (R-EXPRESSIONS)[4] can take a pronominal antecedent just as long as that antecedent is contained within an adjunct clause, or is a possessive pronoun: in (16d), *she* can be interpreted as co-referent with either *Emma* or *Marjolaine*, and the same is true of *her* in (16e), even if co-indexation with *Marjolaine* yields somewhat marginal results. Notice, also, that in (16d) *herself* is unacceptable where it functions as a possessive, even though it was fine in (16a) as an oblique pronoun, and is clearly fully interpretable in this position.

It's all quite exhausting, isn't it?

Contrasts such as these have captivated the attention of competence-based psycholinguists for several reasons. First, there is nothing in the surface form of the utterances themselves that signals which interpretations are possible, and which are impossible: determining co-reference requires complex analysis. Yet in spite of the absence of robust cues, native speakers display striking agreement on the possible interpretations of any given string.[5] Second, apparently in contrast to the cases considered earlier, the alternating judgments on reflexive anaphors and pronouns in (16) do not seem to be contingent upon lexical choice or pragmatic felicity: in virtually any discourse context, with almost any set of predicates, the same co-reference constraints seem to apply. Hence, it looks very much as if there are general rules of construal which all native speakers acquire and use in essentially the same way, in spite of the (apparent) inductive gap between knowledge and experience.

The problem is made even more tantalising by the fact that these rules of construal vary from one language to the next. Consider, for instance, the Japanese equivalents of (16a) and (*16d), given in (17a) and (17b). In contrast to English, example (17a) is unambiguous – *jibun* 'self' can only take a subject NP as its antecedent; (17b), on the other hand, is grammatically acceptable, since *jibun* can function as a possessive pronoun in Japanese:

(17) a. Emma-wa   Mary-ni   jibun-ni tsuite omosiroi   koto-o   hanasi-ta.
          Emma-TOP Mary-DAT   self   about interesting fact-ACC   tell-PAST
          'Emma told Mary something very interesting about herself.'
      b. Emma-wa   Mary-ni   jibun-no yume-ni   tsuite   hanasi-ta.
          Emma-TOP Mary-DAT   self-GEN dream-DAT about   tell-PAST
          'Emma told Mary about self's dream.'

So what is it that native speakers of a language 'know' that enables them to converge on the right set of interpretive judgments in each case? Most psycholinguists who take their lead from generative grammar suppose that these rules of construal are essentially syntactic in nature, that speakers must internally represent and use the PRINCIPLES OF BINDING THEORY to compute co-reference possibilities. In particular, generativists are wont to assume that speakers make reference to the core theoretical construct of C-COMMAND, a hierarchical relationship involving nodes in a phrase-structure tree. See Appendix A (website) for some explication.[6]

A direct consequence of this assumption for language processing is that language users must construct hierarchical analyses of every linear string, otherwise these c-command relations could not be computed. By extension, the assumption forces the conclusion that this propositional syntactic knowledge is autonomously represented and addressed in the course of sentence processing.

In short, if Binding Theory is the correct explanation of how speakers compute co-reference relations, it strongly implies a psychological distinction between the GRAMMAR (statically represented knowledge) and the PARSER. See Figure 6 in Part I above.

The implications for first language acquisition are equally far-reaching: if the generative approach to anaphoric dependencies is correct, then some mental correlate of c-command must be innately represented, since it is clearly not present in the input, and is plausibly unlearnable. Co-reference relations thus offer a potential instance of a POVERTY OF THE STIMULUS problem.

Without drawing any firm conclusions at this point, it is fair to question the adequacy of the standard generative approach, even considered on its own terms (that is to say, non-psychologically). Close examination of the data that are supposed to be covered by each principle has revealed a complex and intricate set of *prima facie* counter-examples. With respect to Principles A and B, for instance, the examples in (18) and (19) show sentences where construal either should be possible, but isn't, or shouldn't be possible, but is. Consider (18a). Here, the reflexive anaphor *themselves* has no antecedent within either the subject noun-phrase that contains it, or within the embedded clause. Principle A of the Binding Theory should therefore block any construal with higher arguments – compare (15a) above – thus rendering (18a) as ungrammatical as (16b). Yet (18a) is perfectly acceptable: as indicated by the subscripts, co-reference is available between *themselves* and *the boys*, and also (more marginally) between *themselves* and *their mothers*. On the other hand, co-reference between the lower pronominal *them* and either of the higher arguments, something that should be readily available by Principle B of the Binding Theory, is marginal at best. To the extent that co-reference is possible in these examples, there is a slight preference for construal with *their mothers* over *the boys* in (18a); this preference is reversed in (18b):

(18) a. The boys$_i$ told their mothers$_k$ that [[pictures of themselves$_{i/??k}$/them$_{??i/?k}$ had been posted on social media]].

    b. The boys$_i$ told their mothers$_j$ that [[John's pictures of themselves$_{*i/*j}$/them$_{??i/?k}$ had been posted on social media]].

The examples in (19) reveal further complexities still. *Prima facie*, the sentence pair in (19a) and (19b) should have the same interpretive possibilities: in both cases, a reflexive anaphor – in this case, the reciprocal *each other* – is contained within the clausal subject; having no c-commanding antecedent for *each other*, the sentence containing it should be ungrammatical. Yet (19a) is considerably more acceptable than (19b); for discussion and analysis, see Pesetsky (1995), Harley (1995), Fujita (1996). Conversely, examples (19c) and (19d) are both marginal with intended co-reference (that is, where *their* is understood as referring to *Bill and Mary*).

(19)   a. ?Each other's jokes made Bill and Mary laugh.
       b. *Each other's parents made Bill and Mary do the washing up.
       c. ?[[Their$_i$] jokes] made [Bill and Mary]$_i$ laugh.
       d. ?[[Their$_i$] parents] made Bill and Mary$_i$ do the washing up.

Note that unless otherwise specified, the acceptability judgments assigned to English sentences are my own. They may not be shared by all native speakers – at least one reviewer disputes the marginality of (19c) and (19d), for example – but they are sincere and consistent across months of revision of this manuscript. It is not a problem that these judgments are not universal; indeed, it proves a significant point. See J is for Judgment below.

For speakers who share my judgments, the anomaly of examples (19c,d) cannot be due to either Principle B or Principle C of the Binding Theory since first, the pronoun *their* is contained within the subject noun-phrase, and thus is itself free (possessive pronouns are in any case immune from Principle B effects, for unclear reasons); second, *their* is unable to c-command *Bill and Mary* from this position, so the (conjoined) NPs [Bill and Mary] are also free throughout.[7]

As for Principle C, research has suggested that co-reference constraints on R-expressions operate across discourse, and even through conversational dyads: see Hankamer (1979); also Morgan (1973), Merchant (2005):

(20)   SPEAKER A: *[pointing to John]* Where do you suppose he$_i$'s going?
       SPEAKER B: I dunno, to the pub, maybe/*To John$_i$'s house, maybe.

The dialogue in (20) appears to show that names cannot be construed as co-referential with a previously mentioned pronoun even where that pronoun appears in a different speaker's utterance. (It should be noted that some linguists would analyse Speaker B's utterance 'To John$_i$'s house' as involving a full clause containing the antecedent *he$_i$'s*, with elision of everything except the prepositional phrase. If this were the correct analysis, then (20) would not constitute a counter-example. In T is for Sentence below, I question the viability of this assumption.)

While none of these counter-examples is original – they have been raised and analysed in previous theoretical work – all suggest that the standard autonomous Binding Theory is a questionable means of characterising rules of construal. The most significant problem here is that co-reference possibilities are inevitably conditioned by lexical choice and pragmatic conditions, even when the surface structural conditions are held constant. This casts doubt on the argument that syntactic relations rigidly determine co-reference possibilities.

Moreover, even if all of these cases could be remedied under a revised version of Binding Theory, we would still require a separate processing theory to deal with the cases of pragmatically determined reference that fall outside any purely structural account. This set of pragmatically determined co-references includes not only the cases that we began with – that is to say, the contrasts in (12), (13) and (16) above, but also those in (21) and (22) below. The examples in (21) show that Principles B and C can be overridden, given the right prosody, while those in (22) show clear restrictions on pronominal binding in constructions involving a sentential topic, unexplained by Principle B; in (22b), for example, co-reference with *John* is quite rigidly excluded – in my judgment, at least – even though *him* cannot be construed with the prominent topic *Mary* because of conventional gender mismatch.

(21)   a.   <u>Everyone</u> loves Raymond, especially <u>Raymond</u>!
      b.   No-one voted for Raymond, even <u>Raymond</u>$_i$ didn't vote for him$_i$.

(22)   a.   As for <u>Raymond</u>$_i$, John$_j$ told Fred$_k$ that no-one likes him$_{i/*j/*k}$.
      b.   As for <u>Mary</u>, John$_j$ told Fred$_k$ that no-one likes him$_{*i/*j/*k}$.

To sum up, there is a significant disconnect between the grammatical constraints that competence-based linguists hypothesise to be represented in speakers' minds and the procedural mechanisms that are independently required to compute co-reference relations online, in varying contexts of utterance (in all of those cases that are not subsumed by some version of Binding Theory). Intuitively, the latter mechanisms take account of notions such as discourse-prominence and 'pre-emption' – that is, co-referential pronouns are dispreferred if reflexive anaphors are available – but don't seem to care overly about structural relations, structural hierarchy or c-command.

Notice, finally, that an adequate explanation of anaphor binding must include a diachronic perspective: as Keenan (2003) discusses, Binding Theory would probably look very different if we still spoke Middle English. This is also true of the phenomena discussed in the next chapter.

> *So I keep you in a flower vase*
> *With your fatalism and your crooked face*
> *With the daisies and the violet brocades*
> And I keep me in a vacant lot   [*myself]
> *In the ivy and the forget-me-nots*
> *Hoping you will come and untangle me one of these days.*
>
> ♫ Josh Ritter, *Come and Find Me* (2002)

Notes

1 It will be clear that the researcher's problem is *not* the reader's problem: figuring out 'who *who* refers to' in a specific context of utterance is a straightforward matter for typical adult readers: it is coming up with the general principles of construal that presents the theoretical difficulty. This mismatch between what linguists and language users consider to be a problem is, of course, a recurrent theme in all areas of cognitive research.

2 To spell this out, example (12a) is at least two ways ambiguous: (i) She [Emma] told Marjolaine that she [Emma] could not leave without her [Marjolaine]'s permission; (ii) She [Emma] told Marjolaine that she [Marjolaine] could not leave without her [Emma]'s permission (the situation indicated by the arrows in Figure 14). At least two other interpretations are excluded: (iii) #She [Emma] told Marjolaine that Emma could not leave without Emma's permission; (iv) #She [Emma] told Marjolaine that Marjolaine could not leave without Marjolaine's permission. Observe, finally, that the initial instance of *she* cannot be co-referential with *Marjolaine* in any of these contexts. I return to this point below.

3 As pointed out to me by Heidi Harley (pers. comm.), there is one rare context where such co-reference is possible, namely, where the first *she* refers to a play director, and where Marjolaine is an actor being told what her (character's) intentions are.

4 Proper names are only a subset of the set of so-called 'R(eferring)-expressions': any specific noun-phrase (e.g. 'The man with the yellow hat', 'the mouse', 'a certain detective') used to refer to an individual or set of individuals in a particular context of utterance counts as an R-expression. See R is for Reference below.

5 At least, there is agreement amongst those native speakers who are typically polled: it is a separate question whether those speakers are representative. Compare Henrich, Heine and Norenzayan (2010).

6 That assumption has been held until recently. Minimalism, having dispensed with syntactic representations in favour of a purely derivational approach to syntax (generalised transformations), has also been forced to abandon the notion of C-COMMAND as a primitive. Attempts have recently been made to derive the effects of Binding through other, derivational, mechanisms: see, for example, Abe (2014).

7 The grammatical acceptability of 'Henry adores his father' shows that English possessive pronouns are generally immune to Principle B effects (see Carnie 2011).

8   (Case #5) 'Be my number two' ... won't you?: The problem of partial generalisations

Le bon dieu est dans le détail.

Gustave Flaubert (attributed)

Does God dwell in the detail(s), as Flaubert had it – or is it the devil that lurks there; alternatively, do the exceptions prove the rule?[1] For some language researchers, the goal of grammatical theory is to derive maximally simple discrete generalisations that allow the linguist (and, by hypothesis, 'the child') to project beyond their verbal experience (the PRIMARY LINGUISTIC DATA).[2] For others, generalisations are crude, broad-brush statements that describe only the most central cases, and which represent a starting-point for deeper empirical investigation, rather than its culmination: see, for example, Elman et al. (1996). On the latter view, if you believe that some grammatical rule has a fully general application within a particular language, or that it can be applied directly to the grammar of a different language, you probably haven't looked closely enough at the phenomenon in question.

The earlier analogy to flight is instructive: humming birds and bats do not fly (algorithmically) like eagles; anyone who supposes they do just hasn't been paying close attention.

A good rule of thumb in evaluating generalisations might seem to be to consider how much work the general rule does: that is, what is the 'balance in extension' between the general rule and the exceptions? If the exceptions account for only a small fraction of the data, say, less than 5 per cent, while the general rule accounts for 95 per cent, we should have little hesitation in endorsing it. If the relationship is more balanced, say 40–60 per cent, we might have some cause for concern, especially if the irregular forms exhibit sub-regularities of their own (so-called 'gang effects': see Stemberger and MacWhinney 1988). And where the general rule only accounts for a small minority of cases – 5 per cent, for example – that cause for concern increases substantially.[3]

Whereas discussion of irregularity in psycholinguistics has traditionally been focused on the acquisition and processing of INFLECTIONAL MORPHOLOGY, the examples discussed in this section involve exceptions to putatively general syntactic rules; specifically, with apparent exceptions to the rules of question formation in Present Day English.

83

A slightly different way of looking at this is not in terms of exceptions – 'exception' is too theory-laden a term – but rather in terms of 'gaps' or 'holes' in the paradigm: my concern here is with interrogative structures that clearly ought to be grammatically acceptable if a general rule applied, but which aren't, as a matter of (contingent) fact. See also v is for von Humboldt below.

The main point to keep in mind here is that whatever view is taken of the existence and/or scope of general rules, there must be some mechanism for learning, marking and storing the exceptions~gaps. Grammatical analysis is a zero-sum game, and unless they are simply swept under the carpet, exceptions~gaps must be represented somewhere in the language processing system. The inevitable price of more Minimalist grammar is an increasingly complex lexicon and/or pragmatics; see Duffield (2014, 2015).

Of course, linguists have long been aware of the fact of syntactic irregularity: nearly a century ago, Edward Sapir's dictum 'All grammars leak' was aimed at just this problem (Sapir 1921). Much more recently, generative linguists were again put on notice of *Irregularity in Syntax* by George Lakoff's seminal 1965 dissertation, published in 1970, under that very title (Lakoff [1965] 1970).

As it turns out, many of the syntactic alternations discussed in Lakoff's thesis are now handled lexically, precisely because of the unpredictable relationships that arise in derivational morphology; see also Chomsky (1970). Two representative cases are given in (23). Lakoff claimed, for example, that while *robber* might be derivationally related to *rob*, *thief* could not be related in the same way to *thieve*; similarly (it was claimed), *handwriting* might be *readable*, but bats are not *swingable*.

(23)   a.   John is a robber/John is a thief. [= (5-5)]
       b.   John robs things/*John thieves things.
       c.   His handwriting can be read/His handwriting is readable. [= (5-6)]
       d.   *This ball is hittable/*This bar is bendable/*This bat is swingable.

Straightaway it should be obvious that Lakoff's judgments do not apply in all varieties of English. In my version of English, for example, 'John robs things' is unacceptable – you can rob *people* or *banks* but not *things* (from people or banks). This is not, however, a general fact about Hiberno-English varieties. For example, Lakoff has support from the Irish author Roddy Doyle: in *Paddy Clarke, Ha, Ha, Ha,* we find the following dialogue:

> – *That's you growing up, you know, she told him. – You'll be very tall.*
> *I never got pains in my legs.*
> – *Very tall. That'll be great, won't it? Great for robbing apples.*
> *That was brilliant. We laughed.*

Roddy Doyle, *Paddy Clarke, Ha, Ha, Ha* (1993)

So, *rob* can take an arbitrary Theme object, for some people. But not for me. Conversely, in many varieties of non-standard English, including the one I grew up with, 'John thieves (things)' is perfectly acceptable. This is supported by the attested forms in (24):

(24) a. 'If <u>she thieves</u> but once, she goes straight back where she came from.'
Val Wood, *Children of the Tide* (2014)

b. 'Greta does not like to let other people pay for her. Some find this strange as she <u>thieves things</u> from others all the time, but when someone offers her anything outright she can't take it.'
Jessica Ziebland, *Greta and Claude* (2010)

As for the cases in (23d), which Lakoff considers unacceptable, these are all unexceptionable, to my ear.

A more interesting kind of exception is illustrated by the examples in (25): here, Lakoff's judgments *of these particular sentence tokens* do seem to apply to all varieties of Present Day English. Yet he was evidently mistaken about the source of the problem: the acceptability of the corresponding examples in (26) speaks against his assertion that such 'verbs do not undergo the passive transformation [categorically]' (Lakoff 1970: 19).

(25) a. John <u>resembles</u> Mary's mother/*Mary's mother is <u>resembled</u> by John.
b. John <u>owes</u> two dollars/*Two dollars are <u>owed</u> by John.
c. Two and two <u>equal</u> four/*Four is <u>equalled</u> by two and two.
d. I <u>meant</u> what I said/*What I said was <u>meant</u> by me.
e. I <u>wanted</u> a catcher's mitt/*A catcher's mitt was <u>wanted</u> by me.

(26) a. [see immediately below]
b. How to buy a car that money is <u>owed</u> on?
c. The return period for a given event is defined as the period of time on the long-term average value at which a given event is <u>equalled</u> or exceeded.[4]
d. What was <u>meant</u> by that statement was quite unclear.
e. What was <u>wanted</u> were people who could speak the Russian language, to participate in an expedition to Chukotka.

If the examples in (26) are fine, then the unacceptability of the starred examples in (26) cannot be due to syntactic ill-formedness, since both sets of examples are described by the same syntactic rules: at least, this was true in the theory that Lakoff adopted, as it is in more recent generative analyses; see Baker, Johnson and Roberts (1989). Hence, prefixing the examples in (26) with an asterisk – the symbol conventionally used to signal a grammatical anomaly – is a misdirection: the anomaly must have a different representational or procedural explanation, most likely one that factors in lexical, collocational and contextual–pragmatic information.

Intuitively, the contrast here is due to the interaction between the thematic relationship between the two arguments on one hand, and the functional value of passivisation, on the other. This difference can be captured in many other grammatical frameworks, but not in standard varieties of generative grammar. Notice that even *resemble* appears to have been passivisable in earlier stages of English: in Thomas Starkey's *Dialogue between Cardinal Pole and Thomas Lupset* (ca. 1529) is found: 'The thing which is resembled to the soul is civil order and politic law, administered by officers and rulers' (see Tillyard 2011).

The crux of the matter is that there is not one passive rule, together with some exceptions; instead, it seems that there exist several related, but ultimately independent, constructions. This at least is how Geoffrey Pullum explains it, in his sharp critique of *Syntactic Structures* (Chomsky 1957); cf. Kiparsky (2013).

The full array [of passive types] contains 24 English passive constructions, of which the SS transformation handles just one: the non-concealed non-adjectival non-prepositional long passive clause as complement of the copula. This one has no special priority or importance relative to the others. If the Passive transformation expressed a true generalization (we shall see below that it does not), it would be expressing a generalization holding over only a very small part of the range inherent in the descriptive task of characterizing English passive clauses.

Geoffrey Pullum, 'Creation myths of generative grammar
and the mathematics of *Syntactic Structures*' (2010)

The cases examined below differ from those discussed by Lakoff inasmuch that they are neither amenable to a purely lexical remedy, however such remedies should be stated, nor do the judgments on them depend on pragmatic factors. Instead, consistent with Pullum's assessment of English passives, speakers' judgments of the following paradigmatic sets seem to co-vary according to constructional properties, including especially the finiteness of the clause in which they appear. As mentioned earlier, finiteness is no longer considered a categorical property in current generative models, though it was in earlier versions of the theory; compare, for example, analyses of the 'Tensed-S Condition' (Chomsky 1973).

So let's return to the Joe Jackson song referenced in the section title, and to its apparently innocuous first line (which begins with the words *Won't you ...* followed the name of the song):[5]

♫ Joe Jackson, *Be my Number Two* (1984)

Like all *won't you*-initial utterances, this string is structurally identical to a negative *Yes-No* question. Yet that is not how the utterance is standardly interpreted: see Searle (1975), also Kiefer (1980). For most adult native speakers,[6] the first line functions primarily as a request or invitation (= '[Please] be my number two'), rather than as a question about a future non-event ('#Is it the case that you will not be my number two'/'#Is it not the case that you will be my number two?' – depending on how negation is interpreted relative to the modal auxiliary).

The utterance is not even particularly negative: its meaning is almost equivalent to the positive request 'Will you be my number two?', albeit the speaker has slightly less hope of his offer being accepted. This kind of 'expletive negation' was much more common in nineteenth-century prose style, as in the excerpt from Alice Bacon's *A Japanese Interior* that was quoted in the Introduction:[7]

[I]f you hear a word that you happen to be familiar with as a noun, you cannot tell whether it is behaving like a noun on this particular occasion, or whether it is not doing the work of a verb or an adjective. [my emphasis: NGD]

Alice M. Bacon, *A Japanese Interior* (1893: 125)

Non-contracted forms of the same utterance behave differently. The sentence in example (27a), for instance, is not generally interpreted as an invitation: either it is strictly interpreted as a negative question, or else – with appropriate intonation – it may be taken as a reproach. Example (27b), on the other hand, is grammatically unacceptable in Present Day English, for reasons I'll return to directly.

Other modal auxiliaries exhibit other interesting effects when inverted, or negated, or both. *May*, for example, resists negative contraction in any position in most varieties of Present Day English: that is to say, *mayn't* is as unacceptable as *amn't*. For a period in the late nineteenth century however, this form was possible, as exemplified in the quotations from Dickens and George Eliot in (27). (Notice that in both examples, the modals are intended epistemically, rather than deontically, and also that in the inverted case in (27b) the utterance functions once again as a request, rather than a negative question.)

(27)   a.   'I mayn't have much head, master, but I've head enough to
            remember those that use me ill.'

                        Charles Dickens, *Barnaby Rudge*, chapter 40 (1841)

       b.   'Now, father,' said Nancy, 'is there any call for you to go home
            to tea? Mayn't you just as well stay with us? – such a beautiful
            evening as it's likely to be.'

                        George Eliot, *Silas Marner*, chapter 17 (1861)

A comparison of two charts – Figures 15 and 16 – confirms that while the overall frequencies of *may* and *might* have changed little in written texts over

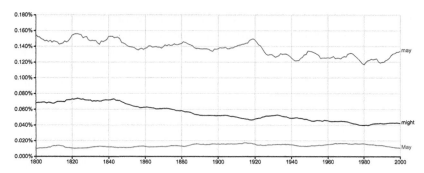

Figure 15 Incidence of *may* and *might* (1800–2000): the figure shows little
change in the frequency of these two forms.

the last 150 years, those of *mayn't* and *mightn't* have fluctuated much more
widely: assuming these measures are representative, Figure 16 clearly implies
that Victorian speakers would probably have agreed with us on the judgments
for (28a) and (28b), but would have assigned reversed judgments for (28c) and
(28d).[8]

(28)   a. The hedgehog may <u>not</u> have done anything to provoke the fox.
       b. The hedgehog might <u>not</u> have done anything/??nothing to provoke the fox.
       c. *Mayn't the hedgehog have done??anything/nothing to provoke the fox?
       d. Mightn't the hedgehog have done?anything/nothing to provoke the fox.

Hence, the grammatical acceptability of sentences containing negative and/or
inverted auxiliaries depends crucially on the particular auxiliary form chosen
as well as on the time frame under consideration.

    Examples (28b) and (28d) also illustrate interpretive differences between
uncontracted and contracted negatives – or rather, between uninverted vs.
inverted *n't*s – namely, that the former license, and indeed require, negative
polarity items (*anything* in place of *nothing*, for speakers of standard varieties
of Present Day English), whereas in the latter case – where the negation is
contracted to an inverted modal – negation need not be interpreted as having
the embedded predicate-phrase in its scope, so allowing for the negative quantifier (*nothing* in place of *anything*). That is to say: 'Mightn't the hedgehog
have done ...' is most naturally interpreted as 'Mightn't it be the case that [the
hedgehog has done nothing to provoke the fox]'; compare 'Might it be the case
that the hedgehog has not done anything to provoke the fox]?' In other words,
inversion introduces a reading that is unavailable – or at least, much harder to
access – in the non-inverted structure. Thus, inversion of *mightn't*, like *won't*,
has obvious interpretive consequences, as well as structural ones.

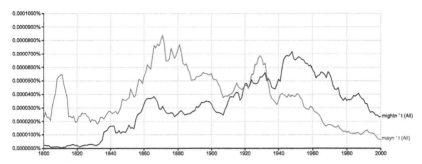

Figure 16 Incidence of *mayn't* and *mightn't* (1800–2000): the former modal, now obsolete, appears to have been more commonly used in the late nineteenth century than was the latter.

Crucially, these interpretive quirks only seem to apply to the modal auxiliaries (*can, may, should, will, might*): *non*-modal auxiliaries (BE and HAVE) dispose of the same range of interpretations whether or not the negative is contracted. This is shown by the examples in (29), where inversion contributes nothing to the semantic force of the auxiliary. Notice, however, that both BE and HAVE auxiliaries share with modals the distributional restriction exemplified in (30), namely, the full negative morpheme must follow the subject.

(29)   a. Isn't he past the point of caring/Is he not past the point of caring?
        b. Haven't you finished your homework yet/Have you not finished
           your homework yet?

(30)   a. *Is not he past the point of caring?
        b. *Have not you finished your homework yet?

Thus far I have been using the term 'inverted' to refer to examples in which the auxiliary element appears as the first clausal constituent, before the subject. This anachronistic terminology reflects the classic Standard Theory analysis of *Yes-No* questions (Chomsky 1957, 1965), which involved a transformational rule of SUBJECT-AUX(ILIARY) INVERSION (SAI) – a structural change (SC) – which reversed the order of the first and second constituents in an underlying structural description (SD). The TGG analysis of SAI is diagrammed in (31):

(31)   a. DS: <u>The guilty hedgehog will</u>   <u>apologise to</u>   <u>the hamster.</u>
        b. SD: 1   2   3   4   5
        c. SC: 1 2 3 4 5 ➜ 2 1 3 4 5
        d. SS: Will the guilty hedgehog apologise to the hamster?

The earlier term has generally been retained in generative discussions in spite of the fact that no actual reversal (metathesis) of syntactic positions is any longer involved. During the 1970s, the analysis of *Yes-No* questions was also extended to include *wh*-questions (constituent questions), as well as questions in embedded clauses. Since the that time, the basic analysis of inversion has remained essentially unaltered: SAI is understood as involving HEAD MOVE-MENT of 'T(ense)' to 'C(omp)', the position occupied by complementisers in embedded clauses; *wh*-movement is construed as a (cyclical) phrasal move-ment to the 'Specifier [position] of CP', a phrasal position to the left of that otherwise occupied by the complementiser. These two transformations are dia-grammed in (32), and instantiated by the examples in (33). Notice especially the complementary distribution of the raised auxiliary in main clauses (33a), and the complementiser *if* in the corresponding embedded clause (33b): hence, the analysis directly captures the fact that T-to-C movement (SAI) is blocked in subordinate clauses containing a complementiser.

(32)

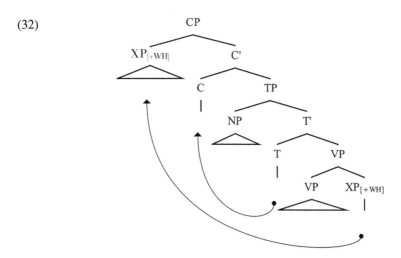

(33) a.   Have   you   ~~have~~   read the book]?
      b. asked [if   you   have   read the book]
      c.   when will   she   ~~will~~   read the book   ~~when~~?
      d. asked [when   she   would   read the book   ~~when~~]

The following transcribed excerpt from Chomsky (2010: 34:25~) confirms the pedigree of the current analysis of English *Yes-No* questions as that first pre-sented over half a century ago: in both cases, the initial position of constitu-ents is determined by principles of semantic-thematic modification, the final position by purely grammatical featural properties; in both cases, the relationship between these two positions ('displacement') is mediated by autonomous syntactic principles.[9]

So ... take the sentence, say, 'Can eagles swim?' ... How do we understand it? ... Well, we're asking ... The word can is actually serving two functions in the sentence – it's what's called 'displaced', meaning two functions ... On the one hand, it's indicating that there's a – it's a – yes or no question; on the other hand, it's connected with swim – you're asking about the capacity to swim – and in fact if you look at it more closely, so, it – semantically – it appears over here [between eagles and swim] it's related to 'Eagles can swim' and it's saying 'Is it true that eagles can swim?' and that's the question. Hm. That also shows up in the inflectional system, not just semantically, so for example, if I had ... if I said ... are ... eagles ... swimming [C. writes are _____ swimming on the chalkboard] the are would have the same relation to the inflection as it has when it appears over here [points to sentence-medial position]: 'Eagles are swimming'. Furthermore, the item that's displaced is actually just the inflection ... You can see that clearly in English where you can move the inflection but not any verbal element, and when you do, you have to invent ... you have to make up a dummy element with no semantic content, namely do ... which carries the inflection ... So this item here [C. points to the auxiliary] actually occurs in two positions: it appears in two positions: it appears in initial position, where it yields the interpretation of a yes-or-no question, and it appears over here, where it ... gains its inflectional properties, and its semantic properties. Let's call that 'displacement' ... This alone is enough to tell us that the structures that are involved are actually some sort of a nominal phrase, and an inflectional element, which is usually called T – T just for tense, but it means all the inflections – and some verbal phrase that's associated with it [i.e. T], and these two things are related ... so this is some kind of a phrase, which is ... an inflectional phrase, and the inflectional element can go out here [C. points to the sentence-initial position] ... and give you displacement ... Well, there's another property of this example, which is universal: you don't pronounce both of the elements: you only pronounce one of them, and the one you pronounce is the hierarchically highest one.

Noam Chomsky, Poverty of Stimulus: Some Unfinished Business (2010)

The movement analysis of questions has remained the centrepiece of generative argumentation and rhetoric: it has inspired a huge number of research experiments in psycholinguistics (e.g. Frazier and Flores d'Arcais 1989, Frazier 1990, Stowe 1986, Sussman and Sedivy 2003, to cite only a handful), and an equally large number of studies in first and second language acquisition; see, for example, Guasti (2004: chapter 6), Crain and Nakayama (1987), White (2003), Juffs and Harrington (1995, 1996). In almost every case, competence-based researchers have unsceptically adopted the assumption that questions – as well as other constructions where constituents that normally appear to the right of the subject are found on the left periphery of the clause – are derived by maximally general movement rules driven by abstract functional features.

The following cases cast some doubt on this core premise; see also H is for Homogeneity below. In considering these examples, it should also be kept in mind that there exist alternative proposals for capturing the relationship between declarative and interrogative structures that do not have recourse to movement rules. This is true even of generative theories that assume the existence of autonomous syntactic rules or principles, such as GPSG, HPSG, LFG, and Relational Grammar. As commentators have repeatedly pointed out, just because you can express a grammatical relationship in terms of movement does not prove that syntactic movement is part of a native speaker's knowledge of grammar, at any level of abstraction. For the purposes of exposition, however, I will provisionally assume the regular movement analysis to be correct.

??What rarely do you find there?

The first phenomenon to be considered is the distribution of a set of English negative adverbials, including *rarely, scarcely, under no circumstances, no sooner, not only* and *not infrequently*. A characteristic property of these expressions is that they seem to trigger SAI whenever they appear clause-initially: this is illustrated by the examples in (34).[10] Klima (1964) was to my knowledge the first to examine these negative adverbial constructions from a generative perspective: in the intervening half-century they have been discussed in numerous papers, including work by Authier (1992), Henry (1995), Schwartz and Vikner (1996) and Hegarty (2005).

(34)   a. Under no circumstances <u>must you</u>/*<u>you must</u> mention this to her.
       b. Not only <u>has he</u>/*<u>he has</u> inherited a bunch of average players, he also has to deal with unrealistic expectations from Spurs fans.[11]
       c. On only a few occasions <u>have I</u> /??<u>I have</u> spent four full hours in meditation within a twenty-four-hour day. (cf. Gattuso 2005)
       d. Never have I/*I have read such a load of nonsense!
       e. No sooner had he/*he had arrived, than she up(ped) and left.

(35)   a. Indisputably <u>they are</u>/*<u>are they</u> my relations; and no less indisputably they live [*do they] live, from a non-Australian perspective, abroad. (cf. James 2000)
       b. Incredibly, <u>he has</u>/*<u>has he</u> solved our problem without leaving his desk.
       c. On a very few occasions, <u>I have</u>/*<u>have I</u> corrected the spellings of place-names that clearly resulted from the transcription process. (McLaurin 2009: ix)

As a comparison between the strings in (34) and (35) makes clear, negative inversion (NI) only applies to a subset of negative expressions: notice, in particular, the minimal contrast between (34c) and (35c). This much is well known. What is less reported is that NI shows more idiosyncratic restrictions: some adverbials are preferred in inverted, others in non-inverted contexts; furthermore, most of these adverbials are associated only with specific auxiliaries and personal pronouns.[12] In this respect, NI constructions are closer to being open-slot idioms than general-purpose syntactic expressions; cf. Jackendoff (1992). However they are analysed, these various restrictions must somehow be mentally represented, either lexically or constructionally, so as to force inversion in the cases in (34), or to block it elsewhere (in the cases in (35), for instance).

NI is significant for another reason. From what was outlined above, if NI recruits the same movement mechanisms as *wh*-movement, it might be expected that in embedded clauses, the adverbial expression would appear in [Spec, CP], also that SAI (T-C) should be blocked in embedded NI contexts, by whatever principles exclude examples such as those in (36):

(36)   a. *She knew [who that would I need to talk to].
       b. *She wondered [where that was he now living.]

The examples in (37), however, defy both of these expectations:

(37)   a. She said (that) <u>under no circumstances</u> *should* I ever tell anyone
          she was …
       b. 'He's said (that) <u>not only</u> *has* he served extraordinarily –
          performed extraordinary service to the US, Jay Carney said that he
          has done remarkable work in his role at the CIA.'[13]
       c. 'He claimed (that) <u>rarely</u> could women acquire the second sight
          needed to see the fairies.'
       d. 'The reason was that <u>rarely</u> had he lost in straight games to the
          Chinese star, if you can win one game …'

The availability of negative inversion in embedded contexts, as well as the position of the negative adverbial to the right of the complementiser, clearly suggest that NI and *wh*-movement target different structural positions.[14] This point is driven home by the observation that NI and *wh*-movement are mutually compatible. At least, this is true of the sole negative expression *under no circumstances* (UNC), as in the examples in (38); see Authier (1992), Schwartz and Vikner (1996).

(38)   a. There will be one guy, <u>who,</u> <u>under no circumstances</u> *should* you
            hit for a boundary …[15]
       b. Now there are places in the world <u>where</u> <u>under no circumstances</u>
            should you drive …
       c. Absolute contraindication exists *when* <u>under no circumstances</u>
            should the drug be used …
       d. … except for this jar, which, <u>under no circumstances</u> *should* you
            touch …

It is worth noting that all of the attested cases of *wh+UNC* involve relative
clauses rather than direct questions. The constructions with *any wh+UNC* combination are also extremely rare overall: for instance, the Google string search
that unearthed (38c) yielded only two hits, as compared with 1.19 million for
the string 'When should you …', and 349,000 for 'Under no circumstances
should you …' when measured separately.

Nevertheless, even though the direct interrogative constructions are
unattested, the questions in (39) appear largely unexceptionable; to my eye,
they are certainly more acceptable than those in (40) or (41):

(39)   a. ?What under no circumstances should [you give to a dog]?
       b. ?Where under no circumstances should [you place a smoke alarm]?
       c. ?When under no circumstances should [you put your head above
            the parapet]?
       d. Who under no circumstances should run a conference]?

(40)   a. ??Under no circumstances what should [you give to a dog]?
       b. ??Under no circumstances where should [you place a smoke alarm]?
       c. ??Under no circumstances when should you [put your head above
            the parapet]?
       d. ??Under no circumstances who should run a conference?

(41)   a. *Under no circumstances should what [you give to a dog]?
       b. *Under no circumstances should where [you place a smoke alarm]?
       c. *Under no circumstances should when [you put your head above
            the parapet]?
       d. ?Under no circumstances should <u>who</u> run a conference]?

(42)   a. ??What should under no circumstances [you give to a dog]?
       b. ??Where should under no circumstances [you place a smoke alarm]?

    c. ??When should under no circumstances [you put your head above
the parapet]?

    d. Who should under no circumstances run a conference?

The acceptability contrasts both across and within these paradigmatic sets raise
a number of interesting theoretical issues: see, in particular, the contrast between
who-subject questions in (39d, 40d, 41d, 42d) and the other *wh*-questions
(examples (a–c)).[16] For the present, the most significant point is that the examples
in (39) appear to show that direct questions can be formed without overt movement
of T to $C_{[wh]}$; indeed, assuming that the judgments in (42a–c) are correct, then full
T-to-$C_{[wh]}$ movement is *less acceptable* in these contexts than partial movement.[17]
Both observations would seem to run contrary to Chomsky's assertion above.

    Consider, finally, the result of embedding the sentences in (39) and (42)
above as complements to *wonder*, as in (43)–(45):

(43) a. ??I wonder [what under no circumstances should you give to a dog.]

      b. ??I wonder [where under no circumstances should you place a
smoke alarm.]

      c. ??I wonder [when under no circumstances should you put your head
above the parapet.]

      d. ?I wonder [who under no circumstances should run a conference]?

(44) a. ??*I wonder [what should under no circumstances you give to a dog.]

      b. ??*I wonder [where should under no circumstances you place a
smoke alarm.]

      c. ??*I wonder [when should under no circumstances you put your
head above the parapet.]

      d. I wonder [who under no circumstances should run a conference].

(45) a. ?I wonder [what under no circumstances you should give to a dog.]

      b. ?I wonder [where under no circumstances you should place a
smoke alarm.]

      c. ?I wonder [when under no circumstances you should put your head
above the parapet.]

      d. ??I wonder [under no circumstances who should run a conference].

      d.´ *I wonder [under no circumstances should who run a conference]

If the assigned judgments hold for other speakers, then the conclusion must be
twofold: not only (!) is 'full SAI' (T to $C_{[wh]}$) dispreferred in the presence of a

fronted negative adverbial in *main* clauses – (39a–c) vs. (??42a–c); but also, even 'short-distance SAI' is blocked in embedded clauses (39a–c) vs. (??43a–c) vs. (?45a–c). The first contrast implies that SAI is not driven by the need to 'check Q-features', since the auxiliary only makes it halfway to C; the second contrast suggests that SAI is driven by 'Force features', since it is completely disallowed in indirect questions; though cf. Rizzi (1997, 2002), Haeberli and Ihsane (2016). The puzzle, however, is that the position the auxiliary naturally ends up in is not one that is most plausibly associated with any kind of illocutionary force.

At best, these contrasts markedly complicate the set of mechanisms required to explain the position of the finite auxiliary in questions, far beyond the explanation given in the 'Can eagles swim?' excerpt quoted above; at worst, they call into question the wisdom of an account based on head movement, or indeed of any formal movement account whatsoever; see also v is for von Humboldt below.

How come you don't say why/Why don't you say how come?

Of course, generative syntacticians have long recognised that there are problems with rules of question formation. At least, we already knew that SAI systematically fails to apply to an apparently heterogeneous subset of main clause *wh*-questions, comprising subject-*wh* questions (46a–b), and *how come* questions, in (46c–d). See also Collins (1991).

(46) a. Who came to see you yesterday?
      b. *Who did come to see you yesterday?[18]
      c. How come you want to study dentistry?
      d. *How come do you want to study dentistry?

In this section, I'll focus exclusively on the issue of *how come*; for some discussion of 'over-regular' subject questions, see Part IV, Chapter 26 below. As suggested by the title above, *why* and *how come* are often interchangeable in informal conversation, in main clauses. Closer consideration of their contexts of use, however, indicates that they are used to ask slightly different questions. For example, the question 'Why don't you like Tom?' seems to imply that the speaker believes the addressee has at least one specific – perhaps principled – reason for disliking Tom (for example, that he has said or done something objectionable in the past); by contrast, 'How come you don't like Tom?' seems to be more concerned with the general circumstances associated with the addressee's dislike of Tom (e.g. you don't like the people he associates with). Alternatively, there may only be a difference in formality between the two interrogative expressions: *how come* being the more colloquial expression, it is perhaps understood as requiring a less precise answer. It is hard to imagine, for instance, a prosecuting barrister asking a trial defendant 'How come you rang Jane Price on four separate occasions, Mr Fox?' General discussion of this question in the Blogosphere is confused.

Whatever is true of main clause semantics, for most native speakers there is a significant difference between the two expressions in embedded contexts, such as those in (47), where *why* is preferred over *how come*:[19]

(47) a. She didn't say why/?how come she needed $40, and I didn't ask.

      b. When asked, he said he didn't know why/?how come she lived that way.

      c. She left me. I don't know why/??how come.

      d. She asked me when I was coming, but not why/??how come.

Perhaps related to this syntactic difference, there is alleged to be an interpretive contrast between the two expressions. Collins (1991) claims that whereas sentence-initial *why* can be construed as a so-called 'long distance question', *how come* can only be understood as modifying the main verb. Compare (48a) and (48b), from a paper by Conroy and Lidz (2007), in which [it is once again claimed] children treat the first question (with *why*) as ambiguous, but not the second (with *how come*):

(48) a. <u>Why</u> did Joe think Monster ate his sandwich?

        – Because he [John] saw his plate was empty.

        – Because he [Monster] was hungry.

     b. <u>How come</u> Joe thought [Monster ate his sandwich]?

        – Because he [John] saw that his plate was empty.

        – #Because he [Monster] was hungry.[20]

But why do these discrepancies exist, and how come (?do) they persist from one generation to the next? How do children acquiring English come to appreciate the difference between the two? Adopting the standard assumption of generalised *wh*-movement leads us to expect one of two possible developmental outcomes. On one hand, the absence of SAI might lead the language learner to treat *how come* as 'base-generated' in a left-peripheral position different from that of other *wh*-expressions: adjoined to the main clause, perhaps, rather than being moved to [Spec, CP]. This would explain (albeit circularly) why *how come* doesn't trigger SAI. However, as we have just seen, there are other regular *wh*-expressions that don't require SAI either, and it is unclear how language learners should distinguish these two classes of exception. What speaks against this possibility, in any case, is the fact that embedded examples with *how come* are attested, even if they are of much lower frequency; see (47a) and (47b) above.

An alternative possibility – still continuing to assume the operation of a general rule to which *how come* is an exception – is that children use the input as INDIRECT NEGATIVE EVIDENCE to induce the fact that *how come* cannot generally be embedded, and so limit their grammar. But 'cannot generally be embedded' is not the kind of (categorical) statement that generative grammar allows for; indeed, it might well be argued that it is not a rule at all. Furthermore, this second explanation predicts that children should go through a stage of using SAI with *how come* before reining it in, something which is unsupported by data on syntactic over-regularisations.

Some researchers have used a version of the second argument to explain why (??how come) many children go through a stage in which they fail to invert the subject in *why* questions, even after they have acquired SAI with other *wh*-expressions. See Labov and Labov (1978), Berk (2003), Thornton (1994); cf. Conroy and Lidz (2007).

But from whichever direction this is viewed, the apparently arbitrary contrast between *what* and *how come* questions raises significant learnability issues for any theory that presupposes a maximally general rule of question formation. Somehow this difference must be represented in English speakers' minds so that it can be available in analysing and producing *why* and *how come* questions. Significantly, this issue does not arise in quite the same way in usage- or performance-based language acquisition, where what is acquired is a closer approximation to ambient patterns of language use.

Why worry?

♫ Dire Straits (Knopfler), *Why Worry?* (1985)

This discussion brings us handily to the other two classes of exception, both of which involve *why* questions. The first is illustrated by the examples in (49), which reveal that – alone among *wh*-expressions – *why* can be combined with a bare non-finite verb-phrase to yield a grammatically acceptable question:[21]

(49) a. Why worry?/Why stay in Boston?/Why not try again, and see what happens?/Why keep on working, now that you have won the lottery?
  b. *Who forget?/*Who spend time with?/*Who talk about linguistics with?
  c. *What eat every day to stay healthy?/*What find delicious?
  d. *When see your parents?/*When take time off?/*When leave home?
  e. *Where send your money?/*Where go on holiday?/*Where live well?
  f. *How come focus on problems like this?

Setting out these contrasts as a sentential paradigm is misleading, however, since (*why* and *why not*) are able to combine with virtually any type of predicate-phrase to generate a kind of 'echo question'. Some relevant examples are given in (50):

(50) a. Why (not) <u>Wednesday</u>?!/Why (not) <u>vitamins</u>?   *why-(not)* NP
     b. Why <u>blue</u>? Why not <u>red</u>?   *why-(not)* AP
     c. Why only <u>possibly</u>? Why not <u>probably</u>?   *why-(not)* AdvP
     d. Why (only) <u>inside the building</u>? Why not <u>outside</u> as well?   *why-(not)* PP
     e. Why <u>or</u>? Why not <u>and</u>?   *why-(not)* Conj

In standard varieties of English, other *wh*-expressions are only able to combine with full clauses, even in those contexts where an elliptical expression would be fully interpretable. The marginal exception – unsurprisingly perhaps – is *how come,* which is occasionally found with non-clausal complements: compare (51a–b):

(51) a. How come <u>Wednesday</u> and not tomorrow?
     b. 'How come <u>blue</u>?' She put her hands on her hips … (Morris 2012)
     c. Possibly? How come only <u>possibly</u>?[22]

Notice that in contrast to *why, how come* never combines directly with *not* to form a constituent. Which inevitably raises the question: *why not* (*how come not?!)?

The contrast is not an arbitrary one, but nor is it predicted by the operation of any synchronic grammatical rule. Instead, a significant part of the explanation for the difference between *why* and *how come* is due to the historical development of these phrases. It is not necessary to go very far back in the history of English to realise that *how come* developed as a fixed expression out of the compositional form *how comes/came* (plus finite clause), in which the original '*wh*-word' was *how*, with *come* functioning as kind of raising predicate (cf. Present Day English 'happen'), undergoing V-C inversion. The source construction can be seen in the following nineteenth-century examples, from works by Charles Dickens and Thomas Hardy, respectively:

'How came he to have fallen asleep, in his clothes, on the sofa in Doctor Manette's consulting-room?'

Charles Dickens, *A Tale of Two Cities* (1859)

'Now, my dear Tess, if I did not know that you are very much excited, and very inexperienced, I should say that remark was not very complimentary. How came you to wish that if you care for me?'

Thomas Hardy, *Tess of the d'Urbervilles* (1891)

At a stroke, this diachronic factor explains most of the apparent idiosyncrasies of (invariant) *how come*, viz., its resistance to appearing in embedded clauses, its failure to trigger inversion, and its prevalence in non-standard, colloquial varieties, as compared with written registers, which tend to be more conservative.[23] The pattern has persisted in the input long after the more general 'rules' that created it were lost.

The problem for competence-based linguists is that this straightforward explanation is not available to them; nor, by (their) hypothesis, is it available to the child acquiring English. Since generative linguists reject the idea that children learn constructions, or indeed pay much attention to the input beyond Saussurean arbitrariness and 'triggering data', there is no principled reason why a child acquiring English should not treat *how come* exactly like *why* (triggering SAI, or appearing in 'sluicing' contexts) or, come to that, why other *wh*-expressions are not generalised to non-clausal complements, like *why* (cf. (49a) vs. (49b–f) above). Yet the fact that children raised in a typical English-language environment learn how to use *how come* correctly from the outset strongly suggests that the input ('E-language') is more important than generativists generally assume; conversely, that rules are much less general than they would be in an ideal system. See G is for Grammar and v is for von Humboldt below.

*Why to go

♫ Snow Patrol, *Chasing Cars* (2006)

The final exception to generalised *wh*-movement also involves English *why*. In this case, the opposite situation obtains: rather than being uniquely available, *why* is the only *wh*-word to be *excluded* from the paradigm. Arguably, this case is the most interesting since there is no obvious functional, pragmatic or historical explanation for the gap, and nothing – other than the simple absence of the construction in the input – to prevent a child learner from generalising to this context. The exception~gap is illustrated by the paradigm in (52). The most natural pre-theoretic description is as follows: in contrast to all other *wh*-expressions, *why* cannot introduce a non-finite indirect question.

(52) a. I wonder/know [who to talk to about this].
  b. She wondered/knew [what to tell him].
  c. She wonders/knows [how (best) to break the news to him].
  d. They wondered/knew [when to speak and when to be silent].
  e. He asked/knew [where to find the exit].
  f. ??*I asked/knew [why to stop eating kiwi-fruit].

Considered in isolation, the relative unacceptability of (52f) might seem unremarkable: after all, as we have just seen, *how come* is also disfavoured in non-initial positions. What is curious, though, is that *why* is perfectly acceptable in *finite* indirect questions, such as those in (53):

(53) a. I know [<u>why</u> the caged bird sings.]
      b. She wonders [<u>why</u> he understands so little of this.]
      c. She knows [<u>why</u> that country has such a dismal tax compliance rate.]
      d. They wondered [<u>why</u> the fruit had been forbidden.]
      e. He asked [<u>why</u> she was looking for the exit.]
      f. I knew [<u>why</u> I should stop eating kiwi-fruit.]

Especially intriguing is the contrast found in the ellipsis ('sluicing') contexts in (54), where the acceptability of the string *but not why* varies according to the finiteness of the implied antecedent phrase: it sounds perfectly fine in (54a), where the antecedent clause is finite, yet exactly the same string is markedly less acceptable in (54b), where the antecedent phrase is analysed as non-finite. This contrast reveals that it is non-finiteness as an abstract grammatical property that constrains the use of the construction, not just a particular sequence of pronounced words.

(54) a. He was told <u>where</u> he was to meet Jane,
             but not <u>why</u> [~~he was to meet Jane~~].
      b. He was told <u>when</u> to meet Jane,
             …??/*but not <u>why</u> [~~to meet Jane~~].
             (…?but not <u>where</u> [~~to meet Jane~~].)

These intuitive judgments closely track the frequency of occurrence of the same strings in Google Books (to consider only the most readily available corpus). Table 3 records the number of Google hits, in thousands, for different combinations of *know+wh+[he/she/they/to]*.

The quantitative difference is striking.[24] Before examining this table, it might have been supposed that indirect questions with *why* are simply much less frequent across the board, for non-structural reasons. However, the contrast between finite and non-finite contexts rules out this possibility: in fact, as Table 3 shows, *why+subject pronoun* strings are actually more numerous (on aggregate) than *who+subject pronoun* strings. No sophisticated statistical analysis is required to determine that the relative distributions in the first three (finite clause) columns are basically equivalent: there may be approximately double the number of hits for masculine over feminine subject pronouns – reflecting, perhaps, the egocentric concerns of typical Internet users – but the pattern is broadly identical

Table 3 *The curious case of* why to *(n = thousands of hits).*

wh-phrase	Finite (know+wh+*she*)	Finite (know+wh+*he*)	Finite (know+wh+*they*)	Finite aggregate	Non-finite (know ... to)
who	1,810	4,760	3,830	10,400	1,600
what	8,990	30,000	36,800	75,790	75,200
where	3,390	9,910	8,400	21,700	25,000
when	873	4,080	3,960	8,913	7,250
why	2,930	5,400	4,360	12,690	92

across the *wh*-expressions in finite clauses. Specifically, in each of the first three columns there are approximately equal numbers of *who* and *why* questions, and roughly double the number of *where* questions, when compared with *why* questions. In all of the finite columns, then, the relative proportions are very similar. Column 5, on the other hand, presents a completely different pattern: non-finite indirect questions with *where* have the highest incidence, while *why* questions virtually disappear. Even restricting the analysis to a comparison of adjunct *wh*-phrases (the bottom three rows: *when* vs. *where* vs. *why*) reveals a clearly significant skewing. Statistically speaking, the frequency distributions observed here are less likely to be due to chance than virtually all of the experimental results discussed in standard psycholinguistics textbooks ($p < 0.00001$). This statistical result requires an explanation.[25]

Whatever the deeper explanation may be, the most obvious grammatical *description* of the exceptional behaviour of *why* is the one given earlier, namely, that 'in contrast to all other *wh*-expressions, *why* cannot introduce a non-finite indirect question'. Which raises the question of whether speakers (implicitly) know this negative constraint; if so, how such knowledge should be represented in a theory that denies the existence of construction-specific rules. If one assumes a maximally general theory of *wh*-movement – as most competence-based psycholinguists do – then the answer to the first part of the question must be that speakers do know this negative constraint, since otherwise non-finite clauses introduced by *why* should enjoy the same privileges that are extended to all other intermediate *wh*-expressions. The problem then becomes how to state the constraint without making reference to construction-specific finiteness, especially since – as we saw in the previous section of this chapter – *why* can occur with almost any predicate-phrase in main clause contexts, including bare (non-finite) verbs (*Why Worry?*); compare once more the examples in (45) and (46) above.

To compound the difficulty, this constraint seems to be peculiar to English: the French, German and Spanish examples in (55), obtained through a Google string search, suggest that there is no universal ban on *why+non-finite* verb in embedded contexts:

(55) a. <u>Je ne sais pas pourquoi faire</u> ce test de grand mère dont je n'ai jamais entendu parler, alors que tu peux aller ...[26]
           'I don't know why [you should] do this old wives' test that I have never heard of, when you can simply go ...'

      b. So pflegt es aber fast immer, <u>ich weiß nicht, warum, zu gehen</u>, und ich habe diese Erfahrung nicht etwa bei einem oder dem andern ... [1776]
           'It almost always happens that, I don't know why [I should] go, and I have this feeling not just on one or two occasions, but ...'

      c. <u>No entiendo por que hacer</u> algo que nadie con un mínimo de compasión haría, se le llama arte.
           'I don't understand why [anyone would] do something that no-one with the slightest compassion would do, in the name of art.'

Reluctant as I am to resort to generativist rhetoric, it is difficult to see how a child equipped with a maximally general set of rules to form *wh*-questions would be able to restrict their grammar so as to carve out this 'language-particular gap' in the system. By contrast, if rules are epiphenomenal – if children and adult learners acquire a grammatical network on the basis of learning individual constructions, and generalise only where this is supported by positive evidence – then arbitrary holes or gaps can develop rather easily inside an otherwise regular system. The following quote by Martin Haspelmath, in his review of Newmeyer (1999), is to the point:

If syntax is described as a network of constructions rather than as a set of rules, then constructions showing different frequencies will be entrenched to different degrees, again with consequences for their structural properties (cf. Bybee & Thompson, 1997). Newmeyer [1999] finds it difficult to conceive of syntax in terms of frequency-sensitive constructions:

'Each time [a] sentence is uttered, do the speaker and hearer really tick off in their mental note pads one more use of each [of the constructions it instantiates]? (p.135).'

The answer is yes, and the difficulty in conceiving of syntax in this way seems to be due exclusively to the long habit of thinking of syntax in a very different way.

Martin Haspelmath, 'Why can't we talk to
each other?' (*Lingua*, 2000: 242–3)

It will be clear that Haspelmath's assertion implies a radically different relationship between representation and processing from that assumed by most competence-based theorists.

Summary

In this chapter I have considered four classes of exception to the putatively general rules of question formation in English, rules that have been uncritically accepted by psycholinguists sympathetic to generative grammar for over half a century. Each of these paradigmatic gaps challenges the idea that learners acquire autonomous grammatical principles largely unconstrained by construction-specific or lexicon-specific properties, and unconditioned by the vagaries of history. The persistence of language-particular gaps~exceptions over generations, I'd suggest, speaks forcefully against the idea that end-state grammatical knowledge is insensitive to frequency distributions in the input. At the very least, data such as these should give us pause in thinking about the relationship between representational and procedural knowledge of syntax.

Contra Chomsky (1981, 1985, and subsequent works), these data suggest that the key problem of language acquisition is *not* the logical one of explaining how the child attains a maximally general grammar when faced with impoverished input – the standard Poverty of the Stimulus argument. On the contrary, the key problem is an empirical one: to explain how a child allegedly equipped with UG is able to cut away so precisely at a maximally general system – here, to carve out the language-particular holes and gaps of the English interrogative system – so as to converge on the ambient patterns in the input, *unless they are attending very closely to that input*: see MacWhinney (2000), amongst others.

A useful allusion here is to the contrast between traditional subtractive production methods and 3D printing technology, in the manufacture of closed objects. Imagine a translucent blue cube (5 cm³), made of some acrylic material. The cube has a uniform solidity, except for one region, exactly 1 cm in from one corner: this area contains a hollow sphere, 0.5 cm in diameter. A little bit of nothing. Such an object is easy to visualise, and simple enough to design: see Figure 17. But how to manufacture it? If one starts with an already solid cube, it is virtually impossible to carve out a perfect sphere – the gap – without disturbing the surrounding material. The only solution consistent with traditional manufacturing is to suppose that the sphere is an inherent property of such cubes *ab initio*: the cubes are cast around a transparent spherical mould, perhaps. But if only some cubes have this property – the English cubes, say, not the French or Spanish ones – then that solution is unavailable. By contrast, if one starts out with nothing except the overall dimensions of the cube, and if each layer of resin is laid down layer upon layer, square millimetre by square millimetre, it is a fairly trivial exercise to create a perfectly hollow sphere, or any other gap, at any arbitrary position within the cube, simply by not injecting resin at those coordinates. The *ab initio* and additive methods will both produce the same 'solid-cube-with-a-hole-inside', but only the additive method can

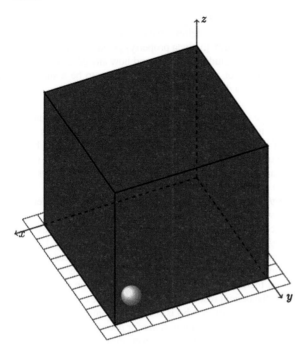

Figure 17 Sphere within a cube: a round hole in a square peg?

be sensitive to local variations in internal topography; in grammatical terms, to microparametric contrasts.

Arguably, what's good for manufacturing cubes is good for grammar, too.

Notes

1 Gregory Titelman, *Random House Dictionary of Popular Proverbs and Sayings*, Random House Reference, 5 March 1996. 'Le bon Dieu est dans le détail' is attributed to Flaubert. More recent attributions of the English version 'God is in the details' to the architect Mies van der Rohe appear to be mistaken; the satanic variant seems to be of even more recent origin. Just to be absolutely clear: I am using the expression '(general) rule' to refer to any autonomous grammatical procedure for deriving grammatically well-formed sentences – or for excluding ill-formed ones; this includes traditional base-rules, transformational rules, generalised transformations, principles and constraints ('Case Filter', 'EPP'), and any other mechanism that is separate from and relatively insensitive to lexical and/or pragmatic information.

2 The neo-Cartesian expression 'the child' dominates generative discussions of language acquisition, as though children were entirely uniform genetically and phenotypically, as if exposure and experience were completely irrelevant to grammatical

development; see H is for Homogeneity below. This is, of course, what many Chomskyan Nativists choose to believe, but to place it in pre-theoretical discussions ('How could the child acquire [a given property] given insufficient exposure?') is to prejudge crucial issues, including whether and how any given child actually comes to know this property – or needs to know it in order to be a successful language user and, supposing they do, whether there is really no evidence of this property in the input.

3 A case in point is the -*s* plural morpheme in Modern Standard German, which essentially only occurs in loanwords and neologisms (*die Taxis* 'the taxis', *zwei Fibs* 'two fips'). In spite of its relative infrequency in German corpora, it has been claimed by some psycholinguists to be the sole rule-generated plural allomorph; see, for example, Marcus, Brinkmann, Clahsen, Wiese and Pinker (1995); cf. Dabrowska (2001).

4 Sources: (26c)   https://water.usgs.gov/edu/100yearflood.html;   (26e)   https:// en.wikipedia.org/wiki/Takigaks_%E2%80%93_Once_Were_Hunters.

5 This 1984 song was Joe Jackson's least successful chart hit, only reaching 70th in the UK singles chart, and failing to chart at all in other countries. Source: http:// en.wikipedia.org/wiki/Joe_Jackson. A possible reason for this lack of success is the use of the term *number two*. The second line makes it clear that the first line is intended as an invitation to someone to replace 'number one' (the singer's previous love). Aside from the obvious fact that 'Please take me on the rebound' is not the best chat-up line, the default readings of *number two* are even less inviting: as (i) the designation for a (naval) officer who is second-in-command; (ii) a euphemism for faeces. Some suggest it this is rhyming slang for *poo*, which unhappily is also a perfect rhyme for the other three verses; however, in my child's English nursery, and in my own memory, *number one(s)*, not *number three*, was a euphemism for *pee*. Regardless, no one wants to be merely an emotional crutch, let alone the by-product of digestion.

6 Google Translate returns a variety of translations, most of which (rather surprisingly) retain the speech act value of the original.

7 In this respect, inverted *won't* resembles the kind of expletive negation found in subjunctive contexts in more literary registers of French, e.g. following the subordinating conjunction *avant que* ('before'), as in (i); see also Newmeyer (1999).

    a. Avant qu'ils <u>ne</u> soient trop grands ...
       before that they NEG be too big
       'Before they become too old [for something] ...'
    b. Je crains que votre ennemi <u>ne</u> revienne.
       I fear that your enemy NEG return
       'I think your enemy is coming back.'

8 The Google Ngram Viewer, which was used to generate these charts, is based predominantly on written texts rather than on (transcripts of) spoken dialogue, but the comparison with positive forms is still instructive. It should be observed that scale of the two charts is completely different, since the absolute frequencies of the negative-contracted forms in written texts are several orders of magnitude lower than those for the affirmative forms. If all four words were plotted against the same *y*-axis, both *mayn't* and *mightn't* would appear as (essentially) flat lines, close to zero.

9 To many generativists, the claim that the theory is little changed in over half a century is a source of pride and satisfaction. While this point of view may be understandable

if linguistics is compared to *haute cuisine* or bespoke tailoring, it is remarkable when compared to other sciences, pure or applied: theories of molecular biology, genetics, cosmology, and pure mathematics have all witnessed remarkable developments, and scientists in those fields who had stuck with outmoded paradigms would be regarded as reactionary at best. More importantly, perhaps, the claim is untrue. As has already mentioned above, Principles and Parameters theory – generative grammar 1981–1995 – had a fundamentally different structure and empirical reach from what preceded and followed it. The history of generative grammar exhibits more cyclicity than continuity.

10 Here, I'll ignore the problem of *do*-support (and its exceptions), and focus solely on SAI and *wh*-movement with modal and aspectual auxiliaries. See Duffield (2013b, 2015).

11 https://twitter.com/JimmyHart_/status/528951205062782978

12 See Duffield (2017b) for some elaboration.

13 Sources: (37b) CNN online, http://edition.cnn.com/TRANSCRIPTS/1211/09/cnr.07.html; (37c) http://goo.gl/GCYOPa (examples with *claim* are extremely rare: this is the only non-quotative hit for the string 'claimed that rarely').

14 This point has generally been accepted in recent generative work concerned with the fine structure of the left periphery. See Rizzi (1997, 2002), see also van Urk and Richards (2013).

15 Sources: (38a) www.bbc.co.uk/dna/606/A50210191; (38b) Vardon-Smith (2014: 349); (38c) Cooper (1991: 39); (38d) Neusner (1995: 158).

16 The acceptability of the (39d, 40d, 41d, 42d) subject version is most consistent with an account in which there is no vacuous movement: i.e. *wh*-subjects do not undergo *wh*-movement in main clauses.

17 There is an alternative explanation for (42d), namely, that *under no circumstances* is treated as a parenthetical expression. While this is quite plausible, it is also *ad hoc*, and fails to explain the unacceptability of the parallel examples in (42a–c).

18 The use of unstressed *do* in assertions was a regular feature of Early Modern English, as has been documented and discussed by many authors: see Ellegård (1953), Roberts (1993), Haeberli and Ihsane (2016). In standard adult varieties of Present Day English, *do*-support is not generally found in subject questions. It *does* occur in child language, however. See Part IV, Chapter 26, for discussion.

19 A Google string search for *didn't say why* yielded thirty-seven pages/346,000 results, compared to four pages for *didn't say how come*, of which only two are legitimate examples; the search for *he doesn't know why she* vs. *he doesn't know how come she* yields 336,000 vs. one (!) example. The great majority of attested cases of embedded *how come* are found in non-standard varieties, including some Midwestern varieties possibly influenced by German. See also http://forum.wordreference.com/showthread.php?t=2024024.

20 Notice that in both cases, the embedded construal of the *wh*-expression is significantly inhibited if a complementiser is inserted (i.e. '??Why did Joe think that Monster ate his sandwich?'). See the discussion of *that*-trace effects in J is for Judgment below.

21 To my knowledge, the theoretical implications of this contrast were first noted by Thomas Roeper (UMass, Amherst): at any rate, it was Tom who first brought it to my attention.

22 Source: www.saxperience.com/forum/archive/index.php/t-285422.html.

23 Even its source, *how came he*, in which the main verb appears to the left of the sub-ject (i.e. SVI, not SAI), is highly conservative: as has been well-documented and analysed, SVI – and main-verb raising in general – was (for the most part) lost at the beginning of the Early Modern English period, Shakespeare's work representing a transition phase. See I is for Internalism (iv) below, and references therein.

24 These figures overstate the actual distributions of non-finite complements, since they include strings where there is a comma or period between the *wh*-expression and non-finite *to* (e.g. 'Why can't I accept that? I want to *know why. To* understand why …'). However, since this applies in some measure to all of the cells in the fourth column, it is a harmless confound: if anything, the skewing would be more pronounced without it.

25 For those less impressed by statistics, it is worth noting that the second most popu-lar set of hits on Google Web for the string 'know why to' is a query from a Korean ESL student, asking why this string is not possible. That student receives no sat-isfactory answer: see www.englishforums.com/English/WhyToInfinite/cpgdw/post.htm.

26 Sources: (55a) https://www.yabiladi.com/forum/test-grossesse-fait-maison-avec-67-5020607.html; (55b) https://books.google.co.jp/book?id=Mjg9AAAAcAAJ; (55c) https://www.xatakaciencia.com/otros/video-tirando-aluminio-fundido-en-un=hormiguero.

9   (Case #6) 'Cwucial questions': Investigating extraction

[I]f we are to prevent the lights going out on our lives once more, we must ask ourselves cwucial questions: Where are we? How did we get here? Why did we come? Where do we want to go? How do we want to get to where we want to go? How far do we have to go before we get to where we want to be? How would we know where we were when we got there? HAVE WE GOT A MAP?! Why did we leave places to get to where we are? Where were we before that we had to leave to get to where we were before we knew we were going to go to where we want to be? Where would we end up if we had the choice? Where would we end up if we didn't have the choice? What would we choose given the choice? Do we have that choice to choose? Or, indeed, can we be choosy about the choice chosen? What are the chooses? – Choices! Do we want to stop now? (rhetorical ...)... Or do we want to go right back to the beginning and start all over again?!

Richard Curtis and Rowan Atkinson, 'Sir Marcus Browning, MP'
(*Live in Belfast*, 1979)

Listening to this after-dinner speech, it very quickly becomes apparent that even though he has absolutely nothing to communicate, Sir Marcus Browning MP is capable of constructing extremely long, and apparently unbounded, questions. Sir Marcus may be a comedic fiction, but his words in all their vacuity are, unfortunately, true to political discourse. He also displays an advanced verbal skill: most second language learners and pre-adolescent children are incapable of producing this kind of verbiage. I suspect that the same lack of ability is true of many adult native speakers, outside the rarified world of linguistics classrooms and psychology laboratories. If not, genuine after-dinner speakers, stand-up comedians and story-tellers (in other cultures) would not be so highly prized for their talent. See C is for Competence~Performance below.

Closer scrutiny of the extract, however, reveals a surprising dearth of grammatical complexity. Though they may be long, Sir Marcus' questions do not involve many 'long-distance dependencies': in almost all cases, the *wh*-word (the FILLER, in traditional psycholinguistic terms) finds its GAP – or, at least, the predicate with which it is associated – almost immediately after the beginning of the sentence; see Pickering and Barry (1991), cf. Nichol and Swinney (1989), Clahsen and Featherston (1999). In examples (56a–d) the source position for the *wh*-constituent is indicated by means of a struck-through copy of the *wh*-word:

(56)   a. Where do we want to <u>go</u> ~~where~~?
     b. How far do we have to <u>go</u> ~~how far~~ before …?
     c. How would we <u>know</u> ~~how~~ where we were …?
     d. Why did we <u>leave places</u> ~~why~~ to get to …?

Ironically, the only utterance that possibly involves a long-distance dependency is one that many syntacticians would categorise as ungrammatical, even though it sounds completely acceptable (as long you don't listen [or read] too closely). The string is repeated in (57):

(57)   <u>Where</u> were we [($_i$_)] before[,] that we had to leave [($_{ii}$_)] to get to where we were before we knew we were going to go to where we want to be?

As indicated, the sentence contains two possible gaps for the initial *where* question: either (i), as a locative argument of the main clause copular verb *were* – call this the 'main-clause construal' – or (ii), as an object complement of the embedded predicate *leave*, a gap contained within the complex relative clause ['that we had to leave (there) … be'] that constitutes the rest of the sentence (the [long-distance] 'embedded-clause construal'). Syntactic problems arise on either construal. On the former analysis – which at first seems to be the more likely of the two – the main issue concerns the fact that locative expressions cannot typically co-occur with restrictive relative clauses, at least not with relative clauses introduced by *that*. This is true even in the absence of *wh*-movement, as is demonstrated by the contrast between (58a) and (58b):

(58)   a. She told you to go (back) <u>there/(*where)</u> (*that you had to leave).
     b. She told you to go (back) <u>to the place</u> that you had to leave.

The examples in (59) show that *wh*-words can head so-called 'free relatives' in English; however, these latter structures are incompatible with initial complementisers. To see this, compare example (59a), with *where*, where the complementiser (*that*) must be omitted, with the standard object relative clause in (59b), where *that* is optional:

(59)   a. She told him to wait <u>where</u> (*that) he had been working, the previous week.
     b. She told him to wait in <u>the room</u> (that) he had been working in, the previous week.

(60)   a.   She waited for him near <u>where</u> they had met (??at) the previous
            week.
       b.   She waited for him near <u>the place</u> that they had met??(at) the
            previous week.

The contrast between (60a) and (60b) suggests a further difference between
these and other relative clauses, namely, that free relatives with *where* do not
allow association with an internal gap. So, in (60a), the *wh*-expression *where*
cannot be associated with a locative argument position inside the relative
clause; this is shown by the marginality of inserting the preposition *at*. On
the other hand, in the semantically equivalent construction in (60b), in which
where is replaced by the NP *the place*, just the opposite effect is observed: regular (restrictive) relative clauses prefer complementisers, and *do* allow association with an internal argument positions. So, in example (60b) the relative
clause not only allows but *requires* insertion of *at* (in order to avoid the object
interpretation '#we had met the place').
    The examples in (61) press home the point that free relatives with *where* are
necessarily 'gapless', in sharp contrast to regular relative clauses:

(61)   a.   We found ourselves back [where [we had been two weeks
            previously]].
       b.   ??We found ourselves back in [the place that [we had been two
            weeks earlier]].[1]
       c.   *We found ourselves back [where [we had discovered two weeks
            earlier]].
       d.   We found ourselves back in [the place (that) [we had discovered two
            weeks earlier]].

In (61a) and (61b), there is no obvious gap within the bracketed string that
needs filling: *be* is a verb that takes no arguments (which is why it functions
so well as a linking verb or auxiliary, more generally). In the free relative version in (61a), the absence of any plausible gap is unproblematic; this follows if
where-free relatives are gapless. In (61b), on the other hand, there is a problem,
since *the place (that)* is identified as a filler (in search of a gap): unless a preposition such as 'to' is inserted, the sentence becomes unacceptable at 'weeks' (at
which point it is clear that *two we ...* is not an object noun-phrase).
    Exactly the opposite judgments obtain in (61c) and (61d). Unlike *be*, *dis-
cover* is a transitive verb that requires an object complement, which means that
the bracketed string in these examples must contain a gap after *discovered*. In
the restrictive relative construction in (61b), that gap is filled unproblemati-
cally by the NP *the place* (or some co-indexed abstract filler). However, example (61c) is unacceptable even though it is perfectly obvious how it should

be interpreted. This contrast appears to confirm that free relatives with *where* are obligatorily gapless.[2]

Summarising the discussion so far, we have seen that (non-embedded) *where* can only be associated with free relatives. These constructions are distinguished from regular relative clauses in permitting no initial complementiser, and in not allowing internal gaps. With this in mind, let us examine (57) again, repeated as (62a):

(62)   a. <u>Where</u> were we before[,] that we had to leave to get to [$_{FR}$ where we were] before we knew we were going to go to [$_{FR}$ where we want to be]?

   b. *Were we WHERE before[,] that we had to leave ...

It should now be evident that the utterance involves at least two (other) free relatives, indicated by the labelled bracketings in (62a). It should also be clearer, on closer examination, that there is no grammatical source/gap for the *wh*-expression in the main clause. As a result, the structure in (62b) is ungrammatical both because of the presence of the complementiser and because of the object gap inside the relative clause. Notice that the sentence fails to improve if *where* is replaced by *there*, or by the bare NP *that place*.

(63)   a. *We were THERE before[,] that we had to leave.

   b. *We were THAT PLACE before, that we had to leave.

On the other hand, the examples in (64) show that direct construal with the position immediately following *leave* yields even worse results, (64a) being intended as a so-called ECHO QUESTION:

(64)   a. ?*We were that we had to leave <u>where</u>?

   b. ??We were that we had to leave there.

   c. ??We were that we had to leave that place.

All of the examples in (64) are fairly poor, to my ear at least. What is more, to the extent that (64b) and (64c) are acceptable, they mean something different from (57), something like 'We were (in such a state) that we had to leave (from) there.' It is thus unlikely that any of these declarative structures can be the source of the question in (62a).

This seems to force us to the conclusion that sentence (62a) is ungrammatical, in the strict sense it has no grammatical derivation. Yet, as noted at the outset, the utterance is perfectly acceptable. Indeed, chances are that most people listening to this sketch had never noticed anything grammatically amiss, until now. (I'm sorry to have spoilt the comedy, for serious effect.) It also seems unlikely that this should be dismissed as a performance error: it is, after all, part of a scripted speech co-written and rehearsed by a skilled comedy writer whose intention was precisely to demonstrate the mismatch between fluency and informational content. Sir Marcus Blanding may be an *eejit*, but he is a verbally able one. So what is going on?

One plausible idea is that readers/listeners treat (57/62a) as though it were the interrogative form of a different type of cleft sentence – parsing 'Where were we that ...?' as though it were 'Where was it that ...?' The examples in (65) show that clefted-*there* sentences *do* allow restrictive relative clauses, both as questions and as declaratives:

(65) a. Where was *(it) <u>that</u> we had to leave ...
      b. It was there <u>that</u> we had to leave?(from).
      c. It was that place <u>that</u> we had to leave.

The same structure is available for argument questions, such as those in (66):

(66) a. Who was *(it) that met us at the airport?
      b. Who was *(it) that they met before leaving the party?
      c. Who was *(it) that you were speaking to? ...
      d. Who was *(it) you gave the book to?
      e. ?Who was *(it) that Amy left Henry for?
      f. ?Who was *(it) that Amy believed the rumour that Henry had been seeing in New York.
      g. Who was *(it) that Amy wondered when Henry could have had time to visit?

The sentences in (66) are interesting in their own right, since long-distance gap-filling seems to be much more acceptable in these structures than in their non-clefted counterparts in (67) (whose unacceptability is standardly accounted for in terms of a grammatical violation of so-called 'island constraints'). Comparing (66e–g) with (67e–g), the latter sentences appear markedly less acceptable:

(67) e. ??Who did Amy leave Henry for?
      f. ??/*Who did Amy believe the rumour that Henry had been seeing in New York.
      g. ??/*Who did Amy wonder when Henry could have had time to visit?

These cases clearly bear further discussion, since the source ambiguity problems concerning long-distance *wh*-movement are as interesting as they are numerous; see Kluender and Kutas (1993), Hofmeister, Casasanto and Sag (2013a), cf. Sprouse, Wagers and Phillips (2012); cf. also Müller (2015) for a recent pragmatics-based approach. For now though, the main lesson to be drawn is that listeners appear not to attend very carefully to the syntactic form of utterances, at least where the syntax is semantically empty.

This highlights an apparent paradox. On one hand, the fact that native speakers generally agree on the very subtle minimal contrasts between the examples in (57)–(67) shows that most of us are capable of fine-grained grammatical analysis, when necessary.[3] Yet the evidence also suggests that we don't always deploy this knowledge in parsing utterances, and that we use more superficial parsing strategies in normal conversation; cf. Phillips, Wagers and Lau (2011). Assuming for the present that 'we' belong to the same community of speakers, this implies two distinct modes of grammatical processing: (i) a 'professional/expert' mode, predominantly used by theoretical linguists, careful copy-editors, and (some) junior high school teachers (as well as by the self-appointed 'grammar police'); (ii) a 'lite' mode used by all of us a good part of the time, which derives analyses of utterances that are 'good enough' to extract the intended message.

As it turns out, just such a distinction has been proposed by a number of different psycholinguists, most notably Fernanda Ferreira and her colleagues at the University of Edinburgh (Ferreira and Patson 2007, Ferreira, Ferraro and Bailey 2002; compare also Frank, Bod and Christiansen 2012, Sanford and Sturt 2012). Similar proposals have been put forward to explain contrasts between native speakers and second language learners (see, for example, Clahsen and Felser 2006). If one or more of these hypotheses prove correct, they have significant implications for models of language comprehension and production, in so far as they suggest that the kinds of theoretical constructs that competence-based theorists care so much about may not be very important in everyday conversation, after all.

Incidentally, the 'Sir Marcus Browning' speech contains another instance of ungrammaticality, one that serves as an appropriate coda to this section:

Because what I'm talking about is life. Because life is the sort of thing … that most of us find it very difficult to avoid.

> Richard Curtis and Rowan Atkinson, 'Sir Marcus
> Browning, MP' (*Live in Belfast*, 1979)

You may have to read these lines a few times to spot the problem.

Notes

1 Example (59b) can be rescued by the insertion of the preposition *in* after *been*, which creates a gap for a locative NP.

2 If you have stuck with the argument so far, well done. If you have found it at all enjoyable, you might want to consider syntax, rather than more psycholinguistics, as your next linguistics course. Either way, this is as technical and involved a grammatical discussion as you're likely to encounter until v is for von Humboldt.

3 Whoever *we* are: this may only be a WEIRD talent: see Henrich, Heine and Norenzayan (2010).

Conclusion to Part II

In this section I have tried to give a sense of the empirical challenges that face any simplistic attempt to integrate static theories of grammatical knowledge with theories of processing and development. It has been shown that even at the most basic observational level it is extremely difficult to decide what aspects of language and linguistic behaviour are best treated declaratively (in terms of stored representations), and which procedurally (in terms of algorithmic rules); or indeed, whether such a sharp distinction is a helpful one in characterising real speakers' knowledge. The case studies also demonstrate that what speakers know about some of the most obvious expressions of their language(s) is much richer, more complex and more subtle than is ever suggested by the facility and casualness of ordinary speech. At the same time, they reveal that much of what we might have supposed to be universal about language is in fact constrained in various ways: by being language-particular, lexically conditioned, or highly specific to a particular context of utterance; usually, all of these things at once. This implies right from the get-go that whatever theories of language acquisition and processing we arrive at should be ones that reflect the dynamic and interactive nature of linguistic behaviour, as well as its inherent complexity, and which allow for the operation of different sets of algorithms in different language varieties.

One size does not fit all.

Part III

Say it ain't so, Joe

Challenging assumptions and idealisations

Introduction: beyond reasonable doubt

Here we have already the beginning of one of the distinctions that cause most trouble in philosophy – the distinction between 'appearance' and 'reality', between what things seem to be and what they are. The painter wants to know what things seem to be, the practical man and the philosopher want to know what they are; but the philosopher's wish to know this is stronger than the practical man's, and is more troubled by knowledge as to the difficulties of answering the question.

Bertrand Russell, The Problems of Philosophy (1912)

HUGH LAURIE: *Can you tell me how to be happy?*
STEPHEN FRY: *How to be happy?*
HUGH LAURIE: *How to be happy.*
STEPHEN FRY: *I'm afraid to say that information may be restricted.*
HUGH LAURIE: *Oh. You do have it, though?*
STEPHEN FRY: *Oh yes.*
HUGH LAURIE: *But it's restricted?*
STEPHEN FRY: *I'm afraid so. Sorry.*
HUGH LAURIE: *Contented?*
STEPHEN FRY: *Yes, thank you.*
HUGH LAURIE: *No, any information on how to be contented?*
STEPHEN FRY: *Oh, I see. Yes, we've got information on that.*
HUGH LAURIE: *Can I have it?*
STEPHEN FRY: *I'm afraid it's a secret.*
HUGH LAURIE: *Oh, go on.*
STEPHEN FRY: *Alright. The secret of contentment is ...*
HUGH LAURIE: *Yes?*
STEPHEN FRY: *... not to ask any questions.*

Stephen Fry and Hugh Laurie, 'Information' sketch
(A Bit of Fry & Laurie, 1990)

In every field of enquiry, researchers assume things to be true that they know to be false simply to get projects off the ground: we call these things IDEALISATIONS. In psycholinguistics, competence-based linguists seem to be happier with idealisations than psychologists, who in turn are happier than speech therapists, for many of the same reasons that mathematicians are happier than architects, and architects than house-builders.

Content with *idealisations*, that is: if Stephen Fry and Hugh Laurie are correct in the sketch above, theoreticians must be a fairly miserable bunch, at least in their professional lives. And what seems desirable to the pure theoretician can be a significant problem if what you're trying to model is an actual speaker's mind, whether it is the mental lexicon of a typically developing five year-old, or the production abilities of a particular aphasic patient, rather than some abstract Cartesian object (the 'language faculty'). Even in psycholinguistics proper, preliminary idealisations are usually harmless, as long as it is not forgotten that this is what they are, and that the real point of the exercise is to explain something much richer and messier. Unfortunately, psycholinguists are no more mindful of this fact than anyone else.

This may have something to do with the fact that models based on ideal assumptions are that much better looking than the real thing. It is probably for the same reason that portraits are often more flattering than unedited photographs, or that some slightly short-sighted people don't wear glasses except when it is a legal requirement. I speak for myself, anyway: airbrushed scenes generally offer a more attractive prospect. As Graham Greene's character Dr Hasselbacher says, in *Our Man in Havana*:

You should dream more, Mr Wormold. Reality in our century is not something to be faced.

Graham Greene, *Our Man in Havana* ([1958] 2004)

Whatever the reason, researchers rarely get around to restoring the messiness and happenstance that would make their models accurate representations of real language users, and instead treat the idealised models as though they told us about something real. In this section I offer a glossary of some of the principal linguistic assumptions and idealisations, which are intended to clarify, but which too often end up achieving the opposite. This is not a glossary in the usual sense, which may be found at the end (or not, depending on space constraints), but rather a means of structuring the conversation so as to give approximately even weight to all of the relevant concepts that need to be discussed.

A (by now familiar) anchoring point for the discussion is Chomsky's early (1965) reference to the 'ideal speaker–listener':

Linguistic theory is concerned primarily with an ideal speaker–listener, in a completely homogeneous speech-community, who know its [the speech community's] language perfectly and is unaffected by such grammatically irrelevant conditions as memory limitations, distractions, shifts of attention and interest, and errors (random or characteristic) in applying his knowledge of this language in actual performance.

Noam Chomsky, *Aspects of the Theory of Syntax* (1965: 3)

While this description was intended to characterise linguistic, as opposed to psycholinguistic, theory, it nevertheless informs the bulk of competence-based psycholinguistic research practice, where it is assumed that – if one could only strip away the other cognitive systems that interact with the language processor in normal language comprehension and production – one would find, within the ideal speaker–listener, a pure system, perfect grammatical knowledge; see also Chomsky (2008). In the following sections, I examine this premise in some detail, and from several different perspectives. For the most part, I do not directly challenge the *status quo* though I'll try to make a case for a more nuanced – more human – approach. In several areas, however, I will question some quite fundamental assumptions, viz.:

- the idea that speakers have internalised an autonomous grammar (as distinct from grammatical knowledge): see G is for Grammar;
- the idea that speakers of a language converge on an essentially uniform and discrete underlying system: see H is for Homogeneity;
- the idea that grammatical acceptability can ever be context-free, or that it is only (or even mainly) about sentences: see J is for Judgment, T is for Sentence;
- the idea that linguistic knowledge is something entirely internal to the mind of an individual: see I is for Internalism, also C is for Competence~Performance;
- the idea that grammatical knowledge involves what Chomsky terms DIS-CRETE INFINITY ('language is a system of infinite generation'); see v is for von Humboldt.

I will also reject two of the current metaphors that inform psycholinguistic research – language as a biological organ, and the mind as a computer – and offer in their place an alternative, namely, language as architecture. For this, see O is for Object of Study. Since each of these counter-arguments requires some bolstering, the relevant sections are markedly longer than the others. I ask the reader's indulgence.

Filtered content: the myth of message extraction

If 'youth is wasted on the young', as George Bernard Shaw quipped, then language is almost certainly wasted on the psycholinguist. The majority of my colleagues approach language the way that a white-coated nutritionist approaches a meal in a *Michelin*-starred restaurant, as a dipsomaniac (or teetotaller) handles a vintage bottle of claret or a perfectly poured pint of stout. Just as a meal is more than its nutritional content, a good wine or beer more than the alcohol it contains, so everyone from the pre-lingual child to the most inarticulate professional footballer 'reflexively knows' that language comprehension is not about stripping away form to extract propositional content, nor is it about resolving every ambiguity. Long before Marshall McLuhan coined the phrase (McLuhan 1964), most everyone had implicitly acknowledged that with respect to spoken language, the 'medium is the [greater part of the] message'. Everyone that is, except the kinds of psycholinguists whose work figures large in standard textbooks.

This critical observation should not be interpreted as a plea for *qualia*, nor for a *Gestalt* approach to language comprehension and production (even if neither of these is necessarily a bad idea). The suggestion is not that no abstraction is involved in processing spoken language, or that language processing can only be understood in holistic terms, or on a case-by-case basis. Quite the contrary: there is reasonably clear experimental evidence to show that different sub-components of the language processor are dedicated to handling different types of information – phonetic, phonological, morphological, lexical syntactic, semantic and pragmatic – and that at least some of these modules can be isolated and studied separately.

As in vision, the impression of a rich and unified phenomenological experience turns out to be due to the operation of many quasi-autonomous processes. When we observe, for example, a wild boar with a grey patch on its snout lying near a stream, this joined-up experience is due to separate mental processes, including separate functional modules responsible for shape, colour and movement detection, for shape identification and recognition, as well as

Figure 18 Wild boar in Okamoto: previously, a common sight in spring and autumn.

for higher-level processes of scene integration. No single part of our brain actually registers the position of a wild boar with a greyish patch on its snout: some parts of the visual system 'see' grey, some may recognise a boar, some detect a static vs. moving object, and so on. (See Riddoch and Humphries 1987 for a fascinating case-study of visual agnosia, which offers good evidence of modularity in this cognitive domain.)

So it is with language, from the moment we start listening to speech: at the same time as we are recognising words, and parsing these into their constituent phrases, we are continuously, if implicitly, aware of the age, gender, voice quality, dialect and register of the speaker, we are monitoring the speaker's choice of grammatical construction, their use of prosody and intonation, the pragmatic implicatures that their utterances convey, not to mention all of the paralinguistic information communicated through non-verbal means (by gestures of different kinds, including facial expressions). In conversation, we rapidly attune to every subtle aspect of the speaker's performance, and adapt our own speech to the particular context of utterance. It is wholly conceivable that all of this information is handled by semi-autonomous sub-modules of the language processor, but however this is achieved, it is all handled nearly simultaneously, in real time, by every competent language user.[1]

And it *all* counts. Language comprehension (and production) involves synthesis of the information from all of these linguistic channels – rather than an abstraction away from everything but the literal message (the PROPOSITIONAL CONTENT). Oftentimes, the literal message may even be irrelevant. As David Byrne of the Talking Heads recently observed of song lyrics:[2]

People ignore them half the time ... In a certain way, it's the sound of the words, the inflection, and the way the song is sung and the way it fits the melody and the way the syllables are on the tongue that has as much of the meaning as the actual, literal words.

David Byrne, 'Song lyrics are overrated' (CNN interview, 2010)

The relative insignificance of the literal message is especially clear in songwriting, most particularly in alliterative contexts. Yves Duteil's whimsical 1974 song *Un Lilas pour Eulalie* is a classic example: you don't need to know any French at all to appreciate this song, all of whose value is lost in translation. Likewise, the lyrics of the Icelandic experimental rock group Sigur Rós are impenetrable to everyone – even to other Icelandic speakers, since they are sung in an invented language (*Vonlenska*) – yet this does not detract from the songs' appeal.

♫ Yves Duteil, Un Lilas pour Eulalie (1974)

The importance of one non-propositional aspect of speech – namely, accent – is directly illustrated in William Boyd's novel *Waiting for Sunrise*. In the extract reproduced below, the protagonist, Lysander Rief, meets his Viennese analyst, an Englishman named Bensimon, for the first time:

'Mr L. U. Rief,' Bensimon said. In the quiet room, Lysander could hear the scratch of his fountain pen. His voice was lightly accented, somewhere from the North of England, Lysander guessed, but honed down so that placing the location was impossible. He was good at accents, Lysander flattered himself – he'd unlock it in a minute or two.

> *'What do the initials stand for?'*
> *'Lysander Ulrich Rief.'*

> *Manchester, Lysander thought – that flat 'A'.*

William Boyd, Waiting for Sunrise (2012: 15–16)

From the very first syllable of their encounter, Rief is concerned to place Bensimon by his accent; only once he has done this can he settle down and listen to what the good doctor has to say. At least among speakers of British and Irish

English, this is a common, near-universal concern whenever one begins a conversation with a stranger.[3] And while some people have a keener ear than others, the ability to locate someone's origins within the first few seconds of listening clearly forms part of almost every native speaker's psycholinguistic competence.

Accent is much more than a source of mild curiosity: it can bind us instantly to another person, or just as quickly, alienate us to such a degree that we cannot – or will not – hear the message beyond it, or in such a way that we treat the message as unreliable.[4] In Seamus Heaney's poem *A Sofa in the Forties*, the poet recalls the wireless news-reader, the 'absolute speaker' (of BBC English):

> *Between him and us*
> *A great gulf was fixed where pronunciation*
> *Reigned tyrannically.*

Seamus Heaney, *A Sofa in the Forties* (1999)

The distancing effect of accent has consequences in legal and forensic contexts, as well: it has been observed that listeners are less inclined to trust nonnative speakers or those who speak with an unfamiliar accent even if they might otherwise be more credible than the equivalent native speaker; cf. Dixon, Mahoney and Cocks (2002). It is unclear whether this is due to foreignness *per se*, or to the difficulty of processing non-native speech; see Lev-Ari and Keysar (2010), also Ω is for Love below ('Comprehensible input') for further discussion. Either way, the alienating effects of accent are undeniable.

Sensitivity to pronunciation is not only reflected in language comprehension. A nice example of conscious adaptation in production can be found in the comparison of two songs by the West Yorkshire singer-songwriter Jake Thackray, who came to public attention in Britain in the 1970s (thanks to his appearances on the BBC comedy/reality show *That's Life*). Born in Leeds, Thackray had studied and lived in France for several years before returning to teach English in his native city, and his songwriting was heavily influenced by francophone *chansonniers*, especially Georges Brassens and Jacques Brel. Although most of Thackray's songs were written in (Yorkshire) English, he also translated a few into French, including *The Black Swan* (*Le Cygne Noir*), a song about drowning one's sorrows 'down t'pub' after a romantic break-up. As well as I can judge, Thackray's pronunciation in the French version of the song is near-native: in particular, his pronunciation of French vowels is native-like, and he produces no final consonants in (masculine) words ending in a written consonant (other than in liaison contexts).[5]

♫ Jake Thackray, *Le Cygne Noir* and *Jumble Sale* (2006)

By contrast, in the English song *Jumble Sale*, Thackray gives to borrowed French words their full Yorkshire values: the French verb *faire* rhymes exactly with *flair* and *dare*, while *art*, *carte* and *heart* are also perfect rhymes: there's not a post-vocalic [r] to be heard, and the final [t]s are all clearly pronounced. This is not simply a matter of French–English code-switching, it is French–Yorkshire code-switching: Thackray's rhymes, his cadences, and lexical choices just don't work so well in many other varieties of English, especially rhotic varieties like mine.

♫ Jake Thackray, *The Last Will and Testament of Jake Thackray* (2006)

Thackray's songs also reflect – and are immediately *understood as reflecting* – different social registers. This is especially clear in the song *The Last Will and Testament of Jake Thackray*. In the second verse, the petit-bourgeois snobbery infused in the vowels of the request for a glass of port wine is directly contrasted with the uninhibited open sounds of the Yorkshire in 'right back', and 'cracking' in the following line.[6]

If you still believe that these things don't matter, try singing any Country & Western song, or popular rock ballad, using Received Pronunciation: if the result doesn't sound preposterous, you are either a non-native speaker or a computer … or else, truly, 'you've got no soul'. (Non-disordered) language users don't abstract away from all of this information in the signal: they take it all in, and understand it as part of the message. An adequate theory of language processing should tell us how this happens.

Ambiguity resolution: the myth of the unambiguous message

In a language as idiomatically stressed as English, opportunities for mis-readings are bound to arise. By a mere backward movement of stress, a verb can become a noun, an act a thing. To refuse, to insist on saying no to what you believe is wrong, becomes at a stroke refuse, an insurmountable pile of garbage.

Ian McEwan, *Amsterdam* (1998)[7]

Another remarkable feature of classical psycholinguistics is its treatment of various kinds of ambiguity. Ambiguity is a pervasive phenomenon at all levels of language processing; indeed, it might well be considered the key phenomenon of psycholinguistic (processing) research, in the same way that variation is the key fact of sociolinguistics. A huge amount of experimental time and effort has been devoted to the question of how listeners and readers deal with different kinds of ambiguity online, and to the types of knowledge that are relevant to the resolution of these ambiguities at different stages of language processing ('the time-course of ambiguity resolution'): see Altmann (1998, 1989). Whether the concern is with mechanisms of phonetic discrimination, spoken word recognition, morphological segmentation, syntactic parsing strategies or pragmatic inferencing, it is usually taken for granted that the aim of the various language processing modules is to resolve local and global ambiguities in such a way as to arrive at a unique 'correct' solution, given the utterance context; though cf. Wasow (2015).

At first blush, this seems to be an innocuous enough ambition, until one considers any sort of skilled language performance, from weak puns, to apparent throw-away lines in songs, to *double entendres*, to innuendo, to sarcasm ... to poetry – whose *raison d'être* resides in the simultaneity of multiple layers of meaning, form and metrical associations.

(If you were misled in parsing the previous sentence, that was the intention.)

Three examples suffice to illustrate the unclosed nature of lexical ambiguity. In cases such as these, it seems, we do not resolve the ambiguities: instead, our minds alternate among them, bouncing back and forth between the preferred and dispreferred readings, the literal and the figurative. Consider, first of all, two riddles from the children's menu in a British chain-restaurant:

(68)   a. Q: Why should you not tell secrets in the kitchen?
               A: Because the potatoes have eyes and the corn has ears!
        b. Q: In which school do you learn to make ice cream?
               A: Sundae School.

Part of what makes these jokes so lame is their very accessibility: the ambiguity is immediately clear, even to a typical eight year-old.

Much more intelligent, but no more obscure to most adults, are the lines from Joni Mitchell's magnificent song *Shades of Scarlett Conquering*. The song's title immediately introduces two parallel themes – *shades* (hues) of red, and *ghosts* of Scarlett (O'Hara in the 1939 epic *Gone with the Wind*). These two themes are developed in parallel throughout the verses – (i) *scarlet / fire / Catholic saints* (evoking purple and cardinal red) / *auburn hair / blood-red embers*; (ii) *Scarlett / cinematic lovers / plantations / ballroom gowns / ghosts of Gable and Flynn / Southern charm* – until they are brought together again in the last four lines of the fourth verse ('Dressed ... fingernails', with a nice play on *cast* in the phrase 'cast iron and frail').

♫ Joni Mitchell, *Shades of Scarlett Conquering* (1975)

Even without the connections drawn by the rhyme and the metre, this is a richly textured piece. The listener does not perceive these separate themes independently, any more than most of us separate out the instruments in the performance of a symphony. (Or even a concerto: a particular instrument may have a prominent role, but a concerto is much more than an extended sonata with background accompaniment.)

Numerous song titles, including those in (69), offer clear instances of two readings being intended simultaneously:

(69) a. *Aladdin Sane* – David Bowie
    b. *Losing my Religion* – REM
    c. *High Fidelity* – Elvis Costello (also Nick Hornby)
    d. *The Stars (Are Out Tonight)* – David Bowie

Take (69b), for example. It has been claimed by REM's Michael Stipe[8] that the phrase 'losing my religion' is only intended with its local vernacular meaning: in the southeastern United States, the phrase has apparently been bleached of its more common interpretation, and signifies little more than losing your patience or temper, coming to the end of your rope. Yet Stipe's assertion is disingenuous: the song would not have become so popular worldwide, had not most English-speaking listeners believed that it referred to a more dramatic loss of faith (religious or otherwise). Surely the writer would have been aware of this.

♫ REM, *Losing My Religion* (1991)

Josh Ritter has a genius for taking a figurative expression and running with its literal interpretation, without losing the metaphor. The following excerpts from his songs *Good Man*, *New Lover* and *Nightmares* offer wonderful demonstrations of this art:

> They shot a Western south of here
> They had him cornered in a canyon
> And even his horse had disappeared
> They say it got run down by a bad, bad man.
>
> You're not a good shot but I'm worse
> And there's so much where we ain't been yet
> So swing up on this little horse
> The only thing we'll hit is sunset.

♫ Josh Ritter, *Good Man* (2006)

> Praise the water under bridges
> Praise the time they say will heal
> Praise the fonder that still grows on the absent heart in fields
> Praise be to this pain these days
> It's all I seem to feel.

♫ Josh Ritter, *New Lover* (2013)

> Nightmares have their dreams as well
> And when they sleep they go to hell
> And drink their fill on lakes of blood

Canter 'cross the skull-paved mud
And nurse their little colts on flies
Their coltish teeth like kitchen knives
And look down from abysmal cliffs
Their dead hair by the lead wind riffed
On denizens too deep to see
Whose own dreams nightmares' nightmares be.

♫ Josh Ritter, *Nightmares* (2013)

(The etymology police may object to the association drawn between bad dreams and horses in *Nightmares* – historically, the 'mare' in nightmare has nothing to do with horses, it means evil spirit or incubus – cf. Dutch *nacht-merrie* – but for most English speakers the two words are naturally related.)

The multi-layered, and continuous, nature of lexical ambiguity is not some special preserve of poets and songwriters: though it may be more prevalent and sophisticated in poetry and song than in usual conversation, unresolved ambiguity is an intrinsic part of typical spoken language comprehension and production, as the children's jokes demonstrate.[9] And though Josh Ritter's lines are clever, they are not subtle or opaque: no complex exegesis is required to divine the intended meanings.

Yet most models of word recognition are constructed to extract only (the verbal equivalent of) the most prominent melodic line, ignoring or deleting any harmonics, counter-melodies and/or metrical structure. Since these other elements very often contribute more than the literal message to the final interpretation, one might consider a processing model that did this efficiently to be a failure, rather than a success. But that is not how it is generally viewed. On the contrary, a model's capacity to rapidly resolve lexical ambiguities, and so to deliver a unique interpretation, are considered self-evident virtues.

Similar considerations apply to syntactic (structural) ambiguities. Here again, there is an implicit assumption in psycholinguistic research that every ambiguous string should be resolved by the language processor, one way or another. In some cases this seems wholly reasonable – perhaps more so than in the lexical cases just discussed. Classic 'attachment' ambiguities, such as those exemplified in (70), only admit one of two mutually exclusive interpretations. In example (70a), for example, the prepositional phrase *in the box* cannot be interpreted simultaneously as being associated with the frog and the table – either the frog starts off in the box (A) or it ends up there (B). In (70b), the phrase *from the lecture theatre* either describes the subject's standpoint (A) or the object participant's (prior) location (B).

(70) a. She set [$_A$ the frog [$_B$ in the box $_A$] on the table $_B$].
      b. She observed [$_A$ [$_B$ the man $_A$] from the lecture theatre $_B$].

Similarly, where two scopal readings offer up contradictory interpretations, as in (71), the ambiguity must be resolved in favour of one or other reading:

(71) a. She didn't come to dinner because she had something better to do: she went to see Arsenal play Manchester City instead.   Because > Not

   b. She didn't come to dinner because she had nothing better to do; after all, she could have gone to see Arsenal play Manchester City.   Not > Because

Most sentence processing models that have been proposed to deal with these kinds of structural ambiguities share the objective of allowing the listener to select the 'correct' analysis by rejecting unwanted alternatives. More recent research, however, suggests that we don't [~~reject unwanted alternatives~~], that is – at least not entirely. For example, reading time experiments by Cai, Sturt and Pickering (2011/2012) lend support to the idea that readers continue to consider non-adopted analyses of ambiguous structures even after they should have been abandoned. See also Ferreira and Dell (2000), Ferreira (2006), Ferreira, Slevc and Rogers (2005); also Roland, Elman and Ferreira (2006), though cf. Parker and Phillips (2016).

   In natural language utterances, one also finds instances where two *overlapping parses* are intended simultaneously: where the listener is first invited to entertain one analysis, and then to re-analyse the final part of that first analysis as non-final, resulting in a 'chaining' through the discourse. In clear contrast to classic 'garden path sentences' – such as those in (72), from Pinker (1994) …

72) a. The cotton clothing is usually made of grows in Mississippi.
   b. The man who hunts ducks out on weekends.
   c. The fat people eat accumulates.

… each link of a chained structure is a legitimate and intended parse.[10]

   The Swedish singer-songwriter Anna Ternheim is superb at this kind of incremental chaining, something beautifully illustrated in her song *Halfway to Fivepoints:*

> *Who's taking you down there?*
> *What's his name, let me know*
> *The price he offers*
> *Round the corner of love.*
>
> *How to get to Fivepoints?*
> *How would I know?*
> *A place so distant*
> *And so long ago.*

♫ Anna Ternheim, *Halfway to Five Points* (2008)

In every verse of this song, we are carried along, each phase ending with the beginning of the next idea. The cycles are schematised in (73):

(73)   [₁ What's his name, [₂ [₃ let me know ₁]
             The price he offers ₂] round the corner of love ₃].
        [₁ [₂ How to get to Fivepoints ₁]
             [₃ [₄ How would I know? ₂] a place so distant? ₃]
             And so long ago ₄].

Another much more familiar example can be found in the refrain to the Beatles' song *Getting Better,* from the *Sgt. Pepper* album. The point to notice about all of these cases is that the chaining process – what might be termed 'second-pass grammaticality' – differs from what is found in a classic garden path utterance, where the first analysis was mistaken and must be rejected: here, the first parse is retained, along with the new analysis.

The possibility of overlapping parses may not appear to be much used in English prose, but something very much like it seems to be a fairly common process in other languages, especially in Mainland Southeast Asian languages. In the Vietnamese sentences in (74), what would otherwise be treated as an embedded clause [₁] is re-parsed as a main clause [₂] – yielding a direct question – through the addition of the final discourse particle *thế* (see Bruening and Tran 2006, cf. Duffield 2014, 2015):[11]

(74)   a. ?Tân vừa chụp hình   [₂ con hổ   [₁ đã dọa ai ₁] *thế* ₂]?
               Tan ADV catch picture   CL tiger   ASP scare who   PRT
               i. *'Who did Tan take a photo of the tiger that scared?'
               ii. 'Tan took a photo of the tiger. Who did it scare?'
        b. ?[₁ Ai [₂ (vừa) bỏ đi ₂] ₁] làm mọi người bối rối   *thế*?
               who ASP leave   make everyone embarrass PRT
               i. *'Who left made everyone embarrassed?'
               ii. 'Who (that just left) made everyone embarrassed?'
        c. ?Tân thua cuộc [₁ vì   [₂ ai   làm hư xe của anh ta ₁] *thế* ₂]?
               Tan lose event   because who do harm car POSS PRN   PRT
               i. *'Who did Tan lose the event because damaged his car?'
               ii. 'Tan lost the event because of … who damaged his car?'

Take (74c), for instance: here, the adjunct *because*-clause, which would otherwise be an 'island' to extraction of the interrogative pronoun *ai* (who), gets reparsed as a main clause through the addition of final *thế* – the initial bracketing [₁] being replaced by the re-parsed bracketing [₂].

It is plausible to think that a similar chaining process is at work in what Doherty (1994, 2013) terms 'subject contact relatives', found in Hiberno-English and other non-standard varieties; see Henry (1995: chapter 6), see also H is for Homogeneity below. In the example in (75), the NP *a woman*, the associate of initial *there*, gets interpreted as the subject of the following subjectless clauses [*came ... said ...*]:

(75)   a. [₁There's [₃ a woman came to see me yesterday₁], [₂ said she wants to buy my car ...₂] ₃]
       b. There's a woman John knows, came to see me, told me that she wants to buy my car ...'

In Doherty's analysis, example (75a) is treated as a presentational cleft [*There's a woman ...*] followed by two relative clauses, each missing their relative pronouns. However, this doesn't match our intuition that, in terms of its discourse function, the second 'relative clause' is interpreted as a main clause: that is to say, (75a) is interpreted in the same way as (76a). This suggests an alternative analysis in which the utterance ends up being analysed with the bracketing [₃], where *there's* gets parsed out (that is, is excluded) on the second pass). On this alternative analysis, the relative clause [₂] is 'promoted to main clause' in the course of parsing. This suggestion is supported by the fact that in the relevant context, the same utterance with relative pronouns sounds strange; compare (75a) with (76b). Notice also that the Definiteness Restriction (see Milsark 1977) disappears whenever the relative pronouns are introduced (76c): that is to say, the noun-phrase following *There's* does not have to be indefinite if it is followed by a relative clause introduced by *that*.

(76)   a. A woman came to see me yesterday. (She said she) wants to buy my car.
       b. [₁There's [₃ a woman that came to see me yesterday₁], [₂ that said she wants to buy my car ...₂] ₃]
       c. [₁There's [₃ the woman that came to see me yesterday₁], [₂ that said she wants to buy my car ...₂]₃]

A reverse instance of this effect, where an initial main clause gets reparsed as a relative, is attested in the following *Belfast Telegraph* video interview, with a local tour guide:[12]

(77)   'Everybody's been on the tour, with their visitors, have enjoyed it ...'

Even if these kinds of syntactic ambiguity are better analysed in some other way, it is almost always the case that strings that are potentially ambiguous are *unambiguous in context*: the ambiguity is immediately pre-empted or resolved by *emphasis and phrasing* (lexical stress, prosody and sentential intonation).[13]

In spoken language, virtually all so-called garden path sentences, including those in (72) above, can easily be disambiguated by such means (. = same prosodic constituent; /, // = pauses):

(78) a. The cotton / **clothing**.is.made.of // grows.in.Mississippi –
          unambiguous relative clause interpretation
      b. The.man.who.hunts // ducks.out/ on.weekends – unambiguous
          relative clause interpretation
      c. The.fat.people // eat.accumulates – unambiguous GP
          interpretation: fat must be an attributive adjective

(Punctuation offers the same service in written texts, as was pointed out by Lynne Truss in her popular, if professionally disdained, book *Eats, Shoots & Leaves* (Truss 2003); cf. Menand (2004).

Figures 19 and 20 show the acoustic contrast between the two readings of (79a) vs. (79b), respectively. In both figures, the word *eat* is represented by the fourth burst from the left: whereas in Figure 19 'eat' is followed by a relatively long stretch of silence (flat line); in Figure 20 (the 'garden path' version), the longer silence precedes *eat*.

(79) a. (The) **fat** // people.eat / accumulates – unambiguous relative
          interpretation
      b. (The) fat.people / eat.accumulates – unambiguous GP
          interpretation (<u>fat</u> must be an attributive pre-nominal adjective)

The disambiguating role of phonetic emphasis – at all levels of linguistic analysis, including lexical tone, word-stress, phrasal prosody and intonation – is hardly a new discovery: its theoretical significance was discussed at least as far back as Newman (1946), see also Bresnan (1971); see Cutler, Dahan and Van Donselaar (1997), Snedeker and Trueswell (2003) for a process-oriented perspective. Within competence-based approaches, theoretical work by Zubizarreta (1998), processing studies by Fodor (1998, 2002), and – perhaps most interestingly – recent work in first language acquisition by de Carvalho et al. (2016), all attest to the use of prosodic information in constraining syntactic analyses.

In spite of this, most experimental studies of sentential ambiguity, as well as many acquisition studies investigating syntactic acquisition, usually abstract away from prosody, yielding models of limited ecological validity. It remains a general assumption that prosody is something secondary – a helpful overlay, rather than a determining factor – in grammatical acceptability. See v is for von Humboldt below.

Crucially, prosody is not only used to signal underlying lexical, morphological and syntactic contrasts: there are cases where phonetic emphasis alone

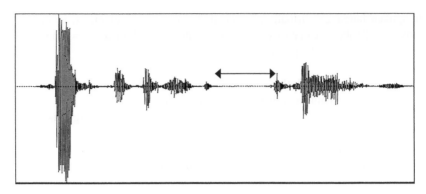

Figure 19 Disambiguating prosody I: ... fat people eat // accumulates.

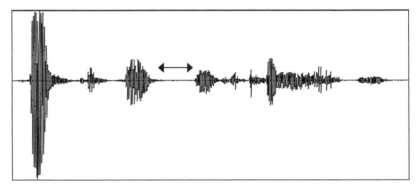

Figure 20 Disambiguating prosody II: ... fat people // eat accumulates.

serves a disambiguating function. Classic examples of this are the notices on the London Underground shown in (80), whose linguistic significance was first noted by Halliday (1970), and which have been discussed by many subsequent researchers, including Gussenhoven (1984), Partee (1991), Krifka et al. (1995), Ladd ([1996] 2008) and Erteschik-Shir (1997):

(80)   a. Dogs must be carried.
        b. Shirts must be worn.

In their written form, both of these sentences are ambiguous: example (80a) either requires all those who have a dog to carry it, or requires everyone wishing to travel to bring a dog; example (80b) either enjoins everyone with a shirt to wear it – as opposed to using it as a seat cover, for instance – or else requires that everyone travelling should wear a shirt. (Implicitly, the message is directed at stereotypical male shirt-wearers: perhaps, it is assumed that blouse-wearers will not go topless on the Underground under any circumstances). When spoken, however, there is no ambiguity in either example: emphasis on the final verb in (81a), and increased stress on the subject in (81b), are sufficient to ensure the intended readings:

(81)   a. Dogs must be <u>carried</u>.
       b. <u>Shirts</u> must be worn.

Though some analysts may dispute the point, there is no obvious lexical or structural difference between the two sentences: prosody alone seems to do all the work.

It is difficult to imagine the research division of any major automobile manufacturing company devoting time to understanding how drivers negotiate complex intersections at night without headlights (or road signs). While it is surely true that startled, squinting drivers resort to various default strategies ('road attachment strategies') when the headlights fail: 'keep straight', 'keep to the nearside lane', 'slow down', etc., this doesn't represent a typical driving situation, and engineers don't design their cars around this contingency. Much the same is true in lexical and syntactic processing: strip out the tones from a tone language, and word recognition becomes much more difficult;[14] remove lexical stress in English, and – as Ian McEwan observes in the quote at the beginning of this section – re ˈfuse [ɹɪˈfjuːz] is hard to distinguish from ˈrefuse [ˈɹɛfjuːs] (though it is worth pointing out that the sibilant is voiced in one case, and voiceless in the other, and that the vowel quality of <e> changes with stress shift); ignore prosody, and it becomes hard to tell where that frog (in example (70)) is … or was … in relation to the box …, or whether a dog is required for travel. But since speakers and listeners use prosody as the night driver or pedestrian uses car headlights, the problem is generally moot.

Naturally, there will always be careless writing that cannot be saved by prosody, as in this piece of sports reporting – not to mention the awful pun in *afoot* – but these are rare exceptions to a massively general rule.

John Guidetti once again demonstrated why moves are afoot to sign him on a permanent basis with a hat trick.

Celtic 6–0 Partick Thistle, BBC Sport, 29 October 2014[15]

In summary, most models of sentence processing proceed from the implicit assumption that the goal of language comprehension is to extract propositional content, and that (in order to do this) listeners abstract away from non-propositional aspects of the verbal message, and quickly resolve any transient ambiguities, to arrive at a unique, context-independent, literal message, using only information proper to each level of language: syntax to resolve syntactic ambiguities, phonology to resolve phonological ambiguities, and so forth. But each of these assumptions is refutable: to the extent that they are challenged, they call into question the validity of the models in which they are instantiated.

Do not forget that it is easier for a rich man to pass through the eye of a needle than it is for a camel to [non-final intonation] ⋯
    ... than it is for a CAMEL to[final falling intonation] ⋯

Richard Curtis and Rowan Atkinson, 'The Wedding:
Vicar's Speech' (1980)

Notes

1 See Friederici (2002), Steinhauer and Drury (2012).

2 David Byrne's CNN interview (April 2010): http://edition.cnn.com/2010/OPINION/04/01/ted.david.byrne/.

3 In spite of having lived abroad for most of my adult life, I fondly imagine that I can still place speakers of Ulster varieties of English to within around 20 miles of their place of birth, at least speakers to the east of the River Bann. This is not, I think a rare ability: it is shared by the majority of the people I grew up with. In the context of the Northern Irish 'Troubles', it might even be viewed as a survival skill (even though one cannot reliably identify members of the unionist or nationalist communities on the basis of accent alone, except probabilistically; see Henry 1995: 8).

4 The same is true of voice quality. It might seem unlikely, for example, that we retain separate representations of every pronunciation of the English word 'dog' – and of all of the other words of English – for each English speaker that we know. Yet we are surprised when someone we know speaks with another's voice, or even in an unexpected fashion ('She doesn't sound herself today'); this implies that we must encode and retain information about the typical voice quality and other speech patterns of other individuals.

5 Unfortunately, republishing fees preclude presentation of Thackray's lyrics directly. The avarice of intermediary music publishers should not stand in the way of your enjoyment: the songs can all be found at www.jakethackray.com.

6 Most linguists would be disturbed by the unscientific use of adjectives in this paragraph. I know I am. Unfortunately, we have not developed any more objective descriptors to use for this aspect of language comprehension and production. There is some consideration of these issues in the emerging field of sociophonetics (see Thomas 2010); up to now, however, there has been little cross-over between this field and experimental psycholinguistics, even less in developmental studies.

7 In spite of its obvious relevance, it is not clear what McEwan intends by the phrase 'idiomatically stressed': the lexical stress rules of English are in the main fairly predictable (Hayes 1982), and are actively used by speakers to segment and analyse speech: see especially Cutler and Norris (1988).

8 Sources: Wikipedia www.nytimes.com/1991/03/13/arts/the-pop-life-122791.html; Stephen Holden, 'The Pop Life', *New York Times* (13 March 1991).

9 See also The Two Ronnies' 'Fork Handles' sketch (1976): https:// en.wikipedia.org/wiki/Four_Candles/.

10 If you mis-parsed this sentence, that was the intention. Normally, though, speakers (writers) do their best to *reduce* ambiguity: as Paul Grice observed, participants in a conversation have the right to assume that they are involved in a cooperative exercise.

11 Axel and Kitziak (2007) discuss a related phenomenon found in German, involving putative cases of long-distance extraction (*wh*-movement), something that is normally grammatically unacceptable: the authors provide diachronic evidence, as well as data from a judgment study, to show that embedded V2 is better analysed in terms of parenthesis than of long-distance extraction.

12 Source: www.belfasttelegraph.co.uk/news/northern-ireland/video-heres-what-you-see-on-belfast-bus-tour-and-not-only-for-visitors-30944326.html.

13 The idea of chaining introduced here finds parallels with the more sophisticated notion 'multidominance' in current Minimalism; see, for example, de Vries (2009) for discussion.

14 This is not a completely artificial exercise. Take Vietnamese, for instance. There are the three major varieties of Vietnamese: Northern (Standard), based on the Hanoi dialect; Central, centred on Hue; and Southern, based on Ho Chi Minh City (Saigon). The Northern variety employs a six-way tonal distinction – neutral, high-rising, low-falling, low-rising, high-broken, low-broken. In the other two major varieties these tonal distinctions have been neutralised to a greater or lesser extent, with the Central dialect exhibiting the most far-reaching neutralisations. As a consequence, there is much more homophony in the Central dialect than in the other varieties. When listening to Central speakers, Northern speaker–listeners are able to compensate for this loss of information by relying on more contextual and pragmatic cues, but for second language learners – at least for *this* one – the absence of tone information means that Central dialect speakers are much harder to understand. The irony, of course, is that having fewer tones makes the Central dialect easier to pronounce, for the same learners.

15 Source: www.bbc.com/sport/football/29718349

When you read you begin with A B C
When you sing you begin with Do Re Mi
The first three notes just happen to be
Do Re Mi, Do Re Mi.

♫ Richard Rodgers and Oscar Hammerstein II, *Do-Re-Mi* (© 1959)

The *Sound of Music* has never been a favourite of mine. I liked it so little the first time I was first taken to see it at the cinema, at the age of five or six, that I yelled until my embarrassed mother took me home; in the intervening decades no number of Christmas repeats have further endeared it to me. In spite of this, like many people of my generation, I probably know the words to every tune, since it was Rodgers and Hammerstein's talent to create 'earworms' twenty or more years before the term was coined.[1] Still, you never know when lyrics will turn out to be useful …

As Oscar Hammerstein II wrote [it], the first three notes *just happen to be*: Do, Re, Mi. *Happen to be:* the choice of Do, Re, Mi appears quite arbitrary.[2] Certainly there's nothing intrinsic to the combination of [d] and [o:] that 'means' a lower note than [re:]. And if the name of the note can also be associated with a deer – a female deer, at that – this is also only due to an arbitrary convention of the English lexicon. English has a whole bunch of monosyllabic words that would have served as well for either referent. If this is not already clear, consider the Japanese version of the song's refrain:

(82)   Do wa donutsu no do   [do as in doughnuts]
        Re wa remon no re   [re as in lemon]
        Mi wa minna no mi   [mi as in *minna* ('everyone')]
        Fa wa faito no fa   [fa as in *fa-i-to* ('fight')]
        So wa aoi sora   [so as in blue *so-ra* ('sky')]
        Ra wa rappa no ra   [ra as in *ra-ppa* ('trumpet')]
        Shi wa shiawase yo   [shi as in *shi-awase* ('happiness')]
            Saa utaimashou   [well, let's sing the song]

Do-Re-Mi, translation by Peggy Hayama (© 2013 Richard Rodgers and Oscar Hammerstein II)

Table 4 *Sound~meaning correspondences in Vietnamese. Match the Vietnamese words (on the left) to their English equivalents (on the right).*[3]

Vietnamese	English
a. bận	1. 'table'
b. bạn	2. 'busy'
c. bàn	3. 'sell'
d. bán	4. 'friend'

The Japanese translation tells us a lot besides the fact that sounds and meanings are generally arbitrarily related. It indicates, for example, that <re> and <le> (= katakana レ) are not distinguished phonemically; that to a Japanese ear, the English loanword <fight> [fa.ı.to] and the Japanese word for trumpet 喇叭 [らっぱ] [ra.p.pa] contain three separate morae – see Introduction above – otherwise the lines would not scan; and that [tiː] (as opposed to [tʃi]) is not a possible Japanese syllable.

Ever since de Saussure, and probably before his students reified the notion by publishing his lectures as *Cours de linguistique générale* (1916), it has been accepted in Western linguistics that the relationship between sound and lexical meaning is largely an arbitrary one (*l'arbitraire du signe*): knowing the phonetic form of a mono-morphemic word does not allow one to infer its meaning, nor *vice versa*.

The arbitrariness of the sign seems particularly clear when we consider words in languages that are historically and areally unrelated to our own. As an example, try to match the four Vietnamese words on the left of Table 4 with the four English translations on the right. Unless you are a speaker of Vietnamese – or possibly, of an areally related language – in which case this is a trivial exercise, the only way that you will arrive at the correct pairings is by chance ($p = (0.25 \times 0.33 \times 0.5 =) 0.042$, in this case).

This doesn't mean that form~meaning correspondences are always unpredictable: within a particular language, words can inherit meaning by association with others; there may also be universals of SOUND SYMBOLISM in certain domains of meaning.

For example, even though Lewis Carroll's 'Jabberwocky' is regularly used to illustrate the arbitrariness of language, there is little question that, at least to an English reader,[4] the nonce words that Carroll creates are imbued with a certain kind of meaning:

> *'Twas brillig, and the slithy toves*
> *Did gyre and gimble in the wabe*

All mimsy were the borogroves
And the mome raths outgrabe.

Lewis Carroll, 'Jabberwocky' (*Through the Looking Glass,*
and What Alice Found There, 1871)

To appreciate how much the English version still conveys, it is useful to compare the verse above with its Modern Irish translation by Nicholas Williams[5] (which is 'all Jabberwocky [Greek?]' to the non-Irish reader):

Bri ollaic a bhí ann; bhí na tóibhí sleo
ag gírleáil 's ag gimleáil ar an taof.
B'an-chuama go deo na borragóibh
is bhí na rádaí miseacha ag braíomh.

A closer read of the original reveals that the non-lexical meaning of the lines derives not only from the grammatical categories (*was, did, in, and, the, were, -s*, etc.) but also from the relative sonority of the nonce words. It is not clear exactly what *toves* might be, but their name and the predicates associated with them *(slithy, gyre* and *gimble*), all sound placid, smooth and rounded, in virtue of their containing a high proportion of voiced plosives, voiced fricatives and nasal consonants. By contrast, the *Jabberwock*, in the verse below, with its claws that *catch*, and the *frumious Bandersnatch*, sound a good deal more hostile, thanks to a high proportion of syllables closed by voiceless stops and affricates [k, t, s, tʃ]. Even the malevolent *Jubjub bird* is most naturally pronounced as though it were written <Jupjup>, that is to say, with final de-voicing:

Beware the Jabberwock, my son!
The jaws that bite, the claws that catch!
Beware the Jubjub bird, and shun
The frumious Bandersnatch!

If your literary education owes more to J. K. Rowling than Lewis Carroll, you might consider instead the proper names in the *Harry Potter* novels: the 'good guys' include *Dumbledore, Dobby, Harry, Hermione, Ron (Weas[z]ley)*; by contrast, the list of 'bad guys' features *Snape*, the *Basilisk, Igor Karkaroff, Bellatrix Lestrange, Lucius* and *Draco Malfoy* and *Stan Shunpike*. Almost without exception, the benevolent characters' names involve sonorant consonants, mostly in open syllables, whereas the names of the evil characters are either 'foreign-sounding', or begin or end in voiceless consonants (often both).

Of course, none of these observations contradicts the basic premise of Saussurean arbitrariness: in any language, one can find thousands of words whose sonority is at odds with their meaning, *stab* and *fish* being fairly blatant cases. It does suggest, however, that sound symbolism might offer a kind of default in the pairing of sounds and meanings. This may even be a universal default. Recent research by Mutsumo Imai and her colleagues shows that English (non-Japanese-speaking) adults are able to guess the meaning of novel Japanese mimetics (e.g. *choka-choka, nosu-nosu*) at significantly higher than chance levels; their results also suggest that the prevalence of sound symbolism in Japanese child-directed speech facilitates young Japanese children's acquisition of verb-meaning; see Imai et al. (2008).

Even words that already have established lexical meanings in English can be co-opted on occasion to take on different ones, as with Sheridan's character Mrs Malaprop (whose creation gave rise to the term MALAPROPISM, and later spawned a niche industry of word-production experiments: see Fay and Cutler (1977), cf. Zwicky (1978/79), Vitevich (1997).[6] This ability of existing words to assume new meanings is richly illustrated in the 1920s song *On the Amazon*, popularised by Don McLean in the late 1970s:[7]

♫ Greatrex Newman, Clifford Grey and Vivian Ellis,
On the Amazon (Mr Cinders)[8]

Listening to this song, the educated listener is clearly aware that prophylactics, hypodermics and stalactites are not predatory animals, that zodiacs can't fly, and that *equinox* is a singular noun, but in the context of the song all of this lexical knowledge is cheerfully ignored, in order to appreciate the intended meanings.

The effects of sound symbolism notwithstanding, it remains true that most words *just happen to* mean what they mean. Yet this arbitrariness is theoretically significant in another respect, since it guarantees that most lexical sound~meaning pairings must be acquired through experience. And this is a crucial fact because vocabulary acquisition constitutes a non-trivial learning challenge, notwithstanding the implicitly dismissive references in some generativist literature. As we have seen already (Part II, Cases #2 and #3 above), words are more than simply labels for pre-existing concepts: significant aspects of the mapping between form and lexical semantics – as well as that between lexical semantic and conceptual representations – must be determined on a language-particular basis, and so must be acquired through interaction with ambient speech. Intensional meanings, supposing they exist as static constructs, must be largely externally derived, as must their pronunciations, on a case-by-case basis.

Moreover, as we shall see later (in G is for Grammar), a significant chunk of what is called (C)-SELECTIONAL INFORMATION varies arbitrarily from one predicate, and from one language variety, to the next. If these subtle and intricate form–meaning relationships can readily be acquired through exposure and interaction, then there is every reason to suppose that (no more subtle and intricate) syntactic generalisations might be acquired in the same way.

Notes

1 According to the Wikipedia entry, the term is a calque on the German expression *Ohrwurm*. Sachs (2007) dates its first English usage to the 1980s, at least twenty-one years after the musical's Broadway premiere.

2 It's not entirely arbitrary. The names of the notes don't *just happen to be* minimal CV syllables: for example, it is extremely unlikely that *Do* could be renamed *thootch*, otherwise the song would be virtually un-singable, not to mention un-translatable. Furthermore – though it may be coincidental – the initial triad sequence [ðʊ-eɪ-i], [ðʊ] being a slightly lower diphthong than [eɪ], which is in turn lower than [iː], in articulatory terms.

3 Answer to Table 4 matching quiz: a = 2, b = 4, c = 1, d = 3.

4 And to Alice, on reading the poem: '"It seems very pretty," she said, when she had finished it, "but it's rather hard to understand!" (You see she didn't like to confess, even to herself, that she couldn't make it out at all.) "Somehow it seems to fill my head with ideas – only I don't exactly know what they are! However, somebody killed something: that's clear, at any rate."'

5 Source: https://en.wikipedia.org/wiki/Jabberwocky.

6 A nice example from comedy is Ronnie Barker's 'Mispronunciation' sketch (www .google.co.jp/search?q=ronnie+barker+mispronunciation). The sketch is as interesting for what Ronnie Barker gets wrong about speech substitution, as for what he gets right.

7 The quoted charge of $60 per 500 copies from one of the rights holders to the lyrics of *On the Amazon* (25 per cent of the US-only rights) prohibits its reproduction here. This is especially unfortunate since all of the other worldwide rights were granted *gratis*. As with the other songs in this book where only the title is presented, full lyrics are freely available online on general lyrics websites.

8 Originally from the 1928 British stage musical *Mr Cinders*, adapted for film in 1934. (Another song from the musical, *Spread a Little Happiness*, was subsequently re-recorded by Sting for the soundtrack of *Brimstone and Treacle* (1982).)

12 C is for Competence~Performance, and Proficiency

HUGH LAURIE: [to screen] *Hello. We're talking about language.*

STEPHEN FRY: *Um... let me start a leveret here: there's language and there's speech. Um, there's chess and there's a game of chess. Mark the difference for me. Mark it please.*

HUGH LAURIE: [to screen] *We've moved on to chess.*

STEPHEN FRY: *Imagine a piano keyboard, eh, 88 keys, only 88 and yet, and yet, hundreds of new melodies, new tunes, new harmonies are being composed upon hundreds of different keyboards every day in Dorset alone. Our language, tiger, our language: hundreds of thousands of available words, frillions of legitimate new ideas, so that I can say the following sentence and be utterly sure that nobody has ever said it before in the history of human communication: 'Hold the newsreader's nose squarely, waiter, or friendly milk will countermand my trousers.' Perfectly ordinary words, but never before put in that precise order. A unique child delivered of a unique mother.*

HUGH LAURIE: [to screen] ...

STEPHEN FRY: *And yet, oh, and yet, we, all of us, spend all our days saying to each other the same things time after weary time: 'I love you', 'Don't go in there', 'Get out!', 'You have no right to say that', 'Stop it!', 'Why should I?', 'That hurt!', 'Help!', 'Marjorie is dead'. Hm? Surely, it's a thought to take out for cream tea on a rainy Sunday afternoon.*

> Stephen Fry and Hugh Laurie, 'Language Conversation'
> (*A Bit of Fry & Laurie*, 1990)

There is some irony in the fact that two of the most important pre-theoretical terms in classical generative linguistics[1] – COMPETENCE and PERFORMANCE – bear so distant a relationship to any popular understanding of their meaning. In other areas of human action, the expressions are interpreted quite differently. If we are told, for example, that someone is a competent driver or pianist, we conclude that their competence is directly expressed in relevant behaviours: a competent motorist is one who can drive a car smoothly and safely in normal traffic conditions, without further instruction, and (more often than not) without causing an accident; the competent pianist is able to play a piece of music of moderate complexity, if not perfectly, then at least without making too many crass errors. If a driver or piano player cannot drive or play to conventionally agreed standards of proficiency we do not judge them 'competent drivers' or 'competent musicians'. It seems nonsensical to say that someone is 'a competent driver in principle, but incompetent in practice'. Intuitively, then, there is a reasonably direct relationship between competence and proficiency; this is reflected in the fact that the corresponding adjectives *competent* and *proficient* are typically regarded as near-synonyms.

Correspondingly, a common understanding of the term *performance* is of some kind of above-average accomplishment. More than mere activity, the word *performance* implies prior practice and/or rehearsal: just as it is odd to say of a musician 'she gave a virtuoso performance, despite having never played the violin before', so it is odd to think of something that is completely natural or spontaneous – unscripted conversation, especially – as any kind of performance whatsoever. (Improvisation in music or comedy is generally a minor variation on a well-rehearsed theme, made to look spontaneous.) Whether in the theatre or in the street, it is usually the actor or street musician that gives the performance, not the audience in the interval, or the passers-by. Even in business-speak, performance implies some measure of extra effort. The assumption that performance involves a measure of artifice is further suggested by the fact that we say things such as 'that interview didn't show what she's really like, she was only performing for the video'.

As confirmation of this, it is worth comparing dictionary entries – even if consulting a dictionary is the first resort of the pedant or second language learner, and the only resort of someone who is both. The Merriam-Webster Dictionary and the Oxford English Dictionary (online editions) offer the following primary definitions of *competence* and *performance*, respectively (respectively):

(83) a. (MW) the ability to do something well: the quality or state of being competent;

b. (OED) the ability to do something successfully or efficiently.

(84) a. (MW) an activity (such as singing a song or acting in a play) that a person or group does to entertain an audience; the way an actor performs a part in a play, movie, etc.: the act of doing a job, an activity, etc.;

b. (OED) An act of presenting a play, concert, or other form of entertainment.

Competence as latent ability then, not 'tacit knowledge'; performance as a (prepared) act, not spontaneous behaviour. Both dictionaries also list the definitions of these words that are specific to linguistics and psychology, but this only underscores the fact that the words are used as terms of art rather than with their ordinary meanings. Which invariably leads to more confusion than insight.

That said, we recognise that there can be a mismatch between latent potential and actual ability in language use. This is especially obvious in the case of acquired neurological deficits. It is clear, for example, that Stephen Hawking, the author of countless books and articles, has an excellent command of language, despite being unable to produce any speech or writing without computer assistance. Intuitively, though, this kind of competence-performance mismatch is relatively 'low-level', related primarily to 'peripheral' motor systems, rather than to 'higher cognition'. (Whether the terms 'higher' and 'low-level' make any real psychological or neurological sense is a different matter: the point is that it seems natural to us to isolate linguistic competence from the other systems that subserve speech production.) Hawking's language production deficit is, we suppose, fundamentally different in kind from that of a global aphasic patient, or of a child with Down's Syndrome. In the latter cases, only sheer ideological commitment would lead anyone to conclude that competence was not impaired, as well as performance.

Within generative linguistics, however, there is no shortage of ideological commitment, much of it sheer: as a result, grammatical competence has come to be construed as an innate capacity that almost entirely divorced from typical linguistic behaviour (normal conversation, for example). First language acquisition theorists in the generative framework routinely assume that infants already have FULL COMPETENCE (in their first language) at birth, several years before their comprehension and production of spoken language even begins to approximate to that of adult native speakers; or indeed, before they show any comprehension or production ability whatsoever, in the ordinary understanding of these terms. Compare Crain and Pietroski (2001). Likewise, many second language acquisition theorists have few qualms about ascribing Full Competence to adult second language learners whose comprehension and production abilities diverge markedly from those of native speakers, attributing the gap between the two groups to 'performance factors'; see White (2003), Schwartz and Sprouse (1996), compare Part IV below, for a response. The clear implication is that, for these researchers, grammatical competence – what was once called 'tacit knowledge' – refers to some mental capacity that is largely dissociated from performance or proficiency.

Not everyone interested in language acquisition subscribes to this arcane view: many people, including myself, would prefer the position of John Lyons ([1965] 1996):

Linguistic competence is the knowledge of particular languages, in virtue of which I am able to produce and understand utterances in those languages.

> John Lyons, 'On competence and performance and related notions'
> (in Brown et al., eds, *Performance and Competence in Second Language Acquisition*, [1965] 1996)

However it is defined, if the notion of competence is to have any theoretical value, it should somehow be demonstrable: it should have empirical content. There must be some non-circular way of interrogating this knowledge such that we can distinguish between competent and less competent users of a language; otherwise, the notion is vacuous, reducing to 'whatever abilities allow (typically developing) children and second language learners to come to understand language in much the same way as adults'.

Competence-based experiments assign special priority to various kinds of 'grammaticality judgments', the implication being that such judgments reflect the competence of a speaker–listener better than other behavioural measures. Yet, as we have seen repeatedly – see especially Cases #5 and #6 above – there are good reasons to doubt this assumption. Indeed, the very idea of autonomous grammatical knowledge is open to question, as I discuss below, especially in G is for Grammar and J is for Judgment. See also Allen and Seidenberg (1999).

Consider now the term PROFICIENCY. It is uncontroversial that adult *second language learners* vary in their language proficiency: a multi-million-dollar language testing industry relies on, and helps to manufacture, this result. But what about native speakers? In other areas of human performance, we have no hesitation in ranking individuals according to their demonstrated ability in examinations or contests. Gaining a cycling proficiency badge doesn't make us Bradley Wiggins, being able to hold a tune doesn't challenge Kiri Te Kanawa, passing Grade IV violin doesn't put us on par with Itzhak Perlman. Yet such minor achievements are still achievements, distinguishing us from others without this level of cycling or musical attainment.

Nor is it the case that a few highly gifted individuals stand out from an otherwise unvariegated herd. The ability to run five kilometres in twenty minutes, for example, may be laughable if you are a professional track athlete,[2] but it nevertheless requires months of training, and a much higher level of fitness and training than is enjoyed by most readers of this book. Similarly, someone who can play a Beethoven sonata is quite evidently a more proficient – arguably, a more competent – pianist than someone who struggles with the work of Ludovico Einaudi; yet even to play *I Giorni* fluently requires a measure of skill and training well beyond that of the absolute beginner. When it comes to native speakers' command of everyday language, on the other hand, many researchers have a near-totalitarian blind spot about proficiency, which leads them to ignore *prima facie* evidence, and which precludes the possibility of obtaining any data that might contradict the assumption that native speakers 'know their language perfectly'.

No doubt, part of the problem here is methodological. In countless language acquisition studies, young children and/or second language learners are compared to (small) control groups of adult native speakers. In almost all of those studies that are published, the control group's results are at close to ceiling levels (> 90 per cent), while the test participants, on average, perform above chance but at significantly lower levels of correct responses than the control group. The conclusion which is usually drawn from these sorts of results is that native speakers' proficiency is uniformly high (essentially perfect), and that this is in virtue of having internalised the same grammatical knowledge: they have 'Full Competence' – *ne plus ultra*.

There are, of course, a range of alternative explanations. The first is that the native speaker controls in such studies may be unrepresentative of native speakers in general, inasmuch as they comprise a metalinguistically sophisticated, charmed, sub-group of English speakers (cf. Henrich, Heine and Norenzayan 2010). It happens that the adult participants in the majority of published studies are comparatively articulate twenty-one-year-old humanities students at more prestigious research universities, while the children involved are typically the equally special, often precocious, offspring of other academics attending university nurseries.

Step outside the Ivory Tower, or the Ivy League, however, and the gap between generativist assumptions and (informed) lay perceptions of grammatical competence becomes more serious – not only for linguists' credibility, but more crucially for social policy. For example, recent news stories in the UK have drawn attention to children starting primary schools with 'failing language skills'. These news stories are based on reports by educational charities and other NGOs, who find that many children – especially boys from poorer backgrounds – lack the language skills necessary to participate in, and to benefit from, classroom activities. The descriptors of 'average language' for five-year-olds reported in a recent *Save The Children Fund* publication (Read 2016) may be somewhat imprecise, but they are essentially grammatical in nature:

- [being] able to understand and talk with new people using well-formed sentences;
- ask[ing] lots of 'why' questions;
- [being] able to understand longer and more complicated sentences;
- [being] able to understand and use most everyday words that adults use;
- explain[ing] what has happened, and why, in an interesting way.

By these measures, 40 per cent of England's poorest boys lag fifteen months behind the average child; more significantly they are 'unlikely ever to catch up', according to the report. Assuming that English is the first language of the children surveyed, and that the sample is valid and representative of a particular segment of British society, the study clearly implies that a significant proportion of typical (i.e. non-disordered) language learners are in fact grammatically incompetent.

Setting this objection aside, there is a separate concern that in many cases ceiling effects are an experimental artifact; in other words, the bar has been set too low. The analogy to running makes this clear. If being able to run five kilometres in twenty-five minutes were taken as the measure of perfect running proficiency, then I would be in the same category as Kenenisa Bekele (see note), even though my best time puffing over this distance is approximately twice as slow as that of the current world record-holder. Obviously, no-one would establish such an easy target in athletics. So why is the bar often set low in acquisition studies? One banal reason is that an SLA research paper is unlikely to get published if the control group displays much less than 90 per cent accuracy: pilot studies where this obtains are generally revised, using different materials; alternatively, individual native speakers who perform badly – two standard deviations below the group mean, for instance – are excluded from the final analysis. See H is for Homogeneity (iii) for some further discussion. In this way, the quantitative results of psycholinguistic studies in second language acquisition tend to confirm the ideological assumption of the 'perfectly proficient native speaker'.

A more interesting possibility, of course, is that ceiling effects may generally quite accurately reflect adult native speakers' proficiency levels: perhaps native speakers really do have 'close to perfect' intuitions about grammatical acceptability. If this is the case, it *could* be – as competence-based theorists assert – a reflection of their perfect competence *ab initio*: Crain and Pietroski (2001). Or it could be the result of twenty years of linguistic experience, both in terms of exposure – more crucially – in terms of interaction; see Long (1996), Brown (2007), Gass and Selinker (2001).

The figure of 10,000 hours is often cited as the magic threshold of expertise – near-perfect performance of a particular skill. In a wide variety of domains of exceptional human performance, from violin playing to table tennis to opera singing, 10,000 hours of practice is deemed a near-sufficient condition for all sorts of virtuoso performance (see, for example, Syed 2011, and references therein). Of course, 10,000 hours of tennis practice alone will not automatically produce another Maria Sharapova, but the difference between county champion and Grand Slam winner may be indistinguishable if the proficiency test in question pits any trained sportswoman against the average Sunday tennis-player.

When we consider practice with language, 10,000 hours is a very low figure, by the most conservative estimates. Even if one assumes, counterfactually, that typical native speakers only start to use language at the age of four, and that they only actively engage in conversation for six hours per day, the average twenty-two year-old native speaker participant in a language experiment will already have notched up approximately 40,000 hours of implicit judgment time (6h*365d*18y), and will have crossed the 10,000 hour threshold by the age of nine. Even discounting all of the internal and external factors that make native speaker interactions much richer than those of typical second language learners – not to mention possible CRITICAL PERIOD effects – the purely numerical gulf of experience that separates native speakers from second language learners is vast. A typical Japanese learner of English receives perhaps two hours of English instruction each school week from the age of twelve or thirteen, with very little of that time being devoted to listening to or producing spoken language (typically much less than 50 per cent in high school). Granting another hour of extra practice each week, the typical twenty-two-year-old Japanese learner of English will have been exposed to just over 1,200 hours of (non-native) English (3h*40w*9y) by the time they participate in the same language experiment, almost none of which involves fluent interactions with peers. At that exposure rate, the Japanese learner would be eighty-five years old before they crossed the 10K hour threshold (except that they would long since have given up trying). Alternatively, if you were to construct an experimental control group by matching hours of exposure, then twenty-two-year-old Japanese second language learners should be paired with a group of four-and-a-half-year-old native speakers (that is to say, with children with six months of naturalistic exposure). Since one could not even elicit judgments from such very young participants using standard computer-based methodologies, it is clear which group would emerge as more proficient.

As ever, there is more than one way to interpret these observations. One could conclude that since adult second language learners actually do relatively well in spite of their limited experience – though not as well as adult native speakers – they must also have access to some *a priori* grammatical knowledge. Some second language researchers might even claim that late learners would perform identically to native speakers if it weren't for the inhibiting/ distracting effects of their first language (cf. Cook 1991). What's more, it is surely the case that other qualitative considerations count for at least as much as hours of interaction: this is confirmed by a huge number of studies (e.g. Kuhl, Tsao and Liu (2003), Roseberry (2009); see also Hambrich and Ullén (2000).[3] Nevertheless, the sheer magnitude of the difference in hours between native speakers and second language learners cannot be dismissed out of hand: one-tenth vs. four times the presumed threshold figure for expertise is a significant contrast in anyone's system of reckoning.

Nor can it be excluded that native speakers' judgments change with experience, that they become more – or less – proficient over time. Indeed, this is also almost certainly true. In the case of loss of proficiency, this erosion of competence is often called LANGUAGE ATTRITION, and is most usually observed in bilingual speakers whose non-native language has become their dominant one: see Schmid (2013, 2016). But if language proficiency varies over time, then logically, at any given point there must be less proficient native speakers. This in turn invites the inference that some native speakers may also be less *competent* than others, either at a particular stage of their lives, or perhaps throughout. See Part IV below.

It should be said that this apparently obvious 'fact' has been challenged. In the area of first language acquisition, for example, some researchers – most prominently, Stephen Crain and his colleagues – have claimed that young children under four years of age exhibit detailed knowledge of complex syntactic and semantic principles, including STRUCTURE-DEPENDENCE (Crain and Nakayama 1987), C-COMMAND (Crain 1991) and De Morgan's laws (Crain and Pietroski 2001): all of this knowledge is supposed to arise in the absence of experience. If such claims were well-supported empirically, then the issue of hours of exposure would become much less significant than it appears to be.

Step away from purely grammatical knowledge, however, and a different picture emerges. First of all, it is evident that not all aspects of language performance are subject to this 'perfect proficiency' filter: it's only with regard to syntax that one finds a rabid reaction. For example, no-one contests that there are huge variations in literary or stylistic ability: Pam Ayres is no Emily Dickinson, Dan Brown no Shakespeare.

> Most pertinently perhaps, J. K. Rowling is no Joseph Conrad. Born Józef Teodor Konrad Korzeniowski, Conrad first learned English as a young adult, and only moved to England in his early twenties: in spite of acquiring English as an adult, this L2 learner is widely regarded as one of the finest English novelists of the twentieth century.

The same wide discrepancies are observed in spoken language performance in the everyday use of the word, which is to say, in rehearsed theatrical performance. There is no interesting comparison, for instance, between Kenneth Branagh's delivery of the St Crispin's Day speech in *Henry V,* and a schoolboy performance of the same lines. Vocabulary size and overall reading comprehension skills are also acknowledged to vary widely among individuals, which is significant because vocabulary size has been clearly shown to co-vary with control of syntactically complex structures in acquisition, processing and aphasia; see Bates and Goodman (1997).

Putting these observations together, it seems only reasonable to suppose that social, cognitive and educational factors also play a crucial role in metalinguistic judgment ability. In fact, there is a fair amount of experimental support for this idea; see especially Gleitman and Gleitman (1979), Dabrowska and Street (2006), also J is for Judgment below. These various considerations point to the conclusion that native speakers do vary in all aspects of their language proficiency, including the ability to give (expert-like) grammaticality judgments. And if this is the case, then the assumption of uniform competence looks to be untenable, at best markedly at variance with observations of typical language users.

A recent introductory textbook on English grammar by Eppler and Ozón (2013) presents the following problem on the use of determiners:

We can immediately tell that the name Harry, *for example, is perfectly happy without a determiner; in fact most English names don't require a determiner, but some do. Which category do the following examples fall into?*

I am cycling along ____ Thames in ____ London, UK.

____ United States of America are bailing out the banks.

____ English Spiros uses is different to ___ English Svetlana uses.

Eva Duran Eppler and Gabriel Ozón, *English Words and
Sentences: An Introduction* (2013: 97)

What is most interesting about this extract is not in fact the issue of determiner placement, as tricky as this may be for many L2 learners. Instead, the concern is with two other anomalies. The first, rather minor, issue has to do with the non-native use of plural agreement in the second quoted example. For me, and I suspect for most native speakers, the term USA refers to a singular entity (the country of American citizens) and so must take singular agreement, unless the states are considered as individuals involved in collective action (e.g. 'The southern states include/*includes ...'). For the authors of the textbook, however, one of whom is an L1 Spanish speaker, this is evidently not the case. (Another small quibble is with the use of the preposition *to*, which is fine for me, but not for many other native speakers.)

The more significant question, however, is this: can one modify the third example and say, felicitously, 'The English I-language Spiros knows is different from the English Svetlana knows'? What about – assuming stereotypical English names – 'The English I-language baby Oliver knows is different from the English baby Olivia knows'? Competence-based linguists should deny this; others might disagree. In I is for Internalism and O is for Object of Study below, I'll argue that the others are right: however deep you dig, we all possess different Englishes.

One final point. It is intuitively clear to the lay reader that all three measures of linguistic knowledge – competence, performance and proficiency – are relative to a particular input or output modality. It is possible to speak a language well without being able to read it, as is typical of five-year-old native speakers of English (not to mention the vast number of speakers of languages lacking a writing system). But the converse also holds: many second language learners can read relatively fluently without being able to understand a (spoken) word. This is especially telling in the case of non-phonetic scripts: Mandarin and Cantonese speakers, for instance, can read the same Chinese menu, despite being unable to understand each others' speech – and even Japanese speakers can make a good stab at distinguishing grilled beef from stir-fried shrimp by checking the *kanji* on the same menu. For learners of languages with alphabetic systems or syllabaries, reading ability can far outstrip spoken language competence. As a second language learner of Swedish, I can hack my way through a Henning Mankell crime mystery with the help of a dictionary; it's also possible to work through the equivalent Danish text, with not much more difficulty. The difference is that I can understand spoken Swedish at a pinch. Spoken Danish, by contrast, might as well be Klingon or Finnish, thanks to the phonetic phenomenon of *stød*, which transforms most Danish syllables into the aural equivalent of cod-liver oil. (For a more scientific discussion, see Basbøll 2005.) Similar contrasts are found with German vs. Dutch, Spanish vs. Portuguese, RP vs. Geordie, and (along a historical dimension) Shakespeare vs. Chaucer.

Intelligibility is a continuous variable, not a discrete fact.

Of course, many psycholinguists discount competence in reading and writing, even as they depend on it to carry out their experiments. Yet the modality-specific nature of competence certainly extends to speaking vs. listening. For many language users, including young children, late learners and atypical language learners, there is a marked contrast – for some individuals, a vast discrepancy – between production and comprehension abilities. This is true of my knowledge of spoken Japanese, for example, and that of my youngest son; see Introduction. Most process-oriented psycholinguists acknowledge the importance of modality in their processing models: in fact, most models of language production are developed independently of comprehension data (and *vice versa*); see, for example, Alario et al. (2006). The same is true in applied linguistics, where language proficiency courses target different skills, independently of one another.

In competence-based acquisition research, on the other hand, it is not unusual to find studies that adopt a modality-neutral approach to grammatical competence. On this view, either the child knows a grammatical property, or she doesn't: passing any kind of test – be it a comprehension task or a test of production – in a way that is comparable to that of an adult native speaker is taken as sufficient evidence of complete internalised knowledge. And comprehension trumps production almost every time: where a language learner is shown to be able to judge sentences correctly, even where their production is systematically non-native-like, competence-based researchers have no qualms in attributing perfect grammatical knowledge to that learner, while at the same time writing off the production failures as 'mere performance' or 'processing errors': see e.g. Hiramatsu and Lillo-Martin (1998), Clahsen and Felser (2006).

From a naïve perspective, this is puzzling: reverting to our opening analogy, it seems extraordinary to say that someone who can barely play a major scale on the piano knows how to play a Chopin nocturne – simply because they can judge whether or not someone else has performed it well.

In conclusion, let's return to the Fry & Laurie excerpt quoted at the beginning of this section. As Stephen Fry so perfectly observes in the sketch, there is a disconnect between the apparently infinite affordances of language ('new melodies, new tunes, new harmonies are being composed upon hundreds of different keyboards every day in Dorset alone') and the 'same things time after weary time' – what most people are actually able to produce, unprompted. This is paradoxical if we all have within us a uniform grammatical competence: inside every chihuahua, as it were, a proud and savage wolf. Yet the mystery is easily, if somewhat depressingly, resolved if there exist two kinds of competence: Lyons' highly variable 'personal competence', on the one hand, and a much richer, inter-subjective and inherently social *langue,* on the other.

It is this idea of a separation between competence and langue that I will develop in the upcoming chapters, especially in H is for Homogeneity, I is for Internalism and J is for Judgment.

Notes

1 This was true until recently. Biolinguistics – with its focus on the initial state of grammar, and the evolutionary precursors to natural language syntax – has little to say about end-state competence, and even less about performance.
2 At the time of writing, the current 5,000 m world records stand at 12:37.35 (men's: Kenenisa Bekele, 2004) and 14:11.15 (women's: Tirunesh Dibaba, 2008).
3 See, for example, the *New York Times* article by Douglas Quenca: 'Quality of words, not quantity, is crucial to language skills, study finds' (16 October 2014).

13 F is for Functions of Language

– Avez-vous jamais été en France?, monsieur Martin, dit Candide.

– Oui, dit Martin, j'ai parcouru plusieurs provinces. Il y en a où la moitié des habitants est folle, quelques-unes où l'on est trop rusé, d'autres où l'on est communément assez doux et assez bête, d'autres où l'on fait le bel esprit; et, dans toutes, la principale occupation est l'amour; la seconde, de médire; et la troisième de dire des sottises.

'Have you ever been to France, Monsieur Martin?' asked Candide.

'Yes,' said Martin, 'I've travelled around various parts of the country. There are some places where half the population is mad, others where they're crafty, others where they are to a man fairly docile and rather stupid, still others where they're full of wit: and, in every province, the main preoccupations are love-making, mudslinging and gossiping, in that order.'

Voltaire, Candide, chapter XXI (1759)

'It is a truth, universally acknowledged …' that the core function of language is to transmit propositional content from one person's mind into the mind of another: or, as the subtitle of Pim Levelt's seminal work, *Speaking*, has it, the function of the language production system is to translate 'from intention to articulation' (Levelt 1989). Universally acknowledged it might be, yet there is a fair amount of evidence to suggest that this is not a truth, but a rather mistaken assumption. (Jane Austen was being ironic, too, of course.) Indeed, to imagine that the purpose of language is to communicate literal messages precisely is rather like believing that the purpose of a knife is to save lives. In the hands of the skilled practitioner (the poet or surgeon, respectively) this may be true – at least on those happy occasions when skill triumphs over chance – but most of us are not lucky poets or surgeons, and the language we use is but a weak approximation to the thoughts and feelings that we wish to convey. As Flaubert noted, in *Madame Bovary*:

Comme si la plénitude de l'âme ne débordait pas quelquefois par les métaphores les plus vides, puisque personne, jamais, ne peut donner l'exacte mesure de ses besoins, ni de ses conceptions, ni de ses douleurs, et que la parole humaine est comme un chaudron fêlé où nous battons des mélodies à faire danser les ours, quand on voudrait attendrir les étoiles.

The fullness of the soul may at times overflow in the most vapid of metaphors, for none of us can ever relay the just measure of their needs or ideas or sorrows. Human speech is like a cracked kettle on which we beat out rhythms for dancing bears, when instead we long to make music that will melt the stars.

Gustave Flaubert, *Madame Bovary*, part 2, chapter 12 (1857)

Naturally, this does not mean that language cannot be used to transmit propositional content. Of course it can, it's just not especially well designed for that purpose.

Spoken language betrays far more than it conveys. Words fail us at both ends of the communicative spectrum: they are either insufficient or redundant. When lovers' eyes meet, when the penitent prays for absolution, when strangers comfort each other in the face of tragedy, what is communicated is beyond language. Words just get in the way; silence (as they say) speaks volumes. As so often, songwriters and poets have expressed it better:

♫ Snow Patrol, *Chasing Cars* (2006)

♫ Depeche Mode, *Enjoy the Silence* (1990)

George Steiner identified the crux of the matter, over fifty years ago:

Language can only deal meaningfully with a special, restricted segment of reality. The rest, and it is presumably the much larger part, is silence.

George Steiner, 'The retreat from the word' (*Kenyon Review*, 1961)

At the other end of the communicative spectrum – moving from the ineffable to the redundant – the universal format of an IKEA instruction sheet, of international road signs, the shared properties of second language learners' compensatory gestures all demonstrate in their own ways that even fairly complex instructions, requests and warnings can be explained wordlessly. Hence, the notion that the prime function of language is to communicate propositional content is at least open to question. This is especially apparent when we consider so-called 'cool medium' languages such as Japanese, where understanding the simplest message requires considerably more inferential effort on the part of the speaker than is needed in a 'hot' language like English: see Huang (1984).[1]

It is not simply the fact that what is most important is largely inexpressible: as we saw in Cases #2 and #3 above, even those ideas that can be adequately conveyed in one language are inextricably embedded in the form–meaning mappings of that particular variety. Perhaps more than any other phenomenon, literary translation gives the lie to the idea that language is a simple carrier of propositional content. The paradox of translation is that what *can* be translated is largely redundant, and what *should* be is usually lost, especially when it comes to poetry – a medium that the Russian–American linguist Roman Jakobson considered to be 'untranslatable … by definition' (Jakobson [1959] 2000). Any fool armed with a dictionary can render a foreign instruction manual for an electrical appliance into comprehensible English – probably no-one will read it anyway – but even a bilingual poet cannot capture the essence of Baudelaire or Dante or Al-Mutanabbi. Translating literature (or poetry or song) is like cleaning silver with sandpaper. Exceptional translations, such as Mike Poulton's (2005) version of Schiller's *Don Carlos,* are hardly translations at all: they are faithful re-imaginings.

Admittedly, languages (including sign languages) have some distinct advantages over icons and gestures, or other systems of communication, when it comes to conveying literal messages. The twentieth-century structuralist linguist Charles Hockett pointed to a number of crucial 'design features' that, he supposed, distinguish natural languages from other forms of communication, especially animal communication.[2] These include: DISPLACEMENT (the ability to talk about things beyond the 'here-and-now', to report past events, to plan future ones, to talk about objects and events that may not, or cannot, come to pass – conditionals, counterfactuals and other unreal events); PRODUCTIVITY (the possibility of producing and understanding entirely novel utterances, by recombining known words using syntactic rules, or by creating new words by using morphological rules, e.g. *purposeless-ness-less-ness* (see below)); and ARBITRARINESS (though see B is for Arbitrariness above). When combined with the property of SPECIALISATION, the observation that language appears to serve no other obvious external function, these design features are weakly consistent with the idea that the function of language is to facilitate literal communication.

But it hardly proves the case. While it may be less ridiculed than Dr Pangloss's interpretation of the external function of the nose, the communicative interpretation of language function has an undeniably *post hoc* air about it:

> *'Il est démontré, disait-il, que les choses ne peuvent être autrement; car tout étant fait pour une fin, tout est nécessairement pour la meilleure fin. Remarquez bien que les nez ont été faits pour porter des lunettes; aussi avons-nous des lunettes.'*

> *'It has been demonstrated,' he said, 'that things cannot be other than they are; since everything has been created for an end, it is necessarily for the best end. Observe, that the nose has been formed to carry spectacles – thus we have spectacles.'*

> Voltaire, *Candide*, chapter I (1759)

Chomsky is especially critical of any communicative basis to language – either synchronically, or in its evolution. In his 2010 CNRS lecture, which has already featured in previous discussions, one finds the following, contemptuous, assertion:

There isn't any reason to believe that human language is a communication system. In fact, there's strong reason to disbelieve it.

Noam Chomsky, *Poverty of Stimulus: Some Unfinished Business* (2010)

As is often the case when rejecting commonly held beliefs, Chomsky offers this comment without any empirical justification. The claim goes unsubstantiated, and seems little short of crazy – until one realises that for Chomsky 'human language' only refers to Universal Grammar, and that Universal Grammar – by 2010, when he gave this lecture – amounts to little more than the recursive function *Merge*. Given such a narrow construal of human language, almost everyone would concur: UG assuredly has nothing whatsoever to do with communication or communicative capacity. It is only in this light that the assertion makes sense.

Still, even if Chomsky's position is extreme, it could still be the case that the communicative function of language is secondary, that language plays some other primary role. An alternative interpretation that is more consistent with linguistic INTERNALISM (see below) has it that the function of language is to permit a certain kind of complex thought.[3] A mind without language – or so the argument goes – might be able to represent first-order (true) beliefs about invisible objects, such as '(I believe that) there is still some cheese left in the fridge', but without recursive syntax we would be unable to represent second- or third-order beliefs, especially false beliefs, such as 'I know [that Jane believes [that there is still some cheese left in the fridge]]', intuited in a context where – unbeknownst to Jane – I had finished off the cheese some time previously; see, for example, Wellman, Cross and Watson (2001) for some discussion.

The idea that knowledge of hierarchical phrase-structure is required to support higher-order predication is encouraged by the observation that the ability to pass so-called THEORY OF MIND tests emerges clearly in young children's minds at around the same time as the ability to produce embedded clauses (de Villiers and Pyers 2002). (There's a complex sentence you won't read again.) Other kinds of thoughts too, may depend crucially on SYNTACTIC RECURSIVITY, the property of embedding grammatical constituents within others of the same kind, as illustrated in (85):

(85)   a. Mary [$_{VP}$ claimed [$_{CP}$ that John [$_{VP}$ believed [$_{CP}$ that Richard had not [$_{VP}$ arrived yet]]]]] (VP~CP recursion)
       b. [$_{NP}$ The ghost [$_{PP}$ of [$_{NP}$ a trace [$_{PP}$ of [$_{NP}$ a pale imitation [$_{PP}$ of you]]]]]] (NP~PP recursion)
       c. [$_{NP}$ [$_{NP}$ [$_{NP}$ [$_{NP}$ John's] friend's] brother's] hamster's] untimely disappearance]]]]] (NP (DP) recursion)

See v is for von Humboldt for further discussion of recursivity. Against this, it has been argued that languages vary widely in the types of recursion they permit; specifically, Everett (2005, 2009) makes the controversial claim that the grammar of Pirahã, a language of the Amazon, lacks nested recursion altogether: see also Evans and Levinson (2009), cf. Nevins, Pesetsky and Rodriguez (2009).[4] And even if it turned out that we needed language to think certain kinds of thoughts, it wouldn't follow – except for a Panglossian – that this is its prime function. It is equally possible that it is a serendipitous side effect of grammatical evolution.

Whatever the function of language may turn out to be, it might seem to be a very poor substitute for telepathy. Life is a perennial – and usually vain – struggle to find just the right words to express what we want to say: if we find them at all, it is generally 'a day late and a dollar short'.

I have really no clear idea what the answer is: it is unlikely that there is one answer. Forced to choose, though, I'd guess that John Keating, the protagonist in Tom Shulman's screenplay *Dead Poets Society*, had it right when he declared that language had been invented for one purpose only: to woo women.[5] Keating's admittedly sexist assertion is at least consistent with Voltaire's assessment of what matters to ordinary people, at the outset to this section. And it makes as much intuitive sense as any other single-factor explanation. Outside of contexts of extreme sexual violence, drunkenness or other loss of control, almost all of you who are reading this book owe your existence to the conversations your biological parents had in the minutes, hours, days and weeks leading to your conception. Beyond basic instinct, sexual attraction owes more to language than to wealth or power: there is a direct causal link between some now-decades-old chat-up line and your being here to read these words. The casual comment has a lot to answer for, as does its failure: if we had only thought of the right words …

♫ The Cure, *Pictures of You* (1990)

If a smart remark can lead to your birth, words can just as surely prevent it. It is language – in the shape of informed consent – that breaks the link between conception and birth. And after you are born, what you or someone else may say can lead directly to your death. Not just through conventional speech acts, such as the pronouncement of a death sentence: even a subtle slip in the wrong context can have lethal consequences. The following comic scene from William Boyd's *Waiting for Sunrise* illustrates just such a possibility:

'… *And all the while, you'd ordered me killed.*'

Massinger looked a bit sick and grimaced.

'*Actually, I didn't, in so many words. Madame Duchesne was going on and on, raising her suspicions about you. So I said –*' *he paused.* '*My French is a bit rusty, you see. I don't know if I made myself totally clear to her. I tried to reassure her and I said words to the effect that we cannot assume that he – you – is not a traitor. It's unlikely, but in the event it was confirmed, you would be treated without compunction.'*

'Pretty difficult to say that in French even if you were fluent.' I said.

'I was a bit out of my depth, you're right. I got confused with "traître" and "traiter", I think.' He looked at me sorrowfully. 'I have this ghastly feeling I said you were a "traître sans pitié" …'

'That's fairly unequivocal. A "merciless traitor".'

'Whereas I was trying to say—'

'I can see where the confusion arose.'

William Boyd, *Waiting for Sunrise* (2012: 289–90)

For more thoughts on language function, see I is for Internalism.

Notes

1 Huang (1984) cites Ross (1982) for the original insight that McLuhan's distinction could be applied to grammatical properties. After only a few years of learning Japanese badly, I have come to the (not entirely flippant) conclusion that Japanese people intuit conversations, that they use spoken language only as a kind of cultural ornamentation, much as the Catholic Church used Latin before Vatican II. If there is any truth to this, it may also hold of other highly homogeneous cultures.

2 See www.revolvy.com/main/index.php?s=Charles F. Hockett&uid=1575.

3 In addition, there are a range of other externalist approaches to language, including those that stress its social and semiotic functions over message-transmission: the work of M. A. K. Halliday (systemic functional linguistics) offers one such approach. It is fair to say that such approaches have received scant attention from psycholinguists, perhaps because of the complexity involved: for Halliday, a semiotic system is one that is simultaneously physical, biological, social and semiotic – four orders of increasing complexity; see e.g. Halliday (2005: 68).

4 The following blog article by Daniel Harbour and associated comments/links offer a useful set of perspectives: http://daniel-harbour.blogspot.jp/2012/03/chomsky-piraha-and-turduckens-of-amazon.html.

5 The precise wording has been changed, for copyright reasons. The screenplay is available in various locations, online.

> *No important national language, at least in the Occidental world, has*
> *complete regularity of grammatical structure, nor is there a single logical*
> *category which is adequately and consistently handled in terms of linguistic*
> *symbolism.*
>
> Edward Sapir, 'The problem of an international
> auxiliary language' ([1907] 2008: 271)

Even outside of generative linguistics, it is almost universally assumed that language users have internalised a grammar, comprising a set of grammatical *rules* that are represented independently of the mental lexicon, and which are also – to some extent at least – independent of 'lower-level' rules of syntactic production and comprehension (parsing rules). The following lines from the Swedish linguist Lars-Gunnar Andersson (1998) exemplify the statements found in virtually every introductory textbook:

> *Let us assume that our knowledge of language consists of the following three*
> *parts: grammar, vocabulary and rules of usage. This means that if you have English as*
> *your first language, you have an English grammar in your head. This grammar makes*
> *your pronunciation and your word order similar to that of other English speakers. You*
> *also have an English vocabulary at your disposal. We don't always find the right words*
> *when we speak, but very often we do (compare how hard it is to find the right word*
> *when speaking a foreign language). You also have a number of rules of usage at your*
> *disposal. These rules tell you when to speak and when to keep quiet, how to address a*
> *person, and how to conduct a telephone conversation.*
>
> Lars Gunnar Andersson, 'Some languages are harder than
> others' (in Bauer and Trudgill, eds, *Language Myths*, 1998)

These assumptions are broadly consistent with the competence-based model of language comprehension that was schematised in Figure 6 above, and which is reproduced here for convenience. There are to be sure important differences between Andersson's rules of 'pronunciation' and the generativist conception of phonology; conversely, Figure 6 does not incorporate social rules of usage. Nevertheless, both perspectives on a speaker's knowledge of language endorse

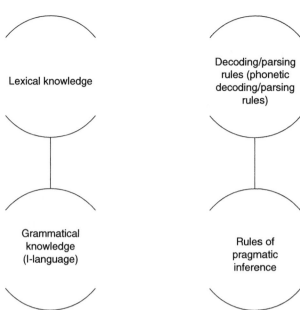

Figure 6 Components of language comprehension: language, perception and Level 1.5.

the notion of grammar as something coherent and dissociable from arbitrary, stored, lexical knowledge (vocabulary).[1]

Nevertheless, despite its common currency, the idea that anyone has internalised a grammar is not obviously correct. It is uncontestable that speakers of a language have internalised *grammatical information*, but any amount of grammatical information – grammatical knowledge, even – does not a grammar make. Not an autonomous one, at any rate. Hopefully, this distinction will become clearer as we proceed.

It turns out that a good deal of what counts as grammatical knowledge must be stored in the lexicon for the simple reason that it is associated with specific lexical items, and that these associations vary from one language to the next, often rather arbitrarily. In this chapter, I'll consider two uncontested instances of 'lexical–grammatical knowledge': GRAMMATICAL GENDER and CATEGORIAL SELECTION (also known as SUBCATEGORISATION).

Take gender first. Notwithstanding some intriguing, but largely peripheral, effects of grammatical gender on semantic construal – see Boroditsky, Schmidt and Phillips (2003), further discussed in Segel and Boroditsky (2011) – there is pretty clear evidence that the classification of inanimate nouns in most Indo-European languages cannot be predicted on the basis of meaning. Table 5

Table 5 *Variation in gender assignment: Spanish, German, Russian.*

English	Spanish	German	Russian
apple	la manzana (f.)	der Apfel (m.)	яблоко (n.)
boot	la bota (f.)	der Stiefel (m.)	ботинок (m.)
fox	el zorro (m.)	der Fuchs (m.)	лиса (f.)
moon	la luna (f.)	der Mond (m.)	луна (f.)
star	la estrella (f.)	der Stern (m.)	звезда (f.)
baby	el bebé (m.)	das Baby (n.)	ребенок (m.)
bridge	el puente (m.)	die Brücke (f.)	мост (m.)
fork	el tenedor (m.)	der Gabel (m.)	вилка (f.)
mouse	el ratón (m.)	die Maus (f.)	мышь (f.)
sun	el sol (m.)	die Sonne (f.)	солнце (n.)
death	la muerte (f.)	der Tod (m.)	смерть (f.)
house	la casa (f.)	das Haus (n.)	дом (m.)

displays a number of common, common nouns that are classified as 'feminine' in one European language but as 'masculine' or 'neuter' in another: in this list, there is not a single instance of across-the-board unanimity.

It is not that gender classification is entirely random, just that lexical meaning is an extremely poor predictor of gender assignment. In German, for example, gender choice is principally determined by morphological and/or phonological shape: almost all stems ending in -*e* (schwa), and all words ending in the nominalising suffixes -*ung*, or -*heit*, or -*keit* are feminine, while nouns formed with the diminutive suffixes -*chen*, -*lein*, as well as many loanwords, are obligatorily neuter. It is for this reason that *Mädchen* 'girl' and *Baby* are neuter, in spite of the fact that girls and babies are obviously animate referents.[2] On the other hand, nothing prepares the L2 learner for the fact that *Wurst* 'sausage', *Maus* 'mouse' and *Butter* are feminine, whereas *Durst* 'thirst' is masculine, and *Haus* 'house' and *Futter* 'animal feed', neuter. See Corbett (1991) for a detailed survey and analysis, while Ibrahim (1973) offers an interesting discussion from a historical perspective. Clearly, this type of quasi-arbitrary grammatical knowledge must be lexically stored, as must the associated inflectional paradigms discussed in Chapter 2 (Tables 1a and 1b above).[3]

Numerous studies have investigated how gender information is acquired and whether/how it is used in language processing, for example, in narrowing down the range of possible noun candidates in spoken word recognition. See van Berkum (1996), cf. Dahan et al. (2000), Bölte and Connine (2004), Spinelli, Meunier and Seigneuric (2006), amongst others; for gender processing by L2 learners, see Sabourin (2003). In all of these studies, the consensus is that gender information must be lexically stored.

The same unpredictableness – or unpredictability? see Aronoff (1976) – applies to grammatical NUMBER-MARKING in English, regarding the question of which nouns may be pluralised and which cannot. It is worth noting that the prescriptive rule taught in second language classrooms, namely, that mass nouns cannot be pluralised – is quite inadequate. Some mass nouns, such as *bread, wine, corn, sand, salt* and *earth* may be pluralised where they denote different types of bread, wine, corn, and so on (86a); other nouns, including *evidence, research* and *information* all resist pluralisation in any context – to second language learners' dismay and frustration (86b,c):

(86) a. 'As a general rule of thumb, pick a lighter bread to go with lighter wines, and heavier <u>breads</u> with more complex wines.'[4]

      b. 'The boy soon developed very good relations with the psychologist, whom he called his "friend". He began to talk to her without falling into his <u>rages</u>.' (cf. *his angers)

      c. 'When defendants are held under harsh conditions, they often will take <u>their frustrations</u> out on their attorney.' (cf. *dismays)

Google Ngram searches reveal that the plural noun *frustrations* is virtually unattested from 1800 to 1920, and that it only rose above a very low threshold in the post-war period. This suggests that for English speakers of the 1930s *frustrations* would have been as grammatically unacceptable as *dismays* is currently. See H is for Homogeneity below.

    A similar arbitrariness affects categorial selection, though *afflicts* might be a better term. In Present Day English, for instance, the verb *say* 'takes' an optional prepositional phrase as an indirect object, together with an obligatory clausal complement, and in that order. Compare (87a) with (87b):

(87) a. She said ([to me]) [that she was waiting for the right opportunity].

      b. She said that she was waiting for the right opportunity (*[to me]).

This arrangement of complements contrasts with that of the (semantically similar) verb *tell*, which requires an 'accusative' indirect object, followed by either a clausal complement or a noun-phrase object; (88a) vs. (88b). Notice that the indirect object of *tell* is optional, where *tell* means 'bear witness', as in (88c); also, that there is an interaction between the position of the indirect object and the semantics of the direct object noun-phrase (89a,b):

(88) a. She told *([me]) [that she was waiting for the right opportunity].

      b. She told?(me) [the whole story].

      c. The scars on his feet told (?us) [a different story].

(89) a. She told her friends [the story/the truth/the plot/?the facts/*the events].
      b. She told the story/?the truth/??the plot/??the facts/*the events to her friends. (Cf. She related the events to her friends.)

Other predicates make even more fine-grained distinctions. Take the predicate WANT, and its cross-linguistic correlates. The English verb *want* selects for a non-finite complement clause regardless of whether the subject of the embedded clause is co-referential with the main clause subject – compare (90a) with (90b); English *want* also rigidly disallows finite clausal complements, as demonstrated by the unacceptability (*90c). Things are different in Dutch and Spanish: whereas complements with co-referential subjects are infinitival as in English (91a/92a), complements with *non*-co-referential subjects are obligatorily finite, with the embedded verb being realised as a subjunctive form in Spanish, and most other Romance varieties: cf. (91b/92b). A third pattern is observed in Greek, Bulgarian, Romanian and other languages of the Balkan SPRACHBUND ('Linguistic Area'): in these languages, the complement clause must be finite even with co-referential subjects, owing to the fact that the verbs of this region have rather carelessly mislaid their infinitival forms; see (93/94).

(90) a. I want <u>to leave</u> you (here).
      b. I want you <u>to leave</u> me (here).
      c. *I want that you <u>leave</u> me (here).

(91) a. Ik wil je <u>loslaten</u>.
      b. *Ik wil je me <u>loslaten</u>.
      c. Ik wil dat je me <u>loslaat</u>.

(92) a. Quiero <u>dejar te</u> aquí.
      b. *Quiero tú <u>dejar me</u> aquí.
      c. Quiero que (tú) me <u>dejes</u> aquí.

(93) a. *искам (аз/ме) те остав тук.[5]
          iskam az/me te octav tuk
          'I want to leave you here.'

      b. *искам ти ме остав тук
          iskam tu me octav tuk
          'I want you to leave me here.'

      c. искам да ме оставиш тук.
          iskam da me octavish tuk
          'I want that you leave me here.'

      d. искам да те оставя тук   (cf. 90–92a)
          iskam da te ostavya tuk
          *'I want that I leave you here.'

(94) a. *θέλω σε   αφή εδώ.
          I.want you leave here
          'I want to leave you here.'
      b. *θέλω (θα/σας) (με) αφή εδώ.
          I.want you   me leave here
          'I want you to leave me here.'
      c. θέλω να   με αφήσεις εδώ.
          I.want that me you.leave here
          'I want that you leave me here.'
      d. θέλω να   σε αφήσω εδώ.
          I.want that you I.leave here
          'I want that I leave you here.'

Finally, consider Vietnamese. The examples in (95) and (96) demonstrate that
Vietnamese lacks the inflectional morphology that readily distinguishes finite
from non-finite forms in most Indo-European languages: this morphological
deficiency makes it hard to determine whether it is more like Greek *sans* inflection, or like English. It turns out, however, that Vietnamese actually patterns with
Dutch and Spanish – the examples in (96) show that independent clausal tense
markers and complementisers are only possible with non-co-referential complements. Yet at first blush Vietnamese seems to pattern like English (excluding
the elements in parenthesis). Taking a less Eurocentric perspective, then, one
might say that the English pattern is more like Vietnamese than it is like any of
the languages to which it is more closely historically or areally related:

(95) a. Tao   muốn bỏ   mày   lại đây.
          PRN.1SG want leave PRN.2SG PREP here
          'I want to leave you here.'
      b. Tao muốn mày   bỏ   tao   lại đây.
          1SG want PRN.2SG leave 1 PRN.1SG PREP here
          'I want you to leave me here.'

(96) a. Tao   muốn (*là) (*sẽ) bỏ   mày   lại   đây.
          PRN.1SG want COMP FUT   leave PRN.2SG PREP here
          'I want to leave you here.'
      b. Tao muốn (là) mày   (sẽ) bỏ   tao   lại đây.
          1SG want COMP PRN.2SG FUT leave 1 PRN.1SG PREP here
          'I want you to leave me here.'

These varying patterns of WANT complementation are summarised in Table 6.
    Faced with such variability, the inescapable conclusion is that this kind of
selectional information must be stored for every predicate (in every language

Table 6 *Cross-linguistic variation in complement clauses with* WANT.

Language/ Complement clause type	(a) non-finite complement with co-referential subject	(b) non-finite complement with non-co-referential subject	(c) finite complement with non-co-referential subject	(d) finite complement with co-referential subject
English	✓	✓	*	*
Dutch	✓	*	✓	*
Spanish	✓	*	✓	*
Bulgarian	*	*	✓	✓
Greek	*	*	✓	✓
Vietnamese	✓	*	✓	*

variety).[6] This is grammatical knowledge to be sure, but it is not autonomous grammatical knowledge of the sort implied by Figure 6 above; instead, it is inextricably linked to some or other lexical predicate.

As it turns out, subcategorisation is only the thin end of the wedge, being no more than a special case of the notion 'in construction with'. Working out from subcategorisation, we observe cross-linguistic differences in what is known as AUXILIARY SELECTION. In most of the Romance and Germanic languages – as well as in earlier stages of English ('The Lord is come') – the present perfect forms of verbs exhibit a well-studied alternation between those predicates that 'select' for a form of HAVE (*avoir, avere, haben, hebben*, etc.), and those that 'select' for a BE-type auxiliary (*être, essere, sein, zijn*, etc.).[7]

In a 2000 article, Antonella Sorace documents what she terms the AUXILIARY SELECTION HIERARCHY, a continuum observed in both language families. At one end of this continuum are found intransitive verbs whose subject arguments are interpreted as having a large amount of control or volition: these verbs, exemplified in (97), are associated with HAVE auxiliaries, particularly where the verb itself denotes a pure activity rather than change of state or location. At the other end, we find telic verbs denoting change of state, particularly those with non-controlling subject arguments: these usually collocate with BE auxiliaries, as in (98).

(97) a. J'ai chanté.   (canonical HAVE verbs)
      b. (Io) ho cantato.
      c. Ich habe gesungen.
         I have sung
         'I have sung.'

(98) a. Elle est arrivée.   (canonical BE verbs)
      b. (Ella) è arrivata.

c. Sie <u>ist</u> angekommen.
   she is arrived
   'She has (literally <u>is</u>) arrived.'

In the middle of the semantic range (where most intransitive verbs are to be found) the picture is much more mixed, with verbs that select BE in one language variety selecting HAVE in another. The following extract from Sorace's paper gives a flavour of the unpredictability of auxiliary selection in this middle region:

In French, verbs of existence consistently select auxiliary avoir. *In German, the majority select* haben *but some exhibit variation, as can be seen in the examples in [(99)], which include verbs of spatial configuration ... Verbs showing similar behaviour include* bestehen *'consist of',* gehören *'belong'. Dutch exhibits some limited variation in auxiliary selection within this verb class: while most verbs of position [(100a)] and existence [(100b)] select* hebben, blijken *('seem') selects the auxiliary* zijn *[(100c)] ... For Dutch and German, the exception is the verb* BE *itself, although [even here] Lieber & Baayen (1997: 815) point out that there is regional variation in Dutch with respect to auxiliary choice with* zijn. *[example numbers changed: NGD]*

Antonella Sorace, 'Gradients in auxiliary selection with
intransitive verbs' (*Language*, 2000: 870)

(99)   a. Das Buch hat mir   gefallen.
          the book   has to.me pleased
          'I liked the book.'

       b. Das hat mir   genügt.
          that has to-me sufficed
          'That was enough for me.'

       c. Das Buch ist/hat auf dem Boden gelegen.
          the book   is/has on the ground   lain
          'The book was lying on the floor.'

       d. Ich bin/Ich habe von ihr abgehangen.
          I am/I have   from her depended
          'I depended on her.'

(100) a. Het beeld heeft op de tafel gestaan.
          the picture has on the table stood
          'The picture stood [sic] on the table.'

       b. Het magische zwaard heeft echt bestaan.
          the magic   sword has   really existed
          'The magic sword really existed.'

       c. Sofie is en goede docente gebleken.
          Sofie is a good teacher   seemed
          'Sofie seemed to be a good teacher.'

As if things weren't involved enough, the picture is further complicated by the fact that the addition of other phrasal constituents, notably directional phrases, may result in a change from HAVE to BE. However, this only occurs in some varieties and/or with certain predicates, and/or in more informal contexts of utterance, and/or where subtly distinct aspectual interpretations are intended. And/or ...

I have deliberately belaboured the discussion of auxiliary selection to demonstrate, first, that grammatical knowledge of acceptable verb use extends well beyond narrow subcategorisation restrictions; second, to show that acceptability judgments are sensitive to the dynamic interaction between all of the various constituents of a given utterance. In this respect, grammatical acceptability looks to be an emergent, and malleable, property of constructions and contexts. Thus, these examples demonstrate that this knowledge is tied – in some cases, quite arbitrarily – to particular verbs in particular languages, often even to specific registers or dialects of what is notionally the 'same language': what is grammatically fully acceptable to an Italian speaker in an informal conversation may be judged unacceptable by the same speaker in respect of the same utterance in written form; see also J is for Judgment below.[8]

The crux of the matter for those who would like to maintain the idea of a distinct grammar is that there is no principled line to be drawn between grammatical knowledge of this lexical-pragmatic kind and those (apparently more general) grammatical properties that might, in principle, be understood as autonomous. And verb selection is just one example of language-particular grammatical knowledge that straddles the theoretical gap between arbitrary lexical knowledge and putatively general rules. We have already seen, in Part II, instances of other general rules being lexically constrained; for example, the phenomenon of 'negative inversion' found with some negative adverbials (*rarely*, *scarcely*) but not with others (*infrequently*, *slightly*), or the exceptional behaviour of *why* among English '*wh*-words'.

It may be argued that all of these cases represent the general situation: rather than *proving* it, the exceptions *are* the rule. 'It's turtles all the way down!' As far as I am aware, there is not a single general 'rule of grammar' (of English, or of any other language variety) that does not come with riders, caveats, lexical and contextual conditions. Sapir was right a century ago, and little has changed in the meantime.

If anything, blind application of (or devotion to) grammatical rules is the hallmark of the 'incompetent' learner, especially of the adult second language learner.[9] In driving, handwriting, medical practice, comedy, as in any other highly skilled activity, going strictly by the book is not a particularly commendable trait. Oliver Wendell Holmes Sr is supposed to have remarked that: 'The young man knows the rules, but the old man knows the exceptions.'

In the context of language acquisition, Holmes' 'old man' may still have his baby teeth: by the age of seven or eight, most typically developing children have abandoned over-regularisation and other spurious generalisations (though see Chapter 26). But if it is true that almost all steady-state grammatical knowledge is ultimately piecemeal, written into our knowledge of lexical items, in construction with one another and with context, then it is fair to ask whether anyone really has – much less needs – an autonomous mental grammar.[10]

Some commentators clearly believe not. MacWhinney (2000) is a particularly articulate sceptic:

In recent years, the biological and epistemological underpinnings of these great symbolic systems have become increasingly shaky and vulnerable. Two basic observational problems faced by all these analyses are the fact that no developmental psychologist ever observed a child learning a rule and that no neuroscientist ever traced the neural substrate of either a rule of a symbol. Similarly, attempts in the 1970s to demonstrate the psychological reality of rules in adults ... yielded uniformly disappointing results. Of course, one could argue that the fact that no one has ever seen the top quark should not prevent us from constructing theories that rely on the reality of this subatomic particle. But analogies of this type are misleading. In fact, carefully controlled experiments with huge collectors of heavy water sunk deep in caves have provided solid tangible evidence of even this most elusive of physical entities. No such solid evidence has ever been provided for either linguistic rules or linguistic symbols.

Brian MacWhinney, 'Connectionism and language learning' (in Barlow and Kemmer, eds, Usage-Based Models of Language, 2000: 122)

In v is for von Humboldt below, I try to address one regularly rehearsed objection to the idea that we can function without grammar, namely, the tricky problem of DISCRETE INFINITY. But this will do to be getting on with. The take-home message of this section should be clear: all rules are generalisations, but it is far from clear that all generalisations are best described by rules.

Notes

1 For generativists, knowledge of grammar *must* be autonomous, since for them it consists in the main of *a priori* knowledge: by hypothesis, UG is (part of) the initial state of the language faculty; as such, it necessarily precedes and informs the acquisition of any lexical vocabulary. Again by hypothesis, core grammar is essentially invariant across different languages, syntactic variation being restricted to lexical properties. In the technical literature, this idea has become known as the BORER-CHOMSKY conjecture, a term first coined in Baker (2008: 353): 'All parameters of variation are attributable to the differences in the features of particular items (e.g., the functional heads) in the lexicon.' Hence, the autonomy of grammar hypothesis is not an empirical question: instead, it is a matter of what Chomsky terms 'virtual

conceptual necessity'. Newmeyer (1999) presents some interesting arguments in support of this idea, which he terms AUTOSYN. But that doesn't make it true.

2 *Das Mädchen* 'girl' is derived from the now obsolete feminine form *die Magd* (cf. Eng. 'maid'). Despite appearances, *der Junge* 'boy' is not an exception to the final schwa ➔ feminine rule; *junge* is, etymologically at least, an attributive adjective meaning 'young' (cf. Eng. 'the little ones'), which declines according to the paradigm set out in Tables 1a and 1b above.

3 Russian and Spanish gender is considerably more perspicuous, in principle at least. Barring some exceptions, the gender of words in both of these languages is related to the final vowel or consonant of the lexical stem: in Spanish, words ending in -a are overwhelmingly feminine, words ending in other vowels or consonants are masculine; in Russian, words ending in -o or -e are typically neuter, those ending in -a or -я are feminine, those ending in consonants or -й are masculine. There is some variability regarding words ending in the 'soft sign' ь. The relative simplicity of Russian gender compared to German vocabulary is more than offset by the associated case alternations: see, for example, http://www.alphadictionary.com/rusgrammar/case .html.

4 Sources: (86a) https://theinternationalkitchen.com/blogs/2014/september/bread-wine-pairings; (86b) Jung ([1954] 1981: 119); (86c) New York Law School *Law Review* (2004), vol. 46, p. 75.

5 I am grateful to my friends Zlatko Anguelov, Jenny Dalalakis and Trang Phan for their help with the Bulgarian, Greek and Vietnamese examples, respectively.

6 Of course, the distribution is not completely arbitrary. As far as I know, no language requires a non-finite complement clause for non-co-referential subjects but a finite one for co-referential subjects (i.e. a*, b✓). In other words, (b✓ ➔ a✓). This is an example of an IMPLICATIONAL UNIVERSAL: see Comrie (1981), Whaley (1998). It is not difficult to see the iconic, functional, reason for this asymmetry: shared subjects lead naturally to restructuring.

7 The first use of 'select', referring to auxiliary selection, is placed in scare quotes, since in terms of theories of phrase-structure, predicates should only be able to select for elements that they govern, i.e. that are within their maximal projection (c-command domain) and not governed more closely by any lower head (minimality). Structurally, auxiliaries govern verbs, not the other way around.

8 It should be noted that some generativists have attempted to capture this variation in terms of 'microparameters', in which differences in auxiliary selection are tied to dialectal differences in the featural specifications of functional heads; see, for example, Roberts and Roussou (2003), Roberts (2007). While this goes some way towards the kind of grammatical customisation necessary to describe the facts, it cannot in principle explain the influence of pragmatic and/or strictly lexical factors, nor does it deal with the observed gradience in judgments in the middle of the hierarchy.

9 See Chapter 26 below.

10 Some neuroscientists have interpreted data from neurophysiological (ERP) studies in support of a separation of autonomous grammatical knowledge from lexical-semantic knowledge, in language processing. Friederici (2002), for example, claims to find discrete dissociations between the 'neural signatures' of grammatical vs.

lexical violations (P600 vs. N400 effects, respectively). If the data were clear, and such interpretations were valid, then this evidence might be taken to demonstrate the 'psychological reality of rules in adults' – or rather, their neurophysiological (Level 3) correlates; see Chapter 3 above. However, the picture is considerably messier than Friederici would have us believe, as shown by a recent meta-analysis undertaken by Steinhauer and Drury (2012). It is fair to say that the (neuroscientific) jury is still out on autonomous rules.

15 H is for Homogeneity

Homogeneity is an ugly, boring word: to call it despicable is to accord it too much value. Homogeneity is a pig's tripe, a sludge, of a word. As for the concept it labels, this is beloved only of strip-mall developers and the fast-food franchises that infest their projects. In nature, homogeneity is as abhorrent as the proverbial vacuum. In human societies, it is associated with soul-destroying constructs: the travesties of 1960s housing estates, suburban tract developments, airline food, and totalitarian urban planning. If what we are trying to explain is some dynamic, natural phenomenon, the assumption of homogeneity has no ecological validity. *Less than zero.*

Chomskyan assumptions about language aside, there is no vital aspect of human culture – or of biology, for that matter – that supports the assumption of homogeneity; see also Sampson (2014). Physical locations, forms of dress, regional cuisine, stereotypes of physical beauty, human sexual relations are all defined by a peculiar, heterogeneous mix of ingredients 'not found elsewhere'. If this were not true, no-one would ever travel or stray (either literally or figuratively) and even more anthropologists would be out of work; indeed, there would be no such field of enquiry. Except in sterile planned communities, such as Levittown, NY, or Milton Keynes, perhaps, we cannot identify a city by its uniform architecture. And though certain styles of architecture may be associated with particular cities – Edinburgh New Town, along with Bath and Dublin, as archetypes of Georgian architecture, for example (see Figure 21) – that is something else: there is no *sui generis* style of architecture common to all of the buildings in London or Paris or Tokyo, say, that distinguishes them from buildings in other cities, such that we could say that every house in Paris looks like a Parisian house, as opposed to a Lyonnaise house, or that this is Düsseldorf-style, not Frankfurt-style.

The same is true of cuisine, dress, notions of beauty; indeed, virtually every aspect of human culture. As for human sexuality – something that presumably has at least as much of a genetic basis as language – it is difficult to imagine a research paper outside of Absurdist theatre or dystopic fiction that would begin:

Figure 21 Georgian architecture: in Dublin, or Edinburgh? (© 2014 Santa Vīnerte, used with permission).

The theory of sexuality is concerned with the ideal sexual partner in a perfectly homogeneous community who knows its rules perfectly.

Even in the most homogeneous social environments, there is a near-obsessive regard for the distinctive. What may appear to the outsider to be undifferentiated uniformity is subject to the finest discriminations by those within the community. To us, one ant looks like any other, one Pacific Coast tributary appears identical to the next one over; but *not* to another ant, or to the next Pacific salmon, respectively. Even in my present home of Japan, one of the most homogeneous societies of the world (Fearon 2003; cf. Patsiurko, Campbell and Hall 2012),[1] parents do not regularly pick up the wrong child at the nursery, employers do not mistake their employees, and Japanese immigration officials are probably no worse at checking passport photographs than those in an ethnically diverse country such as Canada.

The ugly exception to this fine discrimination is soldiery, where, as Wolf Biermann observes in his poem 'Soldat, Soldat': 'Soldaten sehn sich alle gleich/ Lebendig und als Leich [Soldiers all look the same, alive and as corpses].'

Soldat Soldat in grauer Norm
  Soldier, Soldier, in grey norm

Soldat Soldat in Uniform
  Soldier, Soldier, in uniform

Soldat Soldat, ihr seid so viel
  Soldier, Soldier, you are so many

Soldat Soldat, das ist kein Spiel
  Soldier, Soldier, it's not a game

Soldat Soldat, ich finde nicht
  Soldier, Soldier, I can't find

Soldat Soldat, dein Angesicht.
  Soldier, Soldier, your expression

Soldaten sehn sich alle gleich
  Soldiers all look the same

Lebendig und als Leich.
  Alive or as corpses.

Wolf Biermann, *Soldat Soldat*[2] ([1965] 1980)

Outside of the theatre of war, heterogeneity is the norm, and it is anything but grey. Of course, the same is true of speech communities, as sociolinguists and dialectologists have taught since their fields of study were first established. Knowing Sheffield, for example, means not just familiarity with the street references of Arctic Monkeys' lyrics, such as Hunter's Bar in *Fake Tales of San Francisco*; it also means knowing not to be threatened if a bus driver calls you 'love', but to be on your guard if anyone calls you 'pal'. Not everyone lives near Hunter's Bar, and most of the time bus drivers are no more forthcoming than anywhere else. Still, Alex Turner's accent is unmistakably 'Sheffield' if you happen to have lived there, or 'Yorkshire', if you come from Manchester, or 'Northern' if you come from the South ('Southern' if you come from Tyneside) – English if you're not, and very possibly unintelligible if you hail from Ann Arbor, or Durban or Vancouver. See below, also R is for Reference.

♫ Arctic Monkeys, *Fake Tales of San Francisco* (2006)

(i)   Theoretical homogeneity

The theoretical-generative linguist is unmoved by these considerations. It should be clear, though, that when Chomsky asserts 'Linguistic theory is concerned primarily with an ideal speaker–listener, in a completely homogeneous speech-community …' he is not claiming that such communities actually exist, or that his theory would offer any description of them if they did. That would be idiotic. What he is claiming is that it would not make any difference to the structure of the theory (its axioms or theorems) if speech communities in which ideal native speakers were found were completely homogeneous. This is the claim that is worth pursuing.

In his discussion of idealisations, Sorensen (2012) observes of Michael Strevens' book *Depth* (Harvard University Press, 2008):

[I]dealizations [are] indirect *assertions – hyperbole in which the truth is conveyed by falsehood. To idealize away X (gravity, friction, air resistance, electrical influences) is to indirectly deny that X is significant for the purpose at hand. Idealizations are like pointers about politeness; they tell us what ought to be ignored. We can ignore small inaccuracies (because they will not accumulate). We can ignore random errors (because they cancel out). And we can ignore some biases (because the direction of the bias is* against *the conclusion).*

Roy Sorensen, 'Veridical idealizations' (in Frappier et al., eds, *Thought Experiments in Science, Philosophy and the Arts*, 2012: 41)

From a strictly internalist, Level 1 perspective, this makes good sense. Just as the principles of aerodynamics idealise away from the flying objects – the birds, insects, planes, and occasional racing cars – that instantiate them, or the principles of Newtonian physics idealise away from friction, so it is only proper to exclude from a Cartesian theory of grammar any consideration of incidental external factors: this includes the nature of the community in which the ideal speaker–listener puts his/her knowledge of UG to use. Indeed, if linguistic theory is only concerned with *a priori* knowledge, as Chomsky assumes (*a priori*), then it would be nonsensical to try to take these external factors into account. The correctness of a Level 1 theory does not depend on contingent facts: the Euler principles would obtain if all birds and insects flew in the same way, or even if all flying organisms were wiped out tomorrow. And the same applies to grammar, as Chomsky construes it: if it is true, as Chomsky asserts, that '… aside from their mutually unintelligible vocabularies, Earthlings speak a single language' (Pinker 1994: 232), it would be odd to make any appeal to social factors in explaining grammatical knowledge, or to care very much whether there are 6,000 extant varieties of language, or only one. For Chomsky, *contra* John Donne, '[**every man**] is an island, entire of itself'. See I is for Internalism below.

At most – given that individuals acquire different vocabularies and that the content of that vocabulary clearly depends on the speech community into which they are born – one might be concerned with the linguistic experience of individuals. But as for the speech community itself, this is irrelevant. In his linguistics, if not in his politics, Chomsky's view of society as a useful abstract concept is at least as dismissive as Margaret Thatcher's:

... they are casting their problems on society and who is society? There is no such thing! There are individual men and women and there are families and no government can do anything except through people and people look to themselves first.

Margaret Thatcher, interview for *Woman's Own* magazine (1987)

Ne obliviscaris. Naturally, the same argument can be run in reverse, with respect to purely externalist theories: to the urban planner studying patterns of traffic congestion in order to design a better road system, the make and model of individual vehicles is largely irrelevant, the mind-set of the driver even more so; for most traffic models, even the general type of vehicle can be safely abstracted away from – in the evening commute, a Lamborghini is largely indistinguishable in its behaviour from a Toyota Prius or a double-decker bus. In the model, that is. Likewise, to the epidemiologist studying HIV transmission, the political or religious beliefs of the individual are largely irrelevant, even while those of the society at large may be crucial factors in halting the spread of disease.

Similar considerations apply to purely externalist approaches to language. Corpus linguists, as well as more traditional sociolinguists and historical linguists, are able to develop models to explain patterns of language use that idealise away from the random variables attached to individual utterances (or to the speakers/writers that produced them): a tagged corpus of business English, or a study of nineteenth-century Northumbrian English, for example, abstracts away from individual sources, and assumes an external homogeneity. If this were not the case, there would be no college courses on Business English, or on the Historical Dialects of Northern Britain. In most cases, this pure externalisation is harmless, since it is rare for an individual to exert any significant influence on external patterns of language use.

Yet it does happen: had it not been for Chaucer's dialect mixing, and/or Shakespeare's linguistic genius, the English we now know would have been quite different; likewise, apocryphally at least, Modern French, would not have uvular *r*s, but for the urgings of the *Académie française*, est. 1635; cf. Haden (1955). Hence, at both ends of the internalist–externalist spectrum, the assumption of homogeneity is not just acceptable: it is probably the right thing to do. However, what is right for a Level 1 theory of grammar or typography seems rather less helpful when it comes to developing a theory of language acquisition and processing. Suppose, for example, it turns out to be the case – as suggested in G is for Grammar above – that there are no autonomous grammatical rules in the mind of any individual speaker, only provisional generalisations tied to particular lexical entries (or collections of entries). Or, as proposed in I is for Internalism below, suppose that the locus of syntactic variation and change is not the individual speaker, but *langue*, an external construct. Or imagine for a moment, as argued in J is for Judgment, that a speaker's intuitions of grammatical acceptability are virtually always based on linguistic experience and sanctioned by external authority. If any of these things is even partly true, a consideration of the speech community becomes indispensable to understanding linguistic competence. And when we look more closely at what a speech community might be, the assumption of homogeneity is more than detrimental to understanding how language works: it is positively fatal.

The problem here is simply stated: idealising away from behaviour is fine as long as you are trying to explain something else – something larger, more abstract, at a different level of explanation – but it is deeply problematic to idealise away from what you are trying to explain. This applies as much to physics as it does to language. As Sorensen (2012) notes, in the continuation of the previously cited discussion:

Strevens overlooks the distinction between what a modeler assumes and what his model actually entails. Consider one of Strevens' own illustrations, in which he notes that

in explaining the appearance of a rainbow, it is assumed that raindrops are perfect spheres ... In fact, local forces will tend to deform the drops slightly. By assuming zero deformation, the model asserts that deformations within the normal range make no difference to the existence of rainbows. (Strevens 2008, 322)

The modeler may be assuming that zero deformation makes no difference but his model implies that a perfect sphere would trap the light in an internal reflection. Some deformation is essential to allow light to exit the drop. Too much smoothing maroons us on a frictionless plane. We need a little grit to proceed.

Roy Sorensen, 'Veridical idealizations' (2012: 41)

Critics of the generativist approach would probably conclude that more is at stake here than a little grit. Chomsky's idealisations don't just entail ignoring small inaccuracies or random errors (even where the direction of bias is in the direction of the conclusion): they involve the dismissal of all external linguistic behaviour. If what you want to explain is the knowledge that gives rise to this linguistic behaviour, alternatively, if – as I shall argue in I is for Internalism – the external behaviour (*langue*) has a coherence, systematicity and dynamic of its own, independently of individual speakers – then this is probably an idealisation too far.

(ii)   'Morr tung': empirical homogeneity

In a neat little town they call Belfast,
Apprentice to trade I was bound
Many an hour's sweet happiness,
Have I spent in that neat little town.

A sad misfortune came over me,
Which caused me to stray from the land
Far away from my friends and relations,
Betrayed by the black velvet band

Her eyes they shone like diamonds
I thought her the queen of the land
And her hair it hung over her shoulder
Tied up with a black velvet band.

The Black Velvet Band (traditional)

The main focus of the discussion in this section is on the syntax of Belfast English; specifically, on the syntactic properties that distinguish Belfast English from Standard British English (SBrE), as detailed in Alison Henry's 1995 monograph (Oxford University Press). Belfast English is special to me since it is the variety of English that was current in the community in which I grew up. To some readers, this might appear to be a really awkward way of describing 'my native variety of English'; however, the two are distinct notions, as will hopefully become clear.

A native speaker of Belfast English might paraphrase the previous sentence by saying 'Them two things's diffrn', but.' But I wouldn't – at least not unself-consciously – for I'm a native *knower* of Belfast English, not a native *speaker*. Like the German second language learners of English studied by Ingrid Piller (see Ω is for Love below), I can reasonably 'pass for native' under the right circumstances – a night-time taxi-ride from the City Airport, for example – but it's a special performance that has never been part of my usual spoken repertoire. Members of my immediate family speak or spoke Belfast English natively. Two of my uncles and my paternal grandfather worked all their lives as foremen in Harland & Wolff and Shorts (Short & Harland), the shipbuilder and aircraft manufacturer, respectively: these relatives of mine, and all of those men who worked under them, spoke Belfast English. My father's second sister spoke a variety of Belfast English corresponding closely to Henry's description – though one that, by the end of her life, was more Bangor (North Down) than Cregagh. Her younger brother – my father – grew up speaking Belfast English, but by the time I knew him he only had an identifiable Belfast accent, and had lost the lexical or grammatical features that Henry's book addresses.

On the other hand, most of the people that I went to school with, in a middle-class suburb of East Belfast, no more spoke Belfast English than francophones

Figure 22 Images of Belfast (original photographs © 2016 Catrin Rhys, used with permission).

in Outremont – an affluent francophone suburb of Montréal – speak 'Montreal French', or than Radio Canada presenters across Canada speak *joual*. In all cases of real language use, there is a vast amount of sociolectal variation, bordering on DIGLOSSIA. For the most part, middle-class Belfast English differs from Standard English only with respect to accent, and perhaps a handful of local idioms and references.

This relative invariance is evidenced by a recent video interview with Gary Lightbody, the lead singer of Snow Patrol. Gary attended the same school as I did/as me – albeit some twenty years later: accent aside, no non-standard features are in evidence in his responses in this clip.[3]

There is more to these autobiographical facts than name dropping, or the commonplace observation that speech communities are themselves internally heterogeneous, that education, income-level, family background and other contingent factors modulate accent and other dialect features. For the significant point is that in spite of all this variability, there *is* something real and inclusive about Belfast English that all of us from Belfast share, and which distinguishes everyone in the community from English speakers in Dublin or Auckland or Pretoria. I may not *produce* the type of Belfast English that Alison Henry describes, but in common with all of the children that I went to school with, I still possess a 'Belfast English competence' – native-like intuitions about how Belfast English is spoken, which expressions are or are not acceptable, and so on – and this receptive competence generates judgments that are very close to those found in Henry's book.[4]

If this seems paradoxical, it is only because of another idealisation discussed in the next section, namely, that of strict internalism. If grammatical knowledge is taken to be purely internal property, then it is nonsense to suggest that I can share knowledge of a variety I do not speak. However, if knowledge of language (*langue*) is partially external, like knowledge of the streets of one's hometown, then there is no paradox at all. In the place of paradox, however, looms a significant theoretical conclusion, one that is fairly unpalatable to many people: grammatical knowledge must be 'out there', too, part of our inter-subjective reality. See I is for Internalism below.

Before considering some evidence, it's important to acknowledge the homogenising effect of standard orthography, which makes varieties of English seem markedly more uniform than they really are.

Let's start with Chinese since – unusual as it may be in the soundscape of Belfast – it provides a starker illustration of the same problem. The official line, believed by many millions of Chinese citizens, has it that there is one standard variety of Chinese, namely, Mandarin, and a related group of 'dialects' (Wu, Ye, Min, Xiang, Hakka, etc.). The educated response to this claim is that it is linguistic nonsense – at least as false as the idea that French is a dialect of Romanian or that Scottish Gaelic is a dialect of Welsh. The linguistically informed view is that 'Chinese' comprises a diverse selection of distinct language varieties, many of which are only remotely related to Mandarin, and whose principal common feature is a shared logographic writing system (hanzi 漢字).

It will be obvious to anyone not blinkered by ideology that sharing a writing system does not entail sharing a common language. Numerals offer a case in point: most of the world's languages have borrowed Arabic numerals to represent natural numbers, but no-one would suggest that all the world has Standard Arabic as a common language, even just as the language of mathematics. (Compare this to musical notation, which does allow almost all of the world's musicians to read music in the same way.)

Instead of relying on shared orthography to determine relatedness, linguistics students are generally told to rely on mutual intelligibility. The criterion of mutual intelligibility works quite well when politics or geography produces two different writing systems for one set of varieties. Scottish Gaelic and Ulster Irish, for example, were once as mutually intelligible as Glaswegian and Belfast English, yet the former pair have developed distinct orthographies (101), whereas the latter varieties are generally represented by the same standardised writing system – actually, *mis*represented, as we shall see directly.

(101) a. A   bheil   Gàidhlig agaibh? Tha, beagan.
           Q BE.PRESENT Gaelic   to-you   be,   little
           'Do you speak Gaelic?'   'Yes, a little.'

       b. An bhfuil   Gaeilge agaibh? Tá, beagán.
           Q BE.PRESENT Gaelic   to-you   be,   little
           'Do you speak Irish?'   'Yes, a little.'

Similar mismatches are found in the comparison of southern varieties of Swedish (Skåne) and Danish, or – even more strikingly – Hindi and Urdu, which use completely different scripts to represent the same lexical items: Devnagri (for Hindi) vs. Nastaleeq (for Urdu); see Jawaid and Ahmed (2009) for discussion.

It seems somewhat ironic that many of the same English-speaking linguists who clearly explicate the Mandarin/Cantonese vs. Swedish/Danish contrast apply different standards when it comes to English. The fact that literate English speakers have shared a more-or-less common orthography since Caxton and Chaucer – one that accurately represents no-one's native pronunciation – obscures the more significant reality that in the British Isles at least, we have never had a shared spoken variety. Research by Peter Trudgill in the 1970s, revisited in 2001, suggests that no more than 3–5 per cent of the British population are RP (Received Pronunciation) speakers; see Trudgill (2001), and compare Trudgill (2008), for discussion of why it hasn't entirely disappeared. That is to say, more than 95 per cent of the British population speak with an identifiable and distinctive regional accent of some kind; of these, a significant proportion use non-standard lexical or syntactic dialect features in their speech to a greater or lesser extent. Throughout the UK and Ireland run a series of intersecting DIALECT CONTINUA: take any two varieties at sufficient geographical or social distance from another, and you will find unintelligibility.

Significantly, this unintelligibility is hardly ever *mutual*: comprehensibility is invariably uni-directional, with those speaking the more prestigious variety failing to understand their (economically) poorer cousins. Any sociolinguist will confirm that these asymmetries have little to do with inherent linguistic factors; instead, they are overwhelmingly due to imbalances of exposure, and/ or concomitant attitudinal factors.[5] As in the Heaney quote above (A is for Abstraction), Power and Prejudice determine who understands who(m).

The distorting role of orthography operates in both directions: on one hand, there are instances where the standard orthography literally renders dialect contrasts invisible – just like Chinese *hanzi*/漢字 – so that what is incomprehensible in pronunciation appears unproblematic when written down; on the other, there are cases where a more faithful orthographic representation of a given variety reveals it to be all but unintelligible to English-speaking outsiders.

An example of the former is the 'Lift' sketch ('Eleven!') from the satirical television series *Burnistoun*, in which two Glaswegians try to get to the eleventh floor in a lift (US 'elevator') that uses voice recognition technology instead of buttons. The transcript of the first few lines of the sketch, in Standard English orthography, offers no clue whatsoever to the hilarity of the dialogue:

IAIN: *Where's the buttons?*
ROB: *Oh no, they've installed voice-recognition technology in this lift, they have no buttons.*
IAIN: *Voice-recognition technology? In a lift? In Scotland? You ever tried voice-recognition technology?*
ROB: *No.*
IAIN; *They don't do Scottish accents.*
ROB: *Eleven.*
VOICE: *Could you please repeat that?*
IAIN: *Eleven.*
ROB: *Eleven. Eleven.*
IAIN: *Eleven.*
VOICE: *Could you please repeat that?*
ROB: *EL-EV-EN.*
IAIN: *Whose idea was this? You need to try an American accent. E-leven. E-leven.*
ROB: *That sounds Irish, not American.*
IAIN: *No it doesn't! ELEVEN.*
ROB: *Where in America is that: Dublin?*
VOICE: *I'm sorry. Could you please repeat that?*

Robert Florence and Iain Connell, 'Lift' sketch (*Burnistoun*, series 1)

See? Nothing even remotely amusing here. Yet the sketch itself – widely available on YouTube – is brilliant; *cracker*, as I might once have said, a long time ago. Notice in passing that the human characters in the sketch have no problem in understanding the disembodied Standard American recorded voice.

It's a different matter when English is written 'as she is spoke', where perfectly ordinary words are transformed into apparent gibberish (disguised as perfectly ordinary words). *John Pepper's Ulster–English Dictionary* presents this take on dialect variation (Pepper 1981); the samples in (102) also provide a smooth transition to Henry's grammatical data.

(102) a. **jamember**, request to recollect. 'Jamember the day we went to Bangor and you nearly cowped the wee boat?' 'Jamember when you could get to Bangor and back for a bob?'
b. **lion upstairs**, in bed, not yet awake. 'Wud ye luk at the time, and him still lion upstairs?' 'Lion upstairs. That's a question to ask at levin in the morning.'

c. **monney down/up**, just out of bed. 'I'm not at myself yet. Sure monney down.' 'Wait till I get my brain shired. Monney up.'

d. **morr tung**, native language 'When ye hear the morr tung in your ears, ye know yer among frens.' 'The best thing about goin' home on a visit is to be able till lissen till people using their morr tung.'

e. **sweat**, indicates that it is raining. 'Luck at that wire, wud ye? Sweat, as usual.'

f. **thon**, reference to a person or a thing. 'Luck at the far out thon wuns is went in that wee boat.' 'Givvus a quarter of thon carmels at the enn of the shelf.'

John Pepper, John Pepper's Ulster–English Dictionary (1981)

Happy days. Example (102f) at once refers back to Part II, Case #3 – confirming the use of the distal deictic term *thon* for objects that are relatively far from both speaker and listener – and forward to the next section, showing a natural usage of what Henry (1995) calls SINGULAR CONCORD, where plural noun-phrases agree with a singular verb ('thon wuns is went out ...' [= those people have/*has gone out...]). Example (102c) offers the closest orthographic rendering of the English word 'shower' in Northern Irish speech; compare the discussion of <kaitch> in the Introduction.

At this point, the sceptic could point out that all of these examples amount to little more than differences of accent – and, perhaps minor differences in verb conjugation that are well-attested in other varieties of English (*went* in place of *gone*, for example). There is nothing here to challenge the idea that Belfast English and Standard English share a common grammar. The phenomena discussed in Alison Henry's monograph *do* challenge that cosy assumption, but.

Henry discusses five syntactic constructions whose acceptability and associated constraints systematically contrast with those found in all other varieties of English spoken outside of (Northern) Ireland, including Standard British and American English. The set comprises:

(a) subject–verb agreement ('singular concord');
(b) overt-subject imperatives;
(c) *for-to* infinitives;
(d) inversion of auxiliaries in embedded questions;
(e) 'subject contact relatives' (cf. Doherty 1994).

Examples of each construction are given in (103): these are all completely acceptable in Belfast English but mostly unacceptable elsewhere in the English-speaking world. The numbers in square brackets designate the source of these examples in Henry's (1995) monograph:

(103)   a. The eggs *is* probably cracked. [Ch. 2: (63)]
        b. Read *you* it to me. [Ch. 3: (19)]
        c. I don't like the children *for to* be out late. [Ch. 4: (21)]
        d. Every pregnant woman *wonders will* her baby be all right [Ch. 5
        (10b)]
        e. There are *people don't* read books. [Ch. 6: (2)]

For reasons of space, I'll restrict attention to (103b) and (103d) – the inversion constructions – in which a main verb or an auxiliary appears to the left of the subject noun-phrase. These are the sentence types that Henry analyses as involving verb raising to C:[6] see Part II, Case #5 above, for Chomsky's discussion of inversion in Standard English ('Can eagles swim?').

Before examining these constructions more closely, take a quick look at the examples in (104), which minimally contrast with their counterparts in (103) above. Speakers of Belfast English will be able to tell which of these examples is acceptable in their variety, but if you are not one of those happy few, your score is unlikely to be significantly above chance (i.e. around 10/20).

(104)   a. i. *Is* the eggs cracked? [Ch. 2: (3)]
        a. ii. Any animals *isn't* coming. [Ch. 2: (73b)]

        b. i. Read it *you* to me. [Ch. 3: (19)]
        b. ii. Read *you* the book to me. [Ch. 3: (200b)]

        c. i. I don't know whether *for to* go. [Ch. 4: (15)]
        c. ii. Not *for to* go would be foolish. [Ch. 4: (30b)]

        d. i. I asked what *had she* done. [Ch. 5: (76)]
        d. ii. Who did you claim *did he* see? [Ch. 5: (79)]

        e. i. I have one student he speaks four languages [Ch. 6: (28)]
        e. ii. John married the girl he met her on holiday [Ch. 6: (32)][7]

With the exception of the construction in (103d), which is fully part of my idiolect, and – more marginally – (103e), which I can imagine myself saying in the right circumstances, none of the other examples in (103) form part of my personal grammatical competence, in the sense that I would ever think to use them. Yet I know them all as old friends, characteristic of the community in which I grew up. For this reason, my judgments on the sentences in (104) match those given by Henry nearly exactly. If acceptability judgments arise from interrogating I-LANGUAGE, then either I should be as mistaken about the acceptability of the examples in (104) as English speakers raised in a different speech community, or I else should freely use all of the sentences in (103) in my own speech. Since neither is true, it suggests that the premise is false: grammatical judgments must be judgments about something else, something distinct from 'personal competence'. This point is elaborated further in J is for Judgment below.

Let's now take a closer look at the constructions involving inversion – the (b) and (d) examples – examining Henry's treatment of these structures. In both cases, Henry analyses the surface word-order, in terms of '(V-)T-C' raising' as schematised in (105), compare (31) above:

(105)

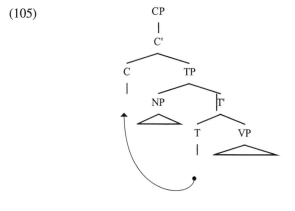

(106) a.   Read   you   ~~read~~   ~~you read~~ it to me]!
        b. wonders   [will   her baby   ~~will~~   be ~~her baby~~ all right]

Henry's phrase-structural assumptions and notation differs in some theoretically significant respects from the diagram in (105), most notably, in the splitting of the functional projection T into 'AgrSP', 'TP' and 'AgrOP', and in the postulation of generalised Object Shift (by which object noun-phrases in English are moved from their base position to some position to the left of the thematic verb-phrase). However, these formal variations are irrelevant to Henry's central claim that Verb-Subject order in (106a) and Aux-Subject order in (106b) are each derived by means of syntactic head movement to C: both of these core claims are accurately diagrammed in the tree in (105).

In the case of embedded interrogatives (106b), it is the auxiliary verb that raises, just as is usually observed in *direct* questions in Standard English; see 'Can eagles swim' again. In the case of overt-subject imperatives (106a), however, it is the main (lexical) verb that raises: this is something that is generally taken to be ungrammatical in standard varieties – though it was freely available up to the Early Modern English period. See I is for Internalism (ii) below.

Henry's analysis raises a number of awkward questions for any generalised transformational approach to inversion. First, it is hard to escape the conclusion that speakers of Belfast English know about 'constructions', rather than about generalised parametric rules. Imperatives and embedded interrogatives in Belfast English may both show inversion, but the kind of inversion involved is quite different in each cases. Notice that for all Belfast English speakers, overt-subject imperatives are incompatible with *do*-support, as evidenced by the unacceptability of (107a). Conversely, main-verb raising is prohibited in embedded questions (107b); in such contexts, *do*-support is obligatory.

(107)   a. *<u>Do</u> you go and read your book! (Cf. Go you and read your book!)
        b. *He wondered <u>went</u> she to the same school as his sister.
            (Cf. He wondered did she go to the same school as his sister.)

Furthermore, even the most basilectal variety of Belfast English prohibits main-verb raising to T in regular declarative and/or matrix interrogative clauses: hence, the examples in (108) are unacceptable for everyone in the community.

(108)   a. *I saw not the film the other night, so I didn't.
            (Cf. I didn't see the film the other night, so I didn't.)
        b. *Found you your wallet?
            (Cf. Did you find your wallet?)

Translating these restrictions into the generative formalism current at the time that Henry's book was written, one would have to say, first, that *just in the case of imperatives* main verbs have 'strong' V-features that must be checked by an abstract imperative element in C, whereas in other cases, the relevant V-features are 'weak'; second, with regard to embedded inversion, that auxiliary verbs in Belfast English embedded clauses have features that must be checked by movement to C. Indeed, this is pretty much what Henry does say (1995: 77):

We have also argued that in imperatives in Belfast English, the main verb raises to C. One question that arises, if this analysis is correct, is why main verbs can raise here, but not in questions, where only be *and* have *raise, other verbs requiring do-support … One would expect that if main verbs cannot raise to C in questions, they should be unable to raise in imperatives: it would be expected that as* do-*support is required in questions with verbs other than* have *or* be, *it would otherwise be required in imperatives, but we have noted that* do-*support is impossible in imperatives. One reason for the lack of* do-*support is that* do *is inserted under Tense, and we have noted that Tense is not instantiated in imperatives; this explains only the lack of* do-*support, however, and not the general availability of verb movement to C. We need to consider why a difference exists between imperatives and other constructions in relation to verb-raising. The answer would seem to lie in the fact that the verb-feature of C and* Agr^{S} *is strong, forcing raising in the syntax. On the contrary, the* v-*features of these nodes are weak in questions, triggering raising in the overt syntax only of those verbs which cannot raise at LF.*

Although the possibility of leaving the subject in situ *can be seen to relate to the general optionality of movement to Spec, Agr ^{S}P, in Belfast English the availability of verb-raising is restricted to imperatives and thus is essentially construction-specific: it involves a statement about the strength of the V-feature of a particular morpheme in C, the imperative morpheme, rather than about C in general. As noted in Chapter 2, the grammar must be able to include statements about the strength or weakness of particular items in a node. Although this increases the power of the grammar, it seems to be empirically necessary; moreover, given the very strongly restricted range of options available within the Minimalist Program, it does not seem it will make parameter-setting unnecessarily difficult. [my emphasis: NGD]*

Alison Henry, *Dialect Variation and Parameter-Setting:
A Study of Belfast English and Standard English* (1995: 77–8)

Alison Henry's discussion of imperatives puts a brave face on a bad situation. Although in purely formal terms her analysis allows her to avoid reference to construction-specific rules, the game would seem to be up: if the most fundamental transformational operations in the grammar are invariably subject to restrictions dictated by invisible formal features, and if these features are privatively associated with one or other grammatical construction, then it would seem that we have construction-specific rules in all but name. (See, however, Pesetsky and Torrego 2001 for an alternative treatment.)

What makes this contrast more damning still is that the theory requires Henry to invoke abstract features on two separate syntactic nodes – C and Agr^S. This is because, in light of the general conditions on head movement in the theory at the time – which is to say, the HEAD MOVEMENT CONSTRAINT of Travis (1984), later the MINIMAL LINK CONDITION (Chomsky 1995) – the verb is not able to move directly to C, skipping intermediate head positions. But this entails that every verb in the language must be alternately specified with strong or weak V-features for Agr^S, as well as for C, depending on the construction. It is far from obvious, to say the least, what kind of Agr^s features should be associated with illocutionary force.[8]

Even more significantly, the two constructions are subject to a variety of distinct constraints, depending on the speaker, as well as on the utterance context. For me – and, I suspect, for many other 'knowers' of BE – overt-subject imperatives are really only acceptable with a handful of high-frequency, mostly intransitive, predicates – as well as with the adverbial idiom 'away you (on, and)...', illustrated in (109):

(109)   a. Away you on!: I'll close up.[9]
        b. Go you and tell your mum we're waiting!
        c. ?Listen you to what I tell you!
        d. ?Read you that book!

  e. ??Handle you that book with care!
  f. *Examine you the contents carefully before disposing of the
     packaging!

My intuitions about embedded inversion involve a quite different set of
restrictions: whereas I find inversion fairly natural with all predicates that
select [+wh] complements (*wonder, ask, enquire, know*, etc.) in the case of
Yes-No questions, inversion is unacceptable where the embedded clauses is
introduced by a fronted *wh*-phrase. Henry notes that there are others like
me: 'for a not insubstantial number of speakers ... the sentences in [(110)]
are ungrammatical':

(110) a. ??She asked [who had I seen].
       b. ??They wondered [what had John done].
       c. ??They couldn't understand [how had she the time to get her hair
          done].
       d. ??They couldn't say [why had they come].

See also McCloskey (2001). For Henry, this contrast between embedded *Yes-
No* and *wh*-questions necessitates a further parametrisation of the grammar,
since the featural properties that trigger movement in the first construction
(107b) must be independent from the features that disallow movement in the
second case (110b), or which force movement in the corresponding matrix
clauses (that is to say, the bracketed portions of the sentences in (110)).
    The picture is yet further complicated by the fact that I find sentences
involving apparent long-distance *wh*-movement with embedded inversion
in the lower clause to be quite acceptable: the sentences in (111) are nearly
perfect for me – at least, they are markedly more acceptable than those in
(110). However, Henry's internalist approach forces her to treat these as of a
piece: this leads to the prediction that speakers should either accept or reject
both kinds of sentence, contrary to fact.

(111) a. Who did you claim did he see?
       b. ??What do you know has John been doing?
          (cf. *Do you know what has John been doing?)

Even if all of these objections could be handled through fine-grained lexical
specification – similar to the specifications argued for in Part II, Case #5 above,
for standard varieties – the irresolvable difficulty for an internalist view is the
fact that speakers of Belfast English cannot be divided into the 'raisers' and
'non-raisers', or the 'singular concordists' and the standard speakers. Instead,
every native speaker of Belfast English implicitly controls a continuum of

grammatical options, which are deployed as the situation requires. It seems unlikely that when I talk to my nephew, I have switched 'on the fly' from a non-raising grammar to a raising grammar ('Go you and tell your mum we're waiting!'), or that if sometimes I invert the subject and auxiliary in embedded questions, and sometimes not, I am alternating between basic parameter-settings. It seems just as implausible to suppose (that) when a speaker who habitually uses singular concord starts to use Standard English agreement – in the context of a court appearance or formal job interview, for example – that she has 'reset' her internal grammar so as to raise subjects to {Spec, Agr_sP}, rather than leaving them in the lower {Spec, TP}. Such dynamism and context-sensitivity is hard to square with the principles of one-time parameter-setting.

Stigmatised syntax is not a discrete property. It is not either present in, or absent from, a particular speech community. The syntactic features of Belfast English are like graffiti on the Parisian RER system: no station is free of it, but prosperous neighbourhoods have considerably less than is found *dans les banlieues*. The only real difference between graffiti and stigmatised syntax of Belfast English is that graffiti is generally produced by younger speakers,[10] whereas in Belfast, at least, the core features of non-standard utterances are the (literal) preserve of the elderly.

It is a case of 'Kilroy was here' (1950s graffito), not a contemporary tagging crew (kru); see Cooper and Chalfant (1984).

The inevitable conclusion, I'd like to suggest, is that grammatical variation is 'out there', in the community, not in our heads: our knowledge of this variation is thus closely aligned with our geographic and social neighbourhoods. And if this is the case, then the assumption of the perfectly 'homogeneous speech community' is anything but harmless, since it effectively precludes any satisfactory description of the locus of (micro-)parametric differences.

(iii)   Methodological homogeneity

HUGH LAURIE: *I'd like some information, please.*
STEPHEN FRY: *Yes. What information would you like?*
HUGH LAURIE: *Well, I don't know. What have you got?*
STEPHEN FRY: *I beg your pardon?*
HUGH LAURIE: *What information have you got?*
STEPHEN FRY: *Well, all sorts.*
HUGH LAURIE: *Such as?*
STEPHEN FRY: *Such as … the average weight of a rabbit.*
HUGH LAURIE: *Well I never knew that.*
STEPHEN FRY: *What?*
HUGH LAURIE: *I never knew rabbits had an average weight.*
STEPHEN: *Oh yes …*

Stephen Fry and Hugh Laurie, 'Information' sketch
(*A Bit of Fry & Laurie*, 2010)

In the sketch, Hugh is right – at least, he is right to be puzzled: individual rabbits don't have an average weight, any more than any particular US household comprises 2.6 persons (we hope), or than that more than a very few people in the UK spend exactly 57.1 minutes getting to work.[11] Mean averages tell us something important about groups, and are useful for guiding social policy, but they don't have much applicability in any specific case.

With respect to language and language processing, the assumption of a third kind of homogeneity is as inevitable as it is perverse. Let's consider finally what might be termed METHODOLOGICAL HOMOGENEITY in experimental psycholinguistics. In spite of regularly criticising Chomsky's idealisation above with regard to the 'ideal speaker–listener, in a homogeneous speech-community', process-oriented psycholinguists need to assume a fair degree of homogeneity within their own communities of speakers – their participant groups – in order to operate. It is of course a different kind of homogeneity that these psycholinguists are interested in, namely, the homogeneity of language processing mechanisms across speakers. Notwithstanding a body of research showing the importance of individual differences in language acquisition (Gleitman and Gleitman 1979, Street and Dabrowska 2014), the overwhelming majority of psycholinguistic models are based on group results, in which outliers are excluded implicitly as performance error (albeit by a neutral mathematical procedure, 'plus or minus two standard deviations'), while central results are taken to be indicative of the processing systems of all individual speaker–listeners. There is thus an ironic parallel between armchair linguists who develop I-language grammars purely on the basis of introspection, and psychologists of language who attribute to individuals processing systems modelled on the basis of averaged group scores. The theoretical linguist may not be confident that his/her judgments will generalise to other speakers of the language under examination, but they are at least the intuitions of an individual mind (assuming they know their own). By contrast, the psychologist can be reasonably sure that the results obtained are representative of the group tested and – provided the experiment has been carried out correctly – has a justified belief that these results should generalise to a wider group of speakers, say, advanced L2 learners of Swedish. But the model that is derived is a model of group performance: the results do not represent any individual's psychology. Yet what is claimed to be being modelled is not some external, social construct – like models of job interviews, or of commuting to work – but the language processing system of every individual represented by the group. Without assuming some reasonable degree of homogeneity, classical psycholinguistics would be a non-starter.

The general methodological assumption is that everyone processes language in approximately the same way. Moreover, it is often assumed – especially by competence-based linguists – that the same processing mechanisms are available to speakers of all languages: languages may contrast in the lexicons and their grammatical structure, but the processing mechanisms are universal. Once again, there is reason to doubt both of these assumptions.

Even within a particular language, individual differences may vitiate experimental results, and the findings derived from them. An example of this was given in a recent journalistic article concerning the processing of metaphorical expressions. At issue in that case was the question of whether hearing an idiom such as 'Amy kicked the bucket' causes the brain to simulate the action of kicking – by stimulating the motor cortex – in the same way as hearing the more literal 'Amy kicked his bag' apparently does (Desai, Binder et al. 2011). Different studies have yielded contradictory results (see Kacinik 2014). Although this may have to do with the differing methods and materials used, it is equally likely to be due to real heterogeneity of representation among the participants tested. As George Lakoff, author of the seminal linguistic study of metaphor – *Women, Fire and Dangerous Things* (1987) – observed:

You say, 'Do you have a mental image? Where is the bucket before it's kicked?' ... Some people say it's upright. Some people say upside down. Some people say you're standing on it. Some people have nothing. You know?! There isn't a systematic connection across people for this. And if you're averaging across subjects, you're probably not going to get anything.

Michael Chorost, 'Your brain on metaphors'
(*Chronicle of Higher Education*, 2014)

This does not undermine the assumption of homogeneity, as long as it is understood as an idealisation. And, as long as variability in the system is relatively constrained, the results of classical psycholinguistics remain valid, up to a point. It is not entirely meaningless to talk of the average weight of a rabbit, either. We may all be individuals, but we participate in and contribute to a significant social identity, inter-subjective reality, of which language (*langue*) is a crucial reflex. And with respect to *langue*, averages are again meaningful.

Notes

1 See https://en.wikipedia.org/wiki/List_of_countries_ranked_by_ethnic_and_cultural_ diversity_level. A significant difficulty with the studies cited is the use of the degree of linguistic homogeneity as an indirect proxy for cultural homogeneity, and a reliance on other sources for measures of ethnic homogeneity.
2 One of several reasons that the translation fails is that the German original is more consistently iambic than the English version can be: the nub of the problem is that 'soldier' is trochaic, whereas 'Soldat' builds an iambic foot. This is an unusual situation: more typically, as with Goethe's *Zauberlehrling* in Chapter 26 below, the opposite issue arises in German–English conversion (i.e. German is trochaic where English requires an iamb).
3 Available at www.youtube.com/watch?v=A4-aqSueT5U

4 I have greater confidence about my judgments of Belfast English than about the blended variety I currently speak: even after thirty-five years, I'm still unsure (of) how to use *shall* like speakers Standard British English, and I can't pronounce *<boots>*.

5 Very little, but not zero: as has been pointed out in various sociolinguistic studies, low-prestige varieties are associated with masking factors in speech production, especially, less differentiation of vowel contrasts, and higher speech rates: non-educated, non-Standard speech may objectively be harder to make sense of than standard varieties; see, for example, Cedergren, Levac and Perreault (1992), Cedergren and Perreault (1994). See also Hawkins (2004) and other contributions to Bernstein (2004).

6 Setting aside the cases of overt-subject imperatives that Henry analyses as Dialect A: see below.

7 Answers: (104ai) unacceptable; (104aii) acceptable (to some speakers); (104bi) acceptable (to some speakers); (104bii) acceptable (to some speakers); (104ci) unacceptable; (104cii) unacceptable; (104di) acceptable; (104dii) acceptable; (104ei) acceptable; (104eii) unacceptable.

8 Doing away with Agr nodes – or exempting head movement from narrow syntax (Chomsky 2001) – doesn't really solve this problem either: it simply transfers the difficulty of explaining 'parametric contrast' to another part of the grammar.

9 Henry treats 'away you' (109a) as a verb in Belfast English, in spite of the fact that it cannot be inflected, or negated, and that it only appears in direct impera-tives (*'Please away you on!'). The phrase has every hallmark of a fixed idiomatic expression, yet Henry's commitment to autonomous syntactic rules (cf. G is for Grammar) and strict internalism (I is for Internalism) prevents her from acknowl-edging this.

10 Source: https://youtube.com/watch?v=hgw2m5w12yg.

11 Source: www.bbc.com/news/uk-38026625

16   I is for Internalism (I-language)

♫ The Who, *Is It in My Head?* (*Quadrophenia*, 1973)

The curse of strict mentalism

One day in the spring of 1960, having had a winter to ruminate over Chomsky's critique of *Verbal Behavior*, psychologists woke up to the idea that language was, in part, an internal phenomenon.

They didn't, of course. Although they might disagree on many issues, it is almost certain that psycholinguists have always shared a belief with theoretical linguists – as with almost anyone else who has thought about the issue seriously – that a significant part of what we call language is in our heads. After all, where else would it be (rhetorical)?! In our kidneys? In our hearts … On our tongues … or lips?![1] Most likely, what really changed when the Cognitive Revolution cast out Behaviourism was not so much the well-accepted notion that knowledge of language was partly internal, but rather a collective attitude to the proposition that *it is only these internally represented aspects of language that have any theoretical significance.* When the COMPETENCE/PERFORMANCE distinction supplanted the Saussurean contrast between LANGUE and PAROLE, things took a dramatic turn: the external products of the language processor – speech and text, discourse, conversation – were henceforth considered irrelevant to theories of the minds that produced them: mere 'performance phenomena', at best, 'impoverished input'. Pure internalism was in the ascendant, and (in many quarters) has remained so ever since.

I'll suggest in the remainder of this section that strict mentalism has been more of a curse than a blessing, and that it is detrimental to any full appreciation of what languages are, and how they work. To understand how, and why, we got here the following paragraphs from McGilvray ([1999] 2014) are worth quoting in full:

Chomsky is what philosophers call an internalist. *With respect to his linguistic science, this is reflected in his view that the science of language is a science of a specific mental faculty that operates inside the head, not of any linguistic phenomena outside the head, such as linguistic behaviour. The external phenomena of language observable in lin-guistic behaviour – the varied and complicated ways that people use language to deal with their world – play a role in constructing a theory of what goes on inside their head, of course; they provide one source of information and evidence. But they are not the subject matter of linguistic theory. So when Chomsky constructs a computational theory of language, he is concerned with the computations (linguistic mental/neural processes) that relate one set of linguistic mental events to another, not with what is outside the head, or with any relationship between these mental events and things or situations outside the head. Indeed, since the theory deals with linguistic mental events alone and supposes that these occur in relative isolation from other mental events (at least until after they 'interface' with other mental events) his linguistic theory is also 'modular': it supposes that the 'language faculty' in which these events take place is relatively iso-lated from other mental faculties. Internalism, however, is primarily a matter of main-taining an inside the head/outside the head distinction: it does not require modularity.*

James McGilvray, *Chomsky: Language, Mind and Politics* ([1999] 2014: 4)

Collins (2011: 137) makes the same point more compactly, with a dose of Latin, as is the wont of some philosophers:

Linguistic Internalism: *The explanations offered by successful linguistic theory nei-ther presuppose nor entail externalia. There are externalia, but they do not enter into explanations of linguistics qua externalia. Linguistics is methodologically solipsistic; its kinds are internalist.*

John Collins, *The Unity of Linguistic Meaning* (2011: 137)

Postponing the question of modularity, I'll focus here on the fundamental issue of internalism. As well as I can determine it, the path to strict mentalism was laid by the final steps – (iv) and (v) – appended to a very familiar logical argument.

(i) Part of what speakers know (that is, have mentally represented) about the language they speak includes a set of highly abstract, intensional proper-ties that have no direct physical correlates: these include knowledge of constituency, recursivity, *c-command*, hierarchical constraints on long-distance dependencies, and so forth.

(ii) All speakers of a given language – perhaps all speakers of all languages – come to know essentially the same abstract properties, in spite of:

   a. significant variability in personal experience (intelligence, educational attainment and socialisation, literacy, and other contingent facts of their upbringing);

   b. the impoverished and incoherent nature of external language (perform-ance/E-language).

(iii) This knowledge – 'knowledge in the absence of experience' – must be innate.

(iv) Linguistic theory is only concerned with explaining these internal properties.

(v) Language in the ordinary sense of the word – what Chomsky calls E-LANGUAGE – plays no explanatory or causal role in linguistic argumentation, and can be dismissed.

Steps (i)–(iii) are, of course, a version of Chomsky's POVERTY OF (THE) STIMULUS (POS) syllogism, which has been rehearsed innumerable times over the last five decades.[2] Step (iv) is a paraphrase of the Chomsky quote with which we started this section: 'Linguistic theory is concerned primarily with an ideal speaker–listener ... performance.' Step (v) is a plausible inference from (iv): if linguistic theory is restricted to internal properties, it makes sense to exclude the external.

The POS argument itself has met with repeated challenges and stiff resistance from all directions, with most opponents criticising some aspect of the minor premise (ii). It is fair to say that these (often trenchant) criticisms have had next to no effect on diehard generativists, with the result that most people have given up trying. Those who have persisted in their criticism have frequently been subject to a barrage of personal flak and invective from some quarters that is as unprofessional as it is upsetting to the recipients (and demeaning to their abusers). Criticising Chomsky is not for the fainthearted, and certainly not for those with a thin skin, or without tenure: far too often, moderate dissent is treated as a form of blasphemy or sedition.[3] So, for present purposes – and with discretion the better part of valour – I'll provisionally grant the following minimal version of the POS argument (steps (i)–(iii)): *some* abstract properties of language are not inducible ➔ language learners appear to converge on these properties, regardless of experience ➔ these properties must be innate.[4] What is at stake here, in any case, are steps (iv) and (v), which are often understood as corollaries of the POS.

The problem is these steps are not corollaries to anything. It just doesn't follow from the fact that *some* properties of language may be innate that *all* grammatical knowledge is internalised, much less that external language can be dismissed as theoretically irrelevant. Steps (iv) and (v) are as much theoretical and methodological assertions as the first two steps in the POS syllogism: there is nothing self-evident about the internalist position.

Curiously, many of those who argue most vociferously against the POS – Christiansen and Chater (2008), for example – nevertheless subscribe to a strictly internalist view of language, and do so with almost as much unreflective zeal as any Chomskyan. Generativists may not have convinced many of their academic opponents of the merits of UG, but they certainly persuaded a generation of cognitive psychologists that all that matters in language is what is abstract, intangible and ineffable. To allude to The Who's song: it may be only generativists who assume that it is *right from the start*, but everyone in the scientific community seems to agree that it's *[only] in my head, [not] in my heart.*

With so many smart people signed up to the doctrine of strict mentalism, it is probably foolish to propose an alternative, especially since the internalist approach allows us to treat language as a closed system (a move that is unquestionably 'a good thing' in anyone's scientific book – until one realises that dynamic biological systems are not closed: see Gould 1987).

In spite of this, I believe that a case can be made for a more outward-facing approach, one in which formal grammatical knowledge is inextricably linked to external language. The fond idea I'd like to propose, following on from the last chapter, is that we know the grammatical properties of English or Japanese or Welsh in the same way that we know the streets of London, or Kobe, or the byways of Gwynedd. External language, on this view, is much more than just incoherent patterns of spontaneously generated, contextually contingent utterances. It is the direct source of our grammatical knowledge, something immeasurably richer, more intricate, and more meaningful, than anything in the mind of a single speaker.

No-one knows their language perfectly any more than anyone knows a large city or stretch of wilderness perfectly, yet every city, every landscape, is perfect in its own contingent and provisional way. We each know *fragments* of language, just as we know fragments of cities. And as we acquire knowledge of different cities at different times in our lives, so our knowledge of grammatical structures is fixed at different points in time and space. This grammatical knowledge is at once deeply personal, and at the same time 'open-source': anyone with my life experience – and love of languages, see Ω is for Love – could have acquired the same inventory of grammatical skills. Like biodiversity, it's all out there, until it's gone, forever; see McCloskey (1997).

They can print statistics and count the populations in hundreds of thousands, but to each man a city consists of no more than a few streets, a few houses, a few people. Remove these few and a city exists no longer except as a pain in the memory, like the pain of an amputated leg no longer there.

Graham Greene, *Our Man in Havana* ([1958] 2004)

Readers with some historical perspective will recognise this conception of linguistic knowledge as coming close to a re-description of the Saussurean notion of *langue*, which de Saussure contrasted with *parole*. In historical surveys of linguistics, *langue* has sometimes been represented as the precursor of *competence*, with *parole* being more closely identified with *performance*. But this is incorrect, as was already pointed out in *Aspects* (Chomsky 1965), where the notion of competence was first introduced.[5] The main reason that there is no continuity between the terms is that (unlike competence) neither *langue* nor *parole* are presumed to be internal to the mind/brain of an individual. For better or worse, they are both 'community assets': essentially external, and intersubjective in nature.

Chomsky is (as usual) dismissive of such externalist concepts: in *Aspects*, he characterises *langue* as 'merely a systematic inventory of items':

> *The distinction I am noting here is related to* the langue–parole *distinction of Saussure; but it is necessary to reject his concept of* langue *as merely a systematic inventory of items and to return rather to the Humboldtian conception of underlying competence as a system of generative processes.*

Noam Chomsky, Aspects of the Theory of Syntax (1965: 4)

Nevertheless, if the arguments of the rest of this chapter go through, there is nothing mere about *langue*: to use a financial metaphor, knowledge of English is the Bank of England, the Bank of Canada, and the Federal Reserve all rolled into one – not just the assets in aggregate, but the banking systems as well. See also v is for von Humboldt below.

In the remainder of the chapter, then, I'll consider four-and-three-quarter arguments that should lead us to prefer *langue* to Chomskyan competence as a viable theoretical construct. If these are sound, then steps (iv) and (v) above must be rejected, even if one continues to accept POS arguments for a very small set of formal properties. In short, I will try to make the case that strict internalism has painted linguistic theory into a corner, and that is time to walk out.

The case for *langue*

In order to make a case for the theoretical utility and coherence of *langue*, it is necessary to shift the goal posts a little with respect to what it is that any speaker has actually internalised. In place of Chomsky's highly restrictive, abstract and aprioristic notions (UG/I-LANGUAGE/NARROW COMPETENCE), I'll explicitly adopt Sir John Lyons' friendlier, more operational definition, which was first introduced in C is for Competence~Performance above, and which is repeated here, for convenience:

> *Linguistic competence is the knowledge of particular languages, in virtue of which I am able to produce and understand utterances in those languages.*

John Lyons, 'On competence and performance and related notions'
(in Brown et al., eds, Performance and Competence in Second
Language Acquisition, [1965] 1996)

That plural -*s* again. As should be clear immediately, this definition implies a much more personal, heterogeneous, permeable and variable kind of knowledge than anything endorsed in the mainstream generativist literature. Some will balk at this imperfection: for others, it seems to make very good sense. *Something so Right*, as Paul Simon once observed, in a different context.

♫ Paul Simon, *Something so Right* (1972)

(i)   Fragments and threads

Language comprehension has often been compared to vision – not just in this book, but elsewhere. There is good reason for this comparison: both involve the internal processing and integration of fragmentary, distal information impinging on our sense organs; both involve discrete, categorical stages of processing – we don't see varying frequencies of light, we see colours; we don't hear vibrations in the air, or Hertz, we hear sounds, or words; both involve the extraction of abstract meaning from a physical signal. The parallels seem obvious.

A crucial difference between the two, however, is that language is a projective and reflexive system: the language processing system generally only operates on and over products of its own creation (utterances, discourse, text). So, while it is reasonable to think that every sighted person shares a broadly similar visual processing system, only a handful of people on earth – identical twins perhaps, living in precisely the same environment – share an identical personal competence language processing system. Indeed, there is no 'generic competence', if John Lyons is correct. Everyone reading this book has an *English* language processing system of some kind, not a language processing system. In virtue of my experience, I have a *Belfast English* processing system, a *Montreal English* processing system, a *Heinian German* processing system, a written *Swedish* processing system, a *downtown Montreal French* processing system, a *Rheinisch German* processing system, a *Restaurant Greek* processing system – I know six useful Modern Greek expressions, four of which are printable – a *Virgilian Latin* processing system, etc. Of course, to call any of these scraps of knowledge 'competences' or 'systems' implies vastly more coherence and separation than is found in the space between my ears. Many of them run into each other at the interstices; indeed some, like my *Spanish* and *Italian* processing systems, are thoroughly confused. When in southwestern Europe, I speak a kind of Common Southern Romance, a *lingua franca australis,* like some character in Umberto Eco's *Name of the Rose*, or a song by Manu Chao, perhaps. It's neither pure nor pretty, but it works well enough.

> *Je ne sais guère, qué voy a hacer*
> *Dov'è vai, mi corazón?*

> After ♫ Manu Chao, *Me Gustas Tu?* (*Próxima Estación: Esperanza,* 2001)

The permeability of what Vivian Cook (e.g. Cook 1995) calls MULTICOMPE-TENCE expresses itself in myriad ways, the most obvious of which is lexical. Take the word *pomegranate*, for (just one) instance. Someone who knows only English would probably treat this word as mono-morphemic, like *crocodile* or *mango*. However, knowing that the French for apple is *pomme*, and for pomegranate, *grenade*, or that the German for pomegranate is *Granatapfel*, forces a re-analysis of the composition of the English word as 'apple grenade'. If one reflected no further, a pomegranate might be thought to be the kind of apple whose seeds exploded like a grenade (cf. Gleitman and Gleitman 1979). Of course, the etymology runs in just the opposite direction: military hand grenades are so-named because they look like pomegranates. The *-granate* part comes from medieval Latin *granatum* 'seeded'. And if you know Italian, instead of French and German, the correct etymology is much more perspicuous: *melograno* 'apple-grain'.

Another nice example of lexical permeability is found in the Jake Thackray song *The Last Will and Testament of Jake Thackray* (already mentioned in A is for Abstraction above). In the first lines of the second verse, Thackray writes about his dying, beginning with two colloquial expressions – to turn up (one's) toes, to rattle (one's) clack. He then adds a third expression: *when I agonise.* This usage of the verb seems strange from a monolingual English perspective, until it is remembered that Thackray was not a 'monolingual English', but also a fluent speaker of French. In Romance, as in earlier stages of English, *agony* means more than psychological discomfort ('She agonised about whether to tell her parents') or extreme physical pain ('I was in agony for weeks'): it means death-throes. *Agony* has undergone semantic weakening in Modern English, yet Thackray is clearly aware of the French sense of the word, even if most of his listeners are not.

♫ Jake Thackray, *The Last Will and Testament of Jake Thackray* (2006)

Languages that are part of our 'personal competence are permeable at a syntactic level also.[6] Native speakers of Vietnamese, for example, who are also L2 learners of English or French, are significantly more likely to use English-like passive constructions in Vietnamese academic writing than monolingual speakers; speakers of Italian who have spent many years in an English environment are more likely to supply overt subject pronouns, where monolingual native speakers would naturally omit them; English L2 learners of German occasionally produce VERB-SECOND orders (see below) when speaking English in a German environment. Generally, the situation where a second language or third language influences a speaker's knowledge of their first language is termed LANGUAGE ATTRITION; see Seliger and Vago (1991), Sorace (2004) and especially Schmid (2013). But while the phenomenon is real, the term is a misnomer, based on the doubtful purist assumption that the language variety we started out with was more 'perfect' before it was modified by foreign influence. Attrition is better viewed as enrichment, or hybridisation.

What's more, we are sometimes unwitting speakers of other languages. In the first episode of James Joyce's *Ulysses*, for instance, the Reverend Mr Haines addresses an old woman in Irish, a language that she doesn't recognise:

> – *Do you understand what he says? Stephen asked her.*
> – *Is it French you are talking, sir? the old woman said to Haines.*
> *Haines spoke to her again a longer speech, confidently.*
> – *Irish, Buck Mulligan said. Is there Gaelic on you?*
> – *I thought it was Irish, she said, by the sound of it. Are you from the West, sir?*
> – *I am an Englishman, Haines answered.*
> – *He's English, Buck Mulligan said, and he thinks we ought to speak Irish in Ireland.*
> – *Sure we ought to, the old woman said, and I'm ashamed I don't speak the language myself. I'm told it's a grand language by them that knows.*
> – *Grand is no name for it, said Buck Mulligan. Wonderful entirely. Fill us out some more tea, Kinch. Would you like a cup, ma'am?*
>
> James Joyce, Little Review 4.11 (1918)

The irony of this exchange is that the way in which the woman asks the question ('Is it French you are talking?') – as well as Buck Mulligan's part in the conversation ('Is there Gaelic on you?' 'Fill us out some more tea ...' 'Grand is no name for it') – is almost pure, relexified Irish; that is to say, Irish syntax with English words attached.

But what about languages we really don't know. Languages that I don't speak don't even impinge on my consciousness. Sitting in a coffee shop in downtown Kobe, what I see (excluding the written language) or feel or taste is much the same as any Japanese customer, but the chatter that I hear is really just background noise. If anything, it helps me to concentrate. By contrast, when two speakers of a variety of English that I *do* recognise enter the same café, I can't help but be distracted by whatever they have to say. For the members of my immediate family, the same environments trigger quite different reactions: since my two older children are native or near-native speakers of Japanese and Sheffield English, *Kobe* Japanese (Kobe-ben) is fully comprehensible, as is Sheffield English, whereas the Belfast English of strangers is largely just noise. (We should really visit more often!)

Yet we all share the same visual perception: if I only noticed European makes of cars when crossing the road in Japan – I jaywalk, I'll admit – I would be dead or seriously injured in less time than it takes to write this sentence.

If personal competence is as fragmentary and ephemeral as suggested by this picture, then where is the rich knowledge of English, or Japanese or Tagalog, this treasure shared by its speakers, such that we can speak of the grammar of English, the French lexicon, the phonology of Standard Russian, and so forth? From a strictly internalist point of view, these things either don't exist – which seems improbable, since countless books have been written about them – or they are simply aggregates of individual competences; this also seems unlikely, given that different varieties of a language involve mutually incompatible specifications; see H is for Homogeneity above. The remaining alternative is that external language (*langue*) is much richer and more coherent than internalists wish to suppose.

Two other inescapable facts about natural languages seem to force us to accept *langue* as a 'virtual conceptual necessity' – to hijack Chomsky's phrase. These are synchronic variation and diachronic (grammatical) change, both of which must have their locus outside of any individual mind. Variation and change are really two sides of the same coin – one being the agent of the other; nevertheless, they can –and will – be considered separately.

(ii)   Verjess Babylon*: the source of grammatical variation*

Let's take grammatical variation first. This was partially addressed in the previous section, with respect to intra-speaker variation in Belfast English. Here, though, the concern is with what has been called 'macro-parametric variation': large-scale generalised differences in phrasal word-order, subject omission, richness of agreement paradigms, binding possibilities, and so on. At least since the seminal work of Joseph Greenberg and others in the 1960s and 1970s (Greenberg 1963), it has been known that language varieties vary fairly systematically along these dimensions; also, that there are a number of interesting implicational relationships holding between particular grammatical phenomena across historically unrelated language varieties. Language typology is just the study of these relationships. See Comrie (1981), Whaley (1998).

To cite just a handful of well-known correlations: languages such as Modern Irish and Standard Arabic that display VSO order in finite clauses almost always show alternate SVO order in non-finite contexts; the VERB-SECOND constraint (a feature of most Germanic languages, except English after 800 CE) is only ever found in root clauses; languages, like French, that allow verbal object agreement (e.g. *Il l'a mise̲ ~ Il l'a mis* 'He put it$_{[fem]}$' vs. 'He put it$_{[masc]}$') always also show verbal agreement with subjects; as discussed in G is for Grammar above, languages that allow infinitival complements of WANT predicates with non-co-referential subjects necessarily allow infinitival complements with co-referential subjects ('I want you to do that' ⊃ 'I want to do that.').

But not *vice versa*, in any of these cases.

While some of these typological properties might be derived from an examination of a particular ambient language, others cannot be. For example, if you happen to be born into a Korean- or Turkish-speaking environment and are never exposed to French, or a language with prepositions (as opposed to postpositions), there is no way to induce the embedded implicational universal in (112), from Hawkins (1983: 66):

(112)   Universal (III): If a language has Prep word order [i.e., has prepositions, rather than postpositions] then, if the adjective follows the noun, the genitive follows the noun; that is, Prep ⊃ (NA ⊃ NG)

John A. Hawkins, *Word Order Universals* (1983: 66)

Implicational universals of this kind cannot be part of anyone's internally represented grammar, since they are derived (and tested) over sets of language types. Nevertheless, statements such as these make clearly testable, empirical predictions about the kinds of word-order that are to be cross-linguistically. If external languages were not real, coherent, structured objects – albeit abstract ones – such predictions would be nonsensical: they would be comparable to predictions about the number of twists on a unicorn's horn, or the fairy-carrying capacity of a pinhead. Clearly, though, there is a real difference between the two kinds of statement: the first involves an empirical prediction about a real-world property – the proposition contained in (112), for instance, is either false or (provisionally) true; by contrast, the shape of unicorns' horns is anyone's guess, and no-one's truth.

Strict internalism allows us no way to observe or describe typological generalisations, yet – ironically – many of these statements are concerned with exactly the range of phenomena that syntactic theory is supposed to explain (traditionally at any rate): see, for example, Travis (1984, 1991). Yet if languages aren't 'out there' – if *langue* is nothing more than a 'systematic inventory of items' – it's not clear what the generalisations could be based on.

(iii)   The Ugly Duckling, *and the stork*

♫ Frank Loesser, *The Ugly Duckling* (popularised by Danny Kaye)

What is at least curious about a strictly internalist approach to language based on a genetic theory of grammar is that exactly *all* of the inherited systematic variation in grammatical structure that we observe has an external source. This makes UG wholly exceptional when compared to other biological systems, where virtually all of the relevant variation in phenotypic expression is due to genetic variation, and where the environment plays no interesting causal role in individual ontological development. Even extreme Lamarckians could not conceive of the idea that the environment might be so absolutely telling. See also N is for Nativism below.

Almost everyone reading this book will know some English version of the *Ugly Duckling* story. Readers of my generation or older may be most familiar with Danny Kaye's rendition of the Frank Loesser song (in the 1952 musical film *Hans Christian Andersen)*, but versions of the allegory can be found in almost every children's anthology of literary folk-tales. Yet probably only a handful of readers will have read the Danish original, published in Copenhagen in 1843. This is a pity, in the present context, since Andersen's original story contains two lessons in genetic inheritance for the price of one. Not only do we find the central redemptive tale of an ugly duckling transformed by his genes into a magnificent swan, but also – right at the outset, almost as a throwaway line – a comment on the genetics of language acquisition, stork style ...

Der var så dejligt ude på landet; det var sommer, kornet stod gult, havren grøn, høet var rejst i stakke nede i de grønne enge, og der gik storken på sine lange, røde ben og snakkede ægyptisk, for det sprog havde han lært af sin moder.

It was so delightful out in the country; it was summer, the corn stood yellow, the oats were green, the hay was set in stooks down in the green meadow, where a stork walked about on his long red legs, speaking Egyptian, for that was the language he had learned from his mother.

Hans Christian Andersen, *Den Grimme Ælling* 'The Ugly Duckling' (1843)

If human children instinctively learned their mother's language as the stork had done, this would be a very different book, and the world a vastly different place. But they don't: human children acquire the language(s) of their community before that of their parents. In this respect, human language is completely different from bird-song (though see Bolhuis, Okanoya and Scharff 2010, Tchernichovski and Marcus 2014). Conversely, if real Danish storks learned to speak as Danish children do, they'd learn Danish, no matter where their mother came from. Except that – as a killjoy ornithologist would tell you – they wouldn't learn any song at all: real storks are mute.

As for the Ugly Duckling, he has no choice in his physiology and appearance, in duckland: being raised among ducks doesn't determine that he'll walk like a duck, or talk like a duck; he can't choose not to be 'ugly for a duck' – and nothing he does will prevent him from becoming a beautiful swan. It doesn't matter how few other swans are around, it doesn't matter if he only feeds on duckweed, or takes quacking lessons for three hours every morning. He's a swan, and he's not about to quack. That's how heredity works.

Except for the *ugly* part, much the same applies to the heredity of my children, who are each what the Japanese call ハーフ *hāfu*. It sounds worse than it is: to many Japanese, *half* in this context is more highly valued than one. Our children were all born in different countries: in the Netherlands (2001), in England (2006), in Japan (2010). As far as phenotypical physical traits are concerned, their place of birth, their ante-natal care, their diet from zero to five years, the people who surrounded them in their pre-school years: beyond minimal conditions for survival, all of these environmental conditions are entirely irrelevant to their physiology or personality. Being *hāfu* means that the two younger children have blonde/light brown hair, that one has golden-brown, the other grey-blue eyes, being *hāfu* means that our eldest child looks significantly more Asian than any of his Irish cousins. He is not one gram more Dutch than the others, however, despite living in Nijmegen for the first four years of his life. His brown eyes and un-Dutch complexion were not altered, even fractionally, by the influence of *hagelslag, stroopwafeln* or *vla*, nor was his innate sense of balance significantly influenced by the experience of riding a bicycle from the age of three. This insensitivity to environmental forces is exactly what one expects of innate characteristics. Indeed, that is a good part of the definition of what innateness is. As Mameli and Bateson (2006) explain it:

A trait is innate if and only if its development doesn't involve the extraction of information from the environment.

> Mateo Mameli and Patrick Bateson, 'Innateness and
> the sciences' (*Biology and Philosophy*, 2006: 159)

By contrast, when it comes to the acquisition of particular languages, the environment is absolutely telling. A fully Japanese child will not acquire knowledge of Japanese grammar twice as well as a ハーフ-child, or have any advantage in learning Japanese over a fully Caucasian one if both are raised in the same environment (for example, as the result of birth adoption). Had we remained in the Netherlands, my eldest son would by now be as fluent a speaker of Dutch as anyone in his school year, in spite of his parentage. And whereas age of first exposure (up to puberty) is a good predictor of native-like proficiency in a second language – Johnson and Newport (1989), Boroditsky (2001), Abrahamsson (2012) – there is no correlation whatsoever between ethnicity and native-like attainment.

Like blood group or eye-colour or handedness, the formal properties of languages vary parametrically and (apparently) categorically; but unlike blood group, eye-colour or handedness, *none* of this variation is in the grammatical genotype of an individual, on anyone's account. Individual language varieties may be transmitted through culture, but they cannot be inherited through our genes. So what remains?

Faced with this obvious dichotomy, the strict internalist has two choices. The first alternative, embraced in the heady days of the Principles and Parameters approach (1981–1993), is to concede that the environment has a sizeable effect, but to construe this as 'triggering data' only. On this view, children are innately endowed with a set of grammatical principles, some of which have alternative parametric settings (±overt *wh*-movement; ±lexical verb raising, ±EPP, etc.), to be fixed by experience. In this way, one can hold on to the notion of a coherent, highly restrictive and innate set of options. A more exuberant variant of this approach is found in some construals of Optimality Theory, which ascribes to UG every possible combination of principles and constraints, which are then ranked on the basis of the input available to the language learner.

But genetics doesn't work this way either. Consider a somewhat misleading – but still useful – analogy from poker: at the point of conception, we are all dealt different hands, we don't each retain a full deck to select cards from on the basis of positive evidence.[7] Matt Ridley makes this point clearly in his book *Genome*. With respect to blood type, for example, we aren't born with the inherent possibility of being A or B, or AB, or O (positive or negative): we have an ABO gene, whose different alleles code for one or other of these options. Similarly, in the domain of personality, we either have relatively 'long copies' of D_4DR genes on chromosome 11, which may result in a low responsiveness to dopamine, and which in turn fosters novelty-seeking behaviours, or we have relatively short copies, in which case a high responsiveness to dopamine may result in our getting our kicks from something much tamer; see Ridley (1999: 165).[8] We are not born genetically equipotential: the choices are made *in utero,* at – or soon after – the point of conception. And so, as Ridley observes:

> *The Human Genome Project is founded upon a fallacy. There is no such thing as 'the human genome'. Neither in time nor in space can such a thing be defined. At hundreds of different loci, scattered throughout the twenty-three chromosomes, there are genes that differ from person to person. Nobody can say that the blood-group A is normal, and that 'O', 'B' and 'AB' are abnormal. So, when the Human Genome Project publishes the sequence of the typical human being, what will it publish for the ABO gene on chromosome 9? The project's declared aim is to publish the average, or 'consensus' sequence of 200 different people. But this would miss the point in the case of the ABO gene, because it is a crucial part of its function that it should not be the same in everybody. Variation is an inherent and integral part of the human – or indeed any – genome.*

> Matt Ridley, *Genome* (1999: 145)

The last line deserves repetition: 'Variation is an inherent and integral part of ... any genome.' This means that if UG is genetic, it can't be invariant. But for Chomsky, and many of his adherents, UG *is* invariant. Consider the following assertion from Boeckx (2006):

> *One thing that a minimalist should resist at all costs is the claim that Rizzi's Relativized Minimality principle (in any of its economy incarnations) [or any similar principle: NGD] is parameterized, meaning that some languages abide by it, while some other languages would be free of its effects. Such a possibility clearly falls out of the set*

of minimalist grammars. Put differently, if Relativized Minimality is a parameter, the
Minimalist Program is not a program worth pursuing.

Cedric Boeckx, *Linguistic Minimalism: Origins, Concepts,*
Methods and Aims (2006: 104–5)

And UG is [also] … 'the theory of the genetic component of the language faculty … that's what it is.' This appears to be a remarkable contradiction.

It will probably not have escaped attention that Matt Ridley is a science-
writer and journalist, not a professional geneticist. The fact that he holds a
doctorate in zoology from Oxford will cut little ice with many of my academic
colleagues, some of whom are broadly contemptuous of science journalism
(especially where they disagree with a journalist's take on a particular issue).
For that reason, it is worth quoting a respected geneticist and science-writer
(not a journalist), Professor Steve Jones of University College, London, who
makes much the same point:

Human genetics was for most of its history more or less restricted to studying pedigrees
which stood out because they contained an abnormality. This limited its ability to trace
patterns of descent to those few families – like the Hapsburgs – who appeared to devi-
ate from the perfect form. Biology has now shown that this perfect form does not exist.
Instead, there is a huge amount of inherited variation. Thousands of inherited charac-
ters [sic] – perfectly normal diversity, not diseases – distinguish each person. There is
so much variety that everyone alive is different, not only from everyone else, but from
everyone who has ever or will ever live … Most of modern genetics is nothing more than
a search for variation.

Steve Jones, *The Language of the Genes: Biology,*
History and the Evolutionary Future (1993: 17)

In short, talk of invariance and genetics in the same breath is oxymoronic –
with or without the PSEUDO-AFFIX. See also Lieberman (2015).

There's also the flipside to this argument, namely, that whereas true genetic
variation is only mediated by sex, variation in ultimate language attainment is
exclusively the result of contingent circumstances. An important consequence
of this is that grammatical knowledge can change within the lifetime of an individual. This is a notion that is patently obvious to second language researchers,
but which seems to slip right by monolingual theoreticians. Thanks to my life
experience I do not speak the English of my parents, but nor do I speak the
English of my ten or twenty-one year-old self. In no other area of biology do
variant genes spread or mutate through association or immersion or random
contact. The leopard cannot change his spots no matter whether he stalks the
dappled fringes of the rain-forest, or is transferred to the grey monotony of a
concrete enclosure. He may change his children's spots (from black to brown)
by mating with a lioness – see the Wikipedia entry for *Leopon* – but he's stuck

with his own. Similarly, sending children on adventure holidays every year will not significantly alter their taste for thrill-seeking experiences: those blessed or cursed with long D_4DR genes will probably continue to love it, while those with short versions of the gene may resent their parents forever for ruining their summers. By contrast, slight shifts in location – moving to another part of the English-speaking world for university or employment, for example – can produce significant changes in our personal grammatical competence: use of the simple past with *yet*, for example, or understanding that *while* can mean *until* (compare 'He won't be back while six' in Sheffield English). At the level of *langue*, being invaded first by Norse-speakers ('Vikings' in what became the *Danelaw*), then by Norman French, has given speakers of Present Day English an ambient language whose grammatical structures are closer to those of Mainland Scandinavian or French than to its Anglo-Saxon/West Germanic roots. One does not have to go as far as the creolists Bailey and Maroldt (1977) ('The French lineage of English') to acknowledge that contact can be at least as important as genetic affiliation in explaining grammatical change. Language contact is 'skin-to-skin', not 'gene to gene'.

There is, of course, an alternative solution to the problem of variation that does not require us to give up strict internalism, and which does not force us to accept *langue* as a coherent social construct.

God did it: *Deus ex machina*.

♫ Wolfgang Niedecken/BAP, *Verjess Babylon* (2011)

In his song *Verjess Babylon* ('Forget Babylon'), the *Kölsch* (Cologne-dialect) folk-rock singer Wolfgang Niedecken reimagines the scene towards the end of the sixth day of Creation, when God suddenly realises that – what with all the other things he has had to attend to – he has forgotten something: to give mankind a language (*Jesses nä, die Minsche hann jo noch kein Sprooch!*).

> *Ja, klar, 'ne Hahn kräht, die Koh määt Muh,*
> > Yeah sure, the cock crows, the cows goes moo
>
> *Un dä Hungk, dä bellt dozo.*
> > And the dog, it can bark too.
>
> *En Katz miaut, der Löwe brüllt,*
> > A cat goes miaow, the lions roar
>
> *Wenn ens jet nit läuf wie bestellt.*
> > When things don't work out as planned before.
>
> *Jesses nä, die Minsche hann jo noch kein Sprooch!*
> > Bejesus, mankind still hasn't a way to speak.
>
> *Das 's mer irj'ndwie durchjejange letzte Woch!...*
> > Somehow it must have slipped my mind last week!

And so he proceeds to think up languages for all the peoples of the Earth:

> *Su krääte Eskimos un Inkas dat,*
> > *And so the Eskimos and the Inkas got*
>
> *Wodrop se schon ihr Levve lang jewaat.*
> > *The thing they'd wanted all their lives.*
>
> *Die Chinese wollte 'n Sprooch, die ohne 'R' usskütt*
> > *The Chinese wanted a language that didn't have any 'r's*
>
> *Un die jeschrivve revolutionär usssieht.*
> > *And which looked revolutionary written down.*
>
> *Kisuaheli, Jamaikanisch un Sanskrit,*
> > *Kiswahili, Jamaican, and Sanskrit too*
>
> *Sprooche, die mer nur 'm Himalaya versteht,*
> > *Languages only people in the Himalayas understand*
>
> *Och Hebräisch, Schwizerdütsch, sujar Latein,*
> > *And Hebrew, Swiss German, even Latin*
>
> *Un ein für die enn Bahrain.*
> > *And one for the folks in Bahrain.*
>
> *Verjess Babylon un dat met däm Turm.*
> > *Forget Babylon and all that Tower stuff*
>
> *Jed Land kritt en Sprooch, ein wöhr nit jenooch.*
> > *Every country gets a language, one wouldn't be enough*
>
> *Verjess Babylon, Hillije Jeist un Jottes Sohn.*
> > *Forget Babylon, Holy Ghost and Son of God*
>
> *Ejal wat et koss, noch benn ich dä Boss!*
> > *Whatever it costs, I'm still the boss!'*

Finally, he arrives back in Germany, and gives to the Hessians and Swabians and Berliners their distinctive dialects; as for Hannover – supposedly the source of Standard German – he can't think of anything very interesting, and Düsseldorf makes no sense anyway. Still, after going around his new world, by the time he gets home to Cologne, he's worn out. So what should he do?

> *So, Lück, wesst ihr wat? Ich hann et jetz satt,*
> *Ich kann ech nimieh, mir deit alles wieh!*
> *Sibbe Daach Akkord, sujet jrenz ahn Mord.*
> *Wiesu sprecht ihr eijentlich nit einfach wie ich?*
>
> > *So, people, d'you know what? I've had enough*
> > *I really can't hack it anymore: everything hurts.*
> > *This Seven Day Contract, it's murder.*
> > *(Tell you what:) Why don't you just speak like me?*

BAP, Verjess Babylon (Halv Su Wild, 2011)

So, there you have a solution to synchronic variation without *langue*. Creationism is always an alternative to real science. But I don't suppose it's any more attractive to most internalists – except perhaps to speakers of (God's own) *Kölsch*.

(iv)   Grammatical change: 'The less we know, the clearer the picture'

It only becomes apparent after a long engagement with the history of the language that the quality and quantity of our data-base shifts massively over time. And the less we know, the clearer the picture.

> Roger Lass, 'Phonology and morphology' (in Hogg and
> Denison, eds, *A History of the English Language*, 2006: 104)

Biological internalism encounters a different kind of challenge when faced with the problem of syntactic change at the level of the speech community, what Labov (1994) refers to as 'communal change'. In fact, this is the same problem viewed from a different perspective. In this case, however, its symptoms are the direct opposite of those found at the level of the individual speaker: rather than happening too quickly – a person's grammatical knowledge changing over his or her lifespan as the result of contact – large-scale grammatical change permeates a speech community much too slowly and gradually to be amenable to any genetic explanation.

The problem is simply stated: if *langue* is a 'mere inventory of items', then language change must be construed in purely internalist terms, as grammar change; cf. Lightfoot (1991). And grammar change, on an internalist view, must be I-LANGUAGE change: children acquiring a language must effect changes by setting grammatical parameters differently from those of previous generations, through 'imperfect learning'. For example, rather than allowing subjects of finite clauses to go unpronounced (as in Italian, and earlier stages of French), the French child in the eighteenth century must have implicitly decided on the basis of the input that these subjects were obligatory; rather than licensing generalised verb raising to C (verb-second) or to tense (as in Modern French), the child learning Standard English must have decided – sometime during the Early Modern English period – that lexical verbs do not raise (unless, that is, that same child is giving orders in Belfast English, or imitating Shakespeare, where verb raising is still an option; see H is for Homogeneity, also J is for Judgment).

The notion that grammatical change is to be explained only in terms of (very early parameter resetting) in first language acquisition is as clever as it is implausible. The two most damning objections to the internalist view of syntactic change are briefly and cogently spelt out in a short article by Jean Aitchison (2003), in which it is claimed, first, that teenagers rather than infants, are the primary agents of grammatical change (see, in particular, Kerswill 1996); second, that change spreads much too slowly through a speech community for it to be usefully conceived of as something internal to any individual. The relevant excerpts are quoted below:

Babies do not initiate changes. Groups of interacting speakers do, particularly adolescents. Any permanent change happens largely via the vocabulary …

No child language event happens sufficiently fast or thoroughly for a parameter to be set or reset in one swoop, however one identifies the various parameters …

[I]n the case of children and change, close-grained sociolinguistic studies have shown that some proposed psycholinguistic explanations [i.e. generative parameter-setting accounts such as that of Roberts (2007): NGD] are a mirage.

> Jean Aitchison, 'Psycholinguistic perspectives on language change' (in Joseph and Janda, eds, *The Handbook of Historical Linguistics*, 2003: 735ff.)

If what Aitchison claims is correct, that is to say if the long-held idea that grammatical change occurs between generations, as the result of young children's imperfect learning – see Paul (1880), Sweet (1899: 74), Andersen (1978: 21), Fromkin and Rodman (1993: 348) – is revealed as false, this undermines to a very large extent the empirical basis of very early parameter-setting.

Aitchison's second charge, that grammatical change plays out over centuries, and that it does so across communities rather than individuals, is no less serious. Even more problematic for a theory to which construction-specific rules are anathema, it looks very much as if syntactic change is a piecemeal business, working its way on a construction-by-construction – even predicate-by-predicate – basis. Catastrophic change is rarely, if ever, observed, probably for the very good reason that it's good to be able to talk to your parents and grandparents, at least occasionally.[9]

James Walker offers a clear statement of the variationists' position:

Whatever the theoretical orientation, all models of language change must acknowledge that change proceeds gradually. In a change from form x to form y there is always a period in which x and y co-exist: that is, there is always a period of variation, which any model of language change must be able to account for. The gradualness of language change presents a problem for those approaches to the study of language that do not recognise variation. These approaches generally view language change as proceeding by re-analysis across generations …

If this model [sic] of language change is correct, we should expect to see change occurring suddenly, across a single generation. Yet an examination of historical data shows that linguistic changes take several generations, or even centuries, to occur. Attempts to resolve this dilemma have argued that the apparent gradualness and variation of language change represent either a set of discrete changes in subsequent generations, or the co-existence of discrete, categorical linguistic systems in the same speech community. However … variation persists no matter how thinly we slice the data. Language change advances via variation. [my emphasis: NGD]

> James Walker, *Variation in Linguistic Systems* (2012: chapter 7)

History of the English Language: Major divisions

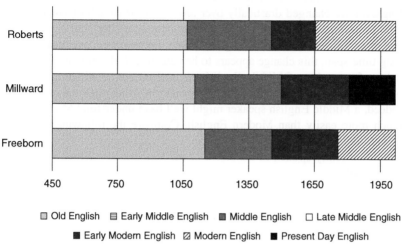

Figure 23 Stages in the history of English.

In support of Walker's claim, let's revisit a phenomenon that has already been rehearsed several times, namely, (lexical) verb-movement and the syntax of inversion, this time from a diachronic perspective.

It is customary to divide the history of English into several distinct epochs, whose more or less discrete beginning- and end-points are signalled by developments external to the language itself. There is broad consensus about where the major transition points are to be found, even if there may be quibbling about the precise dates and the timing of less dramatic developments. Figure 23 compares three different classifications: those of Freeborn (2005), Millward (1989) and Roberts (1993), respectively.

As this figure illustrates, it is generally agreed that those who understood *Beowulf* natively spoke a variety of Old English, that Chaucer's *Canterbury Tales* was written in a variety of Middle English, and that the Early Modern period began at or just before the accession of King Henry VII (1485–1500) and ended sometime in the late seventeenth century. Yet in spite of these discrete labels, it will be clear that historical change in language is continuous: people did not stop speaking Old English, or switch to Anglo-Norman, on the day after the Battle of Hastings; speakers of London English in 1580 (100 years into the Early Modern English period) would have understood Chaucer about as well as we understand Shakespeare; researchers, like Millward (1989), who draw a distinction between Modern and Present Day English do not dispute the ready accessibility of Jane Austen or Charles Dickens to a twenty-first-century reader. For all that, it is undeniable that the basic grammatical structures of English have changed drastically over any 500-year stretch of language history: the selection of specific transition points may be fairly arbitrary, but the fact of significant structural change is certain. Furthermore, over a sufficiently long time-span, this change appears to be categorical: the grammatical knowledge of a speaker of Middle English *circa* 1300 was as different from that of someone born in 1990, as that of a speaker of Modern Dutch or Swedish. Indeed, a Middle English speaker might well have understood Modern Dutch much more easily than Modern English. Compare the following song-lines from Middle English and Modern Frisian (Frŷs), a conservative West Germanic variety currently spoken in the North of the Netherlands. Which is the more accessible?

> *When the nyhtegale singes,*
> > *When the nightingale sings,*
> *The wodes waxen grene,*
> > *The trees grow green,*
> *Lef ant gras ant blosme springes*
> > *Leaf and grass and blossom springs*
> *In Averyl, Y wene;*
> > *In April, I suppose*
> *Ant love is to myn herte gon*
> > *And love has to my heart gone*
> *With one spere so kene*
> > *With a spear so sharp*
> *Nyht ant day my blod hit drynkes*
> > *Night and day my blood it drains*
> *Myn herte deth me tene.*
> > *My heart to death it aches.*

When the Nyhtegale Singes (ca. 1310), Harley MS
2253, British Library

> *De nacht is foarby, de sinne is frij, om heech te gean*
> > *The night has passed, the sun is about to rise*
> *Aanst wurdt it dei, de moarn is te nij, om stil te stean*
> > *Soon it will be day, the morning is too new to be still.*
> *It libben wie wrang, it wachtsjen te lang.*
> > *Life was hard, the waiting so long*
> *Mar 't nimt in kear*
> > *But the tide is turning*
> *Wês mar net bang, nea wer bang, it hoecht net mear.*
> > *Don't be afraid, you don't need to fear ever again.*

de Kast, *In Nije Dei* 'A New Day' (1997)

Here, I'll focus exclusively on the position of the finite verb across a range of syntactic contexts during the period 1300–1900 (from Middle to Modern English, particularly during the Early Modern English period, approximately 1450–1700); for a more theoretical treatment, see Han (2000), and references therein. The Chaucerian examples in (113), together with their Modern English glosses, illustrate the contrasting positions of lexical (main) verbs in five different constructions in the period before and after the rise of '*do*-support', the expletive auxiliary that is now obligatory in inversion and negation contexts in Standard British English: whereas in Middle English the main verb (in italics) appears outside of the verb-phrase, in Modern English, this higher position is now almost always taken by 'dummy *do*':

(113) a. Thanne <u>longen</u> folk to goon on pilgrimages …
         Then do folk long to go on piligrimage …
                        Chaucer, *CT: Prologue* (adverbial-V_2 [transitive])

       b. <u>Seyde</u> he nat thus, 'ne do no fors of dremes'?
         Did he not say (thus) 'do not be troubled of dreams'?
                        Chaucer, *CT: Nun's Priest's Tale*, 121 (negative question)

       c. <u>Woot</u> ye nat, where ther stant a litel toun.
         Don't you know where [that] little town is?
                        Chaucer, *CT: Manciple's Tale*, 1 (adverbial-V_2 [intransitive] Y-N
                                                                                question)

       d. What <u>seith</u> she now? what <u>dooth</u> this queene of love,
         What does she say now? What does she do, this queen of love?
                        Chaucer, *CT: Knight's Tale*, 2664 (affirmative object question)

       e. I <u>saugh</u> nat this yeer so myrie a compaignye / Atones in this
         herberwe as is now
         This year I did not see at any one time as merry a company in this
         inn as now.
                        Chaucer, *CT: General Prologue*, 764 (negative declaratives)

Figure 24 – originally due to Ellegård (1953), see also Ogura (1993), Kroch (1989), Roberts (1993), cf. Kroch (2003) – charts the emergence of *do*-support in five different constructions that previously displayed generalised verb raising (to T or C).

The first thing to consider is the disparities among the various constructions in the trajectories of auxiliary *do*: whereas the incidence of *do*-support rises fairly quickly for affirmative transitives and negative questions, the increase in object question and negative declarative contexts – (113d) and (113e) – is much more gradual. Even by 1700, according to the figure, the majority of

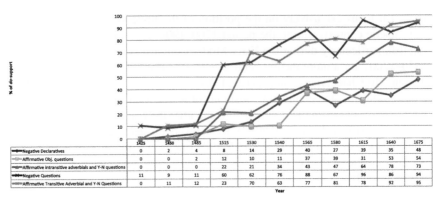

	1425	1450	1485	1515	1530	1540	1565	1580	1615	1640	1675
Negative Declaratives	0	2	4	8	14	29	40	27	39	35	48
Affirmative Obj. questions	0	0	2	12	10	11	37	39	31	53	54
Affirmative Intransitive adverbials and Y-N questions	0	0	0	22	21	34	43	47	64	78	73
Negative Questions	11	9	11	60	62	76	88	67	96	86	94
Affirmative Transitive Adverbial and Y-N Questions	0	11	12	23	70	63	77	81	78	92	95

Year

Figure 24 The rise of *do*-support/demise of main-verb raising (redrawn from Ellegård 1953).

negative declarative sentences appear not to require *do*-support. In the language of Shakespeare (late sixteenth to early seventeenth century), this optionality is partly attributable to the fact that unraised finite verbs were allowed to occur without *do* to the right of negation, as in (114) – from van Gelderen (2000):

(114) a. CAESAR: when to sound your name
            It not <u>concernèd</u> me. (*Antony and Cleopatra*, 2.2.35)

     b. LEONATO: that they themselves not <u>feele</u>
            (*Much Ado About Nothing*, 5.1.22)

     c. HUBERT: whose tongue … not truly <u>speakes</u>
            (*King John*, 4.3.96)

By the end of the seventeenth century, however, virtually all of the complement set consists of persistent main-verb raising past negation.[10] The availability of verb raising over negation in Late Modern English is taken up in Varga (2005), who cites examples from Mary Shelley's *Frankenstein* and Jane Austen's *Pride and Prejudice,* amongst other nineteenth-century works. Some of Varga's examples are reproduced in (115): these show continued use of V_{fin}-*not* order well past the Late Modern period.

(115) a. I <u>closed</u> not my eyes that night. (*Frankenstein*, 1816: 47)
     b. I <u>doubted</u> not that I should ultimately succeed. (*Frankenstein*, 1816: 52)
     c. Yet I <u>seek</u> not a fellow feeling in my misery. (*Frankenstein*, 1816: 209)

The other general point to notice in Figure 24 is that *do*-support is not obligatory in *any* construction throughout the seventeenth century. As other researchers have observed, main-verb raising is fairly commonly available in *Yes-No* questions up to the mid-nineteenth century, at least with certain predicates; see, for example, Warner (2005). Even today, sporadic instances of main-verb raising can still be found in interrogative contexts, such as those in (116), as well as in negative declaratives, in (117):

(116) a. 'I'm thinking of going to the mall later. What say you?' (*Urban Dictionary*)
b. *Where Goes the Heart?* (1958 book title)
c. 'Why comes he not, today?' (*Eliza Cook's Journal*, 1851)

(117) a. He who knows not and knows not that he knows not is a fool; avoid him.
He who knows not and knows that he knows not is a student; teach him.
He who knows and knows not that he knows is asleep; wake him.
He who knows and knows that he knows is a wise man; follow him.
Various attributions: Persian apothegm, Sanskrit saying, Chinese proverb[11]
b. Every man has his secret sorrows which the world <u>knows not</u>; and often times we call a man cold when he is only sad. Henry Wadsworth Longfellow

The normal assumption is that examples like those in (116) and (117) can be written off as archaisms or fossilised forms, and that main-verb raising is no longer part of Present Day English. Though such a move is necessary to preserve the coherence of a strictly internalist perspective – at least one that draws a rigid distinction between arbitrary lexical properties and maximally general rules – it is questionable whether it has much ecological validity. If what we call knowledge of language is as much *langue* as it is personal competence, then grammatical 'archaisms' are as integral a part of the language as any more productive grammatical knowledge. On this view, abstracting away from archaic language in characterising speakers' knowledge of English is akin to abstracting away from St Paul's Cathedral, Westminster Abbey and the Tower in describing people's knowledge of London (just because we don't build that way any more).

Strict internalism requires ahistoricism – the rejection of any appeal to history in explaining current grammatical knowledge. This is the direct legacy of de Saussure's rigid distinction between synchronic and diachronic linguistics, which allowed internalism to develop in the first place. Arguably, it has done more harm than good.

Furthermore, even if one accepts the idea that *do*-support is now categorical where it applies (though see H is for Homogeneity for discussion of Belfast English imperatives), it seems undeniable that finite-verb raising was optional in many of the same contexts for at least 250 years, from 1450 to 1700 – for 400 years (1450 to 1850), if Varga (2005) is correct; though see Haeberli and Ihsane (2016), for a more nuanced approach. By anyone's reckoning, 250–400 years spans more than one generation of speakers. Moreover, the fact that sentences with and without *do*-support are found in the same text – in Shakespeare's plays, within the same speeches – gives the lie to the notion that the apparent gradualness of language change could be due to the 'co-existence of discrete, categorical linguistic systems' in the same speech community (see Walker quote, above, also Kroch 1989: 137). This would seem to confirm what we have already seen in Belfast English, namely, that grammatical optionality is a fact of dynamic language use; cf. Han (2000), Han and Kroch (2000).

Speakers' sentence production, it seems, is not constrained by a rigid set of discrete parameters acquired shortly after birth; on the contrary, their personal competence continuously adapts to the grammatical patterns they observe in the ambient language – the *langue* that surrounds them. *Contra* Lightfoot (1991), Roberts (1985, 2007) and many others, grammatical change appears to be much more the result of the interplay between personal competence and external *langue* than of one-off, 'very early parameter-setting' (VEPS) (Wexler 1998).[12] And if this is really so, the main lesson of historical linguistics may be, as Paul Hopper expresses it:

> there is … no 'grammar' but only 'grammaticalisation' – movements toward structure
>
> Paul Hopper, 'Emergent Grammar' (1987: 148)

If the arguments summarised in the preceding paragraphs are at all convincing, then the assumption of strict internalism must be reconsidered. No-one has personal access to the history of their language: it must be stored elsewhere. In addition, if the argument of the following section goes through, then strict internalism is dead in the water (to use an apt metaphor).

(v)   *Lazarus, resurrect*

> *He opens his eyes falls in love at first sight*
> *With the girl in the doorway.*
> *What beautiful lines and how full of life;*
> *After thousands of years what a face to wake up to.*
>
> *He holds back a sigh as she touches his arm*
> *She dusts off the bed where 'til now he's been sleeping*

And under miles of stone, the dried fig of his heart
Under scarab and bone starts back to its beating.

♫ Josh Ritter, *The Curse* (2010)

In Josh Ritter's bittersweet song *The Curse*, an Ancient Egyptian mummy is revived by the sight of a beautiful archaeologist ... *after thousands of years ... the dried fig of his heart ... starts back to its beating.* The man is restored to life, though – ironically, in the present context – his language is not:

She carries him home in a beautiful boat
He watches the sea from a porthole in stowage
He can hear all she says as she sits by his bed
And one day his lips answer her in her own language ...
Then he talks of the Nile, and the girls in bullrushes.

♫ Josh Ritter, *The Curse* (2010)

This is possibly the only song to try to rhyme *language* with *stowage*. The attempt fails because <-*(u/w)age*> is extra-metrical; lexical stress means that *stow* and *lang* are the final candidates in their respective lines. But it's a tricky one, *language*.

As the title intimates, the mummy's revival comes at a heavy cost. Yet it happens nonetheless. In the material world, humans cannot literally be revived, at least not after thousands of years, for the very good reason that DNA needs an organic host. Even in the fictional world of *Jurassic Park*, there must be some medium in which genetic information can be preserved. So what about languages? Can these be revived?

If strict internalism is correct, then a language is gone forever once the last speaker dies. Long before that, in fact: conventional wisdom has it that a language variety is literally *moribund*, on death row, as soon as children stop acquiring it as a first language. If language is a biological property, it too needs a host, and if there are no speakers, the language must go extinct. Unlike human diseases that can lurk in other organisms even after their last human victim has been quarantined, there are no other viable hosts for (I-) language: if there's one thing we can all agree on, it's that grammatical knowledge is not transmitted by other species. So language death must be forever, on a strictly internalist view.

And right now there's so much death and dying about. A recent paper by Harmon and Loh (2010), following up on Michael Krauss's 1992 wake-up call (Krauss 1992), clearly demonstrates the scale of the problem: the loss of language diversity over the past century dwarfs the (much better publicised) loss of biodiversity. See Jim McCloskey's elegiac article on the subject: McCloskey (1997), also Vidal (2014).

Yet more than once in recent history, a language is *after thousands of years, [brought] back to its beating*. By happy coincidence, the most famous revived tongue is the official language of a country that is a figurative (sometimes literal) stone's throw away from *the Nile, and the girls in bullrushes*. The country is Israel, the language in question Modern Hebrew.

The general consensus is that Modern Hebrew is a revived and extended form of Biblical (Mishnaic) Hebrew. Mishnaic Hebrew died out as a spoken language in the second century CE, and, for nearly 2,000 years Hebrew was no-one's native tongue, being preserved only as a liturgical written language (rather like Mediaeval Latin in the Roman Catholic church, up to Vatican II). Yet currently, as the result of a revitalisation campaign begun in the nineteenth century, a variety of that language is spoken by an estimated nine million speakers. For many speakers, Modern Hebrew is their native language; for many others, it is the only language used in daily communication. And for all of these speakers, the proximate source of Modern (spoken) Hebrew are written texts studied and revitalised by second language learners from the nineteenth century: there has never been a spoken continuum of the kind that gives us French from Vulgar Latin, for example.

The idea that Modern Hebrew is a direct descendant of Mishnaic Hebrew has been challenged by some dissident scholars, notably Wexler (1990), who claims that it is a relexified admixture of Sorbian, and other non-Semitic languages, which did not die out, as Hebrew did. But this rather specious claim is based largely on lexical evidence, as much of the vocabulary of Modern Hebrew comes from Yiddish and other language varieties spoken by European and Russian Jews in the intervening two thousand years. Syntactic properties, on the other hand, are often impervious to lexical borrowing (invasion). The Austro-Asiatic language Vietnamese, for instance, has borrowed more than 50 per cent of its lexicon from Mandarin and other Chinese varieties, yet still retains distinctive grammatical characteristics. As Mark Alves (1999) concludes of Vietnamese:

Based on comparative lexical, phonological, morphological, and syntactic evidence, the influence of Chinese, though lexically significant, is best viewed as structurally superficial ... at each linguistic level, Chinese influence is primarily restricted to non-structural aspects of Vietnamese, and the various linguistic elements of Chinese have been fit onto a primarily Southeast Asian and Mon-Khmer linguistic template.

Mark Alves, 'What's so Chinese about Vietnamese?' (1999)

Modulo the contact languages involved, the same remarks apply to Hebrew: to wit, 'at each linguistic level, [Slavic and Germanic] influence is primarily restricted to non-structural aspects of [Modern Hebrew], and the various linguistic elements of [Slavic and Germanic] have been fit onto a primarily Semitic linguistic template.'

Table 7 *Possessor noun-phrases in Irish and Hebrew ('Construct State').*

Modern Irish	Modern Hebrew
a. (*an) guth láidir [an tsagairt] DET voice strong DET priest-GEN 'the priest's powerful voice'	a.′ *(*ha) beyt ha-yafe ha-mora DET house-m DET-pretty.m DET–teacher-f 'the teacher's pretty house'
b. (*an) guth [an tsagairt láidir] DET voice DET priest-GEN strong 'the strong priest's voice'	b.′ (*ha) beyt **ha-mora ha-yafa** DET house DET teacher-f DET–pretty.f 'the pretty teacher's house'
c. (*an) teach [an tsagairt chiúin] DET house DET priest-GEN quiet 'the quiet priest's house'/*'the priest's quiet house'	c. ′ (*ha) **beyt** ha-mora **ha-yafe** DET house DET teacher-f DET–pretty.m 'the teacher's pretty house'

The syntax of Hebrew noun-phrases, specifically *possessor noun-phrases* – the so-called Construct State – provides a striking example of Hebrew's Semitic lineage: the distinctive form and left-peripheral position of the head noun, the constraints on modifier order, and agreement, are all features of other Semitic varieties (Biblical Hebrew, Classical Arabic, Modern Spoken Arabic, Maltese, etc.), which bear no close similarity to possessor noun-phrases in other Indo-European languages: Ritter (1987, 1988), Borer (1988), Fabri (1993).

Except, as chance would have it, to noun-phrases in Celtic languages, at the other end of Western Europe; cf. Duffield (1996). The comparison in Table 7 shows that possessor noun-phrases in Semitic are structurally distinguished from their Celtic counterparts only by the position of the attributive adjectives modifying the head noun: in Semitic, they appear to the left of the possessor-phrase, whereas in Celtic, they appear to the right (Hebrew data from Ritter 1988: 916).

The structural parallels should be obvious. Modern Irish noun-phrases are not the same as those in Hebrew, but they are much closer than anything found in Slavic. So, unless the Hebrew Construct State was kept alive by the same Irish Christian monks that 'saved Western Civilisation' (see Cahill 1995), and who then helpfully repositioned the adjective-phrase before handing it back – there seems to be little alternative to the idea that – at least with respect to noun-phrase syntax – Hebrew is a Semitic language, raised from the dead.

Although language revival is rare, the case of Modern Hebrew is not unique. Twenty years ago, when I wrote my PhD dissertation on the syntax Modern Ulster Irish, it was established wisdom that its Goidelic cousin, Manx, had 'rattled its proverbial clack' in 1974, with the death of the last native speaker, Ned Madrell. Yet the current Wikipedia entry has it:

In recent years the language has been the subject of revival efforts, so that despite the small number of speakers, the language has become more visible on the island, with increased signage and radio broadcasts. The revival of Manx has been aided by the fact that the language was well recorded; for example, the Bible was translated into Manx, and a number of audio recordings were made of native speakers.

Wikipedia, Manx Language

There are now estimated to be a hundred competent adult speakers of Manx, with more than seventy children in immersion education in the *Bunscoill Ghaelgagh* (Manx elementary school) in St Helen's: a YouTube video literally yells against the idea that Manx is extinct.[13] Crucially, what they are speaking is not relexified English.

Language revitalisation projects have been undertaken in other parts of the world as well, most notably in North America, where the magnitude of language loss over the last two centuries, and the concomitant social, economic and cultural impoverishment, has been much more devastating than in Europe. Two projects deserve particular recognition: seminal work by Jessie Little Doe Baird, together with Ken Hale and Norvin Richards, on Wampanoag (a language of Eastern Massachusetts) which led to a revival of this language in the context of the Wôpanâak Language Reclamation Project; Quirina Geary and Natasha Warner's work, which has yielded a new dictionary of Mutsun (a language of California), which may foster language revival in that region too (Warner, Butler and Geary 2016, Perez 2016). See also the work of Leanne Hinton, and others in California (http://bol.aicls.org/).

Granted, twenty-first-century speakers of Hebrew and Manx may not speak exactly the same way as second-century or nineteenth-century speakers of these varieties, but the same is true of twenty-first-century speakers of English, or of any other language that has been continuously spoken for centuries. In fact, if one restricts attention to formal properties (phonological inventory, morphological affixation, syntactic constructions), Modern Hebrew is measurably closer to second-century Mishnaic Hebrew than Present Day English is to Middle English, let alone to earlier Anglo-Saxon varieties.

There is no tenable internalist solution to language revival. Yet it happens. It doesn't matter that it's as rare as virgin birth. Once is enough, to make the point (cf. Hogenboom 2014).

> *Sweeney: Birth, and copulation, and death.*
> *That's all the facts when you come to brass tacks:*
> *Birth, and copulation, and death.*
> *I've been born, and once is enough.*
> *You don't remember, but I remember,*
> *Once is enough.*

T. S. Eliot, 'Fragment of an Agon' (1927)

(vi)   Afterthought

Chomskyan linguistics offers us an appealing, reductionist ontology: linguistics undoubtedly becomes much simpler and more tractable if language (like vision) is regarded as essentially and exclusively internal, ultimately a biological phenomenon. Yet a massive amount of counter-evidence supports the idea that crucial grammatical properties must be external: aspects of *langue*, rather than of (personal) *competence*. And language – in both of its guises – is causally and dynamically connected to each and every vital aspect of our lives, and to our social and cultural experience.

Much as I dislike the banking industry, it provides a useful analogy: *competence* is to *langue* what personal savings accounts are to a bank – a nationalised one, at any rate: not just to its financial assets, but to the entire system. Linguistically (I dare say grammatically) some of us may be personally richer than others, but if the bank collapses, we are all left destitute. This is why language documentation and preservation is not some frivolous activity; for all of us, it should be an existential concern. It is also why Chomsky's implicitly survivalist attitude to languages – if UG is intact until the last human being dies, the fate of individual languages doesn't really matter – is so profoundly soul-destroying.

> *No man is an island,*
> *Entire of itself,*
> *Every man is a piece of the continent,*
> *A part of the main.*
> *If a clod be washed away by the sea,*
> *Europe is the less.*
> *As well as if a promontory were.*
> *As well as if a manor of thy friend's*
> *Or of thine own were:*
> *Any man's death diminishes me,*
> *Because I am involved in mankind,*
> *And therefore never send to know for whom the bell tolls;*
> *It tolls for thee.*

John Donne, *Meditation XVII* (*Devotions upon Emergent Occasions*, 1624)

For 'man', read 'language': though't may not scan so well, its truth is just as plain.

Notes

1 The final suggestion may not be so absurd as it sounds; see, in particular, Berent, Brem, Zhao et al. (2015), for evidence supporting the idea; cf. also Robson (2014).

2 Don't see P is for Poverty of the Stimulus below: there's nothing there. Do see Pullum and Scholz (2002).

3 A case in point is the generativist response to recent work by Christine Behme (2014), Daniel Everett (2013) and Nicholas Evans (Evans and Levinson 2009).

4 It will be clear from other sections – see specially G is for Grammar, H is for Homogeneity, O is for Object of Study – that I have serious doubts about the viability of POS arguments. Nothing I have seen or experienced in sixteen years as a parent of three children, including one with Down's Syndrome, or in more than twenty-five years as a teacher of languages, readily supports POS arguments. Still, like most of Chomsky's arguments, the logic is impeccable: if one grants steps (i) and (ii), then (iii) must be true. But whatever the truth of (i)–(iii), (iv) and (v) are not true corollaries.

5 Ironically, this seems to have been where the conflation of the terms was first introduced: Chomsky's claiming that *competence* was *not* like *langue* appears to have led others to entertain the proposition that it might be.

6 Or – as the previous sentence demonstrates – final *also* is acceptable to American English speakers, and now to me. It sounds odd in Belfast or Cardiff, but.

7 The analogy is misleading because there are vastly more than fifty-two genetic combinations to choose from; also, because my being assigned five genetic cards does not preclude the assignment of the same cards in other combinations for a different individual.

8 The putative association between D_4DR variants and novelty-seeking behaviour has been challenged, and remains controversial: see, for example, Munafò, Yalcin, Willis-Owen and Flint (2007). The point should still be clear, however.

9 The same may well be true of phonological change. Contrary to the Neogrammarian assumption that sound change operates blindly, affecting all relevant segments in the same way, the theory of LEXICAL DIFFUSION, first proposed by Wang (1969), has it that sound change first affects a single word, or set of words, and only later proliferates throughout the lexicon, through piecemeal changes at different times; cf. Labov (1981). See Campbell (1998) for discussion of the lexical trajectories of the English Great Vowel Shift (GVS).

10 Generativists accept that syntactic changes appear to take time to complete, but argue against the idea that gradualness is theoretically problematic – or even that it has any place within a coherent theory. Roberts (2007: Chapter 4), for example, explicitly claims that gradualness is a mirage.

11 Immediate source: www.xenodochy.org/ex/quotes/knowsnot.html.

12 A different interpretation is proposed by Kroch (1989), and subsequent work. Rather than giving up on discrete grammatical parameters, Kroch locates the optionality of *do*-support in speakers' processing rules: the parser may generate alternative parses even where (underlyingly) speakers have made a discrete grammatical (parametric) choice. Moreover, Kroch argues that most of the variation in the incidence of *do*-support across various constructions is only apparent: if instead of a linear function, one applies a logistic (s-shaped) function, then all of the constructions analysed in Figure 24 show a relatively good fit, the implication being that they may be due to the same discrete grammatical change. See also Vulanović (2010).

13 'A day in the life of the Bunscoill Ghaelgagh' (www.youtube.com/watch?v= 6rUEZ8A-678).

> *[D]oing syntax is a bit like the opposite of writing a poem. It is a truism that one can tell a poet from the following ability: give a poet a poem, and they will make it into a better poem. Well, the way to tell a syntactician is: give them a sentence and they will make it worse. I call this 'shooting for the stars' because when a syntactician has taken a perfectly decent sentence like* 'Lee watched TV all night' *and has twisted it into* *TV was watched all night by Lee *by misapplying to it the most famous rule, or transformation in syntax – PASSIVIZATION – the syntactician prefixes to the wrecked result the symbol* * *(a star) to announce its hopelessness.*
>
> Haj Ross, 'Why to syntax' (2015: 1)

> *A child may pick up a large part of his vocabulary and 'feel' for sentence structure from television, from reading, from listening to adults, etc.*
>
> Noam Chomsky, 'A review of B. F. Skinner's *Verbal Behavior*'
> (*Language*, 1959: 42)

If the theoretical basis of generative linguistics is the Poverty of the Stimulus argument, its empirical foundations are sunk in the mire of 'acceptability judgments': the shared ability of speakers of a given language to draw subtle distinctions between those sentences that they deem grammatically acceptable and those they consider unacceptable.[1] In generativist discussions, these two arguments are often linked: it is just the ability to identify negative constraints on form and interpretation, as exemplified by the sentences in (118) and (119), respectively, that provides the empirical grist to the mill of grammatical innateness: see Crain (1993), Crain and Pietroski (2001).

(118)   a. Who did you say Kate really likes?   [*that*-trace effects]
        b. Who did you say that Kate really likes?
        c. Who did you say really likes Kate?
        d. *Who did you say that really likes Kate?

(119)   a. $Kate_i$ doesn't think that anyone appreciates her_i efforts.   [Condition B effects]
        b. $Kate_i$ doesn't think that anyone appreciates $her_{i/j}$.
        c. (Only) $Kate_i$ appreciates $her_{?i/j}$ efforts.
        d. $Kate_i$ appreciates $her_{*i/j}$

The generativist argument is often expressed in the form of a rhetorical question: if, for example, all mature speakers of a language agree that sentence (118d) is less acceptable than those in (118a–c), or that example (119d) disallows co-reference between *Kate* and *her*, even though the closely related sentences in (119a–c) freely allow this interpretive relationship; and if children are never presented with the information adequate to guarantee convergence on such matters, how else do they acquire this knowledge, other than through innate pre-specification?

As has been touched on elsewhere, there are numerous ways of tackling this rhetorical argument. First, one might challenge the notion of convergence head-on. One could point out, for example, that not all native speakers agree on the relevant judgments across a range of contexts; an obvious case in point was Lakoff's judgments of the examples in (23d) above. Or one could try to show that there is a disconnect between speakers' judgments and their normal linguistic behaviour, suggesting the operation of a prescriptive rule; see the discussion of ... *is She*, below. Or again, it might be demonstrated that such judgments emerge only after an extended period of exposure, once more speaking against innateness. See also H is for Homogeneity.

Alternatively, 'the basic facts' might just be wrong for everyone. Consider the examples (118) once more. This paradigm is supposed to illustrate the operation of the so-called '*that*-trace filter': see Pesetsky (2015) for an overview. Most competence-based researchers present examples (118a) and (118b) as equally acceptable, and claim that (118d) is totally unacceptable: the odd one out. Yet both of these assumptions are open to challenge.

- First, a comparison of Ngram patterns for the strings: 'who said say he/she/they' vs. 'who said say that he/she/they' reveals a clear preference for the former, that is to say, for sentences without the complementiser, across the board. Thus, even before considering whether (118d) merits an asterisk (*), it must be acknowledged that part of the reason for its deviance is the simple presence of the complementiser *that* (independently of any *wh*-trace), as shown in Figure 25.
- It is also generally assumed that unbounded dependencies of this kind (so-called long-distance questions) are in principle free, except where blocked. This too is debatable, given that most 'non-bridge' verbs – that is to say, almost all verbs taking a clausal complement, except *say*, *think*, and *tell* – are barriers to long-distance movement: compare 'Who did you say/??allege/ *mumble that Richard had gone out with?' What's more, '*that*-trace' effects are observable even in the absence of a subject trace. In their discussion of the phenomenon, Aoun et al. (1987) acknowledge that for some native speakers the presence of the complementiser inhibits construal of *wh*-adjuncts (*when*, *where*, *why*, etc.) with positions inside the embedded clause: as a

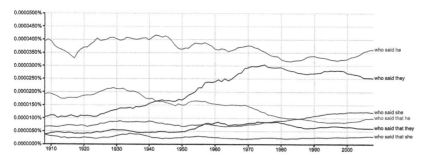

Figure 25 Complementiser deletion in *who* questions 1910–2000.

result, (120a) is ambiguous with respect to the interpretation of *why* (for such speakers), whereas (120b) only admits a main clause interpretation. And the blocking effects of *that* seem to be amplified as more embedded[2] clauses are added ((120b) > > (120c) > (120d) [> = 'more acceptable than']).

(120)   a. Why do you think [Peter bought a new car ~~why~~]?
        b. ?Why do you think [that Peter bought a new car ~~why~~]?
        c. ??Why do you think [Peter said [that Mary had bought a new car ~~why~~]?
        d. ??*Why do you think that Peter said that Mary had bought a new car ~~why~~]?

- On the other side of the argument is the observation that *that*-trace effects are absent from some non-standard English varieties: see Sobin (1987), cf. Sobin (2002); see also Salzmann, Häusler, Bader and Bayer (2013). They are also reduced or eliminated (in all varieties) by the presence of an initial adverbial phrase (Culicover 1993).

When these considerations are taken into account, it becomes much more questionable whether a paradigmatic contrast exists in the first place: if *that* is generally dispreferred where it can be omitted, and if 'extraction' from embedded clauses is dispreferred even when the 'trace position' is non-adjacent to the complementiser (i.e. with non-subjects), it's unclear that there is any such thing as a *that*-trace effect for the learner to be inherently sensitive to. Yet if the phenomenon is an *epi*phenomenon, we don't need to invoke innate principles to explain it.

Rather than enter into data disputes, many acquisition researchers prefer a different tack, namely, to accept convergence, but to challenge the idea of an impoverished environment. If it can be shown that the input is sufficiently rich to give rise to a shared set of uniform judgments – that children, for example, can make use of corrective feedback so as to allow them to rein in their grammatical creativity in just the right way (see Saxton 2010) – this once again precludes the need to invoke innate knowledge of negative constraints.

Either of these general strategies would seem to generate enough reasonable doubt for anyone to be sceptical of Poverty of the Stimulus claims based on paradigmatic contrasts. In this section, I'll outline a third approach, one that is marginally more original – and perhaps more troublesome for defenders of innateness. What I'll question is the source of the judgments themselves – that is to say, what the judgments are judgments *on*. I'll suggest that acceptability judgments are irreducibly sensitive to context: in particular, they are always sensitive to external historical and social context in ways that are incompatible with a strictly internalist approach. Judgments may be 'in our heads', but that doesn't necessarily make them intensional reflexes of I-LANGUAGE: they might just as well be reflexes of an external *langue*. This suggestion is quite explicit in Huddleston and Pullum's (2012) discussion of grammatical acceptability:

> *[T]he evidence we use comes from several sources: our own intuitions as native speakers of the language; the reactions of other native speakers we consult when we are in doubt; data from computer corpora (machine-readable bodies of naturally occurring text), and data presented in dictionaries and other scholarly works on grammar. We alternate between the different sources and cross-check them against each other, since intuitions can be misleading and texts can contain errors. Issues of interpretation often arise.*
>
> Rodney Huddleston, Geoffrey Pullum et al., *The Cambridge Grammar of the English Language* (2002: 11)

Convergent judgments are argued to be at least as much the result of shared social experience, as of shared genes: it is *langue*, rather than competence, that lies at the heart of our judgment ability. Notice that *if* this is true, it implies that 'grammaticality judgments' are no different in kind from other aesthetic judgments: a 'good' sentence is no different from a 'good' design, a 'good view', a 'good taste'; an 'unacceptable sentence' is little different from a 'poor design', 'an ugly view' and 'an inedible meal'. All of these derive as much from shared cultural aesthetics as from biology.

> This is not necessarily to trivialise the notion, or to relativise it. Etcoff (1999), for example, argues convincingly that certain core aspects of our aesthetic judgment are universal, plausibly innate. But it *is* to locate the proximate source of our judgments in ambient language, rather than in I-language.

I'll begin and end the presentation of data exhibits with *Curious George*, my youngest son's morning and evening favourite, and with a favourite of mine, another song by Josh Ritter. These examples serve to illustrate two grammatical phenomena that have occupied me in my theoretical research in recent years: on one hand, the behaviour of modal and aspectual auxiliaries, such as *is*, *has*, *can*, *should*, *will*, *might*, etc. – see Duffield (2013); on the other, the proper characterisation of utterances involving VP-ellipsis, a phenomenon usually described in terms of a transformational rule that elides (deletes) a verb-phrase constituent under some kind of identity with a preceding antecedent phrase, and which was originally discussed in a seminal paper by Hankamer and Sag (1976); see also Duffield, Matsuo and Roberts (2010), Roberts, Matsuo and Duffield (2013); cf. Hardt (1993), Merchant (2001, 2005).

(121)   Allie couldn't wait to board the subway train … So she didn't.

The line in (121) above, adapted from a syntactically parallel one in *Curious George's Subway Adventure*, is amusing in the first place because of the unusually literal use of the expression *couldn't wait*, which normally means 'was very excited at the prospect of', rather than (as here) 'was unable to wait'. The anomaly (and the humour) is further increased by the fact that VP-ellipsis usually picks up the most recent accessible antecedent, here, the VP [*get onto … train*]; in this instance, however, it is the containing VP [*wait to get on … train*] that is accessed. *So she didn't* … means that she didn't *wait*, not that she didn't *get on* to the train. Compare (121) with the more conventional (122):

(122)   George remembered that the man in the yellow hat had told him not to eat another doughnut … So he didn't.
      a. didn't = [eat another doughnut]
      b. didn't = ##[tell him not to eat another doughnut]
      c. didn't = ##[remember that…doughnut].

Other interesting anomalies arise with respect to ellipsis in the lyrics in (123), taken from Josh Ritter's song *A Certain Light*:

(123)   It was hard to think her smile
      Could bring the Springtime
      But it did and now it is.

      The green, green grass
      Is come up green, and it's feeling
      Just the way it did, the very first time.

♫ Josh Ritter, *A Certain Light* (2013)

This verse offers three separate uses of ellipsis, each of which is relatively innocuous in isolation, but which (in the first two cases at least) create grammatical anomalies through their interaction. It is a crying shame to have to spell out wit, but here goes.

> The first instance of *did* is a straightforward case of VP-ellipsis: the intended antecedent verb-phrase is [*bring the Springtime*]. This would be unremarkable but for the fact that the immediately following auxiliary *is* also requires an antecedent, this time a predicate – compare 'Do you think she can ever be successful?'... 'Oh but she *is* [successful], already.' Hence, the intended analysis in the second case is '... now it *is* [Springtime]'. Normally, however, two auxiliaries in quick succession should take the same antecedent; as a result, the phrase is most readily parsed as 'it is [*bring(ing) the Springtime*]', which doesn't work quite so well, and is presumably not what Ritter intended.
>
> The second instance of *did* in the last line illustrates an interesting case of so-called ANTECEDENT-CONTAINED DELETION (ACD, cf. Bouton 1970, Sag 1976, Baltin 1987, Matsuo 1998), in which – as its name implies – the antecedent verb-phrase is contained within the elided constituent, something that should lead to infinite regress. Applying VP-ellipsis here should produce 'did [$_{VP}$ feel just the way it did [$_{VP}$ feel just the way it did [$_{VP}$ feel just the way it did ...∞'
>
> Except that it doesn't ... [$_{VP}$ ~~lead to infinite regress~~]: the sentence feels just fine; see Hackl, Koster-Hale and Varvoutis (2012), cf. Jacobson and Gibson (2014). (There's also the issue of what *it* refers to, but I'll leave that aside for now.)
>
> In addition to the unusual uses of VP-ellipsis here, these lines are also notable for the archaic use of a BE auxiliary (instead of have) with an inchoative verb: that is, *is come up green* instead of the more usual *has come up green*. As Sorace (2000) notes, this flexibility in auxiliary selection is observed across a range of Western Indo-European (Romance and Germanic) languages. See G is for Grammar above.

If those two references are insufficient, you could do worse than examine the final verse of Billy Joel's song *Vienna* – the line beginning *Dream on ...* – for another nice example of non-parallel anaphora, which once again works just fine in context.

♫ Billy Joel, *Vienna* (1977)

According to your background and temperament, this discussion serves to illustrate one of two things. On one hand, it might be taken to show the value of grammatical analysis – how examination of the simplest lines can reveal wondrously subtle and intricate contrasts. On the other, it demonstrates how a piece of gentle wit can be completely ruined by academic worrying, few things being more tedious than having a pedant explain a joke. Or perhaps both: these are certainly not incompatible notions. But whatever you think of the discussion, it's very unlikely that you consider the examples in (121) and (123) to be grammatically anomalous: every competent speaker of English will realise, upon reflection, that there is something unusual about these uses of ellipsis but they are perfectly acceptable, in context.

Besides, there are more egregious cases of ungrammaticality that pass most speakers by. A frequent context of obliviousness to ungrammaticality is historical fiction, in which a modern writer affects an archaic dialect in order to evoke an earlier – sometimes mythical – period. You have to be a fairly educated reader to be greatly disturbed by the (un)grammatical awfulness of the following excerpts from Christopher Paolini's mythical fantasy novel *Eldest*, in (124) and (125):

(124)   In a low whisper he said, 'It is always so; those closest to the heart cause the most pain. <u>Thou will</u> have no dowry from me, snake, nor <u>your</u> mother's inheritance.'

Christopher Paolini, Eldest (2005: 185)

Reading these lines, the anglicist may be struck by the following observations: (i) that use of the subject pronoun *thou* in (124) should trigger second-person agreement (e.g. *thou wilt, thou dost*, etc.); (ii) that *will* is in any case the wrong auxiliary, since in the period that Paolini seeks to evoke – the mediaeval rather than the Early Modern – *will* retained its modal interpretation (cf. German/Dutch *wollen/willen*), so that the future auxiliary should be *shal(t)*; (iii) that the correct possessive form should be *thy* (*your* being an obligatorily plural pronoun until the latter half of the seventeenth century). Yet these facts race right past the ordinary fan of Paolini's fiction.

To see how it should be done, compare Juliet's lines in the following excerpt from Shakespeare's *Romeo and Juliet*:

> *Thou knowest the mask of night is on my face,*
> *Else would a maiden blush bepaint my cheek*   (90)
> *For that which* thou hast *heard me speak tonight.*
> *Fain would I dwell on form; fain, fain deny*
> *What I have spoke. But farewell compliment.*
> *Dost thou love me? I know* thou wilt say *'Ay',*
> *And I will take thy word. Yet, if* thou swear'st,
> Thou mayst *prove false. At lovers' perjuries,*
> *They say, Jove laughs. O gentle Romeo,*
> *If* thou dost *love, pronounce it faithfully:*
> *Or if* thou thinkest *I am too quickly won,*
> *I'll frown, and be perverse, and say thee nay,*   (100)
> *So* thou wilt *woo: but else, not for the world.*

William Shakespeare, Romeo and Juliet (2.2.89–101)

Similarly, in the second extract from *Eldest* reproduced in (125), the possessive pronoun *thine* is ungrammatical, and has always been so: *thine* was – and in certain dialects remains – the pre-vocalic form of *thy*: hence, *thine eyes, thine honour,* but *thy will, thy back, thy horse*:

(125)   'Elves are a queer race; full of light and dark. In the morning they
          drink with you; in the evening, they stab you. Keep <u>thine</u> back to a
          wall, Shadeslayer. Capricious, they are.'
          'I will remember that.'
          'Mmm.' Thor gestured toward the river. 'They plan to travel up Eldor
          lake in boats. What will you do with <u>thine</u> horse? We could return him
          to Tarnag with us.'

Christopher Paolini, Eldest (2005: 170)

The following Shakespearean extract from what is coyly referred to as 'The Scottish Play' demonstrates conventional usage of second person pronoun variants (allomorphs):

> Was the hope drunk
> Wherein you dress'd yourself? hath it slept since?
> And wakes it now, to look so green and pale
> At what it did so freely? From this time
> Such I account thy love. Art thou afeard
> To be the same in thine own act and valour   (40)
> As thou art in desire? Wouldst thou have that
> Which thou esteem'st the ornament of life,
> And live a coward in thine own esteem,
> Letting 'I dare not' wait upon 'I would',
> Like the poor cat i' the adage?

William Shakespeare, Macbeth (1.7.35–45)

As this latter excerpt shows, in Shakespearean English *thine* and *thy* alternate in exactly the same fashion as do the articles *an* and *a* in Modern English. The same readers who are completely unfazed by Paolini's text would look askance at the examples in (126):

(126)   a. He attended a international school, then went to an university in
             Germany.
         b. Will you have a apple or an peach?

Paolini's idiosyncratic uses of pronouns and auxiliaries are only the most obvious symptoms of a chaotic disregard for the 'rules of English grammar' (at any stage of historical development): aside from his use of function words, his arbitrary mixing of finite-verb raising and *do*-support, not to mention a violently anachronistic use of idioms and lexical borrowings from other languages, are enough to raise the blood pressure of any scholar of Middle or Early Modern English. Yet these solecisms were clearly lost on the copy-editors, and on the reviewers of the work (a *Sunday Times* bestseller, praised as 'literary magic' by *People* magazine). And of course they are lost on the ordinary teenage reader, who presumably enjoyed every ungrammatical phrase without demur.

But let's now pretend that you aren't privy to the preceding discussion, and that you have never been vouchsafed exposure to [the] 'authentic work of great talent' (*New York Review of Books*) that is Paolini's *Eldest*. Imagine, instead, that you had been asked to rate the sentences in (127) in order of acceptability (and with apologies to Shakespeare):

(127)   a. Dost thou love me? I know thou <u>wilt</u> say 'Ay',
               And I will take <u>thy</u> word.
        b. Do thou love me? I know thou <u>will</u> say 'Ay',
               And I will take <u>thy</u> word.
        c. Do thou love me? I know thou <u>will</u> say 'Ay',
               And I will take <u>thine</u> word.
        d. Do you love me? I know thou <u>will</u> say 'Ay',
               And I will take <u>your</u> word.

I haven't carried out this experiment yet, but I am happy to bet my dog's next breakfast that the educated reader would rank the original version (127a) above the others, and would consider the 'Paolini versions', in (127c) and (127d), to be sharply unacceptable. Moreover, if in place of a ranked judgment, I were to present only (127a) and (127d) as a minimal contrast and (to) ask naïve participants to place an asterisk next to the less acceptable one I confidently predict close to 100 per cent unanimity in readers' judgments. What makes this interesting is that no-one speaks Early Modern English any more, and that sentence (127d) is much closer to what would be generated by the I-LANGUAGE(S) of readers of this book – supposing such a thing existed – the I-LANGUAGE, not the book or its readers – than the markedly more acceptable sentence (127a).

Ay, there's the rub.

For a more sophisticated variation on the same theme, see 'So that's the way you like it' (*Beyond the Fringe*, 1961).[3]

Naturally, this argument can be run the other way around. It usually is. So now read the sentences in (128) and indicate briefly which you consider grammatically acceptable:

(128)   a. They go to the park every week.
        b. They do go to the park every week.
        c. He goes to the park every week.

> d. He does go to the park every week.
> e. He do go to the park every week.

I haven't carried out this experiment, but I am confident that all native speakers will share the following judgments: to wit, (128a) and (128c) are completely acceptable, while (128b) and (128d) are acceptable only if auxiliary *do(es)* bears contrastive stress, but are otherwise marginal. And (128e) is unacceptable.

Assuming that you agree with these judgments, consider the following extract from John Banville's *The Untouchable*, which really *is* 'an authentic work of great talent':

> *'We had a grand time at the seaside,' Mrs Blenkinsop said to me loudly in her knife-edged Presbyterian voice. 'Isn't that right, Freddie?'*
>
> *Freddie did not look at her, but another, different sort of spasm passed through him, and I knew exactly what he thought of Mrs Blenkinsop.*
>
> *'Aye,' said Andy, 'he do love the strand.'*

John Banville, The Untouchable (1997: 239)

If you judge (128e) unacceptable, then you should have no reason to accept Andy's assertion, viz., *he do love the strand*. The logical conclusion must be that Banville has written an ungrammatical sentence (which has once more escaped the copy-editor's attention).

One reaction to this might be to say something along the lines of: 'I wouldn't say it, but I can imagine others that would: it's a question of dialect.' In some instances, this is a legitimate defence (though it begs many of the same questions about what it is we are judging when we say that a given sentence is acceptable).[4] In this instance, however, the objection fails – at least, I *think* it does. The reason for saying so is that this scene in Banville's novel is set in the fictional village of Carrickdrum, a few miles from Belfast (which is, as you must know by now, the speech community in which I grew up). While I can't say exactly what the correct alternative might be here, I'd guess that 'Aye, he likes the strand, right enough' is more plausible piece of dialogue. (Northern Irish people of a certain age are almost as reticent as the Japanese about using the 'L-word', particularly with reference to inanimate objects.)

Further investigation reveals that the string *he do love* is virtually non-existent in the Google Books corpus (1800–2000). The sole mentions of the phrase are in reference grammars, where it is employed to illustrate the subjunctive mood in subordinate clauses introduced by *if*, and in the following excerpt from Anthony Trollope's *The Prime Minister*, where it is so used:

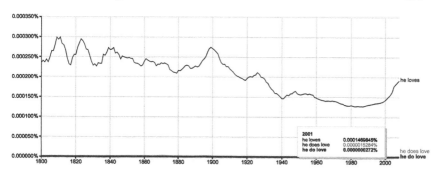

Figure 26 He loves, he does love, he do love.

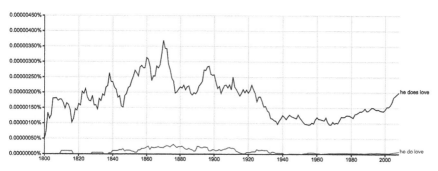

Figure 27 He does love, he do love.

A girl's cheek is never so holy to herself as it is to her lover – if he do love her.

Anthony Trollope, *The Prime Minister* (1876)

The string never appears in a main clause declarative context anywhere in the corpus. By contrast, the Google Ngrams in Figures 26 and 27 show that 'he does love' does (!) occur, although, predictably, it is much less frequent in the corpus than 'he loves'. Even the subjunctive form 'that he love her' has a somewhat higher incidence than 'he do love her', as is shown in Figure 28. (Notice that the *y*-axis scales are different in each figure.)

Generativists are reluctant to accept that frequency might be a good proxy for grammaticality, since it implies the unthinkable: rather than tapping some well-spring of innate grammatical competence, acceptability judgments reference our stored knowledge of ambient language. In other words, what people judge acceptable is a close reflection of what they hear. Still, much of the available evidence suggests that generativists are wrong: not just in this case, but at nearly every turn, there are tight correlations between ambient language and perceived grammaticality. See Bybee and Thompson (1997), Bybee and

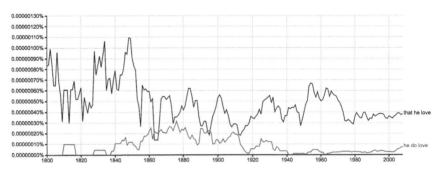

Figure 28 'He do love' vs. 'that he love'.

Hopper (2001b); also Culicover (1998, 1999). If this were not the case, predictive text applications such as the one on my *iPhone 5s* (iOS 8.2) would never be as useful as they are. And unskilled writing would not be full of the 'same old, same old' tropes.

This is not to say that grammatical acceptability is always a reflex of collocational frequency. For example, there are some interesting instances where strings that are never normally attested – structures involving multiple centre-embedding – the strings in (129), for instance – turn out be acceptable to a reader with enough time, and a pencil in hand (> = 'harder to parse than'):

(129)   a. The cat the mouse the hamster caught chased tried to
            escape.   >
        b. The mouse the hamster the cat caught chased tried to
            escape.   >
        c. The mouse [that the hamster [that the cat caught] chased] tried to
            escape.

These are the exceptions, however: to ignore constructional frequency in explaining grammatical acceptability is akin to ignoring life-style factors and diet in explaining obesity (just because the proximate cause, in a small minority of cases, is thyroid dysfunction).

But to return to John Banville's character, Andy. The data presented above, as well as my local intuitions, suggest that Banville got it wrong: Andy's utterances, like those of Paolini's characters, are examples of ungrammatical English (at any time, in any place).

Really, though, who cares? For over two centuries writers no less articulate than Banville, including many of his compatriots – Thomas Sheridan and Synge, for example – have brightly evoked Irish characters by misrepresenting their speech. It is thanks to these authors that we have the term *Stage Irish*. To complain that Banville's character is made to speak ungrammatically when his speech is clearly convincing to every ordinary reader of the novel is nothing short of pedantry. Moreover, if I compare Banville's character – where I pretend to have a judgment – to the Southern Irish boy in Brendán Ó Conaire's translation 'From the Irish' in Flann O'Brien's *Myles before Myles*, where I have none at all, it becomes clear how *ad hoc* such judgments really are:

One day, he took his father aside and asked him a question – a great question that had been lying heavily on his mind for a long time.

'When this old fellow is in bed,' said the lad, 'does his beard be under the bedclothes, or does it be out in the open with the blankets tucked in underneath it?'

'That's a big question,' said the father, 'and I haven't got its solution. But go and ask your mother.'

This the lad did.

Brian O'Nolan (Flann O'Brien, Myles na Gopaleen)
'An Insoluble Question' (*Myles before Myles*, 2011 reprint edition)

The last two literary examples point up another worrying property of our judgment capacity, namely, its susceptibility to authority. If acceptability judgments really tapped some innate competence, then they should be unaffected by the status of the speaker or writer. It is irrelevant how well-qualified or powerful someone is, if they tell you that $2 + 2 = 5$, or that the sun is not shining (when you can plainly see that it is), you will disbelieve them. Notwithstanding the experiences of Winston Smith in *1984,* analytic falsehoods are falsehoods no matter who utters them, and the same holds for many contingent facts of basic perception: I may believe the science teacher who tells me that the sun doesn't really set, or that there isn't 'somewhere over the rainbow', but someone who stands next to me and says that he is two metres taller than I am is not exercising freedom of expression: he is lying, and I am sure of it.

Acceptability judgments don't seem to work that way. When a Japanese second language learner of English writes 'The animal is awaring' or 'The man aware nothing a piece of the puzzle', as in (130), so treating an adjectival predicate as a verb, there is no hesitation in marking it down as an error:

(130)   a. A man is going to play the puzzle. He need to seek a piece of the puzzle. He is refusing because there is only a piece of the puzzle. But the animal is awaring.

Konan University Entrance Examination 2015: English composition section (Anonymous)

   b. This picture show that the monkey think the puzzle is something eat. A man say to the monkey 'This isn't eat. This is one of puzzle.' When a man and the monkey is playing the puzzle, a man aware nothing a piece of the puzzle. It is eaten.

Konan University Entrance Examination 2015: English composition section (Anonymous)

Yet when Shakespeare writes in *Romeo and Juliet* 'Thank me no thankings, nor proud me no prouds', the verb 'to proud' is deemed acceptable, and enters the English literary canon:

> *How, how, how, how? Chopped logic! What is this?*
> *'Proud,' and 'I thank you,' and 'I thank you not,'*
> *And yet 'not proud'? Mistress minion you,*
> *Thank me no thankings, nor proud me no prouds,*
> *But fettle your fine joints gainst Thursday next*
> *To go with Paris to Saint Peter's Church,*
> *Or I will drag thee on a hurdle thither.*

William Shakespeare, Romeo and Juliet (3.4)

Chopped logic, indeed.

Somewhere between the two lies *She,* by the French singer Charles Aznavour (a song later covered by Elvis Costello, and which featured in the romantic comedy *Notting Hill*), in whose final line the singer declares that the meaning of his life ... *is She.*

♫ Charles Aznavour, She (1974)

The grammatical problem with ending the song this way is that nominative pronouns cannot appear in predicate position – or as inverted subjects – in any variety of spoken English; see Heycock (2013).[5] Compare the examples in (131): if (131b) and (131d) are bad for thee/So too must be ... *is she.*

(131)   a. He is the man they are looking for.
        b. *The man they are looking for is he.
        c. 'I am your best hope,' said Fred.
        d. 'Your best hope is *I/?me,' said Fred.

So why is the line acceptable? One obvious reason is end-rhyme and prosody: *is she* rhymes and scans perfectly with *to be* in the previous line: see the discussion of *Play Me* in Part II. The other, less circular, reason is sociolinguistic: I can't prove it, but I suspect that it is because Aznavour represents that most rare of combinations – a foreigner with authority – and an attractive French accent. (Ironically, the song was originally written in L2 English, and only later translated back to French.)

There are several other issues concerning acceptability judgments that deserve a fuller airing, not least the issue of gradience: the fact that every piece of language that one could possibly judge lies on a continuum of acceptability from 'perfect and natural in the context' to 'meaningless word-salad', and that there is no point along this continuum where a sentence switches from being unequivocally acceptable to being categorically terrible. Linguistic judgments are analogue, not digital. This is hardly an original insight, but it is something that is frequently overlooked in (psycholinguistic) practice: see Duffield (2003, 2004).

But that's enough about judgments for the time being ...

[A]nymore, it'd stretch the rhyme
So let me leave this where I started, I'm
Just happy for the first time
In a long time.

♪ Josh Ritter, *A Certain Light* (2013)

Notes

1 This might seem to be an unnecessarily awkward way of saying that speakers are able to 'give grammaticality judgments'. Yet, as many commentators have pointed out, the notion 'grammaticality judgment' is quite problematic; by the end of this section, it should be clearer why this is the case. See Allen and Seidenberg (1999), also Duffield (2003); cf. Schütze (1996), Featherston (2007), Larson (2015).
2 The term 'embedded' here should be taken under advisement: this is surely the standard analysis, but not necessarily the right one. 'Remote' might be a better description. See v is for von Humboldt for further discussion.
3 See http://bufvc.ac.uk/shakespeare/index.php/title/av37391.
4 It is interesting to observe, in this context, that those same linguists who rail against prescriptivism and rote learning – Pinker (1994) and Milroy (1998) deserve special mention here – are often unusually normative in their judgments, and in their own writing style.
5 Notwithstanding the prescriptive concerns of whoever devised the '11-plus' grammar question, cited in Richardson (2016).

> *'When I use a word,' Humpty Dumpty said in rather a scornful tone, 'it means just what I choose it to mean – neither more nor less.'*
>
> *'The question is,' said Alice, 'whether you can make words mean so many different things.'*
>
> *'The question is,' said Humpty Dumpty, 'which is to be master – that's all.'*
>
> Lewis Carroll, *Through the Looking Glass, and What Alice Found There* (1871)

♫ Leonard Cohen, *Democracy* (1992)

Chomskyan Nativism is not unlike American democracy: just as some Americans continue to assume that the United States of America is the only true democracy, so many Minimalists, as well as some competence-based psycholinguists, write as though Chomskyan nativism – with its claims of domain-specificity and grammatical autonomy, and its Poverty of the Stimulus arguments – represented the only viable theoretical approach to mentalist linguistics. An abject example of such zealotry is given by the following quote by Mendívil Giró (2012), in an article criticising Evans and Levinson's (2009) paper, 'The myth of Language Universals':[1]

The 'number one enemy' of Evans & Levinson and, in general, of the FCP [Functional–Cognitivist Paradigm: NGD], is the assumption that human beings have a natural capacity for language (i.e. what traditionally has been called UG).

Mendívil Giró, 'The myth of language diversity' (in Boeckx et al., eds, *Language, from a Biological Point of View*, 2012)

It would be sheer nonsense for anyone to deny that human beings have a natural capacity for language. To attribute such a denial to serious linguistic researchers – even as indirectly as Mendívil Giró does – is at best a red herring, or a straw man: take your figurative pick. In thirty years of research, learning and teaching, having studied under and worked alongside generativist and anti-generativists, formal and functional linguists, philosophers, psychologists, speech pathologists, and medical professionals, I have not met a single academic who does *not* believe that 'human beings have a natural capacity for language'. Really, not one ... Typologists such as Nick Evans and Steven Levinson certainly don't deny the proposition, computational linguistics like Jeff Elman and his colleagues don't; I'm quite sure that psychologists such as Michael Tomasello, Elena Lieven and Lorraine Tyler don't either. Yet many of these researchers reject Chomskyan Nativism (CN). As the field linguist Daniel Everett puts it:

Is [there] anything inborn in humans vital to the learning of language? Of course! Our brains are essential to learning and those cerebral spheres grow out of our genome. Our vocal apparatus is another inborn language-relevant manifestation of our biology.

Everett continues:

[F]inding genetic support for language is not the issue, though debates about nativism often make it seem as though it were. Rather, the question is whether or not there is anything exclusively dedicated to language learning or language form in our genotype. The answer is that we currently know of no such thing, apart from the shape and development of the human vocal tract.

Daniel Everett, Language: The Cultural Tool (2013: 88)

It is evident to anyone who has given the question an ounce of consideration that a human's ability to acquire and use language fluently rests on natural capacities – in the first place cognitive and sensorimotor capacities – all of which are ultimately due to biology/genetics. In this very broad sense, all mentalist linguistics is biolinguistics. Moreover, there is clear and consistent evidence, from the pioneering work of Gopnik (1990), Gopnik and Crago (1991), Vargha-Khadem et al. (1995), involving the 'KE family', to subsequent research by Simon Fisher and colleagues (Max Planck Institute for Psycholinguistics), that particular gene networks – in particular, the FOXP2 transcription factor – are implicated in the ability to produce human speech, as well as other complex vocalisations in other vertebrates, including bird-song; see Fisher et al. (1998), Fisher and Scharff (2009). Given this, I am as convinced as of anything else in this book that 'the pre-requisite for the unique human aptitude for language and speech must be in the DNA of Homo sapiens' (Max Planck Society 2016). But this conviction does not entail any commitment to UG, or any other construct of Chomskyan Nativism. Naturally, it does not preclude the possibility that UG is the right theory, either. But unless you believe in oracles, CN is just one of several higher-level interpretations of the term 'natural capacity for language'; for many people, one of the least biologically plausible. It is also irrelevant to explaining grammatical variation, or the acquisition of end-state grammars, which is a principal concern of this book: see I is for Internalism above; see also O'Grady (2003).

Aside from the hubris of Mendívil Giró's assertion – does he really believe that psychologists and linguists who do not identify nativism with

UG have no alternative conception of innateness? – the comment reveals a implicitly supremacist attitude towards atypical language learners.[2] As the father of a child with Down's Syndrome, I am perhaps more sensitised than some other language researchers, but the issue arises in all cases of atypical language development. If the hallmark of being human is the possession of UG, and if UG is the guarantor of grammatical knowledge – given the alleged deficiencies of the input – then, by implication, those whose language development is hindered or aborted by cognitive and neurological differences such that they cannot understand, produce or judge complex sentences (like this one!) – these individuals must be less than human. If one retreats from this conclusion by claiming that such children do have UG, but that other cognitive or physiological factors prevent them from demonstrating this knowledge in any way, then not only does the claim become largely vacuous, but UG must be de-coupled from the idea of a 'natural capacity for language' (unless 'language' just means UG, in which case the claim is empirically void).

Significantly, children with Down's Syndrome have the same admixture of genes as any other typically developing child: they just have more of them, in the form of an extra twenty-first chromosome. In this respect, DS children are distinct from those with Williams Syndrome, and/or Specific Language Impairment, since both of these conditions have been tied to genetic differences – deletion of 26–28 genes in WS, mutant allele of the FOXP2 transcription factor in SLI – located on chromosome 7.[3] As far as is known, there is nothing anomalous about chromosome 7 in children with DS. Yet they manifestly do have problems with language processing, especially speech production. In addition, the IQ range of children with Down's Syndrome overlaps with that of typically developing, non-disordered children: if lowered general intelligence were a significant masking factor in grammar acquisition – something that generativists in any case deny – then some typically developing children should also show impaired language competence. Perhaps they do: perhaps we should look more closely. But if UG does not guarantee convergence, it has no explanatory function.

Finally, in spite of their difficulties with the processing of multi-word utterances, it is undeniable that children with Down's Syndrome have some 'natural capacity for language', as anyone who communicates with such a child will quickly realise. If anything, pragmatic, metalinguistic and other communication skills – for example, the use of paralinguistic gestures – appear to be enhanced in compensation, relative to those of typically developing children. Still, even if work by Christodoulou and Wexler (2016) suggests that adults with Down's Syndrome know more about morphosyntactic properties (such as case and tense marking) than is suggested by a casual inspection of their spontaneous speech, there is almost no evidence that my son, for instance, 'has UG', or that UG has helped him to use his two languages to any level of proficiency.

If Chomskyan nativism means more than the truism that human beings are innately equipped to learn the language of their community, then – as many commentators have pointed out – there is a need to be much more specific about the epistemic content of UG, and of the ways in which this knowledge interacts with more general cognitive attentional and learning mechanisms. After half a century of research effort, it seems like plainly inadequate hand-waving to conclude that (as quoted earlier):[4]

UG is used in this sense ... the theory of the genetic component of the language faculty ... that's what it is.

Equally serious is the fact that even if some content could be agreed on, the distance between such knowledge and genetics is too great to yield any valid set of explanations. That was the thrust of the argument in Part I.

In his article 'The Ghost of Protagoras' (1987), Stephen Jay Gould points out the problem with sociobiological accounts of cultural evolution:

When sociobiology is injudicious and trades in speculative genetic arguments about specific human behaviours, it speaks nonsense. When it is judicious and implicates genetics only in setting the capacity for broad spectra of culturally conditioned behaviours, then it is not very enlightening. To me, such an irresolvable dilemma only indicates that this latest attempt to reduce the human sciences [to genetics] will have very limited utility.

Stephen Jay Gould, 'The Ghost of Pythagoras'
(*An Urchin in the Storm*, 1987: 68)

These comments, I suggest, apply equally forcefully to theories of language. Some Chomskyans may object that linguistics is not a human science, in this sense. While one can of course define the term as one pleases, such a response strikes me as at best Quixotic, Humpty Dumpty-ish at worst. A little of both, perhaps.

Notes

1 It is not as though I am uncritical of Evans and Levinson's paper: in fact, I have published criticism of it, taking issue with what I see as their misinterpretations of generativist claims about UG; see Duffield (2010), cf. Levinson and Evans (2010) for a response.
2 I don't know of a better term to employ here. Racist is obviously wrong: the attitude uniformly discriminates against atypical learners of every ethnicity, colour and creed.

3 For discussion of Williams Syndrome, see Martens, Wilson and Reutens (2008); for SLI and other Speech Sound Disorders, see Lewis, Shriberg, Freebairn et al. (2006).

4 Some Chomskyan Nativists have attempted to flesh out how one might find evidence for UG reflected in the acquisition process. Stephen Crain's 'Three Hallmarks of Innateness' (Crain 1993) – as well as later work by Crain and Pietroski (2001) – point at the kinds of evidence (albeit mostly circumstantial) that would support CN.

19   O is for Object of Study

'Still, it's a nice place, you must admit ... all this gilt and the elephants. Very nice ... None of your bloody modern bloody architecture ... I tell you: modern architects ... scum of the earth. Whatever building you ask them to design they'll always come up with a lump of concrete that looks like a dustbin with a bicycle on top of it.'

Richard Curtis and Rowan Atkinson, 'Man in Seat 23c'
(Live in Belfast , 1979)

[C]um magnificenter opus perfectum aspicietur, a domini potestate inpensae laudabuntur, cum subtiliter, officinatoris probabitur exactio, cum vero venuste proportionibus et symmetriis habuerit auctoritatem, tunc fuerit gloria architecti.

When a work has been completed in a magnificent fashion, the owner is the one who will be praised for his munificence; when it is carried out with subtlety, the master craftsman will be lauded for his skill of execution; but when the work derives its authority from its proportions and symmetry, the glory will belong to the architect.

Marcus Vitruvius Pollio, De Architectura 'The Ten
Books on Architecture', book VI (30–15 BCE)

All analogies are doomed. Most similes are like nothing else; as for metaphors, some people wouldn't recognise one if it jumped up and bit them on the nose. Yet analogies matter greatly. For as long as they work, they help the researcher to develop a coherent line of research, to anticipate gaps or sudden changes in direction. Only after they fail – as they are sure to do – do we appreciate the damage they have done, the deception they have caused.

A fundamental problem is that it is impossible to speak about metaphors without employing them: indeed, if George Lakoff and Mark Johnson are correct – in their book *Metaphors We Live By* (Lakoff and Johnson 2003) – it's virtually impossible to speak at all. In any situation, though, some metaphors are surely more valuable than others. In this section, I'll briefly discuss two dominant metaphors that I consider bankrupt, or seriously insolvent at best, as well as an allegory enclosed in an aphorism which seems no less problematic. For reasons of space as well as charity ('if you can't say anything nice, don't say nothing at all'), I'll not spend much time examining all that is wrong with these analogies. In their place, I'll offer an alternative that seems to me to offer a more profitable means of explaining language(s) in mind, namely physical architecture.

(i)   Language as a biological organ

[Language is] essentially a kind of an organ of the body on a par with the visual system, or the immune system … or organs of the body.

Noam Chomsky, *Poverty of Stimulus: Some Unfinished Business* (2010); see Chapter 1

Chomsky's assertion struggles to be coherent, but it doesn't struggle hard. Systems are not organs, in any sense of either of the two words; organs are not systems. Organs are anatomical units, collections of physically connected tissues. Some organs, such as the bladder, have a dedicated function within a larger organ system; others subserve a variety of physiological systems. The human tongue is a relevant case in point: primarily an organ for taste and digestion, it has a large number of secondary functions, including, most relevantly, enabling oral speech production.

Since they are anatomically defined, organs have a specified physical location: surgeons can transplant a heart, a liver, an eye, can remove a uterus, a bowel, even part of a brain, without losing a system. (Skin is an anomaly in this regard.) By contrast, it is impossible to transplant the entire visual system, the immune system, the digestive system. Systems are not physically discrete. Indeed, systems are not essentially biological – fortunately for those on kidney dialysis, or equipped with a pacemaker. Systems are concerned with the conversion, and/or relay, of *energy* or *information*, which might be the same thing from a certain perspective. The visual system (as discussed earlier) is concerned with the processing of external bits of information impinging on our retinas, and the conversion of these sensory impulses into sensations, to thoughts about the world. The digestive system is concerned with the transformation of food into increasingly smaller chemical units that get re-absorbed and assimilated into the body at different stages in the process. Every system is functionally defined and operates in relation to other functional systems. See I is for Internalism. In some cases, whether a process belongs to one system or another is a question of perspective and context: the olfactory system, for example, can be viewed as part of the digestive system, or as an attentional system, or sensory system in its own right. Crucially, physiological systems are never named by a specific organ: there is an auditory system, but no 'ear system', a urinary or renal system, but no 'bladder system'.

Nor do organs grow selectively in response to external input (not ontogenetically, at least): children living in quiet environments don't grow bigger ears; children raised in contemporary urban societies don't stop growing molars even when they don't need to chew their food. But speech perception, and language comprehension, does work in just this way: all of the mechanisms of language processing are dynamically attuned to the particular linguistic stimuli they are required to handle.

Given this, it makes no sense to say 'It's essentially a kind of an organ of the body on a par with the visual system.' Language can't essentially be one thing or another: either it's an organ – which seems anatomically improbable, since it has no exclusively physical properties – or it's a system. Or neither. But Chomskyan I-LANGUAGE alone cannot be a system, since biological systems serve some coherent information processing function, involving many complex steps, and I-LANGUAGE, on Chomsky's own definition, explicitly does not have these functional characteristics. Indeed, as was discussed earlier, Chomsky explicitly denies that I-language has any function: see F is for Functions of Language. The human *language system* – the one involved with language comprehension and production – *is* a viable candidate as a biological system, but language processing in this broader and richer sense is not what generativist linguists are typically concerned with.

(ii)   The mind as a computer

A recent essay by the psychologist Robert Epstein, titled 'The empty brain', begins with the following introductory lines:

Your brain does not process information, retrieve knowledge or store memories. In short: your brain is not a computer.

Robert Epstein, 'The empty brain' (Aeon, 2016)

The first sentence leaves no room for compromise: unless the entire field of cognitive science should be consigned to the dustbin, Epstein's assertion is nonsense. It's quite astonishing that anyone, let alone a self-respecting research psychologist, would write such a sentence, even more remarkable that any (non-satirical) outlet would publish it ...

A fuller read of the article, however, suggests that perhaps he didn't ([write it], that is): perhaps this was the fault of a copy-editor trying to serve up a catchy standfirst, without basic understanding of non-right-monotone-increasing contexts; see Szabolcsi and Zwarts (1993).

The property of right-monotone-increasingness sounds complex, but is actually simple to grasp. It refers to the fact that the truth or falsity of a short sentence is usually preserved even when additional material is added (to the right); hence 'right-increasing'. So, for example, if it is true that *Amy likes chocolate [more than anything else in the world]*, then it is true that she likes chocolate (132); if it is true that *Andrew is a liar [and a weasel]*, then it is true that Andrew is a liar. In many instances you can delete the last part of the sentence without altering the truth conditions pertaining to the first part, if uttered in isolation. Some elements, however, block this semantic property: these include adverbs such as *always, never, often* (133), relative clauses (134), and – crucially – clausal negation (135). All of these elements prevent inferences from longer to shorter sentences. Editors should beware of such elements as these.

(132) a. Amy likes chocolate … more than anything else in the world.
　　　 b. Amy likes chocolate.　　[a entails b.]

(133) a. Fred always/never/often eats spaghetti with chopsticks.
　　　 b. Fred always/never/often eats spaghetti.　　[a. does not entail b.]

(134) a. Gerald hates dogs that snap at his ankles.
　　　 b. Gerald hates dogs.　　[a. does not entail b.]

(135) a. Jerry doesn't buy groceries at the supermarket very often.
　　　 b. Jerry doesn't buy groceries at the supermarket.
　　　 c. Jerry doesn't buy groceries very often.
　　　 d. Jerry doesn't buy groceries.　　[a. does not entail b., c. or d.]

Philip and de Villiers (1992) have shown that children as young as four years old are aware of the inferential contrasts exemplified above. Yet this same awareness seems to have been lost on the editorial team that published Epstein's article, since – in the body of the article itself – the closest we find to these preview lines are the following, fairly pedestrian, assertions:

> *We don't* store *words or the rules that tell us how to manipulate them. We don't create* representations *of visual stimuli,* store *them in a short-term memory buffer, and then* transfer *the representation into a long-term memory device. We don't* retrieve *information or images or words from memory registers. Computers do all of these things, but organisms do not.*
>
> Robert Epstein, 'The empty brain' (*Aeon*, 2016)

It's not as though everyone would necessarily agree with all of these claims, but they are for the most part empirical. They are not wholly ridiculous. For example, Epstein is very likely correct to claim that 'we don't store words' in our brain: a huge amount of experimental research on lexical representations suggests that lexical storage and access involves units both smaller or larger than words (roots, stems, multi-word strings, etc.), and that these units are represented in highly distributed dynamic neural networks. Moreover, as any undergraduate student of linguistics has been taught, the very notion of 'word' is incredibly problematic. How many words, for example, are found in the following sentence from Yup'ik Eskimo (from Payne 1997: 28), where, of all the morphemes only *tuntu* ('reindeer') can appear in isolation?

(136)   tuntussurqatarniksaitengqiggtuq
        tuntu-ssur-qatar-ni-ksaite-ngqiggte-uq
        reindeer-hunt-FUT-say-NEG-again-3sg:IND
        'He had not yet said again that he was going to hunt reindeer.'

It also seems unlikely that our brains manipulate autonomous grammatical rules: indeed, there is near-universal agreement across the theoretical spectrum that there are no rules in the traditional sense, at any level of theoretical explanation: see Chapter 3. Finally, no-one supposes (I assume) that the human brain has the physical and functional architecture of a late twentieth-century micro-computer. Hence, Epstein is surely right to claim that we don't store representations 'in a short-term memory buffer, and then transfer [them] into a long-term memory device'. But of course, many computers – including the one I've used to write these paragraphs – don't have that architecture either.

The problem with the 'mind~brain as computer' metaphor is that it is obviously true and patently false, at the same time:

> Where the term 'computer' is understood as any self-contained system that converts information from one state to another in ways that can (in principle) be described algorithmically, then the brain is most certainly a computer, but then so is the stomach, the womb, and every cell in the human body;
>
> Life, Imagination, Planet Earth is computational, in this very broad sense.
>
> If, on the other hand, a computer is defined as a particular kind of programmable (electronic, silicon-based, digital, serial) machine, then the brain is not a computer. Obviously. But then neither is/was Charles Babbage's 'No. 2 Difference Engine', or any other early analytic device based on mechanics rather than electronics. Or any quantum computer, or any computer implemented in an organic medium ...

Assuming that the value of a metaphor is to be measured by how much it enhances our understanding of some phenomenon, the 'brain as computer' metaphor is literally less than useless. It leads to dodgy logic, and should be given up.

(iii)   Foxes and hedgehogs ... windmills too

The fox knows many things, but the hedgehog knows one big thing.

Arilochus

Allegory is a special kind of metaphor, at once cosy and cryptic. It is the kind that provides a useful means of criticising your opponents without incurring a libel suit or a knock on the door in the night, whilst at the same time allowing you to represent yourself as the weaker, more vulnerable – yet ultimately smarter – party: calling someone arrogant or stupid, prideful or selfish will necessarily be interpreted as *ad hominem*, whereas re-telling the classical fable of the hare and the tortoise, or – in this case, referring to the fox and the hedgehog – allows you to taunt others with less fear of retribution. It also allows you to flaunt a classical education. Allegory is the weapon of choice of political dissidents and nerds alike, since no-one can say exactly what it means (even if they think they know).

The meaning of the fox and hedgehog saying is more veiled than most allegories, since Arilochus didn't even provide an accompanying narrative. The general idea is clear, though: it's better to stick to one thing, to strive for coherence in a restricted search area, than to waste one's time with novelty, exploring different paths.

As obviously sound as this might seem, not all scientists endorse such single-mindedness, not everyone adores the hedgehog. Even those like Stephen Jay Gould, who ultimately sides with the spiny creature – his collection of essays *An Urchin in the Storm* is named in its honour – are aware of the problems involved:

I don't think that coherence is an unmixed blessing, or necessarily a virtue at all in our complex world. It forces one to take the hedgehog's part in that overused (and basically uninterpretable) aphorism, attributed to Arilochus and kept alive through the ages from Erasmus to Isaiah Berlin ... Vulpine flexibility may be the greater virtue in such a diverse and dangerous world. Think what the hedgehogs of history, Cortez and Pissarro, for example, might have done with the modern technologies of destruction.

Stephen Jay Gould, *An Urchin in the Storm* (1987: 4)

After over 200 pages of rambling across the linguistic countryside, it would reasonable for the reader to conclude that I run with the fox, and have little time for hedgehogs. That's wrong, though, for I like real hedgehogs well enough. But the *fox-and-hedgehog* metaphor is deadly if it is a licence for continuing to do 'the same damn thing over and over' again, even after it has been shown not to work. Within theoretical linguistics, Arilochus' analogy is typically used to endorse a methodological strategy of ignoring empirical evidence derived from other sources, of pushing a theoretical construct (functional categories, Binding Principles, for example) beyond the bounds of empirical reasonableness, and – not infrequently – denigrating those who draw attention to obvious problems with grammatical theory. The following quotation from Boeckx (2006) is representative:

Foxes know many tricks, hedgehogs only one. Foxes are interested in everything and move easily from one problem to another. Hedgehogs are interested only in a few problems which they consider fundamental, and stick with the same problems for decades. Most of the great discovery [sic] are made by hedgehogs, most of the little discoveries by foxes. Both types of discovery are needed to understand the universe. Science needs both hedgehogs and foxes for its healthy growth – hedgehogs to dig deep into the nature of things, foxes to explore the complicated details of our marvellous world. By its very programmatic nature, minimalism offers an opportunity for everyone to be a hedgehog.

Cedric Boeckx, *Linguistic Minimalism: Origins,*
Concepts, Methods and Aims (2006: 14)

In spite of allowing a place for foxes in scientific enquiry ('Both types of discovery are necessary...'), it seems clear which animal Boeckx considers the more admirable: who would not want to make great discoveries rather than little ones, to dig deep into the nature of things, instead of running around scratching at the surface?

Yet the allegory is basically invalid, not least because hedgehogs are rather stupid creatures, and Minimalists are not. Far from it: of the smartest people I have worked with in my career, most have been generative linguists. (It is true that some generativists share with hedgehogs a nocturnal cycle, as well as a tendency to roll into a prickly ball when attacked, but that doesn't seem to be what Arilochus had in mind – or Boeckx, come to that.) More importantly, the saying downplays the explanatory potential of new vantage points and different perspectives on scientific problems: just because the fox is inquisitive and wide-ranging doesn't mean it can't be single-minded.

Rather than reaching back to antiquity for a useful allegory, one could do worse than stretch a finger towards the world's first novel, Cervantes' *Don Quixote*, to the intellectual tension between the aprioristic windmill-slaying squire Don Quixote and his loyal empiricist servant Sancho Panza:

– ¡Válame Dios – dijo don Quijote –, y qué de necedades vas, Sancho, ensartando! ¿Qué va de lo que tratamos a los refranes que enhilas? Por tu vida, Sancho, que calles; y de aquí adelante, entremétete en espolear a tu asno, y deja de hacello en lo que no te importa. Y entiende con todos tus cinco sentidos que todo cuanto yo he hecho, hago e hiciere, va muy puesto en razón y muy conforme a las reglas de caballería, que las sé mejor que cuantos caballeros las profesaron en el mundo.

– Señor – respondió Sancho –, y ¿es buena regla de caballería que andemos perdidos por estas montañas, sin senda ni camino, buscando a un loco, el cual, después de

hallado, quizá le vendrá en voluntad de acabar lo que dejó comenzado, no de su cuento, sino de la cabeza de vuestra merced y de mis costillas, acabándonoslas de romper de todo punto?

> 'God preserve us!' said Don Quixote, 'what a lot of nonsensical ideas you are stringing together! What have these proverbs you are threading together got to do with the matter at hand? For your own good, Sancho, keep that mouth of yours shut, and stick to jabbing your mule from now on, and keep out of other people's business! Try to realise, with all of your five senses, that everything I have done, am doing, or shall do, is based on strict reason and is in perfect conformity with the rules of chivalry, for I understand these better than all the knights of the world who go around professing them.'

> 'Senor,' replied Sancho, 'is it a good rule of chivalry that we should get lost in these mountains, with no path or roads to guide us, in search of a madman who, once he is found, may well take it into his head to finish off what he started – I don't mean his story, but your worship's head and my ribs – and end up breaking them into small pieces?'

Calla, te digo otra vez, Sancho – dijo don Quijote –; porque te hago saber que no sólo me trae por estas partes el deseo de hallar al loco, cuanto el que tengo de hacer en ellas una hazaña con que he de ganar perpetuo nombre y fama en todo lo descubierto de la tierra; y será tal, que he de echar con ella el sello a todo aquello que puede hacer perfecto y famoso a un andante caballero.

> 'Hold your tongue, I say again, Sancho,' said Don Quixote, 'I'd have you know that it's not so much wanting to find that madman that leads me into these places as the yearning to achieve something there that will earn me eternal fame and renown in all of the known world; and that achievement will set the seal on everything that could make a knight-errant perfect and famous.'

Miguel de Cervantes, *El Ingenioso Hidalgo Don Quijote de la Mancha*, volume 1, chapter 25 (1605–15)

Don Quixote presents us with a much more interesting and ambiguous contrast than any anthropomorphic tale of ruse drawn from antiquity. Quixote may be a delusional character, he may lack worldliness, but he is not stupid; in most respects, he is still more attractive in his madness than his stolid companion, Sancho Panza. Who, then, is the hero of the piece?

(iv)   'An immense invitation'

> Long ago on the ship she asked, 'Why pyramids?'
> He said, 'Think of them as an immense invitation.'
> She asked, 'Are you cursed?'
> He said, 'I think that I'm cured.'
> Then he kissed her, and hoped that she'd forget that question.

♫ Josh Ritter, *The Curse* (2010)

For at least 4,500 years – for more than 2,000 years before Euclid – humans have been constructing Euclidean buildings: squares, rectangles, pentagons,

Figure 29 Umeda Sky Building, Osaka: 'a picture of infinity'.

occasionally circles – any shape, provided it has at least one line of symmetry (except triangular buildings, which don't allow for much internal floor space). Wherever you look, in whatever country, at whatever point in history, the hand of man is revealed by perpendicular lines and regular geometry. See Figure 29 for a particularly interesting modern example: the Umeda Sky Building, in Osaka. If you were looking for circumstantial evidence that humans had arrived from another planet, you need look no further than the buildings we construct and the road systems that connect them. Also ley lines, crop circles, and *feng shui* ...

Human architecture is at least as alienated from the rest of nature as human language is from other systems of animal communication. More so in fact, since it seems redundant to talk about 'human architecture' as opposed to 'architecture' *tout court*; though cf. Hansell (2007). In respect of language, by contrast, only Chomskyans rigidly deny the possibility that other species might have languages, too; hence, for most people the modifier 'human' still does some work, in this context.

So, architecture is at once distinctively human, and remarkably 'unnatural'. In what we call the natural world, certainly at the macroscopic level, there

are no analogues of the parallel lines, right angles and perfect symmetry that
so engage and attract us, in the physical products of the architectural mind.
No other animal species uses natural resources around them to create straight
lines or perpendicularity, nor are there inorganic geological processes that give
rise to ninety-degree angles. Yet every human being reflexively responds to
the parallel and perpendicular in architecture and art – and if extant structures
are a reliable guide, it has always been this way.

> *Euclid alone has looked on Beauty bare.*
> *Let all who prate of Beauty hold their peace,*
> *And lay them prone upon the earth and cease*
> *To ponder on themselves, the while they stare*
> *At nothing, intricately drawn nowhere*
> *In shapes of shifting lineage; let geese*
> *Gabble and hiss, but heroes seek release*
> *From dusty bondage into luminous air.*

Edna St Vincent Millay, 'Sonnet VI' (*American Poetry*, 1922)

Even where Euclidean geometry nearly kills us with its sharp edges, we eschew
natural irregularity. Edmonton, Alberta, is a case in point. Built on a bluff,
the downtown section of the northernmost city in North America comprises
buildings whose most distinctive ecological property is the creation of artificial wind-tunnels in sub-zero temperatures: needless suffering for the minimalist aesthetics of sharp lines. And on the outskirts of the city, the Muttart
Conservatory in winter presents an immense, frigid, invitation: see Figure 30.

The intimate, awe-inspiring, relationship between geometry, architecture
and infinity in the human imagination is encapsulated in these lines from
William Golding's novel, *The Spire*:

Then one morning when he entered the cathedral ('Lift up your heads, O ye Gates')
and stood by the pit where no smell was, he heard a change in the noises from the
vaulting. He strained back his head on his neck, and a grain of sky hit him, smack,
breath-taking, unbelievable, wonderful, blue. As the edges of his small window
sometimes gave a depth and intensity to what he saw through it, so the roof round
this tiny hole made this glimpse into a jewel. Up there, they were laying back the
lead, rolling it back on the rafters. The blue widened and lengthened, joined earth
to heaven, where one day and soon, the geometric lines would leap into a picture
of infinity.

William Golding, *The Spire* (1964)

Some people have interpreted this love of geometric form in theological terms.
In his book *Geometry and Faith*, Thomas Hill, the nineteenth-century clergy-
man and scholar (also twentieth president of Harvard University) considered
the instinctive regard for symmetry as evidence of our being the species closest

Figure 30 Muttart Conservatory of Edmonton (© Camille Tucker, used with permission).

to the mind of God (Hill 2015). In *Equations from God: Pure Mathematics and Victorian Faith*, Daniel Cohen writes about Hill:

Hill traced the process whereby mathematics comes into contact with the ideal, divine patterns of nature and thus gives strength to faith. The process begins simply, he noted, even in childhood. We enjoy symmetry, and this 'perception of beauty in outline is the unconscious perception of geometric law.' The innate love of symmetry is the first step to both mathematical understanding and the comprehension of divine laws, Hill then explained. It shows that we are truly the earthly creatures closest to God: 'The human mind, fettered by the body, seems in such speculations to show its kindred to the Infinite Spirit.'

Daniel Cohen, *Equations from God: Pure Mathematics and Victorian Faith* (2008)

Innate love. As Cohen notes, Hill explicitly adopted an internalist stance in his speculations: at the outset to *Geometry and Faith*, he wrote:

[O]bservation alone can lead to nothing, without insight – without that clearness of inward vision that sees more than the outward fact.

Thomas Hill, *Geometry and Faith* (2015)

This thread of the discussion may lead some people to wonder whether a purely internalist theory of architectural form might be constructed that would abstract away from superficial diversity: 'UG' (G for geometry, this time) or I-ARCHITECTURE perhaps. Confronted with 'knowledge [of architectural form] in the absence of experience' – the only rational, non-metaphysical, response is to invoke innateness arguments.

The argument has at least as much merit as any POS argument for language. Yet I suspect that a purely internalist theory of architecture is unlikely to attract serious attention from academic researchers (even if there may be a few Minimalists who will regard it as a brilliant idea). The reason that it shouldn't catch on is *not* that there are no abstract universals of architecture: it is quite plausible to believe there are. Rather, it is because all of the theoretically interesting aspects of architectural design relate to the wealth of synchronic and diachronic variation, to the ways in which buildings are adapted to the natural and built environment, and to contrasts in aesthetic preferences in building design across different cultures, and across time. Constrained diversity is what is theoretically significant, not Euclidean uniformity.

The same issues of acquisition from the input, the same mysteries of cultural transmission and local continuity, the same problems of imperfection and 'performance error' that arise for language do so for architecture. Yet no-one would resort to a internalist 'parameter-setting model' of architectural design to explain the diachronic differences between Romanesque vs. Gothic styles in European ecclesiastical architecture, or to account for the synchronic contrasts between Romanesque and Byzantine art in eleventh-century Europe. At least I hope not. Most of the truth about architecture is out there, not within us. And this is for the best, particularly if Josh Ritter is right about parallel lines:

> *It's a long way to Heaven, it's closer to Harrisburg*
> *And that's still a long way from the place where we are*
> *And if evil exists, it's a pair of train tracks*
> *And the devil is a railroad car.*

♫ Josh Ritter, *Harrisburg* (2001)

But if the best theory of architecture remains an externalist one, and if – as I've hinted here – architecture offers a better analogy for thinking about how we learn and use language than does biology or applied mathematics, then it seems only reasonable to suppose that the best theory of language will also be at least partially externalist 'in nature', too.

20 P is for Poverty of the Stimulus (good arguments)

This page intentionally left blank

21 R is for (Exophoric) Reference

In this chapter, I briefly examine the problem of exophoric reference, how words are associated with objects beyond speech and text. This may be another fool's errand, since, as was noted earlier, many linguists regard the issue as so intractable as to dismiss it out of hand, alternatively, to leave it to philosophers. (For a good signpost down that road, see Reimer and Michaelson 2016.) I hope you will bear with me, nevertheless.

The simplest way to gain traction on the problem is by assuming that what a word connects to is not some object in the real world,[1] but rather one that sits within our minds – within the conceptual models that we construct to represent objects, situations and events. There is no 'outside' there: the physical existence (or otherwise) of the real-world correlates of pronouns and names is largely irrelevant to their psychological ontology. Of course, this is hardly a novel idea. In cognitive psychology, the notion of mental models can be traced back to the seminal work of Kenneth Craik (1967), work originally published in 1943; since then, it has been pursued and developed by many researchers, including Gentner and Stevens (1983), and Johnson-Laird (1983). (It should be noted that much of this work is more concerned with reasoning and inference than with reference *per se*.)

For concreteness (!), consider again the *Madame Bovary* passage first introduced in Part II (Case #4), which is repeated for convenience below. Whereas the concern in the earlier chapter was with referential dependencies internal to language – anaphoric binding relations – this time the focus is on the sentence-external (exophoric) interpretation of names and pronouns. Specifically, in the case at hand, who or what does *she* or *he* or *Paris,* or *there,* refer to?

Elle$_1$ était à Tostes. Lui$_2$, il$_2$ était à Paris$_3$, maintenant; là-bas!

Comment était ce Paris$_3$? Quel nom$_4$ démesuré! Elle$_5$ se le$_6$ répétait à demi-voix$_7$, pour se$_8$ faire plaisir; il$_9$ sonnait à ses$_{10}$ oreilles comme un bourdon$_{11}$ de cathédrale$_{12}$, il$_{13}$ flamboyait à ses$_{14}$ yeux jusque sur l'étiquette$_{14}$ de ses$_{15}$ pots$_{16}$ de pommade.

La nuit, quand les mareyeurs, dans leurs charrettes, passaient sous ses fenêtres en chantant la Marjolaine, elle s'éveillait, et écoutant le bruit des roues ferrées, qui, à la sortie du pays, s'amortissait vite sur la terre:

– Ils y seront demain! se disait-elle.

She₁ was in Tostes. And as for him₂, he₂ was in Paris now; way over there! What sort of a place was Paris₃? What a boundless name₄. She₅ whispered it₆ to herself₇, because she₈ loved its sound. It₉ resonated in her₁₀ ears like the great bell₁₁ of a cathedral₁₂; it₁₃ radiated from her₁₄ eyes even onto the labels₁₅ of her₁₆ pomade pots₁₇.

At night, when the fish carriers passed by in their carts, beneath her windows, singing the Marjolaine, she would wake up, and hearing the noise of the iron-clad wheels, suddenly muffled, as they left the village, by the dull earth of the country road:

'They will be there tomorrow!' she told herself.

Gustave Flaubert, *Madame Bovary*, chapter 9 (1857)

Intuitively, *she* refers to Emma Bovary (a fictional character), *he* refers to Emma's mental image of her lover (a fiction within a fiction). The pronoun *it* is particularly interesting, in referring not to Paris itself, but to the *name* of the place – the sound of the word, and the images that the pronunciation of the word evoke in Emma's mind. Yet the two are not clearly separated: the stock images of Paris – Notre Dame Cathedral, Paris as City of Lights – are infused into Emma's sub-vocal representation of the name ('It resonated in her ears ... it radiated from her eyes...'). Of all the referents in the text, only Paris has any correlate in the real world: the one illustrated in Figure 31. But this does not give it any distinguished status in the mental model that we construct as we read the passage. Nor does the level of psychological reality privilege one referent over another: to the reader, Emma Bovary is no more salient or accessible than the (more embedded) characters and places in Emma's mind ('second-' or 'third-order' referents). We effortlessly shift perspective as we read the text, moving between these different levels of the model. In the second paragraph, for example, the imagined fishermen (*they*) would be *there* – simultaneously in the Paris they were travelling to, and in the Paris of Emma's imagination – though not, of course, in the reader's imagined Paris, still less in Paris itself.

Some readers of this book will have spent time on *Les Grands Boulevards* (Glanzberg/Plante/Montand) in Paris (France); others may live in (or have visited) the Carolinas (US East Coast states), the inspiration for James Taylor's wonderful evocation *Carolina in my Mind*. A few people may be physically familiar with both locations. Most readers, however, will have no personal knowledge of either Paris or Carolina. But whatever our individual experiences may be, we none of us have any privileged access to *Flaubert's* or *Montand's* Paris or *James Taylor's* Carolina: these are – as Taylor's lyrics make quite explicit – in their own minds, not in the world.

♫ Jacques Glanzberg, Norbert Plante, Yves Montand, *Les Grands Boulevards* (1951)

♫ James Taylor, *Carolina in my Mind* (1968)

Figure 31 *Comment était ce Paris? Quel nom démesuré!* Afternoon view of Paris, from the Eiffel Tower.

Of course, personal experience of a particular time and place may add value to referents. In my own case, many of the places name-checked in Van Morrison's songs have a special resonance, in virtue of the fact that we grew up in the same part of East Belfast (off the Upper Newtownards Road) during the 1960s and 1970s. During my childhood, for example, I was often driven by my mother down *Cyprus Avenue* to visit my grandmother and great-aunt, who lived a couple of streets further into town. As Figure 32 illustrates, Cyprus Avenue remains a quiet tree-lined avenue, with markedly larger and more expensive homes (*mansion[s] on the hill*) than those of the working-class streets to the west: an aspirational symbol, perhaps.

♫ Van Morrison, *Cyprus Avenue* (1968)

♫ Van Morrison, *Ancient Highway* (1995)

Similarly, Morrison's song *Ancient Highway* references the Connswater area at the lower end of the Upper Newtownards Road, whose sights and smells I remember well: every year, at back-to-school time, I'd be taken to Irvine's shoe shop, near East Bread Street (*A street called Bread*), where the now-closed

Figure 32 *Mansions on the hill*: Cyprus Avenue, East Belfast.

Inglis bakery was located, itself just a few streets from where Belfast's most famous son – George Best – grew up (where *Georgie knows best.*)

The map of East Belfast in Figure 33 describes an area of approximately two square kilometres which includes Cyprus Avenue, E. Bread Street, and the one-time homes of Van Morrison, George Best, and my grandmother and her sister, my great-aunt. (The rock guitarist Gary Moore, of *Parisienne Walkways* fame, grew up about a mile further east, just off the Upper Newtownards Road.)

All very interesting, to me at any rate. Yet the fact that my sense of place in Van Morrison's songs is informed by memories of actual houses and streets does not make the least difference to any other reader, or to the validity of their imaginings. In fact, personal knowledge may even preclude a deeper under-standing of song's message: *Cyprus Avenue* is a metaphor before anything else.

The theoretical problem of exophoric reference is certainly intractable if it is primarily understood in terms of ostensive definition, as proposed in W. v. O. Quine's famous book, *Word and Object* ([1960] 2015), perhaps the best-known Behaviourist account of meaning. If, instead, reference is construed as the relationship between word and mental image that is updated and enriched primarily through language, the problem is much reduced, even if it is not eliminated. In particular, this construal allows us to abandon the otherwise

Figure 33 East Belfast: A, Van Morrison's house; B, George Best's house; C,
Cyprus Avenue; D, Bread Street; E, my grandmother's house; F, *our house.*

unhelpful distinction between abstract and concrete referents in a way that better matches our intuitions. To take a mundane example, the referent of 'Andy's
preference for sweet wine' is no more abstract – no less psychologically real –
than 'the shoes that Kathy was wearing yesterday'.

Finally, the internalisation of exophoric reference readily makes sense of the
fact that we effortlessly refer to things that we know do not physically exist.
When George Steiner remarks that ...

*We speak still of 'sunrise' and 'sunset.' We do so as if the Copernican model of the solar
system had not replaced, ineradicably, the Ptolemaic. Vacant metaphors, eroded figures
of speech, inhabit our vocabulary and grammar. They are caught, tenaciously, in the
scaffolding and recesses of our common parlance. There they rattle about like old rags
or ghosts in the attic.*

George Steiner, *Real Presences* (1989: 5).

... he has fallen into the trap of Referentialism. 'Sunrise' and 'sunset' are *not*
vacant metaphors: they are real mental constructs. The fact that the physical solar system doesn't work that way is largely irrelevant to our innate
geocentrism.

No doubt, many philosophers and their students will regard this speculation
about reference as a huge cop-out. This is because by not stepping outside, the
mental models approach avoids many of the difficult issues that plague standard philosophical theories, be they descriptivist theories (Frege [1892] 1952,

Russell [1911] 1917, Searle 1983), 'direct reference' theories (Marcus 1961), causal theories (e.g. Kripke 1980) or some other (e.g. Evans 1982); see Reimer and Michaelson (2016) for detailed discussion. In every case, the problem is not getting outside of *language*, but actually connecting something inside our heads to something outside. Particularly when that something is '[the] black cat … that isn't there':

'Purpose is what we're striving for. We must have purpose. We mustn't be purposeless. We must not exhibit purposenessless. We must be purposelessnessless. Because we don't want to end up, do we? … Because we don't want to end up, do we, like the blind man in the dark room looking for the black cat … that isn't there.'

Richard Curtis and Rowan Atkinson, 'Sir Marcus Browning, MP' (*Live in Belfast*, 1979)

So it may be an evasion. Still, the solipsist in me wonders whether that is the best we can hope for. To take a (final) spatial analogy: suppose you are standing in London's Hyde Park, penniless and without a valid passport, and want to travel to Russia tonight. The local travel agent (a.k.a. philosopher) will tell you it just can't be done: I'll suggest to you that you stroll across Kensington Gardens, walk on a couple more streets to the Russian Embassy, and knock (or ring). If they let you in – you're there.

Note

1 This point has been accepted in the philosophical literature for some time, at least since Wittgenstein: opposition to Referentialism – the idea that meaning involves a direct relationship between a word and some real object (set of objects) in the world – can be further traced to Frege. Indeed, opposition to pure Referentialism is one of the few issues on which Frege, Wittgenstein and Chomsky appear to be in agreement, though see Dobler (2013). Even if I were qualified to enter this philosophical debate, this is not the place for it. All that is important here is the recognition that exophoric reference is in principle just as internal to the speaker as endophoric reference. Paradoxically, exophoric reference is the more abstract, since we can at least point to external reflexes of endophoric reference on a printed page or a tagged spectrogram.

22 T is for Sentence

DUDLEY: *Is that you, Brian?*
PETER: *Yes father.*
DUDLEY: *What time of the night do you call this, then?*
PETER: *It's four o'clock in the morning father.*
DUDLEY: *I'll <u>four o'clock in the morning</u> you, my boy.*

...

PETER: *Father, I don't know why you go on about the drains. You know perfectly well you retired at thirty-one, and haven't been down there since.*
DUDLEY: *I'll <u>haven't been down there since</u> you, my boy.*

...

PETER: *Father, I can't help being an agnostic. I wish I had faith like you.*
DUDLEY: *I'll <u>I wish I had faith like you</u>, my boy.*

...

DUDLEY: *Good Lord! Do you think your mother would have gone off to live with some dirty matelot in Frinton. She worshipped the ground I walked on.*
PETER: *She liked the ground, but she didn't care for you, father.*
DUDLEY: *I'll <u>didn't care for you</u> you, my boy.*

Peter Cook, 'Father & Son' (BBC2, 1966, republished
in *Tragically I was an Only Twin*, Peter Cook 2002)

'Beyond the pale': the hegemony of the sentence

In A is for Abstraction (and Ambiguity), I introduced the possibility of 'chaining' – overlapping and/or extended syntactic analyses, in which a string of words functions, simultaneously, as the completion of one sentence, and the middle or beginning of another. This device is especially prevalent in poetry and song, as in the Anna Ternheim song cited earlier, but it also occurs in speech, where it may be treated either as an afterthought, or – by some psycholinguists – as a performance error. Often both at once, are true.

(As an aside, notice that instead of 'poetry and song' in the previous paragraph, I could have written 'song and poetry'. This would not be ungrammatical (in the generativist sense), but it feels much less natural – or less

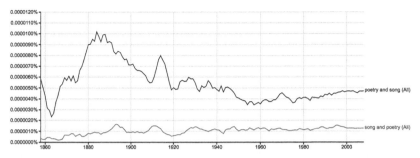

Figure 34 Phrasal acceptability: 'song and poetry' vs. 'poetry and song'.

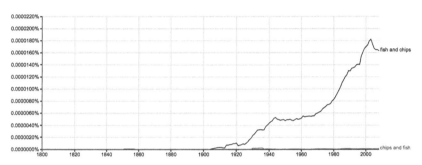

Figure 35 Google Ngram results: 'fish and chips' vs. 'chips and fish'.

hackneyed, depending on your point of view: see J is for Judgment. Very plausibly, the contrast in acceptability is due to the relative frequency of the two collocations, as revealed in the Google Ngram chart in Figure 34: cf. Bybee and Hopper (2001a). This is a subtle contrast, to be sure, especially when compared to 'fish and chips' vs. 'chips and fish' (Figure 35), but it is one to which native speakers are nonetheless sensitive – and at a phrasal, rather than clausal, level.)

But back to chaining. One possible reason that the phenomenon of sentence-chaining receives scant attention in formal linguistics is that the analytic tools that linguists have developed to deal with predominantly hypotactic language are ill-suited to dealing with more paratactic structures, which is to say, with the kinds of structures that are the most typically found in normal conversation. Or flowing text. Such as this one.

This inadequacy is an indirect result of the fact that most linguists have long considered the grammatical sentence – 'TP' in current Minimalist terminology – to be the largest well-regulated domain of linguistic knowledge (in extension). As the functionalist linguists Haiman and Thompson (1988) observe:

Traditional and modern grammarians alike have restricted what they call 'syntax' to the study of what goes on within the boundaries of the prosodic sentence. The limitation is justified by the widespread belief that at the paragraph level, and beyond, anything goes, the ars obligatoria *of grammar yielding to the anarchy of personal style … On the other hand, the nature of clause-combining within a prosodic sentence has always been a central concern of traditional syntax. One has only to glance through the monumental compendious grammars of languages like Latin, Greek, German, French, and English, to be struck by the subtle, painstaking treatment linguists … have lavished on the definition, description and exemplification of various kinds of coordination, parataxis, subordination, hypotaxis, and embedding. The importance of at least the coordination/ subordination distinction is taken for granted in generative grammar, where it underlies important research on deletion and anaphora … There has always been something a little dubious, however, about a research strategy that submits clause combinations to the most searching analysis when there is no prosodic or intonational break between them, and officially ignores virtually synonymous combinations which are separated by such a pause or break.*

John Haiman and Sandra Thompson, *Clause Combining in Grammar and Discourse* (1988: ix)

The dubiousness of this strategy is increased by the fact that, as discussed in A is for Abstraction (and Ambiguity), formal syntactic theories, and the psycholinguistic theories that depend on them, typically abstract away from non-syntactic information (especially lexical prosody and intonation) in explaining grammaticality. See also v is for von Humboldt.

It is important to recognise that not all psycholinguistics are committed to what has been termed the 'clausal hypothesis': since the 1970s, many researchers have pursued an utterance-focused process-oriented approach, arguments for which were first clearly set out nearly forty years ago in a paper by William Marslen-Wilson, Lorraine Tyler and Mark Seidenberg (Marslen-Wilson et al. 1978). See again v is for von Humboldt for a discussion of the difference between sentences and utterances. On these accounts, the distinction between well-formed sentences and acceptable fragments is much less important. However, the majority of those that believe in autonomous grammatical rules assume that such rules only hold sway from the beginning to the end of a sentence, [in print] from the initial capital letter to the final period, the clear implication being that barbaric chaos reigns beyond these boundary markers – not unlike the idea of the Roman *limes*, or medieval Pale; hence, the contempt in certain quarters for the semicolon. This entrenched assumption has led to some counter-intuitive conclusions, in particular, we find repeated denials of the idea that inter-speaker dyads can be as tightly regulated as intra-speaker combinations, for example, the relationship between main and subordinate clauses; where such inter-speaker dyads *are* shown to be constrained by grammatical principles, the discourse itself gets re-analysed so that this effect can thereby be 'internalised', so brought within the scope of sentence grammar.

(If you disliked the structure of the previous paragraph, that was precisely the intention: what is naturally spoken is not necessarily easily read, and *vice versa.*)

This ploy of 'internalising' discourse is demonstrated to good effect in the treatment of so-called 'Condition C effects'. (We're back to Binding Theory, once again – as if working though Part II, Case #4 was not sufficiently tedious.) In marked contrast to Binding Principles A and B, which – as we saw earlier – govern the distribution of anaphors and pronouns – and which do seem to be constrained by the first clausal boundary, Condition C is taken to 'apply throughout': that is to say, a proper name (or other R-expression) must be bound by any syntactically prominent antecedent, no matter the prior distance between the two elements. See Appendix A (website).

The examples in (137)–(138) are supposed to illustrate the operation of this structural principle. In the first pair of examples (137a,b), the noun-phrase *Kate* must be interpreted as disjoint in reference from *she* and *Mrs Cartwright*, respectively, even where it is otherwise conceivable that these noun-phrases could co-refer. The reason that co-indexation is possible in the second pair in (137) is that the pronoun *she* is contained within a subordinate clause, and is therefore not syntactically prominent. Finally, the examples in (138) allow co-reference because the noun-phrase *(the real) Mrs Cartwright* functioning as a predicate here rather than as a referring expression.

(137) a. She$_i$ believes, as does Harry, [that Kate$_{*i}$ is doing her job well].
   b. Mrs Cartwright$_i$ said that [she$_{i/j}$ thought [that Kate$_{*i/*j/k}$ was doing her job well]].
   c. Although she$_i$ is frequently criticised, Kate$_{i/?j}$ is doing her job well, in fact.
   d. Once she$_i$ admitted it, Kate$_{i/?j}$ felt a lot better.

(138) a. Kate$_i$ admitted to Fred that [she$_i$ was the real Mrs Cartwright$_i$]
   b. Kate$_i$ played Mrs Cartwright$_i$ to a tee.

Research by Solan (1983), later refined by Crain and McKee (1985), suggests that children as young as three years old are sensitive to 'Principle C effects' in complex declarative sentences; see also Crain and Thornton (1998).

It turns out, however, that Condition C effects extend beyond the level of the individual utterance to the immediately preceding discourse context. In other words, one speaker's possibilities for co-reference are constrained by

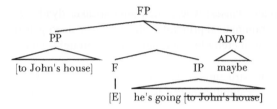

Figure 36 Internalising discourse fragments. Speaker B's fragmentary utterance in (139) is reanalysed as a full clause in which the prepositional phrase is first topicalised before the remainder of the clause gets elided (as formally required by the E-feature under node F). In this way, a copy of the NP John is c-commanded by the structurally more prominent pronoun, yielding a Principle C violation. See Appendix A (website).

the previous speaker's utterance. This was illustrated by the examples in (20) above, repeated here as (139):

(139)   SPEAKER A: *[pointing to John]* Where do you suppose he$_i$'s going?
        SPEAKER B: I dunno, to the pub, maybe/*To John$_i$'s house, maybe.

In this dyad, if speaker B knows that speaker A's *he* is intended to refer to John, s/he cannot use the R-expression *John*: the exchange is only licit if *he* and *John* are taken to refer to different people.

But what do they$_i$ know, exactly, these speakers$_i$?

Notice that if this interpretive restriction is to be explained syntactically, speaker B's utterance must be re-analysed so as to contain the offending pronoun at a more abstract level. This is precisely what Conroy and Thornton (2005) propose: following Merchant (2005), the authors explicitly analyse short answers to questions as involving a complex syntactic derivation in which the full answer is first computed, the fragment is fronted, and the residue subsequently elided: see Figure 36.

   If nothing else, this analysis demonstrates the lengths some researchers will go to to corral phenomena within a sentential frame of reference (pun intended): compare Barton (1986), Sutton, Lukyanenko and Lidz (2011).

   Aside from its unnecessary complexity, the more significant, empirical, problem with the analysis is that it only works sometimes, for Condition C – or rather, the effect that Condition C was formulated to explain – regularly fails to put in an appearance in normal discourse. Consider the following paragraphs adapted from a section in John Steinbeck's *East of Eden*. (For reasons of copyright, the passage has been relexified: the common nouns and other predicates have been replaced; however, the pronouns and syntactic structure match the original perfectly.) In the first paragraph below, *he* and *his* and *their uncle* all refer to the protagonist Elias [Salk] (here, *Elijah*), a name which is only mentioned in the subsequent paragraph:

James and little Matthew would be quiet and attentive while <u>their uncle</u> expounded on how every military commander *had acted and where* they *had failed and what they should have done. And then – <u>he</u> had believed it back then – <u>he</u> had told* Kelly and McCollum *where* they *were mistaken and had urged* them *to accept <u>his</u> view of the thing.* They *almost always rejected his counsel, and only afterwards was <u>he</u> proven to be right.*

There was one thing <u>Elijah</u> did not do, and maybe it was smart of him.

Adapted from John Steinbeck, *East of Eden* ([1952] 2001)

What makes this passage is particularly interesting is that Condition C seems to be violated twice: the quantified noun-phrase *every general* refers to – or at least includes – the (Civil War generals) Grant [Kelly] and McClellan [McCollum], who are mentioned in the immediately following sentence.[1]

One does not have to go as far as literature to find contexts where Condition C effects fail to appear where they should, or apply where they shouldn't. The utterances in (140) show instances of (three kinds of) RIGHT DISLOCATION, a common feature of many varieties of colloquial English, which is treated in detail in Durham (2011). The following are Durham's examples:[2]

(140)   a. They keep good time the cows. [= ex. 1]
        b. Oh he stayed with this other woman John did. [= ex. 4]
        c. She was an Irish lady was my grandma. [= ex. 6]

One would be hard-pressed to analyse any of the above examples such that the following NP is disjoint in reference from the pronoun; in each of these examples, the pronoun not only *can* be interpreted as co-referential with the right-dislocated expression, it seems that it *must* be so interpreted. Similarly, a subtle tweaking of the discourse context in the examples in (139) immediately allows for co-reference. This is shown in (141):

(141)   SPEAKER A: *[pointing towards two men]* Where do you suppose
        he$_i$'s going?
        SPEAKER B: *John$_i$*, you mean?
        SPEAKER A: Yeah …
        SPEAKER B: I dunno, to the pub, maybe, or to his$_i$ house.

Here, in contrast to the exchange in (139), though speaker A intends to refer to John, speaker B is unsure which of the two men is being pointed at. By uttering *John?* speaker B disambiguates the previous act of reference, but in so doing he also violates Condition C (supposing that such a principle exists).

Conversely, co-reference is between *he* and *Charlie* is clearly blocked in the passage in (142), even though the NP *Charlie* is not syntactically bound by any co-indexed element (since both of the preceding pronominal expressions are contained within embedded clauses):

(142)   Of the two men closest to her, Becky knew [that her brother would never do anything like that.] She knew [that he was greedy], yes, but not ruthless, not cruel. *Charlie,* though: Charlie was different.

The most reasonable conclusion to draw from the examples just discussed is that the sentential level plays no special role in determining the co-referential possibilities of proper names or other referring expressions. Even if Principle C could explain constraints on intra-sentential co-reference, we would still need a discourse-level processing theory to account for all of the other cases, and any such theory would necessarily subsume intra-sentential effects as well. As we saw earlier (Part II, Case #4), similar arguments apply to Principles A and B.

So, if not Binding, what other grammatical dependencies justify privileging the sentence as the primary level of analysis (above the word-level)? In J is for Judgment, it was argued that speaker-listeners are able to assign acceptability judgments just as well to sentence fragments as to conversational exchanges and other larger stretches of discourse. In any case, it seems ironic that a grammatical theory that regards reading and writing to be secondary systems should focus exclusively on a particular type of utterance whose only true distinguishing characteristic is that it begins with a capital letter and ends with a full stop, in its written form. The more so when its proponents regularly dismiss any concern with 'proper punctuation' as the petty obsession of small-minded 'language mavens'; see, for example, Pinker (1994) or any introductory textbook discussion of prescriptive grammar. See also v is for von Humboldt below.

A final problem with the idea that sentences (and their hierarchical sub-constituents) are the only valid units of grammar is that many spoken utterances contain elements that have no natural place in clausal syntax, but which nevertheless receive a clear analysis in the minds of native speakers. Some linguists do take these elements into account. Robins (1989: 217), for example, draws a distinction between FAVOURITE and NON-FAVOURITE SENTENCES. The latter class include fragments of various kinds:[3]

[T]hose that are not referable to a longer sentence syntactically, are independent of a previous sentence, and may initiate a discourse or conversation. Sentences of this sort are often exclamatory: John! hello! bother! drat! ... *Others may be gnomic, such* as the more, the merrier, easy come, easy go. *Sentences of this latter type are lexically restricted in most cases, and little or no variation of their particular word content is normally permitted in them; in consequence, they are hardly at all productive.*

R. H. Robins, *General Linguistics* (fourth edition, 1989)

See Duffield (2016) for further discussion. Although there are notable exceptions, e.g. Fillmore, Kay and O'Connor (1988), it is clear which kinds of sentence are the theoreticians' favourite. Yet, as we have seen repeatedly up to now, it is much less obvious where and how to draw the line between the lexically restricted and the generally productive, without resorting to *ad hoc* stipulation. This problem is taken up again in the next chapter, v is for von Humboldt.

Notes

1 Technically, this is not a Principle C violation, since *every military commander* and *they* are contained within a complement clause, and so do not c-command *Kelly* and *McCollum*. However, for those who do not accept the generativist account, the two referential chains [*he*... *Cyrus*], [*they*... *Kelly/McCollum*] appear to be very much of a piece; whatever explains one should extend to the other.
2 Discussion of these constructions can be traced back to Jespersen (1949). Traditionally, regular use of right dislocation in conversation has been associated with Northern varieties of English: Quirk et al. (1985). As Durham (2011) points out, the phenomenon is attested in other varieties as well; certainly, it was a feature of my own speech long before I lived in Yorkshire.
3 Not every language has a separate word for *sentence* – as opposed to *phrase*.

The golden ratio, the shell
The stairs ascending round themselves
The trees rustle as if to kneel and listen
To the heartbeat of a lark or the lark in my heartbeat.

The oxygen in priestly green
The answers dressed in labyrinthine
The telescopes atop the mountains of ecstatic vision listening
To the heartbeat of a lark or the lark in my heartbeat.

> *I am assured, yes I am assured yes*
> *I am assured that peace will come to me*
> *A peace that can yes surpass the speed yes*
> *Of my understanding and my need...*

The meteoric warp and wend
In counterbalance to the spark ever ascending
The arrow time shoots forward though it moves through repetition
To the heartbeat of a lark or the lark in my heartbeat.

What is it that drives the driven snow now?
Upon whose temples will I rest my weary hopes now?
The rain distils down steeples fills the ears of lonely church mice
With the heartbeat of a lark or the lark in my heartbeat.

> *I am assured yes I am assured yes*
> *I am assured that peace will come to me*
> *A peace that can yes surpass the speed yes*
> *Of my understanding and my need.*

♫ Josh Ritter, *Lark* (2010)

'The infinite employment of finite means'

Chomsky regularly cites the eighteenth-to-nineteenth-century German linguist and philosopher Wilhelm von Humboldt for his assertion that language 'makes infinite use of finite means'.[2] The original phrase, reproduced below, comes from the first volume of von Humboldt's collected writings – *Über die Sprache*

('On Language'), published posthumously in 1836. So there is little doubt that von Humboldt did write it, or something very much like it, as Peter Heath's translation in Losonsky (1999) confirms:

Language is quite peculiarly confronted by an unending and truly boundless domain, the essence of all that can be thought. It must therefore **make infinite employment of finite means**, *and is able to do so through the power which produces identity of language and thought. But this also necessarily implies that language should exert its effect in two directions at once, in that it first proceeds outward to the utterance and then also back again to the powers that engender it. Both effects are modified in each particular language by the method observed therein, and so must be taken together in expounding and evaluating that method.*

> Wilhelm von Humboldt, *Über die Sprache* 'On Language' ([1836] 1999: 91)

In spite of this, it is extremely doubtful whether von Humboldt would have endorsed Chomsky's co-opting of the expression: see Borsche (1990), Losonsky (1999). It is fair to say that Chomsky is highly selective in his use of von Humboldt's writings, which would seem to be a prudent strategy, given that the philosopher is also regarded as the 'father of linguistic relativity'.[3] Von Humboldt's unsuitability as a role-model for generativism is apparent in Sapir's discussion of von Humboldt in *Herder's Ursprung der Sprache* (Sapir [1907] 2008): in that article, von Humboldt is shown to be much more concerned with the infinite *variety* of languages than with the generation of infinite sets of sentences.[4]

Peter Losonsky (1999) expresses this tension explicitly:

Chomsky and Humboldt differ sharply about what is infinite about language. A generative grammar is a finite system of rules that generates an infinite set of sentences. So, Chomsky's understanding of Humboldt's idea that language makes infinite use of finite means entails the means are the rules and the uses are the sentences that can be constructed on the basis of the rules. For Humboldt, however, the boundless or infinite domain is 'the essence of all that can be thought', not sentences. So while for Chomsky the infinite domain is sentences, for Humboldt the infinite domain is what language is about or what it expresses.

> Michael Losonsky, *Humboldt: On Language* (1999: xxx)

For this reason, for Chomsky to quote favourably from von Humboldt may be compared to Adam Smith quoting favourably from Rousseau, except that the latter pair were contemporaries. Thatcher from Marx would be a better analogy.

Be that as it may, the property of 'infinite use of finite means' – now regularly termed DISCRETE INFINITY – is considered by many generativists as *the* defining property of I-LANGUAGE. The property has also been used as one of the key arguments for innateness, as well as for a non-gradualist theory of language evolution; see Gould and Eldredge (1977), Gould (2002); cf. Lieberman (2015).

Language is a system of infinite generation, that's not questionable. *And you cannot go from finite to infinite in small steps, so there is no point trying. It can't be done. You cannot go from a system of, say, four-word sentences to unbounded sentences in small steps. So you have to give it up. [my emphasis: NGD]*

Noam Chomsky, *Poverty of Stimulus: Some Unfinished Business* (2010: at 23:30)

Chomsky's assertion is just as relevant to language acquisition as to evolution: if his characterisation of language is correct, then children could not – in principle – learn to generalise from a finite set of utterances to a system exhibiting discrete infinity, any more than early pre-lingual humans could have developed a complex grammar from more primitive, finite systems of communication. You can't get there from here, as they say. This is the POVERTY OF THE STIMULUS writ large. Once again.

The difficulty with this argument is that it seems entirely possible that language (by which Chomsky means syntax) is *not* a system of infinite generation, but is instead a system of finite generation, albeit a large and complicated one. If this is true, then the assertion *is* questionable.

Rather than leaving this as a rhetorical point, which would surely have been the safest – not to mention briefest – course of action, I'll use the last part of this chapter to set out a declarative alternative to arithmetic, something which is also regarded as a system of infinite generation, equally unquestioningly. If a case can be made for a finite knowledge of numbers, it is at least plausible to think that such a system applies to sentences as well.

Before going there, it is worth pointing out a fundamental problem that arises in discussing any kind of infinity, discrete or otherwise: to wit, we are generally not very good at comprehending large numbers, let alone the infinite. See Land (1974: 138). Making even reasonably accurate estimates of large numbers is beyond the average person. Most observers, for example, can tell the difference between a crowd of a hundred and one of a thousand, but distinguishing 19,100 from 20,000 (the same numerical difference) is considerably more difficult, unless that crowd is arranged in uniform rows – in which case one is counting rows, not individuals.

To appreciate this point, have a look at Figure 37, and see whether you can estimate the size of this 1918 crowd. Is it closest to (a) 5,000, (b) 10,000, (c) 20,000 or (d) 30,000? Now examine the detail from the same photograph in Figure 38. Do you see (a) 100, (b) 300, (c) 700 or (d) 1,000 spectators?

According to the proximate source of these photographs (http://longstreet .typepad.com/thesciencebookstore/2008/11/the-detail-in-teh-detail-boxing-scene-viewed-by-20000-soldiers-1918.html), the correct answers are (c) and

Figure 37 Spectators at a boxing match (1918).

Figure 38 Spectators at a boxing match (1918 [detail]).

Table 8 *Guesstimation: large numbers are a real problem for normal people.*

	Q1				Q2				Q3
% of correct scores	45%				58%				–
Score distribution (*n*)	(a)	(b)	(c)	(d)	(a)	(b)	(c)	(d)	
	4	4	**11**	5	6	**14**	3	1	
Mean score/result	(18,125)				(313)				4,173,756,333
Median score/result	(20,000)				(300)				1,000,000
Standard deviation	(8,316.2)				(189.86)				21,220,227.32
Mean estimate (excluding outliers)	–				–				7,397,913

(b), respectively. In spite of the fact that neither problem is inherently difficult or complex, a quick survey among my first-year students (*n* = 24) reveals contrastive patterns of estimation in the two cases: whereas 58 per cent of students chose the correct answer for the detail picture (with most of the remainder choosing the lower figure), the estimates for the whole scene were more widely distributed; fewer than half (45 per cent) chose the correct answer for is this question. Notice that this is for a multiple-choice question with only four possible answers. See Table 8 (and note 5).

And when it comes to numbers of units above 5,000 or so, reason seems to desert us. The final question in my short survey asked students to estimate the number of grains in a 10 kg sack of uncooked rice (a common object in Japanese homes). We know objectively that it must be a relatively constrained figure – fewer than a million perhaps, more than 50,000 – but really, we have no precise notion: in the survey (Question 3) students' estimates varied from 12,000 to 100 billion (or 30 million, if one truly wild guess is excluded). Just visualising the problem causes some people to experience a certain queasiness; see Wikipedia entry for *Trypophobia*.[5]

If large *finite* numbers are difficult, our minds shut down almost entirely at the thought of the infinite. To some, like Douglas Adams, infinity is merely 'flat and uninteresting'; to others – particularly those of us tormented in childhood by religious stories of fire and brimstone – it is too terrifying to contemplate, for long. Either way, the best (or worst) that we can imagine is 'very, very, very big':

The car shot forward straight into the circle of light, and suddenly Arthur had a fairly clear idea of what infinity looked like. It wasn't infinity in fact. Infinity itself looks flat and uninteresting. Looking up into the night sky is looking into infinity – distance is incomprehensible and therefore meaningless. The chamber into which the aircar emerged was anything but infinite, it was just very very very big, so big that it gave the impression of infinity far better than infinity itself.

Douglas Adams, *The Hitchhiker's Guide to the Galaxy*, chapter XXIV ([1979] 2009)

Between the estimable (<~ 1,000) and the incomprehensibly numerous lies everything else; quite literally every thing (see www.youtube.com/results?search_query=size+of+the+universe, for some literal, astronomical comparisons). In the case of language, some relatively large numbers include: the number of words known to an average ten year-old; the number of words heard or produced by a speaker in an average month; the number of uses of 'the' by a speaker of English in his or her lifetime; the number of words in this book so far. (One nice irony is that the on-screen word-count feature of my word-processing application stops calculating when the total length of a document exceeds 99,000 words, something that happened a while back.)

Except for the first of these 'interesting facts', all of the other figures are assumed to refer to external reality (*parole*): as such, they are irrelevant to internalist construal of language: see I is for Internalism above. It turns out, though, that what is supposed to demonstrate the 'infinite use of finite means' – namely, the set of all grammatically well-formed sentences – is also an external fact (especially, if the conclusions of J is for Judgment are correct). Yet this forms a crucial part of Chomsky's argument for language as a recursive rule system, presumably an internal and intensional construct.

By language, of course, Chomsky means grammar. That point should by now be tediously obvious. And with respect to grammar, it all depends on *what* is being generated. In countless introductory syntax lectures, at least since the mid-1960s, linguistics instructors have rehearsed (and students have absorbed) the following syllogistic argument:

(1) A grammar of a given language *L* is nothing more than an explicit characterisation of all and only the grammatical sentences of *L*. The simplest such grammatical description would be an exhaustive *List Grammar* (a grammar 'in extension'): one could simply write down all of the grammatical sentences of *L*. Grammar as inventory.

(2) This simple approach is not tenable for natural languages, however, because [it is claimed]:

a. there is no principled limit either on absolute sentence length ('same-level' recursion; see below) or on depth of embedding ('nested recursion') ...

> *And it goes on indefinitely ... You can have a hundred-word sentence, a 10,000-word sentence, and so on.*
>
> Noam Chomsky, *Poverty of Stimulus: Some Unfinished Business* (2010); see Chapter 1

b. even if there were a principled limit on utterance length, say, 100 words, there would still be an infinite number of grammatical sentences since

(i) there are innumerable ways of combining the words in our lexicon at any point in time (see C is for Competence~Performance); and (ii) the lexicon is itself is infinitely expandable ...[6]

So let's buckle down, shall we? Purpose is what we're striving for. We must have purpose. *We mustn't be* purposeless. *We must not exhibit* purposelessness. *We must not be* purposelessnessless.

Richard Curtis and Rowan Atkinson, 'Sir Marcus
Browning, MP' (*Live in Belfast*, 1979)

(3) Assuming the correctness of (2), the grammar of a language must instead include a recursive rule system of some kind: a 'grammar in intension'.

Once one accepts the minor premises of this argument, the question is not *whether* grammar involves recursive rules, but *which* is the best recursive grammar for the job. The logical sleight of hand is easy to miss. For if either part of the minor premise (2) is false, there is no logical reason to accept the conclusion. Naturally, it could still be the case that language users have internalised a recursive rule system but – as George and Ira Gershwin wrote in *Porgy and Bess* – 'It ain't necessarily so.'

(Come to think of it, the Gershwins' song could well serve as the refrain for every letter of this section, from A to Ω.)

'Or shall I don a blue?': utterances vs. sentences

Let's take parts (2a) and (2b) of the minor premise in turn. First of all, we can ask whether there is a principled limit to sentence length: can you really have a 10,000 word sentence, as Chomsky asserts? In order to properly address this claim, it is vital to distinguish SENTENCES – the abstract objects that are (putatively) generated by a syntactic rule system – from UTTERANCES, the strings of words that people produce in speech or writing, which may be shorter or longer than sentences. See also T is for Sentence above. There can be no doubt that the two notions are closely related inasmuch as utterances are typically reflexes of sentences (or *vice versa*, depending on your theoretical commitments). Yet they differ from each other in several crucial respects, and as a consequence, there is no logical inference from the finiteness (or otherwise) of utterances to that of sentences. In other words, even if utterances turned out to be infinite, this wouldn't tell us anything about the infinitude of sentences.

Among their contrastive properties is the INTERNAL/EXTERNAL distinction, which has been an ongoing concern of this book: sentences (in comprehension) arise through an interaction between internally represented grammatical knowledge ('personal competence') and the environment, while utterances remain fundamentally external objects – *parole*, in Saussurean terms.

Utterances exist for everyone, as pre-theoretical objects. If I travel to Budapest, I will be exposed to a huge number of Hungarian utterances, tuning into a Hungarian radio station, I will be assailed by Hungarian input, but without some internalised knowledge of this language – however partial, see I is for Internalism – I will never in my life 'hear a sentence of Hungarian'. Ignoring the effects of sound symbolism and intonation, utterances are meaningless pre-analytic strings. Regardless of whether you are a speaker of Spanish or Vietnamese or Irish, there are three utterances in (143). I've unhelpfully removed the spaces between words, so obscuring the segmentation, to make this point clearer.

(143)   a. Delasierramorena,
           cielitolindovienenbajando,
           Unpardeojitosnegros,
           cielitolindodecontrabando.

                             Cielito Lindo, nineteenth-century Mexico

        b. Ngườiơingườiờđừng về
           Ngườivêemvầntrông theo,
           Trôngnướcnướcchảy,
           Trôngbèobèotrôi.

                      Người ơi người ở đừng về, traditional Vietnamese

        c. Thíosiláranghleanna, Tráthnónabeagaréir
           Agusandrúcht'nadheora geala, Inaluíarbharranfhéir
           Seacasadhdomhsaanainnir, Abáillegnúisispearsa
           Sísheolmostuaimchunseachráin
           Tráthnónabeagaréir.

                             Tráthnóna beag aréir, traditional Irish

        ♫ Clannad, *Tráthnóna beag aréir* (1996)

Only if you are speaker ('knower') of one or more of these languages will you be able to identify the *sentences* in these examples. As it turns out – these being extracts from songs – there are almost no instances of complete sentences, in the generativist sense, in any of these lines. See T is for sentence above. There are, however, many well-formed sentence fragments, grammatically acceptable constituent phrases that serve as well to convey propositional content – at least to the speaker of Spanish, Vietnamese or Irish, respectively.[7]

Another key difference between the two terms is that utterances may be ambiguous, but sentences never are. To speak of an 'ambiguous sentence' is loose talk: see A is for Abstraction (and Ambiguity) above. To see this, consider an example that is familiar from every basic introduction to semantics: 'Everyone loves someone.' This string has at least two interpretations in English: a 'linear scope' reading, corresponding to the surface order, which asserts that every individual is such that s/he loves at least one person (possibly him- or herself); and an 'inverse scope' reading, where there is a particular individual that everyone loves. Those with a preference for pseudo-mathematical formulae may like to express these readings as in (144): although it adds no real clarification, it looks somehow impressive to the uninitiated:

(144)   a. $\forall x \, (\exists y \, [x \text{ loves } y])$
          b. $\exists y \, (\forall x \, [x \text{ loves } y])$

While there are other ways of handling this interpretive contrast, it is often assumed in the generative literature that each of these readings is associated with a particular structural description (that is, a sentence), with the inverse scope reading involving an additional transformational step in the derivation: see May (1977, 1985); cf. Aoun and Li (1989, 1993). Whatever the precise technical treatment may be, any truly ambiguous utterance involves more than one sentential analysis, on a generativist approach.

Having once drawn these distinctions, let's now see whether there are natural bounds to either *utterance length* or *sentence length,* respectively. Notice at the outset the one-way implication here: if one can define the longest utterance, there must be a longest sentence. But the reverse does not hold: even if it turns out that there is no principled restriction on utterance length, there may or may not be an upper bound on sentences.

In order to address the question of utterance length consider the final section of 'Molly Bloom's soliloquy', the name given to the final chapter of James Joyce's *Ulysses* (1922 edition). At 3,669 words, this segment is widely celebrated as one of the longest printed 'sentences' in world literature: the other segments of the soliloquy vary in length between 920 and 5,941 words. As utterances go, 3,669 words is an impressive length, to be sure, but it is a lot closer to the ordinary than to the infinite – infinitely closer, in fact. The first 150-odd words of the 3,669 segment are reproduced below. Or they *would* be, but for the barking vicissitudes of international copyright law, as a result of which I am unable to republish – at least until 2030, in the US – what is freely available for reproduction throughout the rest of the world (except Spain), and may be read on the Internet (see www.gutenberg.org, amongst other places). In their stead, I offer 145 words of my own bowdlerised version:

No its no right of his has he no courtesy nor no deportment nor one thing in his character grabbing me behind like that by the arse for that I missed calling him Eamonn the eejit that cant tell verse from a turnip thats what comes from their not being kept where they belong leaving off his socks and trousers here on the table before me unabashed

without so much as by your leave and sticking out rude as you like still in that part of a
shirt they put on for the respect like a lawyer or a barber or those old sycophants from
the time of the caesars sure hes not wrong in his way to spend his time messing around
youd be as well off in bed with what with an ox Jesus he might have better conversation
an old ox might ...

Compare James Joyce, Ulysses (1922: chapter 18)

The last 3,669-word segment of Molly Bloom's soliloquy is an utterance, not a sentence, and the only thing that makes the final paragraph of the chapter one of the longest anythings in the Irish literary canon is the absence of overt punctuation: periods, commas, initial capital letters, and the like. It is clear to every human reader – though perhaps not to the parsing algorithms of Google Translate – that the 145-word string above is composed of a large number of easily identifiable 'multi-word phrases', which we might otherwise call sentences (though, strictly speaking, they are the *reflexes* of sentences), such that we can agree that (145a) is an acceptable parse of these words, whereas (145b) is not.

(145)   a.   No, it's no right of his. Has he no courtesy nor no deportment nor one thing in his character? Grabbing me behind like that by the arse for that I missed calling him Eamonn! The eejit, that can't tell verse from a turnip! That's what comes from their not being kept where they belong, leaving off his socks and trousers here on the table before me, unabashed, without so much as 'by your leave', and sticking out, rude as you like, still in that part of a shirt they put on for the respect, like a lawyer or a barber, or those old sycophants from the time of the Caesars. Sure, he's not wrong in his way to spend his time messing around. You'd be as well off in bed ... with what? With an ox! Jesus: he might have better conversation, an old ox might ...

       b.   No its no right of his has. He no courtesy nor no deportment? Nor one thing in his character grabbing me behind. Like that by the arse, for that I missed?! Calling him Eamonn the eejit. That can't tell verse from a turnip, that's what! Comes from their not being kept. Where they belong, leaving off his socks and trousers here on the table, before me unabashed without so much. As by your leave and sticking out rude, as you like still in that. Part of a shirt they put on for, the respect like a lawyer or a barber or those old sycophants. From the time of the Caesars, sure he's not. Wrong in his way to spend his time. Messing around you'd be as well, off in bed with what with an ox, Jesus. He might have better conversation. An old ox might ...

Figure 39 Akashi–Kaikyō suspension bridge, looking east.

With respect to (in)finity, utterances are like suspension bridges: there may be no principled limit on the absolute length of a multi-span bridge, but there *are* physically definable limits on the lengths of each of the spans that constitute the bridge from end to end. Compare Joyce's original passage with the following stream of consciousness:

My in-laws live in a suburb of Kobe evocatively named Asagiri morning mist situated about three kilometres from the Kobe end of the Akashi–Kaikyō suspension bridge which links Kobe to Awaji Island and which the bridge not the island is the longest of its kind in the world with a span of 1,991 metres (6,532 feet) see Figure 39 it shouldn't have been quite that long the construction project was begun in 1988 and by 1995 the two towers were completed standing at a planned distance of 1,990 metres but then came the great Hanshin earthquake which was first mentioned about 240 pages ago and which had its epicentre on Awaji Island as a result of this the earthquake not the island what became the main span was stretched by one metre more than the architects and the construction engineers and the Japanese government had bargained for I should imagine. [150 words].

The immediately preceding passage shows that James Joyce is not the only one to be able to write long utterances (though his are no doubt more effective). The only formal difference between the adapted extract from *Ulysses* and my description of the Akashi bridge project which curiously is not in Akashi prefecture the bridge not the project the name is mysterious unless one knows that *Kaikyō* means marine channel or strait is that I have provided capital letters for proper names. I could go on like this for a long time, but it would soon become really, really, really annoying. Really. Annoying.

The relevant question here is how much longer a single-span suspension bridge could be, given currently available materials, before it collapsed under its own weight and stresses. Twice as long? Four times? I'm not a structural engineer, but it seems obvious that there is a set of possible values, *within a finite range*; in other words, the answer is not 'infinitely longer': cf. Yngve (1960, 1986). There is not one single value (say, 3.67

kilometres) since the answer depends on a complex range of interacting variables: inherent factors include the tensile strength of cables, the height and composition of the towers, the composition of the supporting bedrock, plus any non-linear effects of scale (the world's tallest buildings are subject to inherent and contingent forces that never affect buildings below several hundred metres); contingent factors will include wind strength and direction at the chosen location, marine currents, as well as the budget of the country or municipality financing it. Some projects are physically feasible, but the materials or skills necessary to achieve extra length are unaffordable. Nevertheless, all of these factors can be modelled to provide a range of maximum distances per span. One possible equation, which is based only on inherent variables, is:

$$L = (M/Dg)\cos(A),$$

where L is the length of the span, M is the maximum stress on the cables, D is the cable density, g is acceleration due to gravity, and A is the angle between the cable and the vertical support (the tower).[8] To beat the previous record, you can't simply pour more concrete, weld on an extra few metres of cable, or hope that the next seismic event will stretch things a bit further.

The suggestion here is that the same is true of clauses and sentences ('utterance spans') within utterances. Except in very special, carefully supported contexts, such as legal contracts and tax law, the 'spans' within normal utterances – the stretches between major pauses, conventionally indicated by semicolons, colons or full stops – rarely exceed ten or so words. It is perhaps no coincidence that the *total* MLU (mean length of utterance) of typically developing eight year-old children is around eight words, less for those with developmental disorders; see Rice et al. (2010).

Moreover, where utterances are extended at their ends ($n + 1$), this is invariably achieved by coordination or simple adjunction, or by apposition, none of which call on recursive rules.

With the span~bridge distinction in mind, let's look at Molly Bloom's soliloquy once again. (For copyright reasons, you'll need to consult your own copy, or look on the Internet: I can only present fragments here.) Examination of the whole of this 3,996-word extract reveals very few examples of embedded recursion, or indeed of embedding *of any kind*. Yes. Table 9 provides a breakdown of the final 500 words of the chapter, reproduced below, where MWP (multi-word phrase) replaces 'sentence' as a timing unit. In the table, MWPs are sub-classified into *main clauses*, i.e. root clauses containing a finite verb, *embedded clauses, adjunct clauses* – those containing a non-finite predicate and any associated arguments – and *fragments* (bare phrases: arguments without predicates, predicates without arguments).

After that

              for   yes

     because

pleasure   asked

        sailors

washing

           poor   the

laughing   shawls

                                    Arabs

          fowl   Larby

                          and

                  bulls

turbans   asking

glancing

                                        castanets

                  Algeciras

serene

           queer

yellow

                          girl   a

                  shall

                                    again

        and   I

                              ... I will Yes

This – as you may read elsewhere – is exquisite prose, but it is not infinite, it rolls in short waves, as each dissipates, another arrives – relenting, hardly crashing – until we are soaked in the rhythm of Molly's surrender. Acceptance

Table 9 *Multi-word phrase-structure in the last 500 words of Molly Bloom's soliloquy. See Appendix C (website) for details.*

MWP	Number	Mean length
Main clauses	23	8.65
Embedded clauses (including verbal complements, restrictive relative clauses)	11	
Embedded clauses with depth $n \geq 1$	1	
Adjunct clauses	18	13.66*
Bare phrases	35	5.84
Overall	88	8.5
Percentage of MWPs introduced by 'and'	50%	11.34
Percentage of unembedded MWPs with no finite predicate	61%	–
Extensions by coordination*	29	–
Extensions by adjunction*	9	–
Extensions by tail recursion	0	–

is too weak a word, by far. 'I will Yes' marks the climax. The finite conclusion. And the tide recedes.

The statistics presented in Table 9 might be revised up or down, depending on precisely how the text is parsed, nevertheless, the basic patterns are probably correctly reported. Nor is there any reason to think that the last 500 words are unrepresentative of the soliloquy as a whole.

Assuming this extract is indeed representative, the table offers three significant results.

- First, fewer than a third of the MWPs in the sample (23/88) contain finite predicates; all of the other standalone phrases either contain non-finite verbs, or no predicate at all. This means that less than half of this material could be generated by the base-rules of Standard Theory – or of any successor to that theory that requires well-formed main clauses in adult language to contain a finite predicate; cf. Wexler (1994). Yet few would claim that *Ulysses* is not, or is only one third, grammatical English.

- Second, the average length of the standalone phrases is 8.6 words, a figure that includes (in approximately 50 per cent of the cases) the initial conjunction 'and'; if one subtracts these conjunctions, the mean length of an MWP in the soliloquy is almost identical to the MLU of children's utterances reported in Rice et al. (2010). The implication of this second result is clear: Joyce may have composed a prodigiously long utterance, but each span is no longer, on average, than those produced by a typically developing eight-year-old child.

- The third point to observe is that almost all instances of sentence extension in the Ulysses extract involve the conjunction 'and' (which here *conjoins,* but does not *coordinate*); more pertinently, there are *no* instances of nested recursion being used to extend any span.

Introducing new adjunct clauses with non-coordinative *and* is a stock feature of almost all non-standard Englishes, especially in narratives, as is illustrated by the examples in (146); cf. also Duffield (1993). It is also – probably by no coincidence – a prominent feature of Modern Irish, as discussed in Chung and McCloskey (1987), from which the examples in (146) are taken:

(146) a. 'Wud ye luk at the time, *and him still upstairs!*' (= 102b)

      b. 'Well, some things they said *was* funny, – yes, and mighty witty too, I ain't denying that, – but all the same it warn't fair nor brave, all them people pitching on one, *and they so glib and sharp, and him without any gift of talk to answer back with.*'

                    Mark Twain, *Tom Sawyer Abroad*, chapter 2 (1894)

      c. 'What if he's on his way to heaven, *and him without feet?*'

                    Jess Smith, *Sookin' Berries* (2008 [ebook 2013])

      d. [B]ut it seems they wandered about the country part of the night, *and them lying down in the place which I used to call my bower,* they were weary and overslept themselves.

                    Daniel Defoe, *The Farther Adventures of Robinson Crusoe*, chapter 3 (1719)

(147) a. Tháinig sé isteach [*agus é   iontach sásta leis féin*].
          came he inside   and him very pleased with self
          'He came inside, looking [lit. and him] very pleased with himself.'

      b. Níor   dúirt sé mórán, [*ach é   ag obair leis   go.ciúin*].
          NEG-PAST said he much   but him PROG. work with.3SG quietly
          'He didn't say much, but worked quietly by himself [lit. but him working quietly]'

              Sandra Chung and James McCloskey, 'Government, barriers and small clauses in Modern Irish' (*Linguistic Inquiry*, 1987)

The acceptability of the strings in (146) implies that non-finite clauses are able function as independent clauses, and that they can contain overt lexical subjects unlicensed by tense. The theoretical significance of utterances like these lies in the fact that they seem to break the link between finiteness and 'case assignment' to subject noun-phrases that is a cornerstone of the generative approach; see e.g. Pesetsky and Torrego (2001), also Bobaljik and Wurmbrand (2008). Perhaps the most relevant point here, however, is that you don't need a recursive rule system of the generativist kind to handle extension through conjunction, or through apposition. Indeed, conjunction and apposition have proved quite resistant to any satisfactory treatment in generative grammar, since they appear to violate a basic principle of phrase-structure, namely, endocentricity – the idea that every phrasal constituent should have a unique head. To illustrate, consider the examples in (148): while it's intuitively clear that *Frank* is the 'head' of the subject noun-phrase in (148a), it's much less obvious what the status of the same name is in (148b) or (148c):

(148)   a. <u>Frank</u> gave away his fortune.
        b. The architect, <u>Frank</u> Lloyd Wright, was well-known throughout the world.
        c. So long, <u>Frank</u> Lloyd Wright.
        d. He was a wild one, that <u>Frank</u>!

Similar problems arise with respect to conjunction, as we shall see directly.

This (extended) discussion indicates that even if utterances might be infinitely extendable in principle, this is only generally possible by tacking on extra spans, and – as we have just seen – span length seems to be rather tightly constrained, to around eight words, excluding conjunctions. In short (!), if there is such a thing as discrete infinity, there is no hint of it in the longest utterances of Irish English literature. It should therefore be clear that there is a wide disparity between utterance length and sentence or clause length, where the latter terms correspond much more closely to spans than to bridges. To use a different engineering analogy, there may be no longest wall, but there surely is a longest brick. Hence, the fact that some utterances can be quite long tells us nothing at all about the possible length of sentences, as generated by grammatical rules, or any other procedure involving formal recursion.

This conclusion should give us pause before we accept Chomsky's assertion, repeated again:

And it goes on indefinitely ... You can have a hundred-word sentence, a 10,000-word sentence, and so on.

> Noam Chomsky, *Poverty of Stimulus: Some Unfinished Business*
> (2010); see Chapter 1

Recursion: what is it good for, anyway?

It's not true that life is one damn thing after another; it's one damn thing over and over.

> Edna St Vincent Millay, *The Letters of Edna St. Vincent Millay* (1952)

The tenor of this quotation – as well as her poem on Euclid (see O is for Object of Study above) – implies that St Vincent Millay and Chomsky might well have got(ten) along very well. Which doesn't mean that her philosophy was correct. If it's true, as suggested by the analysis of Molly Bloom's soliloquy, that utterances are most regularly extended *via* (non-coordinative) conjunction or apposition, and that clause length is usually fairly tightly restricted (to fewer than ten words), then it's reasonable to ask what role recursive functions actually play in grammatical descriptions: alternatively, whether other parsing procedures – for example, immediate structural priming (cf. Ferreira and Bock 2006), might not offer a better characterisation of the structural regularities underlying iterated phrasal sequences. Come to that, why did anyone suppose that recursive rules were good for something in the first place?[9]

In this subsection and the next, I will argue that generativist recursive rules are not up to the task of describing natural iteration, especially non-constituent iteration, in a significant class of English utterances. It will also be observed that semantic and prosodic factors (especially considerations of foot structure) often outrank purely structural constraints in determining acceptable word-order.

At the outset, it's useful to distinguish three kinds of iteration found in natural English utterances: these are illustrated in (149)–(151). First, the examples in (149) illustrate what might be termed 'same-level phrasal recursion' (SLR), in which what appear to be constituent phrases of the same syntactic category (PP, NP, AP, etc.) are juxtaposed in linear sequence:

(149)   a. She asked us to [meet her [$_{PP}$ at five o'clock] [$_{PP}$ outside the cinema] [$_{PP}$ after the conference]]. ('PP-iteration')
        b. She bought [$_{NP}$ apples], [$_{NP}$ some grapes], and [$_{NP}$ a pineapple]: [$_{NP}$ all sorts of fruit]. ('NP-iteration')
        c. She promised [that she would come over], [that she would bring the money], [that everything would work out for us better from now on]. ('CP-iteration')

Next, in the examples in (150), we find 1-subjacent or 'nested recursion' (NR), where a recurring constituent phrase-type is apparently embedded inside the complement of its complement.[10] This is the type of recursion that generativists typically focus on, yet it is by far the least frequent source of long sentences in normal text: beyond the confines of syntax textbooks – the 'reptile houses' of natural discourse – multiply embedded clauses are a seriously endangered species.

(150)   a. Mary [$_{VP}$ claimed [$_{CP}$ that John [$_{VP}$ believed [$_{CP}$ that Richard had not [$_{VP}$ arrived yet]]]]] ('VP~CP recursion')
        b. Everything that they do is [$_{NP}$ the ghost [$_{PP}$ of [$_{NP}$ a trace [$_{PP}$ of [$_{NP}$ a pale imitation [$_{PP}$ of you]]]]]] ('NP/PP recursion') (Josh Ritter, *Kathleen*)
        c. Delilah regretted [$_{NP}$ [$_{NP}$ [$_{NP}$ [$_{NP}$ John's] friend's] brother's] hamster's] untimely disappearance]]]]] ('NP/(NP) recursion')[11]

A point to observe in passing is that canonical examples of nested recursion almost always involve identical category iteration: not only do the phrasal categories recur, so do all of their sub-constituents. While this strong parallelism is most striking in nursery rhymes ('The house that Jack built', for example), the constraint can also be found in prose examples, where a simple change of verb-argument structure, agreement properties, or the addition of adjunct modifiers may affect the acceptability of the sentence: cf. Frazier et al. (1984), Knoeferle and Crocker (2009), Callahan, Shapiro and Love (2010).

Finally, in (151) are displayed instances of 'simple loop recursion' (SLR), where an identical word, or partial constituent, is 're-cycled', repeated, replaced, in an adjacent position [just as in this sentence].

(151) a. She [should not], [could not], with her car,
        She [will not], [shall not], to a bar.
        She should not drive them [out of town],
        She should not drive them [in a gown].
        [Not to the zoo!] [Not for some tea],
        [Not to McGrew] [And not for me!]
                        Dr Kleuss, *Bad Rhymes and Spam* (after Dr Seuss,
                                            Green Eggs and Ham)
     b. It was just [[very] [very] [very] [big]], [[so] [big] that it gave the
        impression of infinity far better than infinity itself]
                        Douglas Adams, *The Hitchhiker's Guide to the Galaxy*,
                                            chapter XXIV ([1979] 2009)
     c. One idea is not enough. Without [ten, twenty, thirty] ideas, you will
        never [ever, ever, ever] succeed.
     d. An extraordinary, [incredibly convoluted], yet [weirdly simple],
        though [still intriguing], while [hardly obscure], but [nevertheless
        beguiling] analysis of the human condition.

By no coincidence, the names of first and third types reduce to the same abbreviation: temporarily, I'll distinguish between SLR$_1$ and SLR$_2$, though it should be clear where this argument is going.

From this point forward, barring some speculations on hamster wheels at the end of the section, the focus will be on the proper treatment (of both kinds) of SLR: the 'dark matter' of syntactic theory. Many more able syntacticians than$_{??}$I/$_?$me have devoted years of their lives to the analysis of different types of Nested Recursion, and I have little to add to their scholarship.

A key property that distinguishes same-level recursion (SLR$_1$) from nested recursion (NR) would seem to be orderability: in the former construction, the repeated phrases can usually be reordered with no loss of acceptability, and without altering propositional content. This can be seen by contrasting the clauses and phrases in (149a) and (150a,c) above with the remodelled examples in (152a) and (153a,c), respectively (here '=' means 'propositionally equivalent to'):[12]

(152) a.i   She asked us to [meet her [$_{PP}$ outside the cinema] [$_{PP}$ at five o'clock] [$_{PP}$ after the conference]] (= 149a)

a.ii   She asked us to [meet her [$_{PP}$ after the conference], [$_{PP}$ outside the cinema] [$_{PP}$ at five o'clock]] (= 149a)

(153) a.i   John [$_{VP}$ believed [$_{CP}$ that Mary [$_{VP}$ claimed [$_{CP}$ that Richard had not [$_{VP}$ arrived yet]]]]] – VP~CP recursion (≠ 150a)

a.ii.   *Mary [$_{VP}$ claimed [$_{CP}$ that Richard had not [$_{VP}$ arrived yet [$_{CP}$ that John [$_{VP}$ believed]]]]] – VP~CP recursion (≠ 150a)

c.i.   [$_{NP}$ [$_{NP}$ [$_{NP}$ [$_{NP}$ John's] friend's] hamster's] brother's] untimely disappearance – NP~(DP) recursion (≠ 150c)

c.ii.   *[$_{NP}$ [$_{NP}$ [$_{NP}$ his friend's] John's] brother's] untimely disappearance – NP~(DP) recursion ((≠ 150c)

Many utterances seem to fall between the two kinds, however. These are contexts in which one or more of the repeated phrases is optional, but in spite of the absence of any standard complementation (selectional) constraints, the order of the repeated phrases is sharply delimited. One such example is given in (154a). On the one hand, this example patterns with other cases of SLR$_1$, in that any one of the bracketed strings can be omitted without loss of grammatical acceptability. On the other hand, in common with the nested recursion sentences in (150), re-ordering of any of the repeated strings leads to unacceptability; this is demonstrated by the anomaly of examples (154b) and (154c).

(154) a.   When an event like this takes place, we bear a responsibility to seize [$_{NP}$ the opportunity [$_{XP?}$ to stop], [$_{XP?}$ to reflect on] and [$_{XP}$ to reform] [$_{NP}$ our attitudes [$_{PP}$ towards fellow believers] and [$_{PP}$ towards those whose souls we aim to claim for Jesus]]]

Valerie Hobbs, 'An overview and assessment of the OPC General Assembly in the appeal of John Carrick' (*The Aquila Report*, 24 June 2015)[13]

b.   #*We bear a responsibility to seize the opportunity [$_{XP?}$ to reflect on], [$_{XP?}$ to stop$_?$] and [$_{XP?}$ to reform$_?$] …

c.   #*We bear a responsibility to seize the opportunity [$_{XP}$ to reform$_?$], [$_{XP}$ to reflect on$_?$] and [$_{XP?}$ to stop$_?$] …

The restrictions observed here are partly due to a kind of (extended) 'selection', or better 'anti-selection': since the first XP contains an intransitive verb, it is prevented from intervening between the other two verbs and their shared object complement [$_{N\,P}$ *our attitudes...Jesus*]. (This restriction is suspended, however, in contexts where the object is extracted, as long as the predicates follow a 'natural course of events': see Lakoff 1986.) The anomalies in (154b) and (154c) are also due in part to the rules of CONVERSATIONAL AND CONVENTIONAL IMPLICATURE (Grice [1975] 1989), according to which order of mention is supposed to reflect the order of events referred to: in this particular example, it is good to stop before reflecting, and to reflect before making reforms, rather than another way around.

Let's consider the syntax of (154a) more closely. The analytic problem here concerns what kind of phrasal constituent (supposing it *is* a constituent) is iterated, and where this constituent ends – hence the 'XP?' label, and the question-marks on the right brackets. Intuitively, the repeated string is some kind of verbal phrase, yet it is one that *includes* the non-finite morpheme *to* – which most generative analyses place in T/(AUX), hence outside the syntactic verb-phrase – but which at the same time *excludes* the shared object complement (*... attitudes ... Jesus*). The fact that the two XP strings are substitutable, albeit with some change of meaning, strongly suggests that they are parallel constituents. In spite of this, example (154a) is not easily amenable to any regular hierarchical analysis, either in terms of more traditional PS rules of the Extended Standard Theory (EST), or in terms of a Minimalist analysis.

Within the EST framework, the sentence is (barely) consistent with the base-rules in (155), provided that *to* is taken to be some kind of verbal affix [*Af*-V], and that *reflect on* is treated as a complex verb [V-Prt], rather than a verb+preposition string:

(155)   S   →   NP (AUX) VP
        VP   →   V* (NP) (ConjP)
        NP   →   D N S*/VP*
        ConjP   →   XP Conj XP

Observe that these rules call on the so-called Kleene star symbol (*), an asterisk immediately *following* a designated phrasal category which signifies that the tagged element may be re-written more than once. It is possible to use this symbol to generate the other SLR cases in (149): thus, examples (149a–c) are describable using the VP-expansion rules in (156a–c), respectively.

(156)   a. VP   →   V NP (PP)*
        b. VP   →   V (NP)*
        c. VP   →   V CP*

But 'possible' does not necessarily mean desirable. A well-known problem is that rules involving Kleene stars massively over-generate, producing many more unacceptable utterances than acceptable ones; these include the unacceptable cases in (157b) and (157d) and those in (158):

(157)   a. The girl went to London, to the musical.
        b. *The girl went (to the musical), (to London).
        c. She bought two apples, some grapes and a pineapple.
        d. ??She bought two apples, some grapes.
(158)   a. *When$_i$ did she ask us to meet her at five o'clock t$_i$? [= after the conference?] (cf. 149a)
        b. *What$_i$ did she buy t$_i$, some grapes, and a pineapple? (cf. 149b)
        c. *What$_i$ did she promise that she would bring the money, t$_i$? (cf. 149c)

The unacceptability of the examples in (158) is a particular problem. If the declarative sentences in (157a,c) are acceptable, there should be no reason, on a movement analysis of *wh*-questions, why one could not question one of the two temporal adjuncts in (158a), or one of a set of possible objects (158b,c). Yet both sentences are strongly unacceptable, there being no perceivable gap for the *wh*-item to fill. Compare also Part II, Case #6 above.

Kleene star rules also prove inadequate in explaining the contrasts in (159). In undergraduate introductions to syntax the unacceptability of a sentence like (159a) is accounted for by saying that *put* requires (subcategorises) a prepositional phrase: the PS rule in (156a) does allow for this, yet the acceptability of example (159b) shows that (semantic) selection can be satisfied by a Theme object plus *any* type of phrase specifying location – not only a prepositional phrase, but a particle like *down*, or an adverbial element like *there* (or both, though only in one particular order). Thus, the rule in (156a) both over-generates and under-generates: it is plainly not up to the job of describing acceptable constituency.

(159)   a. *Can you put it?
        b. Can you put it (down, there?/down there/*there down)
        c. He gave every employee their paycheck.
        d. *He gave every paycheck$_i$ his employees$_i$.

Similarly, the phrase-structure rule in (156b) incorrectly predicts the equal acceptability of (159c) and (159d), yet – as has been conclusively demonstrated: see, for example, Larson (1988) – 'double-object constructions' of the kind illustrated here are asymmetrical, the first ('Goal') NP necessarily having scope over the ('Theme') phrase that follows it.

For these reasons – like the *Zauberlehrling*'s magic spell, mentioned in Chapter 26 below – Kleene stars turn out to be much more trouble than they're worth, as a solution to same-level recursion.

The shortcomings of PS rules (with or without Kleene stars) have been known for decades. However, the situation is only a little better when we try to apply later versions of generative theory to the analysis at hand. The issue is simple: on a GB/Minimalist approach, there seems to be no grammatically licit structural derivation available for (154a), unless one abandons the binary-branching assumption that is an essential part of the Minimalist structure-building algorithm *Merge*. Given that (binary) *Merge* is posited precisely to capture the putative 'fact of discrete infinity', this is scarcely a principle that generativists would be willing to give up. Indeed, for some syntacticians, it is all that they have left.

The phrase-marker in (160) represents the best possible (good faith) attempt to analyse the sentence in (154a) in a manner consistent with standard Minimalist assumptions. In the interests of readers' sanity – also because it is a doomed solution in any case – only the rightward section of the utterance is analysed:[14]

(160)

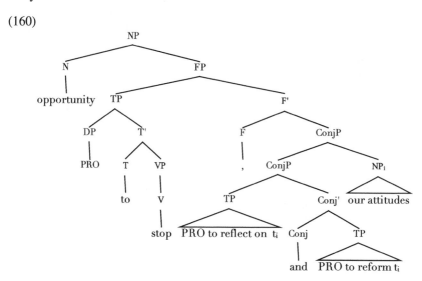

Quite apart from the fact that there is little empirical justification either for 'FP' – unless commas should now be accorded syntactic status – or for treating the co-coordinative conjunction 'and' as a syntactic head (though see Kayne 1994, and subsequent work), the analysis schematised in (160) faces other more serious empirical problems. Chief among these is that the first of the three conjuncts can also be replaced by a transitive predicate taking the string-final NP as an object: cf. (161a) (indeed, any number of transitive predicates may be iterated in first position). Alternatively, the final conjunct may be intransitive, as in (161b). Only (161c) is obviously unacceptable.

(161)   a. the opportunity to identify [], to reflect on [] and to reform [our
            attitudes].
        b. the opportunity to reflect on []?(and) to reform [our attitudes],
            and then to start over.
        c. *the opportunity to reflect on []?to start over, and to reform [our
            attitudes].

Second, given the standard 'Right Node Raising (RNR)' analysis of the object-sharing involved in these structures – see Ross (1967), Hankamer (1971), Postal (1974), also Sabbagh (2007) – the derivation in (160) cannot be the correct analysis, since RNR of objects requires both conjuncts to be VPs at the same syntactic level, whereas the phrase-marker in (161) involves asymmetrical TP conjuncts.

It's also worth pointing out that disjoint reference effects (Condition C effects) are observed even though no *c-command* relationship obtains between any of the object positions in this structure: the contrasting examples in (162) clearly illustrate the bar on object co-reference. See Appendix A (website). If co-reference restrictions are to be read off syntactic structures, then the tree in (160) cannot be the right analysis of these strings. But nor can any other structure employing binary *Merge*. This point may be moot, given that we have already observed the limitations of a structural account of co-reference relations; see Case #4 and T is for Sentence above. Still, if structures generated by binary *Merge* cannot explain movement and binding possibilities in the case of same-level recursion (SLR$_1$), it's reasonable to ask what the operation is good for.[15]

(162)   a. *the opportunity to identify <u>them</u>$_i$, to reflect on [] and to reform
            [<u>our attitudes</u>$_i$]
        b. *the opportunity to reflect on <u>them</u>$_i$ (and) to reform [<u>our attitudes</u>$_i$]
            and then to try again.
        c. the opportunity to reflect on our attitudes (and) to reform [them]
            and then to try again.

Generative rules fare no better when it comes to handling the cases of simple loop recursion (SLR$_2$) in (151), in which a single lexical category or partial constituent is iterated, often for rhetorical effect. Take the *Dr Seuss* parody in (151a), for example. According to most standard generative treatments *should not, could not, will not*, etc. (in the first two lines) must be non-constituents: this is because finite modals are generally assumed to occupy T, whereas negation is either assigned to its own functional projection or else is analysed as a VP adjunct. The grammatically licit options are schematised in (163a) and (163b), respectively; in neither case does the modal form a constituent with *not*:

(163) (a)

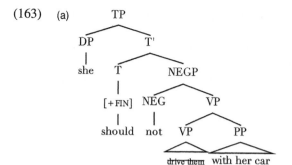

(b)

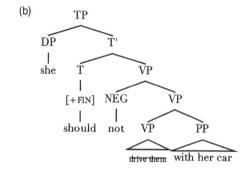

Consequently, the only viable analysis using *Merge* that allows for the modal+*not* string to be repeated is one that involves iterated VP-ellipsis: something like (164). Although it is technically possible to treat the 'Dr Kleuss' examples in hierarchical terms – by first generating and then deleting a full VP constituent in each case – the only real justification for such an analysis is a blind commitment to syntactic constituency rules.

(164)

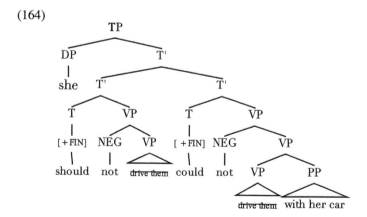

A final problem with this kind of analysis is that *not* is understood in directly modifying the PPs (*with her car, to a bar*, etc.), rather than the elided verb-phrase, and this interpretation is incompatible with the VPE analysis in (164). What is more, the repeated strings in the last two lines of the verse are grammatically unacceptable in full clauses, as is shown by the unacceptability of the examples in (165). Yet it is fairly clear that they are well-formed phrases in this context.

(165)   a.   *(She should drive them) not to the zoo.
        b.   *(She should drive them), and not with me!

With enough ingenuity (or violence) it is always possible to fit a square peg in a round hole, but the result is rarely pretty, and never honest.

Intuitively, the correct recursive analysis of *should not, could not* is much, much (!) simpler, namely, the string is repeated under 'partial category reduplication': in linear terms, we would say that the parse is looped, in phrase-structural terms, the same sequence of categories is recycled. These alternatives are schematised in (166):

(166)

SLR: She $\left|\;\left\|\begin{matrix}should\ not\\ could\ not\end{matrix}\right\|\right.$ with her car

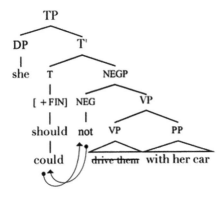

A similar lack of 'plausible constituency' applies to single-word iteration, illustrated in examples (151b) and (151c) above. In these particular cases, the issue is one of generalisability: this kind of repetition is so lexically restricted that it makes no sense to construct a general rule to describe it. In the case of example (151b), for instance, what works for high-frequency emphatic, bi-syllabic, trochaic adverbs like *very, really* and *truly* does not even extend to other degree modifiers – at least if my judgments, as indicated in (167), are typical – much less to VP-adverbials in general, as shown by the examples in (168).

(167) a. She is really, really sorry/*very really sorry/*really, very, sorry.[16]
       b. ??The store is [[extremely], [unusually], busy] for the time of year.
           cf. The store is extremely busy for the time of year/ The store
           is unusually busy for the time of year.
(168) a. ??She was quietly, quickly, carefully writing the letter.
           cf. She was quietly writing the letter, quickly and carefully.
       b. ??She rarely, quickly, wrote letters.[17]
           cf. She rarely wrote letters quickly/?She quickly wrote letters,
           rarely.

Similarly, numeral quantifiers such as those in (151c) can only be repeated if
they form a formulaic (rising) sequence, as evidenced by the strangeness of the
phrases in (169):

(169) a. ??She had three or two things she wanted to discuss with me.
       b. ??She has many, thirty, twenty ideas about the new project.
       c. *She cannot find more than one, a, the, (single) solution to this
           problem.

A dungeon deep: non-syntactic factors affecting word-order

Even the more productive cases of single-word iteration – those that Kleene
star notation was originally invoked to describe – are subject to strict ordering
constraints, usually based on semantics. Take attributive Adjective Ordering
Restrictions (AOR). A long tradition of work, dating back to Bloomfield (1933),
has shown that attributive adjectives are sequenced relative to the head noun
according to the semantic hierarchy given in (170), from Laenzlinger (2005);
see also Crisma (1990), Sproat and Shih (1991) and especially Teodorescu
(2006). The effect of this hierarchy is to render all of the alternative adjective
orders in (170b–d) anomalous at best:

(170) [quantif. ordinal > cardinal] > [speak-orient subjective comment >
       evidential] > [scalar physical property size > length > height > speed
       > depth > width] > [measure weight > temperature > wetness > age]
       > [non-scalar physical property shape > colour > nationality/origin
       > material]
       a. her two, large, round, black, Chinese boxes
       b. #her Chinese, two, black, round, large boxes
       c. #her black, Chinese, large, round boxes
       d. #her round, black, Chinese, large boxes

As shown by the examples in (171), from Sproat and Shih (1991), the same
restrictions are observed in other languages (though they systematically fail to

apply where attributive adjectives are expressed as reduced relative clauses, rather than as bare modifiers). Most interesting, perhaps, is the Arabic example in (172), where it has been claimed that the canonical order is a mirror-image of that found in Romance and Germanic (see Fassi Fehri 1999), cf. Duffield (1996)); if this claim is substantiated, the contrast would show that the constraint is not one of simple linear precedence *per se*, but of relative proximity to the head noun.

(171)   a. i   suoi due altri bei   grandi quadri$_i$ tondi grigi t_i
            the his two other nice big   pictures round grey
            'his two other nice big round grey pictures'
        b. mes trois beaux   grands fauteuils$_i$ rouges t_i
            my three beautiful big   armchairs red
            'my three beautiful big red chairs'
        c. ihre drei   außergewöhnliche dreieckige rote französische
            Bücher
            her three extraordinary   triangular red french   books
            'her three extraordinary triangular red French books'
(172)   l-kitaab-u   l-ʔaxḍar-u   ṣ-ṣaġiir-u
            the-book-NOM the-green-NOM the-little-NOM
            'the little green book'

The main theoretical consequence of this cross-linguistic 'semantic hierarchy' is that iterated attributive adjectives cannot be adequately described by the recursive syntactic rules in (173): the phrase-structure rule in (173a), for example, does not even approach what Chomsky used to call 'observational adequacy', with respect to pre-nominal adjective placement:

(173)   a. NP   →   (Det) (AP*) N [PP*/CP]
        b. AP   →   (ADVP*) A (NP)
        c. PP   →   P NP

PS rules aside, the more serious problem for derivational accounts of modification based on external *Merge* is that Adjective Ordering Restrictions are not capturable in terms of semantic or categorial selection. This is because attributive adjectives bear a dependency relation to the head noun, but no selectional relationship to each other. Given this, the only way to describe these precedence relations syntactically would seem to be in representational terms, by means of a set of templates – a syntactic cartography – since blind derivational rules allow no 'look-ahead' or extrinsic ordering.

Even where semantics does not determine the position of attributive adjectives, prosody and euphony can play a more significant role than syntactic placement rules. In typical sentences, simple attributive adjectives must appear pre-nominally in English, but in songs – and poetry especially – post-nominal adjectives are preferred where they contribute to iambic foot structure. A nice example of this is found in the first verse of Gordon Lightfoot's classic song *If You Could Read My Mind.* (For rights reasons, it is not possible to reproduce the verse verbatim: thus, except for the relevant items, all other words are replaced by xxxx's, with strong syllables indicated in bold):

> *If you could read my mind [xxxx],*
> *Xxxx x xxxx xx xxxxxx xxxxx tell.*
> *Xxxx xxxx xx xxx xxxx mo[vie],*
> *Xxxx x xxxxx xxxx x xxxxxxx well.*
> *Xx x castle dark xx x fortress strong*
> *Xxx chains xxxx xx feet.*
> *Xxx xxxx xxxx xxxxx xx xx*
> *xxx X xxxx xxxxx xx xxx xxxx*
> *Xx xxxx xx X'xx x xxxx xxxx xxx xxx xxx.*

♫ Gordon Lightfoot, *If You Could Read My Mind* (1970)

In each verse, only the second and fourth lines have an end-rhyme (A~B~C~B~D~E~F~G~H), so there is no segmental reason why normal adjective order could not be followed in the fifth line; that is to say, the line might just as well have ended with the last rime of <fortress> [ɛs], as with the [ɔŋ] of . The conditioning factor here is IAMBIC foot structure, which explains why (174a) is unacceptable in the context, whereas (174b) offers a satisfactory alternative (keeping in mind that both *love* and *-vie* in *movie* are extra-metrical, in lines 1 and 3, and so downstressed):

(174) a. ??In a **dark cast**le or a **strong pri**son
          With shackles **on** my **wrists**.
       b. On a **barr**en **hill** or a **desert plain**
          With shackles **on** my **wrists**.

It is worth pointing out that the same iambicity constraint accounts directly for almost all of the non-canonical *not*+finite-verb orders found in Shakespeare's plays that van Gelderen (2000) analyses in terms of abstract feature-raising: see I is for Internalism (iii) above. For convenience, the examples are repeated here as (175):

(175) a. CAESAR: when to sound your name
          It **not** *concernèd* **me.** (*Antony and Cleopatra*, 2.2.35)
       b. LEONATO: that **they** thems**elves** not **feele** (*Much Ado About Nothing*, 5.1.22)
       c. HUBERT: whose tongue … not **tru**ly **speakes** (*King John*, 4.3.96)

Here, as in almost every example cited in van Gelderen's article, post-verbal placement of *not* (and/or dummy *do*-insertion) would derail the final iambs.

The issues raised by the last few examples are well encapsulated in the following excerpt from Truman Capote's novella *Breakfast at Tiffany's*. In fact, almost any sufficiently well-written piece of prose would serve as well: it is only in the clichés of syntax textbooks that same-level recursion is unproblematic, for going unmentioned. Capote's paragraph is obviously acceptable to generations of English native speakers, yet its eight lines are packed with same-level recursions, including two clear 'grammatical violations' – strings that should not be iterable, given standard generative assumptions.

He was a middle-aged child that had never shed its baby fat, though some gifted tailor had almost succeeded in camouflaging his plump and spankable bottom. His face, [$_{NP}$ a zero filled with [$_{A1}$ pretty] [$_{A2}$ miniature] features], had [$_{XP}$ an unused], [$_{XP}$ a virginal] quality ...

... The man's name was Rutherfurd ('Rusty') Trawler. In 1908, he lost both his parents, [$_{YP1}$ his father the victim of an anarchist], and [$_{YP2}$ his mother of shock], which double misfortune had made Rusty [$_{NP1}$ an orphan]$_i$, [$_{NP2}$ a millionaire]$_j$, and [$_{NP3}$ a celebrity]$_k$ [all$_{i,j,k}$ at the age of five].

Truman Capote, *Breakfast at Tiffany's* (1958)

There is an article's worth of discussion in this excerpt, including a proper description of anaphoric quantifier *all* in the last line, none of whose antecedents is a true referring expression. The most immediately relevant challenge, however, is presented by the two iterated strings 'XP' and 'YP', extracted in (176):

(176) a. [$_{XP1}$ an unused], [$_{XP2}$ a virginal], quality

      b. [$_{YP1}$ his father the victim of an anarchist], and [$_{YP2}$ his mother of shock]

In (176a), it is obvious that the two sub-constituents of XP are a determiner and an adjective; also, that these Determiner-Adjective iterations modify the final noun *quality*. This creates a tension: on the one hand, the principle of endocentricity dictates that XP must either be a DP or an AP, not an NP; it can't be the noun that it modifies at a distance. Yet English (in contrast to German, for example) doesn't allow this kind of nominal ellipsis – that's what we have the pro-form *one* for ('an unused *(one)'). Hence, the phrase must be strictly ungrammatical. The iterated sequence is perfectly acceptable, however. Its discourse function is also clear. The main reason that the determiner is repeated is that Capote is 'having a second go' at defining the precise quality of

Rusty's face: it is not that it was unused *and* virginal, which a simple list would have implied, but rather that whatever quality it had was something partially suggested by both of these attributes, neither being quite right. This semantic hesitancy is combined with a morpho-phonological constraint: *unused* begins with a vowel, so requires *an*, *virginal* does not, so *a* is the required form of the article. Given this clash, no stylistic choice is available other than to use both: *an*, then *a*.

A different problem arises with respect to the phrase labelled YP, in (176b). Here, the repeated phrase – whatever its proper analysis – is naturally understood as an elided version of its antecedent (177a): that is to say, what is reconstructed is (177b):

(177)   a. [$_{YP1}$ his father [the victim of an anarchist]], and
        b. [$_{YP2}$ his mother [the victim] of shock]

In this context, the noun *victim* is the only possible predicate with which the modifier *of shock* can be associated; **He lost his mother of shock* is not grammatically acceptable. Yet under a generative analysis, it should be impossible to delete or move a head noun plus determiner (*the victim*) without also deleting or moving its syntactic complement (*of shock*), as in (177). This is a point pressed home repeatedly in every elementary introduction to constituency-based syntax; see, for example, Carnie (2011). (Note that measure phrases are an exception in this regard; cf. (178b).)

(178)   a. *I want the box *of chocolates* and you the box *of ice cream.*
        b. ?*How many kilos* did you buy *of potatoes?*
        c. *A lot* was what we got into *of trouble.*

The conclusion of the last few pages would to be that hierarchical phrase-structure rules (with or without the addition of Kleene star notation) are ill-suited – to use a charitable adjective – to describing either kind of SLR, which may now be spelled out as 'simple linear recursion'. This is unfortunate, since SLR is the most productive way of extending sentences in natural languages, by a long shot. Indeed, for many speakers and writers, it is the *only* way to 'keep on going', most of the time. Given this inadequacy, it follows that even if recursive rules are employed to handle nested recursion (NR), one would still need a separate syntactic sub-theory to deal with SLR: that theory would need to incorporate semantic, phonological, prosodic and pragmatic–contextual information. The thing is, as was the case with endophoric reference (Binding Theory: see Part II, Case 4), it is not unreasonable to think that an adequate theory of SLR will subsume nested recursion as well.

Afterthought: Snowflake's journeys ($2\pi rn + 10$ cm)

To those people who have hacked through the preceding arguments in this section, and are still reading, my thanks. The worst is over. Nearly. Before heading towards the light(er) (entertainment) of Part IV, I want to consider one final question concerning recursivity, namely, whether 'discrete infinity' might not really be infinite after all: just very, very, very big ...

In lieu of which, some final thoughts on nested recursion. In fact, the thoughts concern our family hamster – now *ex*-hamster – Snowflake: there's a lesson in most everything, once you think about it closely.

> **$2\pi rn + 10$ cm.** 'Sitting opposite me, as I write this piece, is my son's hamster. Since she arrived from the pet shop three years ago, Snowflake has rarely been taken out of her cage, and has never been allowed to stray beyond the confines of the living room. Even these short excursions were cancelled after we got a dog. So, in terms of movement along a two-dimensional plane, Snowflake has never travelled more than a few metres away from her nest. Yet thanks to her wheel, she runs great distances every night: for up to 90 minutes, from around 1:30 in the morning, Snowflake races furiously, as fanatically as any human gym rat, in search of only she knows what. Calculating exactly how far she travels is not difficult, in principle: the distance must be equal to the inner circumference of the wheel ($2\pi r$) times the number of circuits (n), plus 10 cm – the distance from her nest to the wheel and back. I have not done the actual calculation since there are easier things to do in the wee hours than count the rotations of a hamster wheel. In any case, in a nice demonstration of the Observer Effect, Snowflake doesn't run if she sees someone watching her. However, assistance is at hand: Wikipedia helpfully informs me that 'it is not uncommon to record distances of 9 km (5.6 mi) being run in one night'. Arbitrarily assuming that Snowflake only covers half that distance each night – she's a dwarf hamster with a small wheel – this still amounts to over 30 kilometres per week, a considerable distance for a creature who spends 99 per cent of her life behind bars.

Which, naturally enough led me to thinking about apparently unbounded movement. What if multiple-embedding (nested recursion) does not involve hierarchical structure at all, but is simply a case of 'running the wheel', 'looping the loop'? What if nested recursion is as linear as the other cases of SLR? If it is possible to iterate non-constituents through simple linear recursion, it is not wholly ridiculous to suppose to think that what look like hierarchical constituents could be treated in the same way. At a first approximation, for

$$\left\|\begin{array}{l}1.\ \textit{Mary claimed that}\\2.\ \textit{John believed that}\end{array}\right\|\ \text{Richard had not arrived yet.}$$

$$\text{Everything that they do is}\ \left\|\begin{array}{l}1.\ \textit{the ghost of}\\2.\ \textit{a trace of}\\3.\ \textit{a pale imitation of}\end{array}\right\|\ \text{you.}$$

$$\text{Delilah regretted John's}\ \left\|\begin{array}{l}1.\ \textit{friend's}\\2.\ \textit{brother's}\\3.\ \textit{hamster's}\end{array}\right\|\ \text{untimely disappearance.}$$

Figure 40 A linear alternative to nested recursion.

example, the nested recursion examples in (150) above might be analysed as in Figure 40; 'long-distance' questions could be handled in a similar fashion.

Mathematical linguists – and especially computationalists – have been here before. What is proposed here is not significantly different from the kinds of AUGMENTED TRANSITION NETWORK discussed in Winograd (1983), except that many of those models assume that hierarchical information is also encoded. The trick must then be to derive what look like hierarchical effects by means of linear annotations: supposing that could be achieved, we could unify SLR and NR.

Which, if successful, wouldn't leave a lot for *Merge* to do. Needless to say, this prospect is more attractive to some than to others. To those of us with a horror of the infinite, though, it is no small comfort.

'Cependant, qui sait? La terre a des limites, mais la bêtise humaine est infinie!'

But, who knows? The earth has limits, but human stupidity is infinite!

Gustave Flaubert, in Guy de Maupassant, *Des Vers* (1880)

Notes

1 Whether v is really for von Humboldt is debatable in an English context. See the References. We don't usually say that v is for van Beethoven or von Goethe. But it suits my purposes here.

2 Advance warning: to illustrate the point, almost every 'sentence' in this section is longer than it really needs to be, this one included.

3 It is telling that the full title is *On the diversity [Verschiedenheit] of Human Language Construction and its Influence on the Mental Development of the Human Species*. Nothing in this title suggests a deep concern for universal principles; quite the opposite, in fact.

4 A favoured rhetorical ploy in Chomsky's more general writings is to ascribe thorny meta-theoretical problems to other intellectual figures: besides *von Humboldt's*

problem, Chomsky advances *Plato's problem*, *Orwell's problem* (Chomsky 1985), and latterly *Darwin's problem*. A cynic might question the motives behind such attributions, whose principal effect is to lend greater historical authority and legitimacy to the associated claims.

5   The best answer supplied for Question 3 was 'around 500,000'. (If Answers.com is to be believed, the correct answer is 365,900 (= 1,829,500 ÷ 5.) Give or take. The median estimate in my survey was exactly double this figure. The figures in the first two columns are in parentheses because they are spurious: since this was a forced-choice, multiple-choice task involving ordinal data, it is illegitimate to calculate mean scores or standard deviations in this way. No-one, for example, could have chosen 15,500 or 23,000; hence, the probability of choosing the right answer by chance is 0.25, so the means/SDs are meaningless. All that one can do is to compare the patterns of responses for Questions 2 and 3.

6   The argument usually also involves what is misleadingly termed LINGUISTIC CREATIVITY: speakers are able to understand and produce novel combinations of words: '"Hold the newsreader's nose squarely, waiter, or friendly milk will countermand my trousers." Perfectly ordinary words, but never before put in that precise order.' See C is for Competence~Performance above. There is a world of difference, however, between 'frillions' of sentences, and an infinite set: in the limit, a *de facto* finite grammatical system is learnable from the input whereas an infinite grammar is not.

7   For a while, in the mid-1980s, Chomsky had a use for some kinds of sentence fragments: he called these Complete Functional Complex(es) (CFC). But CFCs had to include a predicate and its arguments; sentence fragment is a much broader notion.

8   See www.brantacan.co.uk/longspan1.htm for a more detailed explication.

9   **Warning**. The following sub-section involves discussion of formal rules and contains graphic images of a technical nature. Readers of a sensitive disposition, especially those who are allergic to pseudo-mathematical formalisms, may prefer to omit this section entirely. Look away now. The same advice applies to true formalists – mathematicians and logicians, for example – though for different reasons.

10 Note the adverbial hedge *apparently*: it is not obvious that semantic complementation necessarily requires a hierarchical syntactic analysis.

11 It may appear from the bracketing as if (150c) is a case of direct, rather than 1-subjacent, recursion: it seems to be an NP embedding an NP modifier. However, under an interpretation of the 'DP-hypothesis' following Abney (1987), in which possessor-phrases are DPs, originating in the Specifier position of the containing NP, multiple possessor-phrases involve DP~NP alternations and are thus assimilable to the other examples in (150).

12 This would seem to be related to the fact that SLR phrases are typically adjuncts, whereas NR phrases normally involve selected arguments. The correlation only works one-way, however: though it is true that that selected complements cannot be re-ordered without change of meaning, as shown by examples (153a), this is also true of many adjunct phrases, e.g. (153c) (assuming '[to stop], [to reflect] and [to reform] ...' are unselected adjuncts of *opportunity*).

13 Source: http://theaquilareport.com/an-overview-and-assessment-of-the-opc-general-assembly-in-the-appeal-of-john-carrick.

14 Other analyses are of course possible. In particular, one could argue that the constituents marked TP are larger than this (CPs embedding TPs) or – very much more probably – smaller (VP-like constituents).

15 To compound the difficulty, notice that even the lexical (selectional) rules of English fail to capture the fact that the non-finite relative clause following *opportunity* is obligatory in this case: nouns such as *right* and *opportunity* pragmatically require a 'complement' even though nouns in general are supposed to only optionally select complements.

    a. She had always wanted to go to Spain. Last month, she was given that opportunity.

    b. A: #You will never have the opportunity.

       B: Huh? What opportunity? To do what??

    c. You have no right #(to say that)!

16 *Really very sorry* is fine if *really* is taken to modify [very sorry]; but it can't be used intersectively to modify *sorry* directly (it can't mean she is both *very sorry* and *really sorry*).

17 *Rarely quickly* in (168b) is acceptable if the first adverbial modifies the second: = 'it was rare that she wrote letters quickly'. However, the intersective reading, where both adverbials independently modify the head noun, is blocked when both appear pre-nominally.

The Angel of the Holy Grail saw Galahad come riding,
So he took the Holy Grail off the shelf.
And inside the Holy Chapel made for Holy Grail hiding,
The Angel could be seen to smile to himself.

'If you're the Great Sir Galahad from now on,' said the Angel,
May all angels call me blessed of my race.
If you're not the Great Sir Galahad I warn you, keep on riding,
And if you are I pray you'll let me see your face ...'

♫ Josh Ritter, *Galahad* (2011)

Any serious scientist would have stopped at the previous letter. But there you are: either I'm not that serious, or I'm not a scientist. Possibly both. Or maybe serious science has been misconstrued. So here is (the) Omega, the twenty-fourth, and final letter of the Greek alphabet.

Whatever may be its contribution to the 'initial state of the language faculty', the secret of successful (end-state) language acquisition is not UG, I believe. It is:

Selflessness, love and comprehensible input

I could leave it there, but it would seem more mystical or psychoanalytical than is intended. So here are some pointers:

• Sometime between 1999 and 2001, when I worked as a guest researcher at the Max Planck Institute for Psycholinguistics in Nijmegen, I met my friend Clive Perdue, a great human being and an equally estimable linguist. Before his untimely death – death is rarely timely, but his came far too soon – he had taught and inspired several generations of linguists, both in Nijmegen and in his near-native Paris, where he was a CNRS professor. I may have learned more about alternative approaches to second language acquisition from a few short conversations with Clive and from his friend and colleague Wolfgang Klein – another *doctor mirabilis* of the MPI – than from any other source. (To my mind, Klein and Perdue (1997) is one of the most significant papers on language acquisition written in the last thirty years.) What left the greatest impression on me, however, was an offhand remark Clive made early in 2001. I was wondering aloud why it was that so few second language learners were able to 'pass for native' in spite of years of exposure and not a little effort and expense.

– Why do you suppose they'd *want* to?' he asked me.

- *And it stoned me.* I genuinely could not imagine not wanting to learn a language so well that native speakers of that language might consider me one of them, if only for five minutes of free conversation. I have loved other language varieties from the instant of first exposure: from the first time in the darkened 'audiovisual room' of my preparatory school, when my French, teacher turned on the projector, and started the tape containing Part 1 of *Bonjour Line* (Gauvenet et al. 1963).[1] In my memory (*aux yeux du souvenir*), every episode began with the same greeting:

« *Bonjour Line* »

« *Bonjour Monsieur (le professeur)* »

- From that instant in 1970, I was hooked, and have remained so ever since, losing myself in other people's languages as other people lose themselves in food or fashion, music, sport, or (I dare say) coding or higher mathematics.

- Success in anything worthwhile is a natural outcome of passion for that thing, a love of process, not an end in itself. If your only motivation to study a foreign language is to pass an exam, to gain a qualification, to get a job, the chances of passing for native are slim. Why would you *want* to? And it's quite impossible to succeed at anything you fear, or hold in contempt. Yet until Clive's comment, it really hadn't occurred to me – despite the overwhelming evidence of the attitudes amongst my own students – that most second language learners just don't love languages as I do.

- Love of language, however important, is not sufficient. To master a language, you have to love its speakers, either individually or as a community. The insufficiency of pure love of language for its own sake is starkly illustrated by the case of Christopher, an autistic savant studied in the 1980s by a team of researchers from University College, London. (Those researchers included Neil Smith, Ianthe Tsimpli, Jamal Ouhalla – and Gary Morgan, who features in the BBC documentary 'Why Do We Talk?' that was mentioned in the Introduction). Christopher has a phenomenal ability to learn new vocabulary items across a wide range of languages, including Berber, Bengali, Czech, Gujarati, Nahuatl and Serbian: he is able to identify the source of words presented to him, and can correctly form short root sentences in a number of (mostly SVO) languages. As remarkable as this is, however, Christopher's talent yields a very restricted kind of linguistic knowledge. It is unlikely that he could articulate – or even become aware of – the difference in meaning between English *water* and Japanese *o-mizu* (Part II, Case #2), or that he knows that an aspect marker may appear in the complement clause of Vietnamese with a non-co-referential subject but not with a co-referential subject (see G is for Grammar above), or that he understands the differences in psychological perspective between the Japanese verbs あげる (*ageru*) and くれる (*kureru*), both of which translate as 'give' in English. Christopher is not a 'natural linguist' any more than Raymond (in the Barry Levinson movie Rain Man) is a 'natural mathematician'. And because he is unable to engage in normal conversation, to empathise with those in his community, to engage in normal social relationships, Christopher's language (in any language) remains highly circumscribed – however much joy he seems to experience in acquiring exotic new labels for concepts. This is vocabulary acquisition as stamp-collecting.

- Of course, as has been rehearsed *ad nauseam*, the standard generativist claim is that all typically developing children come to know their language perfectly. Although I've argued above that there is much more significant variability in end-state competence than is generally acknowledged, it's certainly the case that most children acquire the language(s) of their speech communities effortlessly, that they attain a grammatical steady state by around six years of age, and that they behave linguistically pretty much like adults before they reach puberty. Yet young children do not show any obvious passion for language itself. Indeed, it has been claimed by Edwards and Kirkpatrick (1999) that children's metalinguistic skills only emerge at around seven to eight years. This is highly disputable: Gombert (1992) puts it earlier, around five to six years, and most generative researchers would put it earlier still (see, for example, Hiramatsu and Lillo-Martin 1998). My own experience of bilingual infants suggests some degree of meta-linguistic awareness from the very beginning of language development. At all events, love of language *per se,* in the sense intended here, seems not to be essential the first time around.

- What most young children have in its place, however, is an instinctive love of others: as children, we all want to make friends, to fit in, to belong. No matter how common mean-spiritedness may be amongst adults, the *infant* misanthrope is a very rare bird. And to communicate with those we love, and want to love us, we have to find the right words. Love me, love my language. *Reach out … and touch faith.*

♫ David Bowie, *There is a Happy Land* (1967)

- You don't need to be a genius, or a Buddhist monk, to recognise that a deep love of language and love of others entail the same natural property: selflessness. Selfish love is not love. It is perhaps not coincidental that the putative 'critical period' for language acquisition has been claimed to end – see Abrahamsson (2012), though cf. Schmid (2016) – just as we begin to 'find our selves' as adolescents and young adults, and that up to that point, accommodating to a new social, cultural or linguistic environment is relatively straightforward. For an English four-year-old, moving to Japan and learning Japanese is no big deal; she has invested very little of herself in English *langue*. For a child moving at age ten, relocation proves that much harder, while for someone in their seventies, it is almost inconceivably difficult. With normally socialised children, language is the key element in establishing, developing and maintaining personal and social identity. And unless you are a strict internalist,[2] the personal and the social are theoretically and practically inextricable. This is not to deny that some core aspects of language acquisition may be biologically determined independently of social interaction: the localisation of speech perception in the first year of life (Werker and Tees 1984) is an obvious example. See also Spelke and Kinzler (2007), as well as the pioneering work of Renée Baillargeon, for evidence of innate cognition more generally (Baillargeon 1987, 2002, Baillargeon, Scott and Bian 2016). Nevertheless, there does seem to be an interesting relationship *in adolescence* between the establishment of social identity and facility with non-native language acquisition, as Rampton (1995, 1999) discusses; see also Kerswill (1996). Empathy also appears to be crucial: see Gardner (2010: 114), also Brown (2007). It seems foolish to dismiss these connections out of hand.

- Though I have no clear evidence, I am willing to bet my dog's dinner – his breakfast having been wagered earlier in the book – that there is a reliable negative correlation between egotism (and its social cousin, national chauvinism) on one hand, and second language attainment, on the other. It's certainly the case that right-of-centre politicians in the UK and elsewhere are not renowned for their fluency in foreign languages. Whether or not this prediction is borne out, many non-native speakers of English who pass for native in certain social contexts nevertheless choose to retain their 'foreign accent' in other situations. Going fully native involves too much of a sacrifice of identity. It is also unnecessary, unless you are a spy (or escaping a past life, perhaps). This – though not the espionage part – is one of the findings of a significant paper by Ingrid Piller, whose results imply that near-nativeness in certain contexts is much more ubiquitous than is generally supposed, even if total assimilation is quite rare (Piller 2002).
- And, of course, near-nativeness – like the successful stick insect – is very hard to spot.
- COMPREHENSIBLE INPUT is a term from the field of applied linguistics/second language acquisition, coined by the linguist Steven Krashen in the 1970s.[3] In the context of Krashen's theory, 'comprehensible input' has a particular definition: assuming that second language competence develops in a strictly

monotonic fashion, starting small and gradually growing larger, input is said to be comprehensible if it is just on the edge of – or one step beyond – a learner's current level of competence ('$i + 1$' input); Krashen (1977).

- Notwithstanding significant criticisms (e.g. Gregg 1984, Swain 1985, White 1987, Loschky 2008 and others), Krashen's general idea makes a good deal of intuitive sense, and a properly developed version of the hypothesis goes a considerable way to explaining the differences in outcomes between typical child and adult learners.

  – Spend any time with pre-school children, and you will very soon realise what *Allie Whoops* (Curious George's country friend in the PBS children's series) learns, after sitting all afternoon in a chicken house: to wit, '[being a chicken], it's not very interesting!' (See Kathy Waugh/Joe Fallon *Curious George: George Meets Allie Whoops* (01:35–55).) Though our own children may be a source of endless fascination, other people's three and four-year-olds are really not great conversationalists; as a group, they are hardly more captivating than chickens. But they talk a lot, endlessly repeating and recasting the same short utterances, until gradually they become at least as interesting as Allie herself.

  – Adult second language learners, on the other hand, have pressing communicative needs that go far beyond $i + 1$: explaining in a second language why you need a refund, checking that the soup of the day is based on a vegetable stock, or is free of pork, negotiating an entry visa with an unhelpful immigration official, going on a date, letting someone down gently: these all require $i + 20^+$ resources. It is plausible to suppose that if we acquired second languages stepwise, we would end up with grammatical networks that were more integrated, sophisticated, and less piecemeal – in other words, more native-like – than is typically observed in SLA.

- This idea is supported by research on computational language learning. In his discussion of artificial learning networks, Jeff Elman demonstrates just how crucial it is to 'start small':

Put simply, the network was unable to learn the complex grammar when trained from the outset with the full 'adult' language. However, when the training data were selected such that simple sentences were presented first, the network succeeded not only in mastering these, but then going on to master the complex sentences as well.

Jeff Elman, 'Learning and development in neural networks:
The importance of starting small' (Cognition, 1993: 78)

- Comprehensible input can also be understood more broadly to refer not just to inherent properties of the ambient language (reduced grammatical and lexical complexity, for example), but also to transient aspects of language performance. Once again, it is obvious that even the simplest utterances can be made incomprehensible by combinations of physical, cognitive and affective factors. Under masking conditions of various kinds, even the simplest utterances can become unintelligible: speaking too loudly, or too softly for the human ear, for example ...[4] Nor can we understand very well what someone is saying when they are screaming loudly, or brandishing a weapon, or when we have to cross oncoming traffic in rush-hour in the rain, or more generally, when we are distracted by the competing demands of another sense. And what is relatively clear to the adult native-listener may be incomprehensible to the young child, second language learner, or atypical language learner.

- It is difficult to prove that these proposed ingredients of successful language learning are necessary, much less sufficient, conditions. It is not an easy task to operationalise selflessness, for example, even if we have a clear intuitive appreciation of what constitutes a selfless act. And it may be impossible in practice to create the conditions for $n + 1$ learning in second language teaching: adult L2 learners may simply be too heterogeneous or too impatient. However, it *is* reasonably obvious how one would go about *disproving* these hypotheses: to that extent at least, they are more viable and at least as useful than any claims about the role of UG in language acquisition, based on Poverty of the Stimulus arguments.

So just maybe: *All you need is love.*

> *There's no ghosts in the graveyard*
> *That's not where they live*
> *They float in between us*
> *'what is' and 'what if'*
> *And cast our own shadows*
> *Before our own eyes*
> *You don't get them up here though*
> *They don't come up high.*

> *Joy to the city*
> *The parking lot lights*
> *The lion of evening*
> *With the rain in its eyes*
> *Joy to the freeway*
> *Joy to the cars*
> *And joy to you baby, wherever you are*
> *Tonight, tonight, tonight*
> *Tonight, tonight, tonight.*

♬ Josh Ritter, *Joy to You, Baby* (2013)

Notes

1 See Rivenc (2003: 103), Gauvenet, Hassan, Gross and Mason (1963). As this Facebook discussion reveals, I am not the only one of my generation so

influenced by this French series: https:www.facebook.com/223951797632697/ photos/a.224250504269493.70960.223951797632697/504850079542866.

2 By internalist here, I mean an academic who adopts a particular philosophical position – Chomsky being the archetypal example – but also someone within the autistic
spectrum, who has difficulties in social interaction. The two groups are not always
sharply dissociated.

3 An early lecture by Krashen on the Input Hypothesis can be found here: www
.youtube.com/results?search_query=stephen+krashen.

4 See 'End of the World' sketch (*Secret Policeman's Ball* version), available on
YouTube.

Conclusion to Part III: 'The last thing ...'

It's quite interesting, because the coal was made in a very unusual way. You see God blew all the trees down. He didn't say 'Let's have some coal,' as he could have done – he had all the right contacts. No, he got this great wind going, you see, and blew down all the trees, then over a period of three million years he changed it into coal – gradually, over a period of three million years so it wasn't noticeable to the average passer by. It was all part of the scheme, but people at the time did not see it that way. People under the trees did not say 'Hurrah, coal in three million years.' No, they said 'Oh dear, oh dear, trees falling on us – that's the last thing we want.' And of course their wish was granted.

Peter Cook, 'Sitting on the Bench' (*Beyond the Fringe*, 1961, republished in *Tragically I was an Only Twin*, Peter Cook 2002)

After 150-odd pages of Part III, the last thing anyone needs is a recapitulation of what has already been discussed. Which of course, as Peter Cook might well have concluded, is the last thing they'll get. To preclude unnecessary delay, though, I'll summarise the glossary of idealisations in twenty-four (or so) lines: see Table 10. Readers looking for more clarification of any of these are encouraged to read the relevant sections again; see website for updates on the 'missing letters'. For each term is also indicated what I take to be the standard position adopted by proponents of competence-based, and process-oriented approaches to psycholinguistic research: CBA and POA, respectively. As ever, there are a wide variety of possible views, but to simplify matters, the table is coded according to four discrete values: −4 = strongly disagree; −2 = broadly disagree; 2 = broadly agree; 4 = strongly agree.[1]

You can take this test for yourself: if your mean score is greater than 2.5 with a small standard deviation, the chances are that you will be sympathetic to a strongly competence-based interpretation of the experimental results presented in standard psycholinguistic textbooks. On the other hand, if your score is around 0 (1 to −1) – once again with a small standard deviation – it is more likely that you will prefer results consistent with a process-oriented approach. As for the outliers: if your score is greater than 3.75 you are in all probability a Wicked Ideologue: an equally ideological advisor can suggest plenty of alternative reading – Boeckx (2009) would seem to be an excellent place to start – but you won't benefit from reading further in this book, since no disconfirming empirical evidence will lead you to change your mind. (Indeed, it's astonishing that you've got(ten) this far.) At the other end of the scale, if you scored less than −2.5 (that is, between −2.5 and −4), you either haven't understood what has been presented to this point, or you are a troll. Either way, just like the

Table 10 'The last thing . . .': a summary of idealisations.

Letter	Keyword	Basic assumption/idealisation	CBA score	POA score
A	Abstraction	Language processing involves abstracting away from all information in the signal except the literal message (propositional content)	2	–2
A	Ambiguity	Language processing involves resolving ambiguities as quickly and efficiently as possible	4	2
B	Arbitrariness	Most of language, especially vocabulary, involves an arbitrary pairing of sound and meaning; sound symbolism/iconicity effects are peripheral and largely trivial	4	2
C	Competence	In principle, there is a useful distinction to be drawn between linguistic competence and language performance; performance data are not theoretically interesting in their own right, but only for what they tell us about internalised language ('language in intension')	4	–2
C	Convergence	Vocabulary size aside, speakers of a given language variety end up with essentially the same grammatical knowledge	4	2
D	Domain-specificity	Linguistic knowledge is autonomous from other kinds of cognition (both in acquisition and processing)	4	–2
E	Informational Encapsulation	Different kinds of linguistic information are stored and processed separately, initially at least	4	–2
F	Functions of Language	It makes little sense to think of language in terms of its external functions: the fact that language is used to communicate has no bearing on 'language in intension'	4	–4
F	Frequency	Effects of frequency (at all levels of language use) have no significant effect either on end-state grammatical knowledge, or on the time-course of language acquisition	4	–4
G	Grammar	Every mature speaker of a language has internalised a set of grammatical rules; this set of rules is autonomous of the lexicon (vocabulary items)	2	–2

H	Homogeneity	Even though actual speakers vary to some extent in what they know about their language, and how they use it, it is a harmless idealisation to suppose that speakers and speech communities are essentially homogeneous	2	2
I	Internalism	Knowledge of language is an internal phenomenon: the external products of the language processing system – speech, text, conversation, discourse – are of no theoretical interest, except as (imperfect) reflections of that system	4	2
J	Judgment	Introspective judgments (concerning grammatical acceptability) provide a reliable source of evidence about linguistic competence. Judgments are grounded in internal competence, not external *langue*	4	–2
K	Perfect Knowledge	Children learning their first language quickly attain a steady end-state competence; aside from vocabulary, speakers' knowledge of language does not show significant development after early childhood	4	2
M	Modularity	'The human mind is modular: the "language faculty" is relatively isolated from other mental faculties'	4	(–2*)
N	(Chomskyan) Nativism	Nativism means Chomskyan Nativism: to deny the existence of UG is to reject the idea that some aspects of language are innately determined	4	(–4)
O	Object of Study	Psycholinguistics is no different from any other branch of cognitive psychology; it is amenable to the same investigative methods; analogies to digital computing and/or biological development are valid and helpful	4	4
P	Poverty of the Stimulus	Poverty of the Stimulus arguments form part of an adequate explanation of language acquisition	4	–4
R	Exophoric Reference	Referentialism, the notion that the meaning of an expression can be explained in terms of the physical object it stands for, is deeply problematic	4	4
S	(de) Saussure	De Saussure's insistence on a rigorous distinction between *synchronic* and *diachronic* can be usefully applied to psycholinguistics: language processing is best explained ahistorically	4	2
T	Sentence (TP)	The privileged status accorded to the grammatical sentence is theoretically and empirically justified: speakers/listeners treat sentences differently from smaller or larger units of text	4	2

(continued)

Table 10 (*continued*)

Letter	Keyword	Basic assumption/idealisation	CBA score	POA score
U	Universals of Processing	Though speakers of different languages may vary in their lexical and grammatical knowledge, the processing mechanisms that instantiate such knowledge are largely invariant cross-linguistically	2	–2
v	von Humboldt (discrete infinity)	'Language is a system of infinite generation'	4	2
W	Weird	Most psychological research is based on the behaviour of WEIRD participants: Western, Educated adults (and children) from Industrialised, Rich, and Democratic societies. This is not a problem	2	–2
X	Equal CompleXity	In principle, all languages – as well as different varieties of the same language – are equally complex, and equally processable by native speakers	4	–2
Ω	Love	*All you need is love …*	–	–
A–Z		Mean	3.6	0.173913043
		SD	–0.816496581	–2.622493156
			p < 0.0001	

ideologue, you should stop now. Finally, if your mean score is further from zero than ±4, you'd do well to check your arithmetic.[2]

Now that's settled, we can move on ...

Notes

1 The fact that zero is not a possible value helps to sharpen the picture a little, though it skews the mean (towards a positive result in this case.) I'm aware of the fact even if zero was included, that it's not strictly legitimate to run a *t-test* on Likert scale (ordinal) data, even if this is commonly observed in practice. See de Winter and Dodou (2010) for discussion and some justification.

2 The numbers with asterisks are not included in the final tally, since there is too much individual variation to make this score representative. With respect to INTERNALISM, for instance, some process-oriented researchers are very strict internalists, while others adopt a much more interactionist approach to processing and acquisition.

Part IV

A Tale of Two Cities

What atypical learners tell us about (end-state) grammars, language and convergence

25 'I ain't bovvered': Lauren's French

Introduction to second language acquisition: final examination

Answer all questions

Total 100 marks

1. Examine the following excerpt from Catherine Tate and Aschlin Ditta's 'French Class' sketch: What grammatical knowledge has been internalised to allow educated speakers of English to understand this 'bit of French'? (300 words, 50 marks)

TEACHER: Right, Lauren, that's enough. I'm not going to stand here and listen to this kind of xenophobic abuse from a stupid girl who is too ignorant to even learn the language, let alone understand the people. I will fail you for this test, which means you will get an F for the entire module.

LAUREN: *[pause]* Suis-je bovvered? *(pronounced [bɔ 'vɛːɹd])*

TEACHER: What?

LAUREN: Suis-je bovvered, though?

TEACHER: Lauren...

LAUREN: *[pointing to face]* Regardez mon visage.

TEACHER: Comment?

...

LAUREN: *[still pointing]* Regardez mon visage *[circular motion indicating whole face]* est-ce que mon visage est bovvered?

TEACHER: Non, mais...

LAUREN: Non, parce que je suis pas bovvered.

TEACHER: Lauren, your behaviour is absolutely appalling. Do you behave like this at home?

LAUREN: *[angry]* Est-ce que vous disrespectez ma famille?

TEACHER: Quoi?

LAUREN: Est-ce que vous appelez ma mère une pykie?

TEACHER: Non.

LAUREN: Est-ce que vous appelez mon père un gyppo?

TEACHER: Pas du tout!

LAUREN: *[pointing to face again, talking quickly]* Regardez. Visage. Regardez. Est-ce que mon visage est bovvered? Je suis pas bovvered. *[Teacher attempts to interrupt through Lauren's speech, with no success]* Regardez mon visage, pas bovvered, pas bovvered, pas bovvered. Thierry Henri, c'est pas bovvered, pas

> bovvered, pas bovvered, regardez mon visage, frère jacques, frère jacques, je
> suis pas bovvered, pas bovvered, un kilo de pommes, un kilo de pommes, pas
> bovvered, où est le syndicat d'initiative, je suis pas bovvered, pas bovvered,
> 'Allo 'Allo ... René, René, René, regardez mon visage, je pas bovvered *[rais-*
> *ing voice, slowly]* ...I ain't – bovvered!

Catherine Tate and Aschlin Ditta, 'French Class'
sketch (*The Catherine Tate Show*)

Studying this brilliant comedy sketch – in particular, attempting to characterise
Lauren's knowledge of English and French – suggests a radically different perspective on language acquisition and processing than does Chomsky's idealisation, repeated here, for the very last time:

> *Linguistic theory is concerned primarily with an ideal speaker-listener, in a completely*
> *homogeneous speech-community, who know its [the speech community's] language*
> *perfectly and is unaffected by such grammatically irrelevant conditions as memory*
> *limitations, distractions, shifts of attention and interest, and errors (random or charac-*
> *teristic) in applying his knowledge of this language in actual performance.*

Noam Chomsky, *Aspects of the Theory of Syntax* (1965: 3)

Let us start with some basic questions about Lauren's performance, or better,
Catherine Tate's performance of Lauren's lines, since unlike most transcripts,
this shows performance in both the conventional and technical senses of the
word. Are there any obvious 'performance errors' (false starts, hesitations,
slips of the tongue, and the like)? The answer is clearly negative. Lauren is
an extremely fluent speaker: she may repeat phrases *Regardez mon visage.*
Regardez mon visage, or pause for dramatic effect, but these are intentional,
essentially perfect, aspects of her linguistic performance. We might then ask
whether her performance is grammatically acceptable. The right answer to this
question is less clear, but if there *is* a problem, it mostly arises with respect
to the more English parts of her lines: Lauren speaks a non-standard variety
of English, in which 'I ain't a French oral' and 'I ain't bovvered' are normal
ways of speaking. As for the French utterances, these are just as acceptable
and correct in context as the English ones. A native Parisian French speaker
would surely have a different pronunciation from Lauren, and would probably not use non-words like *disrespecter* or *bovverd* [bɔˈvɛːɹd] or *gyppo*. (The
verb *to disrespect* has been borrowed from English into non-standard Dutch
disrespecteren, but is not possible in French as far as I am aware.) In general, it
appears that, accent aside, Lauren's French is fluent and grammatically acceptable: verbs are correctly conjugated; determiners and possessive pronouns and
articles agree in number and gender with their head nouns (*ma famille, mon*
visage, ma mère, mon père, le syndicat, un kilo); questions and imperatives
show correct word-order and constructional marker (*Regardez mon visage.*
Est-ce que vous disrespectez ma famille?); the negation marker *pas* is correctly

positioned after the auxiliary verb (*je suis pas bovvered*), and so on. Lauren's pronunciation and vocabulary choices may not be native-like, but that is precisely where the humour lies: if Lauren code-switched to 'perfect French' – or to a language less familiar to English speakers, much of the comic effect would be lost. Overall then, Lauren's performance is highly proficient. If anything, her French output at a morpho-syntactic level is closer to Standard French than her English output is to Standard English: this is hardly surprising, considering the input available to her in GCSE French class-rooms in English secondary schools. As we shall see in the next section, grammatical (over-) regularity can be viewed as a diagnostic of insufficient input and interaction.

Now let's consider some questions of implicit linguistic knowledge. Does Lauren – or rather, the kind of French learner exemplified by Lauren – know French perfectly? Has three or more years of French instruction enabled her to internalise an autonomous grammar of French alongside that of English? Does this explain her ability to produce fluent utterances? Does she know, for instance, that French subject pronouns obligatorily encliticise to finite auxiliaries in direct questions, but that full noun-phrases do not – giving rise to the minimal contrasts in (179) – or that, in contrast to English, third person possessive pronouns agree in number and gender with their head noun, rather than matching the gender and number features of their antecedents, as shown by the contrasts in (180)?

(179) a. Quelqu'un, a-t-il   une paire de chaussures   que je pourrais
           emprunter?
           Someone,   has-t-he a pair   of shoes   that I could borrow
           'Has anyone a pair of shoes that I can borrow?'
       b. * Quelqu'un, a il une paire de chaussures que je pourrais
           emprunter?
           Someone,   has he a pair of shoes   that I could borrow
           'Does anyone have a pair of shoes that I can borrow?'
       c. * A quelqu'un une paire de chaussures que je pourrais emprunter?
           Has someone, a pair   of shoes   that I could   borrow
           'Has anyone a pair of shoes that I can borrow?'[1]

(180) a. Il a   rendu visite à sa/*son   tante   à Nantes.
           He has visited to 3POSS.FEM/3POSS.MASC aunt(fem) in Nantes
           'He visited his (lit. her) aunt in Nantes.'
       b. Elle a rendu visite à *sa/son   oncle   à   Rennes.
           She has   visited to   3.POSS.FEM/3.POSS.MASC uncle(masc) in Rennes
           'She visited her (lit. his) uncle in Rennes.'

Does she know, in addition, that *wh*-phrases only optionally move to the beginning of the clause in spoken French (181), or that higher registers of French allow what is called Complex Inversion, illustrated in (182), from Sportiche (1995); see also Rizzi and Roberts (1989), cf. Kayne and Pollock (2008)?

(181) a. T'fais quoi, là?
           you do what, there
           'What ya doing, there?' (*You doing what there?)
       b. Qu'est-ce que tu fais là?
           What-is-it that you do, there
           'What are you doing, there?'

(182) a. Depuis quand Jean est-il malade?
           since   when John is-he sick
           'Since when has John been ill?'
       b. *Depuis quand est Jean malade?
       c. *Depuis quand Jean est malade?
       d. *Jean est-il malade depuis quand?
       e. *Depuis quand Jean a-t-il été malade?

Intuitively, the answer to all of these questions is 'No'. Although it cannot be
excluded outright, there is no reason to suppose that Lauren has internalised
any of these generalisations about French, almost certainly not the latter two.
For the most part, her production consists of stock phrases familiar to her –
as they are to generations of British school children – through introductory
French textbooks and classroom role-plays (*un kilo de pommes, où est le syndicat d'initiative?*), nursery songs (*Frère Jacques*), (former) Premier League
footballers (*Thierry Henri!*) and references to an English television sit-com set
in wartime France (*Allô, Allô!, René, René!*). On the basis of the final outburst,
one might conclude that Lauren knows no French grammar at all, just a smat-
tering of Anglo-French vocabulary. And yet, whatever she knows gives her
the capacity her to generalise sufficiently from the fixed expressions of GCSE
textbooks to generate new, grammatically acceptable, utterances. Expressions
such as *Est-ce vous appelez mon père un gyppo?* are not to be found in any
French textbook, or nor do they appear in any corpus of spoken French.
Likewise, *Est-ce que vous disrepectez ma famille?* is not a question that will
ever come naturally from the mouth of any native Parisian, yet it is an instance
of spontaneous, grammatically well-formed French. Equally importantly, it is
not simply 'Frenchified English': although the verb *disrespecter* is very likely
a instance of lexical transfer, the use of a second person plural pronoun for a
singular referent (*vous*), the plural agreement-marking on the verb, the interrogative complementiser (*Est-ce que*), and the gender agreement on the possessive pronoun (*ma famille, mon père*) are all non-English grammatical features.
What's more, Lauren's pronunciation in the French parts of her monologue
better approximates to French phonology than to her native English: <bov-
vered> [bɔˈvɛːɹd] in (*suis pas bovvered*) shows a postvocalic [r] – albeit an
English [ɹ], rather than French uvular [ʁ] – final stress, and full pronunciation

of the second vowel: in the London speech that Lauren represents, by contrast, there are no post-vocalic [r]s of any kind, stress is penultimate in bi-syllabic words, and the second vowel of such words is reduced to schwa: [ˈbɒvəd].

Thus, while no-one would maintain that Lauren knows French perfectly, it is just as clear that Lauren does know some French, including some 'rules of French grammar'. She knows a bit: *un p'tit peu*. And that is the same *p'tit peu* that most British second language learners of French also know. Which is just the point: if the same sketch involved Lauren speaking Vietnamese or Scottish Gaelic instead of French, her code-switching wouldn't even raise more than a bemused half-smile. The sketch thus trades on the implicit assumption that (except for the propositional content) Lauren speaks 'our kind of French'.

We can go on from this to ask a further question: is it conceivable that with more exposure and interaction a student of Lauren's ability could learn how to use sentences involving Complex Inversion correctly, or even to master the intricacies of the *passé antérieur* and other literary tenses, to the same level of proficiency as an educated native speaker of French?

If the answer to this question is affirmative, then it would seem that one *can* go from partial to more native-like control of complex syntax in an incremental fashion, proceeding from small local generalisations to a more general system of grammatical knowledge. It is not necessary to have a fully specified grammatical system in advance. (Notice that we are agreed that Lauren probably does not possess perfect grammatical knowledge of French at this stage.) If, on the other hand, the answer is negative, then it is reasonable to ask at what point incremental learning of grammar stops: what kinds of structures are beyond Lauren's second language competence in principle? Either way, the question is an empirical one, at least with respect to Lauren's real-world counterparts: by probing learners' knowledge of ever more complex structures, we can determine the point at which L2 learners' knowledge fails to converge on native speaker judgments, presumably without the benefit of UG.

Finally, if the correct characterisation of Lauren's knowledge of French is that she has a partial grammar of French, what should be said about her knowledge of English? Is there any reason to suppose that Lauren – more significantly, real speakers like Lauren – know English grammar perfectly, in virtue of their biological endowment? Is the difference between Lauren's knowledge of English and of French a qualitative one, or simply a matter of degree?

This last question puts linguists – especially generative acquisitionists – in something of a logical bind. The simplest way out is to claim that the mechanisms of first and second language acquisition are fundamentally different from one another: that whereas L1 is determined by UG, yielding a perfect I-language (end-state grammar), second language acquisition is guided by a different set of principles. In other words, there is a clear discontinuity between the two kinds of language learning, which means we cannot draw any conclusions about first language development on the basis of SLA.

Ironically, most competence-based researchers in SLA roundly reject what might be called the DISCONTINUITY HYPOTHESIS, versions of which have been proposed by various authors, including Bley-Vroman (1990), Bley-Vroman, Felix and Ioup (1988), Clahsen and Muysken (1986), Pienemann (1998), Paradis (2009). White (1996, 2003), for example, is one of those who insist that there is no fundamental difference in the grammars attainable by children and adult second language learners: since she and others assume that UG informs first language acquisition, considerations of Economy of Explanation ('Occam's razor') lead her to conclude that UG is operative in second language acquisition, too. This is the so-called 'Full Access hypothesis': see also Schwartz and Sprouse (1996), Epstein, Flynn and Martohardjono (1996).

Yet continuity arguments cut both ways. If it turns out that one can in fact move from a more partial to a less partial (native-like) grammar in second language acquisition without the benefit of UG, there is no reason (other than ideological commitment) to suppose that the same is not also true of first language acquisition. On reflection, it seems that almost everything hangs on the assumption of CONVERGENCE. If all native speakers ultimately converge on the same grammatical knowledge, regardless of their education and experience, and interaction, then Nativist arguments prevail; there must be an inductive gap between experience and attainment. However, if convergence is only ever partial and variable, if speakers' underlying competence varies even a fraction as much as their variable performance suggests, as I suggested earlier (H is for Homogeneity, I is for Internalism), then considerations of economy force us to eliminate UG from first language acquisition as well.

Note

1 Notice that the English translation of (179c) is grammatically acceptable in some varieties of British English, but completely unacceptable in others.

In Goethe's poem *Der Zauberlehrling* ('The Sorcerer's Apprentice'), the eponymous *Lehrling* takes advantage of his master's absence to try out a few spells, in order to make light of his cleaning chores. At first everything works wonderfully – as one expects of wonders – but things very quickly get out of control, as the water continues to gush forth, and the broom and cleaning towels stop obeying his commands: what at first offered a quick remedy becomes a nuisance, then an existential threat. In *Zauberlehrling* 'go swimmingly' becomes a literal expression; the apprentice only wanted a clean floor, not to drown in a flooded room. The following extracts summarise his predicament:

Hat der alte Hexenmeister	*So, the old magician then*
sich doch einmal weggegeben!	*Has taken himself off for once!*
Und nun sollen seine Geister	*And now, his spirits, live they shall*
auch nach meinem Willen leben.	*To follow only my commands.*
...	
Walle! walle!	*Flow now! Flow!*
Manche Strecke,	*In many streams*
daß, zum Zwecke,	*Let water flow on*
Wasser fließe	*To that purpose*
und mit reichem, vollem Schwalle	*And in rich, and gushing surges*
zu dem Bade sich ergieße.	*Spew its way into the bath.*
Und nun komm, du alter Besen!	*Now come you here, you old broomstick*
Nimm die schlechten Lumpenhüllen;	*and take these filthy bits of cloth;*
bist schon lange Knecht gewesen:	*You've been a slave for long years now:*
nun erfülle meinen Willen!	*High time that you obeyed my will!*
...	
Seht, er läuft zum Ufer nieder,	*See how he runs down to the river*
Wahrlich! ist schon an dem Flusse,	*Already down there by the water*

und mit Blitzesschnelle wieder	*And at lightning speed returning*
ist er hier mit raschem Gusse.	*He's straight back, his buckets teaming.*
Schon zum zweiten Male!	*And off a second time!*
Wie das Becken schwillt!	*How that pool is swelling*
Wie sich jede Schale	*How each and every ladle is*
voll mit Wasser füllt!	*full of water, brimming!*
Stehe! stehe! denn wir haben	*Stop now! Stop! We've had enough*
deiner Gaben vollgemessen! –	*Of these gifts bestowed so well*
Ach, ich merk es! Wehe! wehe!	*But now I see: oh heck, oh no!*
Hab ich doch das Wort vergessen!	*I clean forgot the magic spell!*
Ach, das Wort, worauf am Ende	*Oh, those words that should return him*
er das wird, was er gewesen.	*To the thing he used to be.*
Ach, er läuft und bringt behende!	*Still he runs and fetches nimbly!*
Wärst du doch der alte Besen!	*The old broom's what I'd like to see!*
Immer neue Güsse	*Constant flows of water*
bringt er schnell herein,	*Ushered quick inside*
Ach! und hundert Flüsse	*Form a hundred rivers*
stürzen auf mich ein!	*Cascading on my head!*

...

Goethe, *Der Zauberlehrling* 'The Sorcerer's Apprentice' ([1798] 1827)

What Goethe's poem beautifully illustrates is the problem of over-generation: although spells – or as one might say, rules – certainly speed things up at first, they can be more bothersome than helpful in the end, if left unconstrained. A little magic is wonderful, but too much can be a (Midas) curse.

In my middle son's case, the issue is not household chores, or royal alchemy, but grammatical rules. And the problem is not that he hasn't learnt them, but that he has acquired them rather too well. *Acquire* is probably the wrong word here, since the generalisations in question were never out there: *come up with* might be better. As has already been noted several times, many children pass through a stage in which they over-generalise certain kinds of grammatical alternation, of which over-regularisations of English irregular plurals and past-tense forms are perhaps the most intensively studied examples. The incidence and duration of morphological over-regularisation is not known precisely – estimates vary considerably – but there seems to be general agreement that it is typically relatively short-lived and self-limiting; see Marcus et al. (1992).[1]

Rather less attention has been paid to syntactic over-regularisation, except, notably, in the case of verb-argument structure; see Bowerman (1982, 1988), Brooks et al. (1999), Ambridge et al. (2013). My son's errors are unusual inasmuch as they do not involve false over-generalisations beyond a lexically restricted base, but instead demonstrate what happens when what seem to be purely syntactic generalisations are allowed to run amok. Compare Part II, Case #5 above.

Adrian's English is non-standard in several respects. Here, I'll mostly restrict attention to question formation, more specifically, to three constructions where his production deviates most sharply from typical eight year-olds: subject questions, negative questions, and indirect questions with inversion. I'll also examine his use of modal auxiliaries. Taking subject questions first, consider the examples in (183), which cover a thirty-one month period from February 2013 to September 2015:

(183) a. What did happen to she?   (13 Feb. 2013)
       b. Who did stand on my foot?   (26 Feb. 2013)
       c. Who does want the last one?   (4 Apr. 2013)
       d. Who did stick it on?   (12 Apr. 2013)
       e. What did happen? Who did come?   (17 Jul. 2013)
       f. What did happen to the cracked bottle?   (11 Jan. 2014)
       g. Who did burp ...? oh, the dog   (29 Dec. 2014)
       h. Dad, who did throw away that towel?   (31 Mar. 2015)
       i. Guess what Austin did throw down the
          stairs and hit the cello?   (4 Apr. 2015)
       j. Who does like shopping channels?! ...
          so annoying, shopping channels   (27 Sept. 2015)

The penultimate example (183i) is especially interesting since, in addition to *do*-support with subject questions – the core problem here – the utterance also shows simultaneous 'extraction' from two different grammatical positions: 'What did he throw down the stairs?' (object question); 'What hit the cello?' (subject question). It is important to keep in mind that *do/did* is unstressed in all of these contexts: these are not cases of contrastive/emphatic *do*. Equally importantly, this over-extension of unstressed *do* only applies in interrogative constructions: it is not found in regular declarative clauses.

The other cases of a 'question-spell gone wrong' are exemplified in (184) and (185), which are probably of a piece: the examples in (184) show auxiliary forms repeated to support negation, while those in (185) show other kinds of 'stranded affix' rescued by the presence of an extra auxiliary, or attached directly to the verb.

(Note that I am using the term 'stranded' purely descriptively here; no movement analysis is necessarily implied, though of course it can't be excluded, either.)

(184) a. Why does he doesn't like to go uphill? (25 Jan. 2015)
   b. Why does John don't want Mutley in his room? (×2, 9 June 2015)
(185) a. How does it be cleaned? (9 Dec. 2013)
   b. Why does Mutley's hair comes [sic] off, like that? (20 Mar. 2015)
   c. What is Isaac's father's job is? (1 Apr. 2015)
   d. Why do Oji kouen has a panda [=picture] on everything? (7 Feb. 2015)

Finally, in respect of interrogatives, observe the over-extension of 'subject-auxiliary inversion' to embedded contexts (compare Part II, Case #5 above):

(186) a. I know where am I going. (8 Apr. 2013)
   b. Can you tell me where is it gone? (11 Jan. 2013)
   c. [pointing to a map] This is where are we, right? (12 Dec. 2013)

In no case is there external support for the over-generalisation – none of these is plausibly a case of cross-linguistic influence from Japanese (a language without inversion or *do*-support), or from my variety of English. Moreover, in every case the 'perfect error' persisted over two years of data collection, and showed little sign of retreating in favour of the more standard, less regular, version of English to which my son was exposed on a daily basis. Until one day it slipped away. (I cannot guarantee that Adrian *never* used the expected forms of these expressions during the two-year period – almost by definition, we tend not to notice 'normal syntax', and clearly I have not transcribed every utterance. Still, I am reasonably confident that 'correct usage' during this time was highly infrequent at best, and that there was no obvious competition, or optionality, in his use of subject question *do*-support and embedded inversion.)

Parallel considerations hold for constructions involving modal auxiliaries. With a very few exceptions,[2] no contemporary variety of English – and certainly none that Adrian has ever encountered – allows non-finite modal expressions:

(187) a. If I'm in England, I will definitely can read it. (14 Oct. 2014)
   b. I don't hate *all* kinds of fish. I might can eat it. (18 Nov. 2014)
   c. If I lived in England, I might can read better. (23 Jan. 2015)
   d. He might have eat something in the shrine. And he might have throw up. (13 Feb. 2015)

    e. I think Mutley might can walk like that without a leash. (13 Feb. 2015)

    f. I might not can't eat that. (26 Feb. 2015)

    g. This is oma:ri [?]: I used to can do it. (28 Feb. 2015)

    h. If his back goes bad, his legs go bad, and he might can't walk. (16 Mar. 2015)

Example (187b) is not a case of double negation: what Adrian intends by this utterance is that it is possible, unusual as it may be for him, that he will be able to eat this particular kind of fish, he thinks. What these examples evidently demonstrate is that in developing knowledge of English, Adrian is able to generalise beyond the input to produce novel forms that he has never heard before. This is just as well, since for the last five years, from the time we moved to Japan in 2010, the only models he has had for his English are me – and to a lesser extent – his mother and older brother; otherwise, his peer group consists predominantly of monolingual Japanese speakers.

Of course, no-one denies that children have some capacity to generalise and so to project beyond the 'primary linguistic data': every halfway viable theory of grammatical development must incorporate and explain this kind of creativity. (The Behaviourist psychologist who claims that we acquire language purely through imitation only exists as a bogey man in certain generativist discussions.) What is at stake, therefore, is not whether children are creative in this way, but whether this creativity affords any evidence of the existence or workings of Universal Grammar. For this to be the case, there should be some asymmetry in the pattern of deviation from the ambient language such that over-generalisation only ever occurs in the direction of greater regularity: it should not increase the irregularity in the system of alternations. If we only consider the paradigmatic data in (183–187), we might suppose that Adrian knows a general syntactic rule – certainly, his behaviour can be described that way. However, as has been noted several times before, just because all rules are generalisations does not mean that all generalisations are rules. The significant point to realise is that these deviations from the kind of English Adrian hears are all mixed up with a set of other 'errors' that depart from that same English model along a variety of more idiosyncratic, and more language-specific, trajectories.

To see this, let's finish the exam:

2. Examine the following data from Adrian's speech corpus: Try to decide which false generalisations tend towards greater regularity, which toward greater entropy; also which of these errors, if any, can be explained by reference to languages other than English. (300 words, 50 marks)

I. a. Don't get 'em out, I'm putting in them. (14 Feb. 2013)

    b. Everyone waves at me. I was waven at by a police-man. (10 Mar. 2013)

    c. Yumi has seen the hamster. She's more bigger than last time she seed her. (2 Feb. 2013)

    d. That's the thing so you don't get shotten. (8 Apr. 2013)

    e. If you have you know … an octopus … no, a jellyfish … and if you get stungen, and you put on vinegar, will it help? (23 Apr. 2013)

    f. I let goed it. (24 Apr. 2013)

    g. He will [fall down] … if he doesn't be careful! (21 May 2013)

    h. They [= the sharks] get put in the box and get brang to the jail. (13 Jul. 2013)

    i. Mum, did you took the picture when the dog and me's on my lap? (3 Sept. 2013)

    j. He's cleaning out the smoking-can. (4 Sept. 2013)

    k. I pulled one wack out of my ear, but there are still some more. (9 Dec. 2013)

    l. I'm changing the animals' food that they eat them from. [Minecraft] (14 Jan. 2014)

    m. There's a weird girl in a marrying dress to have her picture tooken. [cosplay photo shoot] (25 May 2014)

    n. Do you think driving is better for mans or for womans? (29 Aug 2014)

    o. [John], we brang the hamsters back. (13 Sept. 2014)

    p. Dad, what would the football person say if I drawed this in black and white and taked it to the football place?

    q. Am I allowed to spin you? You span me yesterday. [playing with remote controlled cars] (13 Sept. 2014)

    r. So that place has less more toys than me?! (5 Oct. 2014)

    s. I have to get my cold checken, and my ears checked, too. (22 Oct. 2014)

    t. That's the fakest clock I ever seen in my life. (22 Oct. 2014)

    u. Dad, did I tell you the story that Ms Shiobara's chihuahua got tak – tooken away by a [sic] eagle? No, … I did?

    v. I carefulled very hard to not use much 'u's. (16 Nov. 2014)

    x. He can't drink water right after eating, can he? … yeah … I'm just washing out it [=the bowl]. (18 Nov. 2014)

    y. Can you cut this in half, so that I can cut this easilier [=more easily]? (18 Nov. 2014)

    z. I'll just wait until it [= loose tooth] come outs by itself. (3 Jan. 2015)

    aa. N: You have to give me a hand, though …

        A: I've already gaven you one hand, how many hand do you need? (26 Mar. 2015)

END OF EXAMINATION

It should be emphasised that the latter examples have not been specially selected to make an argument: aside from a handful of cases that clearly show CLI effects from Japanese, these constitute the total remainder of the *Adrianish* corpus that – together with the examples in (183–187) – make up the entire set of transcribed utterances. (Three children and two full-time jobs don't leave us parents a lot of time for extensive diary studies.)

The examples reveal interesting systematicities in Adrian's deviance: for example, almost all passive participles are marked with *-en*, while active perfect participles are generally affixed with *-ed*; some phrasal and compound verbs are treated as single units (let-go*ed*, come-out*s*). And there are other morphological generalisations that tend toward greater regularity: 'mans' for *men*, womans for *women*, 'taked' for *took*, 'dangerousest' for *most dangerous* and – rather charmingly – 'wack' for (one piece of) *wax*. But set against these over-regularisations, are a comparable number of systematic deviations that tend towards greater irregularity: 'over-irregularisations', as it were. These include irregular verb-forms such as ('doesn't be careful', 'stungen', 'brang', 'did you took …?', 'shotten', 'tooken', 'seed', 'gaven', 'span', etc.). In addition to these inflectional errors, Adrian produces unacceptable syntactic patterns. For example, he allows weak object pronouns to appear after the particle in phrasal verb constructions, where the correct attachment of the *-ing* affix suggests that he has analysed these verbs as two-part forms: (i.e. *I'm putting in them, I'm washing out it*). These examples are particularly interesting because there is no variety of English – or other Germanic varieties with phrasal verbs – where weak pronouns are allowed to remain to the left of verb-particles, in contrast to heavier noun-phrases (though whether this is due to syntactic or processing reasons is a matter of debate: Johnson 1991, cf. Hawkins 1995, 2001). Similarly, nominative pronouns are never normally permitted in oblique contexts. In most generative studies of pronoun acquisition – see e.g. Deprez and Pierce (1993) – it is claimed that 'default accusative' usage ('me' for *I*, 'him' for *he*, 'them' for *they*, etc.) may precede the acquisition of nominative pronouns in finite clauses, but that once these are acquired, they are not used incorrectly. At least in this small corpus, that expectation is not borne out ('What did happen to she?').

Notes

1 My experience of listening to my older son and his school-friends between the ages of six and ten suggests that morphological over-regularisation errors are much more persistent – particularly with less frequent forms, e.g. *catched* for *caught*, *teached* for *taught* – than is generally claimed in the literature.
2 See Nagel (1989), Battistela (1991) and Trudgill (1990), all cited in Roberts (1993).

Conclusion to Part IV: A Tale of Two Cities (London and Kobe)

♫ Dire Straits, *Brothers in Arms* (1985)

In many respects, Lauren and Adrian represent polar opposites in any continuum of language learning: Lauren, the reluctant second language learner with a truly appalling attitude, whose French output is cobbled together from hackneyed phrases and rudimentary sentence fragments; Adrian, a first language learner, whose English is generally as fluent and natural as any other native speaker. Except that it's perfect – *too perfect*. The irony is that Adrian's English only exists because he is 'an ideal speaker–listener … in a perfectly homogeneous speech community', which is to say, his own. Had we stayed in imperfect England in 2010, instead of moving to Japan just after he turned four, there is every reason to think that his English would be as unremarkable as that of his older brother, who moved here at age ten after five years at a Sheffield primary school. This fact gives the lie to the idealisation of homogeneity (see above): to acquire a language perfectly requires external imperfection. It seems that it really *does* matter who you talk to.

In spite of these disparities, the fictional Lauren and the (blessedly) very real Adrian have a lot in common. Both have clearly developed an ability to generalise beyond the input, to produce novel sentences that speakers of the two languages would readily understand. The majority of both speakers' productions are grammatically well formed at most levels of analysis: probably, most non-linguists would not even notice the errors that Adrian makes. It is foreseeable that both could ultimately 'pass for native speakers' given sufficient input and interaction. Yet, from a strictly learning-theoretic perspective, Adrian's problem is much harder to solve than Lauren's: given that his English is better than any of his peers or teachers, in the absence of negative evidence, it's not guaranteed that he will ever succeed in getting *back to where [he] once belonged*.

Lauren might not be *bov'aired*, but still – perhaps *because* of that – she might have better cards.

Epilogue

Io non saprò certamente mai consigliarvi a secondare il bizzarro pensiero, che vi è nato, di fantasticare intorno alla lingua universale.

I would assuredly never advise you to pursue the bizarre conceit, engendered in you, of exploring the fantasy of a universal language.

Francesco Soave, *Riflessioni intorno all'istituzione di una lingua universale* (1774, quoted in Eco 1993)

In science, great ideas often run in advance of evidence. When an idea pays off, we regard its originator as a genius, and wonder why other scientists were so foolish as to ignore his or her (literal) prescience. More often than not, however, novel ideas are fond delusions – 'bizarre conceits', to re-use Francesco Soave's phrase: where they seduce a community of scholars, we ask why the same scientists were in such thrall to claims lacking any substance, to the emperor's new clothes. In more autocratic and/or theocratic societies, the answers to the latter question are easy to find: awe of authority – or fear of challenging orthodoxy – are understandable reasons to toe an irrational line. *Who's (not) afraid of the Spanish Inquisition?* Of course, if the evidence for a given theoretical construct is never forthcoming – or alternatively, if what we are trying to explain turns out to be adequately explained without recourse to that construct – then should we persist in holding to that idea we are no longer dealing with science, but with mythology or cult religion.

In 1794, 150 years before Watson and Crick's 1953 article on the structure of DNA revolutionised scientific – and later popular – understanding of life on Earth, Erasmus Darwin (Charles Darwin's grandfather) wrote:

As the earth and ocean were probably peopled with vegetable productions long before the existence of animals; and many families of these animals long before other families of them, shall we conjecture that one and the same kind of living filaments is and has been the cause of all organic life?

Erasmus Darwin, *Zoonomia, or The Laws of Organic Life* (1794, cited in Ridley 1999)

In 1667, around 150 years before Erasmus Darwin was being so fantastically prescient, the German alchemist-physician Johann Becher advanced what became known as the PHLOGISTON THEORY OF COMBUSTION, to explain the chemistry of burning and rusting. According to this theory, combustion involved the release of a fundamental fire-like element, which Becher named *terra pinguis*; the substance was later renamed *phlogiston* by Georg Eric Stahl. Phlogiston theory was only finally refuted by Antoine Lavoisier ('the father of modern chemistry') in the 1780s, just a few years before Erasmus Darwin's speculation was published.

Becher is now viewed – if he is viewed at all – as a middling scientist, a vaguely ridiculous figure. The following quote from Bill Bryson's book *A Short History of Nearly Everything* is instructive:

Chemistry as an earnest and respectable science is often said to date from 1661, when Robert Boyle of Oxford published The Sceptical Chymist *– the first work to distinguish between chemists and alchemists – but it was a slow and often erratic transition. Into the eighteenth century scholars could feel oddly comfortable in both camps – like the German Johann Becher, who produced sober and unexceptional work on mineralogy called* Physica Subterranea, *but who also was certain that, given the right materials, he could make himself invisible.*

Bill Bryson, *A Short History of Nearly Everything*, chapter 7 (2005)

These historical precedents imply that we need to wait another 150 years to find out whether UG is more like DNA – a 'living filament' running through all human language – or whether it is like phlogiston, an irrelevant, distracting, myth. (Becher, of course, may have the last laugh: he was mistaken about *terra pinguis*, but it turns out that given the right materials it *is* now possible to make objects invisible, albeit tiny ones. See, for example, Greenleaf, Lassas and Uhlmann 2003, Gabrielli, Cardenas, Poitras et al. 2009.)

The joy and frustration of scientific enquiry is that we don't know the answers. Professor Brian Cox, one of the UK's most popular scientists, recently rehearsed the important, but often misappropriated, saying: 'the three most important words in science are "We don't know"'.

What is important about this phrase is the clear implication that those who claim certain knowledge of anything are not scientists, but priests or imams, quacks or oracles. The phrase is misappropriated when taken by those opposed to science – a different group of fundamentalists, relativists and ignorant sceptics, who also believe they know the truth – as an assertion that all explanations are equally valid. It's hard to tell, as Joseph Campbell mused in the prefatory quote, which group really gets the message.

All we can do is follow the evidence, and act in good faith. T. S. Eliot said it better, in the continuation of the same poem that was quoted in the Introduction:

And what there is to conquer
By strength and submission, has already been discovered
Once or twice, or several times, by men whom one cannot hope
To emulate – but there is no competition –
There is only the fight to recover what has been lost
And found and lost again and again: and now, under conditions
That seem unpropitious.
But perhaps neither gain nor loss.
For us, there is only the trying.
The rest is not our business.

T. S. Eliot, 'East Coker' (*Four Quartets*, 1943)

Acknowledgments, credits and permissions

Though this section appears at the end, there will be some that will look here first: should they find their name missing from the list, the book will be returned to the shelf unread – and immediately devalued in their estimation. If you are one of those prospective readers, rest assured that the book wasn't written for you. (Carly Simon wrote something similar, over forty years ago.) There may also be others who will find themselves thanked or credited without really knowing why; in a few cases, this recognition will bring more unease than satisfaction. Guilt by association is a fearful thing.

I wish to thank four different groups of people that have made this book possible: (i) my teachers; (ii) the authors, poets, songwriters and comedians that have helped me to make sense of the world – including the world of linguistics; (iii) the publishers, agents and other intermediaries who have supported this project by granting licences to republish material, for free or at nominal charge; (iv) those whom I love most, who have inspired this work in different ways, and stuck with me on the journey.

By teachers I include all those who have made a significant difference to my understanding of languages and linguistics, whether or not they were employed as educators at the time: the group includes school teachers, lecturers, professors, classmates, colleagues, students and other academics I have met on the way. I rarely appreciated what I had learned from them until later – sometimes only after decades of further study and teaching. It doesn't matter whether I spent an hour or a year or more in someone's company, but to be included on the list, it is crucial that we actually shared the same physical space at some point.[1]

So, in approximate chronological order (of first encounter), I'd like to thank: E. T. (Ted) Cooke, Tom Garrett, Raoul Larmour, R. F. K. Lucas, David Young (DBY) (Cabin Hill School and Campbell College, Belfast); J. Cremona, David Greene, Peter Johnson, Stephen Levinson, Terry Moore, Francis Nolan, Nigel Vincent, Paul Warren (University of Cambridge, Modern and Medieval Languages Tripos); Max Coltheart, Martin Davies, Sam Gutenplan, Margaret Harris, Barry Smith (Birkbeck and University College, London); Elaine

337

Andersen, Joseph Aoun, Doug Biber, Patricia Clancy, Bernard Comrie, Ed Finegan, James Paul Gee, Jack Hawkins, Nina Hyams, Larry Hyman, Osvaldo Jaeggli,[†] Ed Keenan, Steve Krashen, Audrey Li, Doug Pulleyblank, Mark Seidenberg, Tim Stowell, Jean-Roger Vergnaud,[†] Maria Luisa Zubizarreta; Elabbas Benmamoun, Heather Goad, Charlotte Reinholtz (University of Southern California/UCLA); Lolly Tyler, William Marslen-Wilson (University of Cambridge); Josef Bayer, Harald Clahsen, Sonja Eisenbeiß, Ray Fabri, Jim Kilbury, Sebastian Löbner, Teresa Parodi, Dieter Wunderlich (Heinrich-Heine-Universität, Düsseldorf); Julie Auger, Mark Baker, Jonathan Bobaljik, Charles Boberg, Martha Crago, Fred Genessee, Brendan Gillon, Myrna Gopnik, Eithne Guilfoyle, Alan Juffs, James McGilvray, Maire Noonam, Michel Paradis, Roumyana Slabakova, Lisa Travis, Lydia White, Susi Wurmbrand (McGill University); Melissa Bowerman, Penny Brown, Anne Cutler, Marianne Gullberg, Eric Kellerman, Ans van Kemenade, Sotaro Kita, Wolfgang Klein, Stephen Levinson (again!), Pieter Muysken, Clive Perdue, Leah Roberts, Natasha Warner (Max Planck Institute for Psycholinguistics, and Radboud University, Nijmegen); Joan Beal, Ewa Dabrowska, Valerie Hobbs, Stephen Laurence, Olivier Pascalis, Trang Phan, Michael Siegal, Rosemary Varley, Gareth Walker (University of Sheffield). Along the way I have also learned a great deal from interactions with David Adger, Martin Atkinson, Robert Bley-Vroman, Lisa Cheng, Grev Corbett, Stephen Crain, Claudia Felser, Lyn Frazier, Lila Gleitman, Helen Goodluck, Liliane Haegeman, Caroline Heycock, Alison Henry, Norbert Hornstein, Richard Kayne, Howard Lasnik, Jim McCloskey, Ian McKay, Gary Marcus, Andrew Martin, Ayumi Matsuo, Asya Pereltsvaig, Colin Phillips, Pierre Pica, Masha Polinsky, Shana Poplack, Ian Roberts, Tom Roeper, Haj Ross, Jeff Runner, Laura Sabourin, Bonnie Schwartz, Pieter Seuren, Dan Slobin, William Snyder, Antonella Sorace, Rint Sybesma, Dylan Tsai, Ianthe Tsimpli, Michael Ullman, Santa Vīnerte, Amy Weinberg, Ken Wexler and Deirdre Wilson. We may not always have agreed on much at the time – some may not even have realised I was even paying attention – but their input has been invaluable, and while no-one but me is responsible for the resulting pig's ear, all deserve my gratitude for affording a wider perspective. I feel extremely privileged to have enjoyed such a long, and interesting education.

If you have arrived at this section by the long route, it should have become clear (quite early on) that I love languages much more than I care about their proper analysis. Unlike some of my close friends and colleagues, academia has never been a calling for me, more a career *faute de mieux*. Partly for this reason, although fellow academics enjoy my respect, my greater admiration will always be reserved for those that are most creative with words, whose gifts offer deeper insights into the human condition than into the mind~brain. It is the chance to experience and share this other creativity with my students that gets me to work in the morning, and helps me through my life. Obtaining all of the permissions necessary to republish the third-party material in this book has been an unimaginably arduous struggle: the job has involved thousands of emails, and over a year of daily effort, to secure only around 70 per cent of the third-party material cited in the original manuscript. In some cases, even where publishers granted permissions on generous terms, the fact that there were any terms at all precluded publication, so circumspect are the legal professionals involved. In the course of this quest, I discovered a great deal about the (under) world of publishing – music publishing, in particular – that is ugly, petty and avaricious. Not to mention wickedly anti-competitive: 'MFN' is a particularly contemptible notion.[2] In short, the system is awful, as are a small number of people that work in it (whose names are excluded here). This makes me all the more grateful to the great majority of publishers and agents that I contacted – and the living artists or authors whom they contacted on my behalf – who proved supportive of the project, and were extremely helpful to me (even in those cases where the system made it impossible for them to grant permissions at an affordable cost). My sincere thanks, therefore, go to the following (in order of appearance in the book).

- Living authors/artists and their agents/representatives/publishers' representatives:
  - Non-academic: Josh Ritter (Erik Gilbert); David Byrne (Ella Griffiths); Roddy Doyle (Sarah Laskin); Val Wood; Jessica Ziebland; Rowan Atkinson and Richard Curtis (Lucy Fairney, Danielle Walker); Stephen Fry and Hugh Laurie (Jo Crocker, David Evans); William Boyd (Claire Weatherhead, UK; Peter London, US); Ian McEwan (Madeleine Dunnigan, UK; Alicia Dercole, US); Anna Ternheim; Wolf Biermann (Pamela Biermann); Robert Florence, Iain Connell (Tracy McPherson); Michael Chorost (Ethan Bassoff); Matt Ridley (UK; Peter London, US); Wolfgang Niedecken (Vera Mommertz-Schmitz); de Kast (Lindsay MacPherson); Christopher Paolini (Sherri Hinchey); John Banville (Emma, UK; Allison Jakobovic, US); Jess Smith (Peter Burns); Catherine Tate and Aschlin Ditta (Maxine Fletcher); Bill Bryson (Alicia Adercole).
  - Academic: Gary Marcus; Keith Devlin (Joan Ashe); Noam Chomsky (Catherine Balladur, Hamida Demirdache, Pierre Pica, Antony Arnove; CNRS); Laura Stingelin (Elsevier); Johan Rooryck; George Steiner (Alicia Misarti); Lars Gunnar Andersson (Alex Bradshaw, Anne Porter); Antonella Sorace (Alyson Reed); Brian MacWhinney (Dana Peters); Roy Sorensen (Diana Taylor); Alison Henry (Ben Kennedy); James McGilvray; John Collins (Diana Taylor); Ties Nijssen (Springer); Cedric Boeckx; Steve Jones (Patricia Pecegueiro, UK; Peter London, US); Jean Aitchison (Paulette Goldweber); James Walker (Diana Taylor); Haj Ross; Daniel Everett (Alia McKellar); Robert Epstein (Ali Hawken); Daniel

Cohen (Shannon A. McCullough); John Haiman and Sandra Thompson (Ineke Elskamp); R. H. Robins (Laura Templeman); Valerie Hobbs.

- Representatives of the estates of the following authors/artists and/or their agents/representatives/publishers' representatives (non-academic):
  – T. S. Eliot (Emma Cheshire, UK; Ron Hussey, US); Joseph Campbell (Michael Lambert); Peter Cook (Georgia Glover); C. S. Lewis (Claire Taylor); Robert Benchley (Nat Benchley); Frank Land (Violett Plessz); Stephen Jay Gould (Robert Shatzkin); Graham Greene (David Evans); Seamus Heaney (Emma Cheshire, UK; Victoria Fox, US); Richard Rodgers and Oscar Hammerstein II (Mike Williams); Margaret Thatcher (Chris Collins); John Pepper [Fred Gamble] (John Murphy); Brian O'Nolan [Flann O'Brien] (Anthony Farrell); Edna St Vincent Millay (Frederick T. Courtright, Edna St Vincent Millay Society); William Golding (Emma Cheshire, UK; Ron Hussey, US); Douglas Adams (Alicia Dercole); Truman Capote (Alex Bradshaw, Madeleine Hartley, UK; Sherri Hinchey, US).

- Others whose generous assistance led to the securing of permissions, or who helped in some other way, along the road (academic and non-academic):
  – Charlotte Stricker (Overamstel), Rint Sybesma and Monika Schmid, for help with Frisian and German translations of request letters; Alex Bradshaw (Penguin UK); Ben Kennedy (OUP); Claire Taylor, and especially my content editor Dan Brown, and copy-editor Glennis Starling (CUP); Ron Unz; Georgia Glover, Dave Evans (David Higham Agency); Catrin Rhys, Camille Tucker and Santa Vīnerte, for royalty-free photographs of Belfast, Edmonton and Edinburgh (yes, it was Edinburgh!), respectively; Neil Strickland and Brad Baxter, for setting me straighter on mathematics; Hannah Clark (Music Sales), for helping to point me in the right direction. The permissions team at Penguin Random House US deserve particular recognition: given the size of their operation, the service was comparatively prompt and unfailingly helpful.

I am grateful to the Readers, anonymous or otherwise, who have been involved at various stages of the project, helping me to remedy at least some of the pratfalls of the original manuscript. Of those whose identity I know, I'd especially like to thank my friends Sonja Eisenbeiß and Natasha Warner. I'd also like to thank Maggie Tallerman and Paul Stevens (Palgrave MacMillan), for supporting this project in its early stages, and for letting me go when our interests diverged.

The faculty and administration of Konan University, in particular my departmental colleagues, have played a significant role in the process by providing a respectful, collegial and supportive environment in which to write. Most importantly, they have granted me trust and space (compare von Humboldt's *Einsamkeit und Freiheit*), two things completely lacking in my experience of

UK academia. As evidence of this: in six years of employment at Konan, I have never once been asked to report on my research activities, or to justify my work in the mindless accountability reviews that distort research and inhibit scholarship in many other places. I very much hope that they will feel that their confidence has been well placed.

People matter most, but places make a huge difference too. And so I can't conclude without a nod to Montreal, Düsseldorf, Nijmegen, Sheffield, Kobe and of course Belfast, whose sounds, streets, light and latitude have shaped my world-view more than I ever would have imagined. Like Joe Jackson, the ambivalence I feel toward my native city does not detract from an underlying affection. Perhaps I could have written the same book had I come from Luton or Exeter, Winnipeg or Melbourne. But somehow I doubt it.

♫ Joe Jackson, *Home Town* (1986)

I dedicate this book to those who are dearest to me, to my family in Northern Ireland and here in Japan. I am forever grateful to my mother, Norma Duffield, for instilling a love of literature and theatre, as well as a deeper appreciation of the ineffable, and to my father, Gordon Duffield, for teaching me (without instruction) how to write, and of the prime importance of kindness and decency. Though he died before this book was even started, those who knew him will clearly see his abiding influence. As for my immediate family in Japan, my wife Ayumi and my children, no words can fully express my gratitude for their love and forbearance, as well as – in Ayumi's case – for her practical support these last few years. Indeed, after this, 'no words' may be the best thing, entirely: whatever selfish pleasure I may have derived from the business of writing, it has been a huge distraction from the more important things in family life. I dedicate this book to all of my family, with deep love, and in grateful consideration.

Republication licences

Approximately 40 per cent of the third-party material used is out of copyright in all territories where this book is published. In the other cases, except those that directly fall under more general fair use/fair dealing provisions (e.g. MIT Press Fair Use provisions, STM regulations), permission to republish with worldwide distribution has been sought from all relevant rights holders. Where permission has been granted under fair use, without limits, fees or conditions, the bibliographical reference serves as the credit. Other credits are given below, in order of appearance in the book. (In those cases where more than one excerpt from a particular work is used, the credits appear together at the first use of the work.)

I am grateful to the individuals tagged with each credit for their invaluable help in receiving my requests, in contacting authors and granting licences; in almost all cases, at no charge. Thanks to them, it has been possible to use more than 60 per cent of the quotes that appeared in the original manuscript (the remainder were either unaffordable – in the case of most song lyrics – or could not be published, in cases where one or other of the rights holder(s) did not reply in time).

- Excerpt from *The Language of Mathematics* by Frank Land. Published in 1974 by John Murray, an imprint of Hodder & Stoughton. Used with publisher's consent. [Original copyright holder untraceable]
- Lyrics from *Give Me Back My Name* by Talking Heads (Weymouth/Frantz/Harrison/Byrne), used by permission of David Byrne. (Ella Griffiths)
- Excerpt from *Children of the Tide* by Val Wood, published by Bantam Press. Reproduced by permission of The Random House Group Ltd. (Sofia Wennerstrom)
- Excerpt from *Greta & Claude*, written and published by Jessica Ziebland. Republished by permission of the author.
- Excerpts from 'Sir Marcus Browning, MP', 'The Wedding: Vicar's Speech' and 'Man in Seat 23c' written by Richard Curtis and Rowan Atkinson, reprinted by permission of the writers. (Lucy Fairney, Danielle Walker)
- Excerpts from *A Bit of Fry & Laurie* ('Information' sketch, 'Language Conversation') by Stephen Fry and Hugh Laurie. Copyright © 1990 Stephen Fry and Hugh Laurie. Published by Mandarin Books. (David Evans)
- Excerpts from *Our Man in Havana* by Graham Greene. Originally published in 1958 by Heinemann. Vintage Classics edition, copyright © 2001. Used with permission of David Higham agency. (David Evans)
- Quote from a 2010 CNN Interview by David Byrne (http://edition.cnn.com/2010/opinion/04/01/ted.david.byrne/). Copyright © David Byrne 2010, used by permission of The Wylie Agency (UK) Ltd. (Ella Griffiths)
- Excerpts from William Boyd's *Waiting for Sunrise* © William Boyd, 2012, Bloomsbury Publishing Plc, used with permission (all territories except US, Philippines, open market) (Claire Weatherhead). Brief quotes from pp. 13, 238 from *Waiting for Sunrise* by William Boyd. Copyright © William Boyd. Reprinted by permission of HarperCollins Publishers (US, Philippines, open market). (Peter London)
- Excerpt from 'A Sofa in the Forties' from *The Opened Ground: Selected Poems 1966–1996* by Seamus Heaney, previously published in *The Spirit Level*. Copyright © 1999 (reprint edition) Farrar, Straus and Giroux. (Victoria Fox). Originally published in the UK in *The Spirit Level* by Faber & Faber, copyright © 1996. (Emma Cheshire)
- Excerpt from *Amsterdam* by Ian McEwan. Published by Jonathan Cape 1998. Copyright © Ian McEwan. Reproduced by permission of the author c/o Rogers, Coleridge and White Ltd, 20 Powis Mews, W11 1JN (British Commonwealth and Canada). (RCW, Madeleine Dunnigan; Random House, USA – fair use)
- Lyrics from *Good Man*, *New Lover* and *Nightmares*, composed and written by Josh Ritter, reprinted by permission of Rural Songs. (Josh Ritter, Erik Gilbert)

- Excerpt from 'Psycholinguistic perspectives on language change' by Jean Aitchison. Copyright © 2003. In Brian D. Joseph and Richard D. Janda, eds, *The Handbook of Historical Linguistics*, Blackwell Publishing Ltd, Malden, MA and Oxford. (Paulette Goldweber).
- Excerpt from *Variation in Linguistic Systems* by James Walker. Copyright © 2012. Reproduced by permission of Taylor & Francis Group, LLC, a division of Informa PLC. (Diana Taylor)
- Lyrics from *In Nije Dei* composed by de Kast, reprinted by permission of Nettwerk Canada. (Lindsay Macpherson)
- Lyrics from *The Curse* and *A Certain Light* composed and written by Josh Ritter, reprinted by permission of Rural Songs. (Erik Gilbert)
- Edna St Vincent Millay, excerpt from 'Euclid Alone Has Looked on Beauty Bare' from *Collected Poems*. Copyright © 1923, 1951 by Edna St Vincent Millay and Norma Millay Ellis. Also, excerpt from *The Letters of Edna St Vincent Millay* (MacDougall ed.), copyright © 1952. Reprinted with the permission of The Permissions Company, Inc., on behalf of Holly Peppe, Literary Executor, The Millay Society. www.millay.org (Fred T. Courtright)
- Excerpts from *The Spire* by William Golding. Reprinted by permission of Faber & Faber (Worldwide ex-US – Fair Dealing) (Emma Cheshire). Copyright © 1964 and renewed 1992 by William Golding. Reprinted by permission of Houghton Mifflin Harcourt Publishing Company. All rights reserved (USA only). (Ron Hussey)
- Excerpts from *Equations from God: Pure Mathematics and Victorian Faith* by Daniel J. Cohen. Copyright © 2007 The Johns Hopkins University Press. Reprinted with permission of Johns Hopkins University Press. (Shannon A. McCullough)
- Lyrics from *Harrisburg* and *Lark*, both composed and written by Josh Ritter, reprinted by permission of Rural Songs. (Erik Gilbert)
- Excerpt from *Breakfast at Tiffany's* by Truman Capote (Hamish Hamilton, 1958). Copyright © Truman Capote, 1958. Reproduced by permission of Penguin Books Ltd/Random House. (Madeleine Hartley, UK; Sherri Hinchey, US)
- Lyrics from *Galahad* and *Joy to You, Baby*, composed and written by Josh Ritter, reprinted by permission of Rural Songs. (Erik Gilbert)
- Excerpt from 'Sitting on the Bench' by Peter Cook (1961 sketch, republished in *Tragically I was an Only Twin*, Cook 2002, St Martin's Press), with permission of David Higham Agency. (Georgia Glover)
- Excerpt from Catherine Tate and Aschlin Ditta, 'French Class' sketch from *The Catherine Tate Show,* series 3, © 2006 Tiger Aspect Productions for the BBC. (Maxine Fletcher)

I'll end this book where I began – with all due thanks to Josh Ritter, and with the final part of his inspirational *Bone of Song*:

> *Then I saw on a white space that was left*
> *A blessing written older than the rest.*
> *It said: 'Leave me here, I care not for wealth or fame*
> *I'll remember your song, but I'll forget your name.'*
>
> > *The words that I sang blew off like the leaves in the wind*
> > *and perched like birds in the branches before landing on the bone again.*
>
> *Then the bone was quiet, it said no more to me*
> *So I wrapped it in the ribbons of a sycamore tree.*
> *And as night had come I turned around and headed home*
> *With a lightness in my step and a song in my bones.*
>
> > *'Lucky are you who finds me in the wilderness*
> > *I am the only unquiet ghost that does not seek rest.'*

♫ Josh Ritter, *Bone of Song* (2003)

Notes

1 This is why, for instance, despite my obvious indebtedness to Noam Chomsky – not only because of his massive influence on Western thought in general, but also because most of the members of my PhD dissertation committee were his former students – his name does not appear in the list.

2 MFN stands for 'most favo(u)red nation', also *Money for Nothing* (Knopfler). Much the same thing, as it turns out.

References

Abe, J. (2014). *A Movement Theory of Anaphora*. Studies in Generative Grammar, vol. 120. Boston, MA, and Berlin: Walter de Gruyter.

Abney, S. (1987). The English noun-phrase in its sentential aspect. PhD dissertation, Massachusetts Institute of Technology.

Abrahamsson, N. (2012). Age of onset and native-like L2 ultimate attainment of morphosyntactic and phonetic intuition. *Studies in Second Language Acquisition* 34: 187–214.

Adger, D. (2013). Constructions are not explanations. *Lingbuzz* 001675. http://ling.auf.net/lingbuzz/001675

Aitchison, J. (2003). Psycholinguistic perspectives on language change. In B. Joseph and R. Janda, eds, *The Handbook of Historical Linguistics*, pp. 736–43. Oxford: Blackwell.

Akhtar, N. and Tomasello, M. (1997). Young children's productivity with word order and verb morphology. *Developmental Psychology* 33 (6): 952–65.

Alario, F.-X., Costa, A., Ferreira, S. V. and Pickering, M. J. (2006). Architectures, representations and processes of language production. *Language and Cognitive Processes* 21: 777–89.

Allen, J. and Seidenberg, M. S. (1999). The emergence of grammaticality in connectionist networks. In B. MacWhinney, ed., *The Emergence of Language*, pp. 115–52. Mahwah, NJ: Lawrence Erlbaum.

Altmann, G. T. M. (1989). Parsing and interpretation: An introduction. *Language and Cognitive Processes* 4: SI1–SI19.

(1998). Ambiguity in sentence processing. *Trends in Cognitive Science* 2 (4): 146–51.

Alves, M. (1999). What's so Chinese about Vietnamese? In G. Thurgood, ed., *Papers from the Ninth Annual Meeting of the South East Asian Linguistics Society 1999*, pp. 221–41. Arizona: Arizona State University.

Ambridge, B., Pine, J. M., Rowland, C. F., Chang, F. and Bidgood, A. (2013). The retreat from overgeneralization in child language acquisition: Word learning, morphology, and verb argument structure. *Wiley Interdisciplinary Reviews: Cognitive Science* 4 (1): 47–62.

Andersen, H. (1978). Perceptual and conceptual factors in abductive innovations. In J. Fisiak, ed., *Recent Developments in Historical Phonology*, pp. 1–22. The Hague: Mouton.

Andersson, L.-G. (1998). Some languages are harder than others. In L. Bauer and P. Trudgill, eds, *Language Myths*, pp. 50–7. London: Penguin.

Andics, A., Gábor, A., Gácsi, M., Faragó, T., Szabó, D. and Miklósi, Á. (2016). Neural mechanisms for lexical processing in dogs. *Science* 353 (6303): 1030–32.

Andreou, G. and Katsarou, D. (2013). Language learning in children with Down Syndrome: Receptive and expressive morphosyntactic abilities. *Procedia: Social and Behavioral Sciences* 93: 921–4.

Aoun, J., Hornstein, N., Lightfoot, D. and Weinberg, A. (1987). Two types of locality. *Linguistic Inquiry* 18: 537–78.

Aoun, J. and Li, Y.-H. A. (1989). Scope and constituency. *Linguistic Inquiry* 20: 141–72.

(1993). *The Syntax of Scope.* Cambridge, MA: MIT Press.

Aronoff, M. (1976). *Word Formation in Generative Grammar.* Cambridge, MA: MIT Press.

Authier, J.-M. (1992). Iterated CPs and embedded topicalization. *Linguistic Inquiry* 23: 329–36.

Axel, K. and Kitziak, T. (2007). Contributing to the extraction/parenthesis debate: Judgement data and historical data. In S. Featherston and W. Sternefeld, eds, *Roots: Linguistics in Search of its Evidential Base*, pp. 29–52. Berlin: Mouton de Gruyter.

Bacon, R. (E. Nolan, ed.) (1902). *Grammatica Graeca [Greek Grammar].* Cambridge: Cambridge University Press.

Bailey, C.-J. N. and Maroldt, K. (1977). The French lineage of English. In J. Meisel, ed., *Pidgins – Creoles – Languages in Contact*, pp. 21–53. Tübingen: Günther Narr.

Baillargeon, R. (1987). Object permanence in 3½-and 4½-month-old infants. *Developmental Psychology* 23: 655–64.

(2002). The acquisition of physical knowledge in infancy: A summary in eight lessons. In U. Goswami, ed., *Blackwell Handbook of Childhood Cognitive Development*, pp. 46–83. Oxford: Blackwell.

Baillargeon, R., Scott, R. M. and Bian, L. (2016). Psychological reasoning in infancy. *Annual Review of Psychology* 67: 159–86.

Baker, M. (2001). *The Atoms of Language: The Mind's Hidden Rules of Grammar.* New York: Basic Books.

(2008). The macroparameter in a microparametric world. In T. Biberauer, ed., *The Limits of Syntactic Variation*, pp. 351–73. Amsterdam and Philadelphia: John Benjamins.

Baker, M., Johnson, K. and Roberts, I. (1989). Passive arguments raised. *Linguistic Inquiry* 20: 219–51.

Baltin, M. (1987). Do antecedent-contained deletions exist? *Linguistic Inquiry* 18: 579–95.

Barlow, M. and Kemmer, S. (2000). *Usage-Based Models of Language.* Stanford, CA: Center for the Study of Language and Information.

Barton, E. (1986). Interacting models: Constituent structures and constituent utterances. In A. M. Farley, P. T. Farley and K.-E. McCullough, eds, *CLS 22: Papers from the Parasession on Pragmatics and Grammatical Theory*, pp. 140–51. Chicago: Chicago Linguistic Society.

Basbøll, H. (2005). *The Phonology of Danish.* Oxford: Oxford University Press.

Bates, E. and Goodman, J. C. (1997). On the inseparability of grammar and the lexicon: Evidence from acquisition, aphasia and realtime processing. *Language and Cognitive Processes* 12 (5/6): 507–84.

Bauer, H. H. (1994). *Scientific Literacy and the Myth of the Scientific Method*. Urbana-Champaign, IL: University of Illinois Press.

Behme, C. (2013). Remarks on recursive misrepresentations by Legate et al. (2013). *Lingbuzz* 001840. http://ling.auf.net/lingbuzz/001840

(2014). A 'Galilean' science of language. *Journal of Linguistics* 50: 671–704.

Berent, I., Brem, A.-K., Zhao, X., Seligson, E., Pan, H., Epstein, J., Stern, E., Galaburda, A. M. and Pascual-Leone, A. (2015). Role of the motor system in language knowledge. *Proceedings of the National Academy of Sciences* 112: 1983–8.

Berk, S. (2003). Why *why* is different. In B. Beachley, A. Brown and F. Conlin, eds, *Boston University Conference on Language Development*, vol. 27, pp. 127–37. Somerville, MA: Cascadilla Press.

Berko, J. (1958). The child's learning of English morphology. *Word* 14: 150–77.

Berko, J. and Brown, R. (1960). Word association and the acquisition of grammar. *Child Development* 31: 1–14.

van Berkum, J. J. A. (1996). *The Psycholinguistics of Grammatical Gender*. Nijmegen: Nijmegen University Press.

Bernstein, B. (2004). *Class, Codes and Control*, vol. 2: *Applied Studies Towards a Sociology of Language*. Abingdon, UK, and New York: Routledge. Originally published 1973.

Bever, T. G. (1970). The cognitive basis for linguistic structures. In J. R. Hays, ed., *The Development of Language*, pp. 279–362. New York: Wiley.

Bever, T. G. and McElree, B. (1988). Empty categories access their antecedents during comprehension. *Linguistic Inquiry* 19: 34–43.

Bley-Vroman, R. (1990). The logical problem of foreign language learning. *Linguistic Analysis* 20: 3–49.

Bley-Vroman, R., Felix, S. and Ioup, G. (1988). The accessibility of Universal Grammar in adult language learning. *Second Language Research* 4: 1–32.

Bloomfield, L. (1933). *Language*. New York: Holt, Rinehart and Winston.

Bobaljik, J. (2012). *Universals of Comparative Morphology*. Cambridge, MA: MIT Press.

(2015). Distributed morphology. Manuscript, University of Connecticut.

Bobaljik, J. and Wurmbrand, S. (2008). Case in GB/minimalism. In A. Malchukov and A. Spencer, eds, *Handbook of Case*, pp. 44–58. Oxford: Oxford University Press.

Bock, K. (1986). Syntactic persistence in language production. *Cognitive Psychology* 18: 355–87.

Boeckx, C. (2006). *Linguistic Minimalism: Origins, Concepts, Methods and Aims*. Oxford: Oxford University Press.

(2008). *Bare Syntax*. Oxford: Oxford University Press.

(2009). *Language in Cognition: Uncovering Mental Structures and the Rule Behind Them*. Malden, MA: Wiley-Blackwell.

Bolhuis, J. J., Okanoya, K. and Scharff, C. (2010). Twitter evolution: Converging mechanisms in birdsong and human speech. *Nature Reviews Neuroscience* 11: 747–59.

Bölte, J. and Connine, C. M. (2004). Grammatical gender in spoken word recognition in German. *Perception & Psychophysics* 66: 1018–32.

Bonet, E. and Harbour, D. (2012). Contextual allomorphy. In J. Trommer, ed., *The Morphology and Phonology of Exponence*, pp. 195–235. Oxford: Oxford University Press.

Bonneville-Roussy, A., Rentfrow, P. J., Xu, M. K. and Potter, J. (2013). Music through the ages: Trends in musical engagement and preferences from adolescence through middle adulthood. *Journal of Personality and Social Psychology* 105: 703–17.

Borer, H. (1988). On the morphological parallelism between compounds and constructs. *Yearbook of Morphology* 1: 45–66.

Boroditsky, L. (2001). Does language shape thought?: Mandarin and English speakers' conceptions of time. *Cognitive Psychology* 43: 1–22.

Boroditsky, L., Schmidt, L. A. and Phillips, W. (2003). Sex, syntax, and semantics. In D. Gentner and S. Goldin-Meadow, eds, *Language in Mind: Advances in the Study of Language and Cognition*, pp. 61–79. Cambridge, MA: MIT Press.

Borsche, T. (1990). *Wilhelm Von Humboldt*. Munich: C. H. Beck.

Bouton, L. F. (1970). Antecedent-contained pro-forms. In M. A. Campbell, J. Lindholm, A. Davison, W. Fisher, L. Furbee, J. Lovins, E. Maxwell, J. Reighard and S. Straight, eds, *Proceedings of Sixth Regional Meeting of the Chicago Linguistic Society*, pp. 154–67. Chicago: University of Chicago.

Bowerman, M. (1982). Reorganizational processes in lexical and syntactic development. In E. Wanner and L. Gleitman, eds, *Language Acquisition: The State of the Art*, pp. 319–46. Cambridge: Cambridge University Press.

(1988). The 'no negative evidence' problem: How do children avoid constructing an overly general grammar? In J. A. Hawkins, ed., *Explaining Language Universals*, pp. 73–104. Oxford: Blackwell.

Bowerman, M. and Choi, S. (2001). Shaping meanings for language: Universal and language-specific in the acquisition of spatial semantic categories. In M. Bowerman and S. Levinson, eds, *Language Acquisition and Conceptual Development*, pp. 475–511. Cambridge: Cambridge University Press.

Bransford, J. D. and Franks, J. J. (1971). The abstraction of linguistic ideas. *Cognitive Psychology* 2: 231–350.

Bresnan, J. (1971). Sentence stress and syntactic transformations. *Language* 47 (2): 257–81.

Brooks, P. J., Tomasello, M., Dodson, K. and Lewis, L. B. (1999). Young children's overgeneralizations with fixed transitivity verbs. *Child Development* 70: 1325–37.

Brown, C. (1997). Acquisition of segmental structure: Consequences for speech perception and second language acquisition. PhD thesis, Department of Linguistics, McGill University.

(2000). The interrelation between speech perception and phonological acquisition from infant to adult. In J. Archibald, ed., *Second Language Acquisition and Linguistic Theory*, pp. 4–63. Malden, MA: Blackwell.

Brown, H. D. (2007). *Principles of Language Learning and Teaching*. New York: Longman.

Bruening, B. and Tran, T. (2006). Wh-questions in Vietnamese. *Journal of East Asian Linguistics* 15: 319–41.

Bryson, B. (2005). *A Short History of Nearly Everything*. New York: Broadway Books/ Random House.

Bybee, J. (2010). *Language, Usage and Cognition*. Cambridge: Cambridge University Press.

Bybee, J. and Hopper, P. J., eds (2001a). *Frequency and the Emergence of Linguistic Structure*. Amsterdam: John Benjamins.

Bybee, J. and Hopper, P. J. (2001b). Introduction to frequency and the emergence of linguistic structure. In J. L. Bybee and P. J. Hopper, eds, *Frequency and the Emergence of Linguistic Structure*, pp. 1–24. Amsterdam: John Benjamins.

Bybee, J. and Thompson, S. A. (1997). Three frequency effects in syntax. In *Proceedings of the Annual Meeting of Berkeley Linguistics Society: General Session and Parasession on Pragmatics and Grammatical Structure*, pp. 378–88. Berkeley, CA: Berkeley Linguistics Society.

Byrne, D. (2010). Song lyrics are overrated. *CNN Online*.

Cahill, L. and Gazdar, G. (1999). German noun inflection. *Journal of Linguistics* 35: 1–42.

Cahill, T. (1995). *How the Irish Saved Civilization: The Untold Story of Ireland's Heroic Role from the Fall of Rome to the Rise of Medieval Europe*. New York and London: Anchor Books/Doubleday.

Cai, Z., Sturt, P. and Pickering, M. (2011/2012). The effect of non-adopted analyses on sentence processing. *Language, Cognition and Neuroscience* 27: 1286–311.

Callahan, S. M., Shapiro, L. P. and Love, T. (2010). Parallelism effects and verb activation: The sustained reactivation hypothesis. *Journal of Psycholinguistic Research* 39: 101–18.

Campbell, J. (2013). *Thou Art That: Transforming Religious Metaphor*. Novato, CA: New World Library.

Campbell, L. (1998). *Historical Linguistics: An Introduction*. Cambridge, MA: MIT Press.

Campbell, R. N. (2006). Language development: Pre-scientific studies. In K. Brown, ed., *Encyclopedia of Languages and Linguistics*, pp. 391–4. Oxford: Elsevier.

Cappelen, H. and Lepore, E. (2005). A tall tale: In defense of semantic minimalism and speech act pluralism. In G. Preyer and G. Peter, eds, *Contextualism in Philosophy: Knowledge, Meaning, and Truth*, pp. 197–220. Oxford: Oxford University Press.

Carnie, A. (2011). *Syntax: A Generative Introduction*, second edition. Oxford: Wiley-Blackwell.

Cedergren, H. J., Levac, L. and Perreault, H. (1992). Durational effects of prosodic structure in spontaneous spoken French. *The Journal of the Acoustical Society of America* 91 (4): 2387.

Cedergren, H. J., and Perreault, H. (1994). Speech rate and syllable timing in spontaneous speech. In *Proceedings of ICSLP '94, Yokohama*, vol. 3, 1087–90. Tokyo: Acoustical Society of Japan.

Chien, Y.-C. and Wexler, K. (1990). Children's knowledge of locality conditions in binding as evidence for the modularity of syntax and pragmatics. *Language Acquisition* 1: 225–95.

Chierchia, G. (1995). *Dynamics of Meaning: Anaphora, Presupposition and the Theory of Grammar*. Chicago: University of Chicago Press.

Choi, S. ([2009] 2015). Language specific spatial semantics and cognition: Developmental patterns in English and Korean. In C. Lee, G. B. Simpson and Y. Kim, eds, *The Handbook of East Asian Psycholinguistics*, pp. 107–26. Cambridge: Cambridge University Press.

Chomsky, N. (1957). *Syntactic Structures*. The Hague: Mouton.

(1959). A review of B. F. Skinner's *Verbal Behavior*. *Language* 35: 26–58.

(1965). *Aspects of the Theory of Syntax*. Cambridge, MA: MIT Press.

(1970). Remarks on nominalization. In R. Jacobs and P. Rosenbaum, eds, *Readings in Transformational Grammar*, pp. 184–221. Waltham, MA: Ginn and Co.

(1973). Conditions on transformations. In S. R. Anderson and P. Kiparsky, eds, *A Festschrift for Morris Halle*, pp. 232–85. New York: Holt, Rinehart and Winston.

(1977). *Essays on Form and Interpretation*. Amsterdam: Elsevier/North-Holland.

(1981). *Lectures on Government and Binding: The Pisa Lectures*, vol. 9. Dordrecht: Foris.

(1985). *Knowledge of Language: Its Nature, Origin, and Use*. New York: Praeger.

(1988). *Language and Problems of Knowledge: The Managua Lectures*. Current Studies in Linguistics, vol. 16. Cambridge, MA: MIT Press.

(1995). *The Minimalist Program*. Cambridge, MA: MIT Press.

(2001). Derivation by phrase. In M. Kenstowicz, ed., *Ken Hale: A Life in Language*. Cambridge, MA: MIT Press.

(2005). Three factors in language design. *Linguistic Inquiry* 36: 1–22.

(2008). On phases. In R. Freidin, C. Otero and M. L. Zubizarreta, eds, *Foundational Issues in Linguistic Theory: Essays in Honor of Jean-Roger Vergnaud*, pp. 133–66. Cambridge, MA: MIT Press.

(2010). *Poverty of Stimulus: Some Unfinished Business*. Paris: CNRS Images.

Chomsky, N., Belletti, A. and Rizzi, L. (2002). *On Nature and Language*. Cambridge: Cambridge University Press.

Chorost, M. (2014). Your brain on metaphors. *Chronicle of Higher Education*. http://chronicle.com/article/Your-Brain-on-Metaphors/148495/

Christiansen, M. H. and Chater, N. (2008). Language as shaped by the brain. *Behavioral and Brain Sciences* 31: 489–509.

Christodoulou, C. and Wexler, K. (2016). The morphosyntactic development of case in Down Syndrome. *Lingua* 184: 25–52.

Chung, S. and McCloskey, J. (1987). Government, barriers and small clauses in Modern Irish. *Linguistic Inquiry* 18: 173–237.

Cinque, G. (1999). *Adverbs and Functional Heads: A Cross-Linguistic Perspective*. New York: Oxford University Press.

(2002). Mapping Functional Structure. In G. Cinque, ed., *Functional Structure in the IP and DP*, pp. 3–11. New York: Oxford University Press.

(2005). Deriving Greenberg's Universal 20 and its exceptions. *Linguistic Inquiry* 36: 315–32.

Clahsen, H. and Featherston, S. (1999). Antecedent priming at trace positions: Evidence from German scrambling. *Journal of Psycholinguistic Research* 28: 415–37.

Clahsen, H. and Felser, C. (2006). Grammatical processing in language learners. *Applied Psycholinguistics* 27: 3–42.

Clahsen, H. and Muysken, P. (1986). The availability of Universal Grammar to adult and child learners: A study of the acquisition of German word order. *Second Language Research* 2: 93–119.

Clark, E. V. (1993). *The Lexicon in Acquisition*. Cambridge: Cambridge University Press.

Cocker, E. (1736). *Cocker's Arithmetick, Perused and Published by J. Hawkins*, 48th edition. London: John Hawkins.

Cohen, D. (2008). *Equations from God: Pure Mathematics and Victorian Faith*. Baltimore, MD: The Johns Hopkins University Press.

Collins, C. (1991). Why and how come. In *MIT Working Papers in Linguistics*, pp. 31–45. Cambridge, MA: MIT Working Papers in Linguistics.

Collins, J. (2011). *The Unity of Linguistic Meaning*. Oxford: Oxford University Press.

Coltheart, M. (2013). How can functional neuroimaging inform cognitive theories? *Perspectives on Psychological Science* 8: 98–103.

Coltheart, M., Rastle, K., Perry, C., Langdon, R. and Ziegler, J. (2001). DRC: A dual route cascaded model of visual word recognition and reading aloud. *Psychological Review* 108: 204–56.

Comrie, B. (1981). *Language Universals and Linguistic Typology*, second edition. Chicago: University of Chicago Press.

Conroy, A. and Lidz, J. (2007). Production/comprehension asymmetry in children's *why* questions. In A. Belikova et al., eds, *Proceedings of the 2nd Conference on Language Acquisition North America (Galana)*, pp. 73–83. Somerville, MA: Cascadilla Press.

Conroy, A. and Thornton, R. (2005). Children's knowledge of Principle C in discourse. In Y. Otsu, ed., *Proceedings of the Sixth Tokyo Conference on Psycholinguistics*, pp. 69–94. Tokyo: Hituzi Syobu.

Conway Morris, S. (2003). *Life's Solution: Inevitable Humans in a Lonely Universe*. Cambridge: Cambridge University Press.

Cook, V. (1991). The poverty-of-the-stimulus argument and multicompetence. *Second Language Research* 7: 103–17.

 (1995). Multicompetence and effects of age. In D. Singleton and Z. Lengyl, eds, *The Age Factor in Second Language Acquisition*. Clevedon, UK: Multilingual Matters.

Cooper, J. (1991). *Drug-Related Problems in Geriatric Nursing Home Patients*. New York: Pharmaceutical Products Press.

Cooper, M. and Chalfant, H. (1984). *Subway Art*. New York: Henry Holt and Company.

Corbett, G. G. (1991). *Gender, Cambridge Textbooks in Linguistics*. Cambridge: Cambridge University Press.

Corbett, G. and Fraser, N. (1993). Network morphology: A DATR account of Russian nominal inflection. *Journal of Linguistics* 29: 113–42.

Cornips, L. and Corrigan, K., eds (2005). *Syntax and Variation: Reconciling the Biological and the Social*. Amsterdam and Philadelphia: John Benjamins.

Craik, K. J. W. (1967). *The Nature of Explanation*. Cambridge: Cambridge University Press. (Original edition, 1943.)

Crain, S. (1991). Language acquisition in the absence of experience. *Behavioral and Brain Sciences* 14: 597–612.

 (1993). Language acquisition in the absence of experience. In P. Bloom, ed., *Language Acquisition: Core Readings*, pp. 364–409. New York: Harvester Wheatsheaf.

Crain, S. and McKee, C. (1985). The acquisition of structural restrictions on anaphora. In S. Berman, J.-W. Choe and J. McDonough, eds, *Proceedings of NELS 15*, pp. 94–110. Amherst, MA: GLSA Publications.

Crain, S. and Nakayama, M. (1987). Structure dependence in grammar formation. *Language* 63: 522–43.

Crain, S. and Pietroski, P. (2001). Nature, nurture and Universal Grammar. *Linguistics and Philosophy* 24: 139–86.

Crain, S. and Thornton, R. (1998). *Investigations in Universal Grammar: A Guide to Experiments on the Acquisition of Syntax*. Cambridge, MA: MIT Press.

Crisma, P. (1990). Functional categories inside the noun phrase: A study on the distribution of nominal modifiers. Tesi di Laurea, University of Venice.

Croft, W. (2001). *Radical Construction Grammar: Syntactic Theory in Typological Perspective*. Oxford: Oxford University Press.

Culicover, P. (1993). Evidence against ECP accounts of the *that*-trace effect. *Linguistic Inquiry* 24: 557–61.

(1998). The minimalist impulse. In P. W. Culicover and L. McNally, eds, *The Limits of Syntax*, pp. 44–77. New York: Academic Press.

(1999). *Syntactic Nuts: Hard Cases, Syntactic Theory and Language Acquisition*. Oxford: Oxford University Press.

Culicover, P. and Jackendoff, R. (2005). *Simpler Syntax*. Oxford: Oxford University Press.

Cutler, A., ed. (2005). *Twenty-First Century Psycholinguistics: Four Cornerstones*. Mahwah, NJ: Lawrence Erlbaum.

Cutler, A. (2015). *Native Listening: Language Experience and the Recognition of Spoken Words*. Cambridge, MA: MIT Press.

Cutler, A., Dahan, D. and Van Donselaar, W. (1997). Prosody in the comprehension of spoken language: A literature review. *Language and Speech* 40: 141–201.

Cutler, A. and Norris, D. (1988). The role of strong syllables in segmentation for lexical access. *Journal of Experimental Psychology: Human Perception and Performance* 14: 113–21.

Cutler, A. and Otake, T. (1994). Mora or phoneme? Further evidence for language-specific listening. *Journal of Memory and Language* 33: 824–844.

Dabrowska, E. (2001). Learning a morphological system without a default: the Polish genitive. *Journal of Child Language* 28: 545–74.

Dabrowska, E. and Street, J. (2006). Individual differences in language attainment: Comprehension of passive sentences by native and non-native English speakers. *Language Sciences* 28: 604–15.

Dahan, D., Swingley, D., Tanenhaus, M. and Magnuson, J. S. (2000). Linguistic gender and spoken-word recognition in French. *Journal of Memory and Language* 42: 465–80.

Darwin, E. (1794). *Zoonomia, or the Laws of Organic Life*, vol. II (third edition 1801). London: J. Johnson. Cited in Ridley (1999: 12).

de Carvalho, A., Lidz, J., Tieu, L., Bleam, T. and Christophe, A. (2016). English-speaking preschoolers can use phrasal prosody for syntactic parsing. *The Journal of the Acoustical Society of America* 139 (6): EL216-EL22.

de Villiers, J. D. and Pyers, J. E. (2002). Complements to cognition: A longitudinal study of the relationship between complex syntax and false-belief-understanding. *Cognitive Development* 17: 1037–60.

Dehaene, S. and Cohen, L. (1991). Two mental calculation systems: A case study of severe acalculia with preserved approximation. *Neuropsychologia* 29: 1045–54.

Deprez, V. and Pierce, A. (1993). Negation and functional projections in early grammar. *Linguistic Inquiry* 24: 25–67.

Desai, R. H., Binder, J. R., Conant, L. L., Mano, Q. R. and Seidenberg, M. S. (2011). The neural career of sensory-motor metaphors. *Journal of Cognitive Neuroscience* 23: 2376–86.

Devlin, K. (1998). *The Language of Mathematics: Making the Invisible Visible.* New York: Henry Holt and Company.

Dixon, J. A., Mahoney, B. and Cocks, R. (2002). Accents of guilt? Effects of regional accent, 'race' and crime type on attributions of guilt. *Journal of Language and Social Psychology* 21: 162–8.

Dobler, T. (2013). Ever the twain shall meet? *Croatian Journal of Philosophy* XIII (38): 293–311.

Doherty, C. (1994). The syntax of subject contact relatives. In K. Beals, ed., *Proceedings of the Twenty-Ninth Meeting of the Chicago Linguistic Society*, pp. 55–65. Chicago: University of Chicago Press.

(2013). *Clauses without 'That': The Case for Bare Sentential Complementation in English.* Abingdon, UK, and New York: Routledge. Originally published in 2000 by Garland Publishing.

Dromi, E. (1987). *Early Lexical Development.* Cambridge: Cambridge University Press.

Duffield, N. (1993). On Case-checking and NPI licensing in Hiberno-English. *Rivista di Linguistica* 5: 215–44.

(1996). On structural invariance and lexical diversity in VSO languages: Arguments from Irish noun-phrases. In R. Borsley and I. Roberts, eds, *The Syntax of the Celtic Languages*, pp. 314–40. Cambridge: Cambridge University Press.

(2003). Measures of competent gradience. In R. van Hout, A. Hulk, F. Kuiken and R. Towell, eds, *The Lexicon–Syntax Interface in Second Language Acquisition*, pp. 97–127. Amsterdam and Philadelphia: John Benjamins.

(2004). Implications of competent gradience. *Moderne Sprachen* 45: 95–117.

(2010). Roll up for the mystery tour! *Lingua* 120: 2673–5.

(2013). On polarity emphasis, assertion and mood in English and Vietnamese. *Lingua* 137: 248–70.

(2014). Shake can well. *Lingbuzz* 002119. http://ling.auf.net/lingbuzz/002119

(2015). On what projects. *Lingbuzz* 002429. http://ling.auf.net/lingbuzz/002429

(2016). Seeing names, hearing faces: A cross-modal investigation of perceptual narrowing in second language learners. Paper presented at PacSLRF 2016, Chuo University, Tokyo.

(2017a). On what projects in Vietnamese. *Journal of East Asian Lingusitics* (in press).

(2017b). Which *Other Race Effect*? Cross-linguistic and cross-modal asymmetries in perceptual narrowing. Manuscript, Konan University.

Duffield, N., Matsuo, A. and Roberts, L. (2010). Factoring out the parallelism effect in VP-ellipsis: English vs. Dutch contrasts. *Second Language Research* 25 (4), 427–67.

Durham, M. (2011). Right dislocation in Northern England: Frequency and use – perception meets reality. *English World-Wide* 32 (3): 257–79.

Durrell, M. (2011). *Hammer's German Grammar and Usage*, fifth edition. Abingdon, UK, and New York: Routledge.

Eco, U. (1993). *La Ricerca Della Lingua Perfetta.* Rome and Bari: Editori Laterza.

Edwards, H. T. and Kirkpatrick, A. G. (1999). Metalinguistic awareness in children: A developmental progression. *Journal of Psycholinguistic Research* 28: 313–29.

Einstein, A. (1934). On the method of theoretical physics: The Herbert Spencer lecture. *Philosophy of Science* 1 (2): 163–9.

Eisenbeiss, S. (2000). The acquisition of the determiner phrase in German child language. In M.-A. Friedemann and L. Rizzi, eds, *The Acquisition of Syntax*. London: Longman.

(2002). Merkmalsgesteuerter Grammatikerwerb: Eine Untersuchung zum Erwerb der Struktur und Flexion von Nominalphrasen. PhD dissertation, Linguistics Department, Heinrich Heine-Universität, Düsseldorf.

Ellegård, A. (1953). *The Auxiliary Do: The Establishment and Regulation of Its Use in English*. Gothenburg Studies in English, vols 2, 3. Stockholm: Almqvist & Wiksell.

Ellis, A. W. and Young, A. W. (1988). *Human Cognitive Neuropsychology*. Hove: Lawrence Erlbaum.

Elman, J. L. (1993). Learning and development in neural networks: The importance of starting small. *Cognition* 48: 71–99.

Elman, J. L., Bates, E. A., Johnson, M. H., Karmiloff-Smith, A., Parisi, D. and Plunkett, K. (1996). *Rethinking Innateness: A Connectionist Perspective on Development*. Cambridge, MA: MIT Press.

Embick, D. and Marantz, A. (2005). Cognitive neuroscience and the English past tense: Comments on the paper by Ullman et al. *Brain and Language* 93: 243–7.

Embick, D. and Noyer, R. (2007). Distributed morphology and the syntax–morphology interface. In G. Ramchand and C. Reiss, eds, *Oxford Handbook of Linguistic Interfaces*, pp. 289–324. Oxford: Oxford University Press.

Embick, D. and Poeppel, D. (2015). Towards a computational(ist) neurobiology of language: Correlational, integrated, and explanatory neurolinguistics. *Language, Cognition and Neuroscience* 30: 357–66.

Eppler, E. D. and Ozón, G. (2013). *English Words and Sentences: An Introduction*. Cambridge: Cambridge University Press.

Epstein, S. D., Flynn, S. and Martohardjono, G. (1996). Second language acquisition: Theoretical and experimental issues in contemporary research. *Brain and Behavioral Sciences* 19: 677–714.

Epstein, S. D. and Seely, T. D. (2006). *Derivations in Minimalism*. Cambridge: Cambridge University Press.

Erteschik-Shir, N. (1997). *The Dynamics of Focus Structure*. Cambridge: Cambridge University Press.

Etcoff, N. (1999). *Survival of the Prettiest: The Science of Beauty*. London: Abacus Books.

Evans, G. (1982). *The Varieties of Reference*. Oxford: Oxford University Press.

Evans, N. and Levinson, S. (2009). The myth of Language Universals: Language diversity and its importance for cognitive science. *Behavioral and Brain Sciences* 32: 429–92.

Everett, D. L. (2005). Cultural constraints on grammar and cognition in Pirahã. *Current Anthropology* 46: 621–46.

(2009). Pirahã culture and grammar: A response to some criticisms. *Language* 85: 405–42.

(2013). *Language: The Cultural Tool*. London: Profile Books.

Eysenck, M. (1984). *A Handbook of Cognitive Psychology*. London and Hillsdale, NJ: Lawrence Erlbaum.

Fabri, R. (1993). *Kongruenz und die Grammatik des Maltesischen [Agreement and the Grammar of Maltese]*. Tübingen: Max Niemeyer Verlag.

Fassi Fehri, A. (1999). Arabic modifying adjectives and DP structures. *Studia Linguistica* 53: 105–54.

Fay, D. and Cutler, A. (1977). Malapropisms and the structure of the mental lexicon. *Linguistic Inquiry* 8: 505–20.

Fearon, J. D. (2003). Ethnic and cultural diversity by country. *Journal of Economic Growth* 8: 195–222.

Featherston, S. (2001). *Empty Categories in Sentence Processing*. Linguistik Aktuell/ Linguistics Today, vol. 43. Amsterdam: John Benjamins.

(2007). Data in generative grammar: The stick and the carrot. *Theoretical Linguistics* 33: 269–318.

Ferreira, F., Ferraro, V. and Bailey, K. G. D. (2002). Good-enough representations in language comprehension. *Current Directions in Psychological Science* 11: 11–5.

Ferreira, F. and Patson, N. D. (2007). The 'good enough' approach to language comprehension. *Language and Linguistics Compass* 1: 71–83.

Ferreira, V. S. (2006). How are speakers' linguistic choices affected by ambiguity? In A. S. Meyer, A. Krott and L. R. Wheeldon, eds, *Automaticity and Control in Language Processing*, pp. 63–92. Hove: Psychology Press.

Ferreira, V. S. and Bock, K. (2006). The functions of structural priming. *Language and Cognitive Processes* 21: 1011–29.

Ferreira, V. S. and Dell, G. S. (2000). The effect of ambiguity and lexical availability on syntactic and lexical production. *Cognitive Psychology* 40: 296–340.

Ferreira, V. S., Slevc, L. R. and Rogers, E. S. (2005). How do speakers avoid ambiguous linguistic expressions? *Cognition* 96: 263–94.

Fillmore, C. J., Kay, P. and O'Connor, M. C. (1988). Regularity and Idiomaticity in grammatical constructions: The case of *let alone*. *Language* 64: 501–38.

Fisher, S. E. and Scharff, C. (2009). FOXP2 as a molecular window into speech and language. *Trends in Genetics* 25: 166–77.

Fisher, S. E., Vargha-Khadem, F., Watkins, K. E., Monaco, A. P. and Pembrey, M. E. (1998). Localisation of a gene implicated in a severe speech and language disorder. *Nat Genet* 18: 168–70.

Flege, J. E., Takagi, N. and Mann, V. (1996). Lexical familiarity and English-language experience affects Japanese adults' perception of /ɹ/ and /L/. *Journal of the Acoustical Society of America* 99: 1161–73.

Flege, J. E., Yeni-Komshian, G. H. and Liu, S. (1999). Age constraints on second language acquisition. *Journal of Memory and Language* 41: 78–104.

Fodor, J. A. (1975). *The Language of Thought*. Cambridge, MA: Harvard University Press.

(1981). The present status of the innateness controversy. In *RePresentations: Philosophical Essays on the Foundations of Cognitive Science*. Cambridge, MA: MIT Press.

(1998). *Concepts: Where Cognitive Science Went Wrong*. New York: Oxford University Press.

Fodor, J. A., Bever, T. G. and Garrett, M. F. (1974). *The Psychology of Language*. New York: McGraw-Hill.

Fodor, J. A. and Garrett, M. F. (1967). Some syntactic determinants of sentential complexity. *Perception & Psychophysics* 2: 289–96.

Fodor, J. D. (1998). Learning to parse? *Journal of Psycholinguistic Research* 27: 285–319.

(2002). Prosodic disambiguation in silent reading. In M. Hirotani, ed., *Proceedings of NELS 32*, vol. 1, pp. 113–32. Amherst, MA: GLSA Publications.

Foley, W. A. and Van Valin, R. D. (1984). *Functional Syntax and Universal Grammar*. Cambridge: Cambridge University Press.

Frank, S. L., Bod, R. and Christiansen, M. H. (2012). How hierarchical is language use? *Proceedings of the Royal Society B* 279: 4522–31.

Fraser, N. and Corbett, G. (1997). Defaults in Arapesh. *Lingua* 103: 25–57.

Frazier, L. (1990). Exploring the architecture of the language processing System. In G. T. M. Altmann, ed., *Cognitive Models of Speech Processing*, pp. 409–33. Cambridge, MA: MIT Press.

Frazier, L. and Flores d'Arcais, G. (1989). Filler driven parsing: A study of gap filling in Dutch. *Journal of Memory and Language* 28: 331–44.

Frazier, L., Taft, L., Roeper, T., Clifton, C. and Ehrlich, K. (1984). Parallel structure: A source of facilitation in sentence comprehension. *Memory and Cognition* 12: 421–30.

Freeborn, D. (2005). *From Old English to Standard English: A Course Book in Language Variations across Time*. London: Palgrave Macmillan.

Frege, G. ([1892] 1952). On sense and reference. In P. Geach and M. Black, eds, *Translations from the Philosophical Writings of Gottlob Frege*. Oxford: Blackwell.

Friederici, A. D. (2002). Towards a neural basis of auditory sentence processing. *Trends in Cognitive Sciences* 6: 78–84.

Fromkin, V. and Rodman, R. (1993). *An Introduction to Language*, fifth edition. New York: Harcourt Brace Jovanovich.

Fruchter, J., Stockall, L. and Marantz, A. (2013). MEG masked priming evidence for form-based decomposition of irregular verbs. *Frontiers in Human Neuroscience* 7: 798.

Fujita, K. (1996). Double objects, causatives and derivational economy. *Linguistic Inquiry* 27: 146–73.

Gabrielli, L. H., Cardenas, J., Poitras, C. B. and Lipson, M. (2009). Cloaking at optical frequencies. arXiv:0904.3508v1 [physics.optics].

Gardner, R. C. (2010). *Motivation and Second Language Acquisition*. New York: Peter Lang.

Gass, S. M. and Selinker, L. (2001). *Second Language Acquisition: An Introductory Course*. Abingdon, UK, and New York: Routledge.

Gattuso, J. (2005). *The Lotus Still Blooms: Sacred Buddhist Teachings for the Western Mind*. New York: Jeremy P. Tarcher/Penguin USA.

Gauvenet, H., Hassan, M., Gross, H. and Mason, B. (1963). *Bonjour Line: An Audio-Visual French Course for Children Starting at Primary Level*. London: G.G. Harrap.

van Gelderen, E. (2000). The absence of verb-movement and the role of C: Some negative constructions in Shakespeare. *Studia Linguistica* 54: 412–23.

Gentner, D. and Stevens, A. L., eds (1983). *Mental Models*. New York and London: Psychology Press.

Geuder, W. and Weisgerber, M. (2006). Manner and causation in movement verbs. In C. Ebert and C. Endriss, eds, *Proceedings of Sinn und Bedeutung 10*, pp. 125–38. ZAS Papers in Linguistics. Berlin: Zentrum für Allgemeine Sprachwissenschaft, Sprachtypologie und Universalienforschung.

Gibson, E., Piantadosi, S. T. and Fedorenko, E. (2013). Quantitative methods in syntax/ semantics research: A response to Sprouse and Almeida (2013). *Language and Cognitive Processes* 28: 229–40.

Gladwell, M. (2013). *David and Goliath: Underdogs, Misfits and the Art of Battling Giants*. New York: Little, Brown and Company.

Gleitman, H. and Gleitman, L. R. (1979). Language use and language judgment. In C. J. Fillmore, D. Kempler and W. S. Wang, eds, *Individual Differences in Language Ability and Language Behavior*, pp. 103–26. New York: Academic Press.

Goddard, C. and Wierzbicka, A. (2002). Semantic primes and Universal Grammar. In C. Goddard and A. Wierzbicka, eds, *Meaning and Universal Grammar: Theory and Empirical Findings*, pp. 41–85. Amsterdam and Philadelphia: John Benjamins.

Goethe, J. W. von ([1821] 1907). *Maximen und Reflexionen, Aphorismen und Aufzeichnungen: Nach den Handschriften des Goethe-und-Schiller-Archivs*, vol. 3: *Aus Kunst und Altertum*. Edited by M. Hecker. Weimar: Verlag der Goethe-Gesellschaft.

Goldberg, A. E. (1995). *Construction Grammar: A Construction Grammar Approach to Argument Structure*. Chicago: University of Chicago Press.

  (2006). *Constructions at Work: The Nature of Generalization in Language*. Oxford: Oxford University Press.

Gombert, J. E. (1992). *Metalinguistic Development*. Translated by T. Pownall. New York: Harvester Wheatsheaf.

Goodluck, H. and Zweig, E. (2013). Introduction: Formal vs. processing explanations of linguistic phenomena. *Language and Cognitive Processes* 28: 1–8.

Gopnik, M. (1990). Feature-blind grammar and dysphasia. *Nature* 344: 715.

Gopnik, M. and Crago, M. B. (1991). Familial aggregation of a developmental language disorder. *Cognition* 39: 1–50.

Goto, H. (1971). Auditory perception by normal Japanese adults of the sounds 'L' and 'R'. *Neuropsychologia* 9: 317–23.

Gould, S. J. (1987). *An Urchin in the Storm*. London: W. W. Norton and Company.

  (2002). *The Structure of Evolutionary Theory*. Cambridge, MA: Harvard University Press.

Gould, S. J. and Eldredge, N. (1977). Punctuated equilibria: The tempo and mode of evolution reconsidered. *Paleobiology* 3: 115–51.

Greenberg, J. H. (1963). Some universals of grammar with particular reference to the order of meaningful elements. In J. H Greenberg, ed., *Universals of Language*, pp. 58–90. Cambridge, MA: MIT Press.

Greenleaf, A., Lassas, M. and Uhlmann, G. (2003). Anisotropic conductivities that cannot be detected by EIT. *Physiol. Meas.* 24: 413–19.

Gregg, K. R. (1984). Krashen's monitor and Occam's razor. *Applied Linguistics* 5: 79–100.

Grice, H. P. ([1975] 1989). Logic and conversation. In P. Cole and J. L. Morgan, eds, *Syntax and Semantics III: Speech Acts*, pp. 41–58. New York: Academic Press.

Guasti, M.-T. (2004). *Language Acquisition: The Growth of Grammar*. Cambridge, MA: MIT Press.

Gussenhoven, C. (1984). *On the Grammar and Semantics of Sentence Accents*. Dordrecht: Foris.

Hackl, M., Koster-Hale, J. and Varvoutis, J. (2012). Quantification and ACD: Evidence from real time sentence processing. *Journal of Semantics* 29: 145–206.

Haden, E. F. (1955). The uvular r in French. *Language* 31: 504–10.

Haeberli, E. and Ihsane, T. (2016). Revisiting the loss of verb movement in the history of English. *Natural Language & Linguistic Theory* 34: 497–542.

Haiman, J. and Thompson, S. A., eds (1988). *Clause Combining in Grammar and Discourse*. Typological Studies in Language, vol. 18. Amsterdam and Philadelphia: John Benjamins.

Halliday, M. A. K. (1970). *A Course in Spoken English: Intonation*. Oxford: Oxford University Press.

(2005). *On Grammar*. London: Bloomsbury Academic.

Hambrich, D. Z., Macnamara, B.N., Campitelli, G., Ullén, F., and Mosing, M. A. (2016). Beyond born vs. made: a new look at expertise. In B. H. Hall, ed., *Psychology of Learning and Motivation*, vol. 64, pp. 1–55. Cambridge, MA: Academic Press.

Han, C.-H. (2000). The evolution of *do*-support in English imperatives. In S. Pintzuk, G. Tsoulas and A. R. Warner, eds, *Diachronic Syntax: Models and Mechanisms*, pp. 275–95. Oxford: Oxford University Press.

Han, C.-H. and Kroch, A. S. (2000). The rise of *do*-support in English: Implications for clause-structure. In M. Hirotani, A. Coetzee, N. Hall and J.-Y. Kim, eds, *Proceedings of NELS 30*, pp. 311–26. Amherst, MA: GLSA Publications.

Hankamer, J. (1971). Deletion in coordinate structures. PhD dissertation, Yale University.

(1979). *Deletion in Coordinate Structures*. New York: Garland.

Hankamer, J. and Sag, I. (1976). Deep and surface anaphora. *Linguistic Inquiry* 7: 391–428.

Hansell, M. (2007). *Built by Animals: The Natural History of Animal Architecture*. Oxford: Oxford University Press.

Harbour, D. (2015). Untitled (segment). *More than Words: Morphology and the Universality of language*. Symposium at NYU Abu Dhabi Institute. www.youtube.com/watch?v=39Gpbm9qgzs

Hardt, D. (1993). Verb phrase ellipsis: Form, meaning and processing. PhD dissertation, Computer and Information Science, University of Pennsylvania.

Harley, H. (1995). Subjects, events, and licensing. PhD dissertation, Department of Linguistics and Philosophy, Massachusetts Institute of Technology.

Harmon, D. and Loh, J. (2010). The index of linguistic diversity: A new quantitative measure of trends in the status of the world's languages. *Language Documentation & Conservation* 4: 97–151.

Harris, M. and Coltheart, M. (1986). *Language Processing in Adults and Children*. London: Routledge and Kegan Paul.

Hartshorne, J. K. and Ullman, M. T. (2006). Why do girls say 'holded' more than boys? *Developmental Science* 9: 21–32.

Haspelmath, M. (2000). Why can't we talk to each other? *Lingua* 110: 235–55.

Hawkins, J. A. (1983). *Word Order Universals*. New York: Academic Press.

(1995). *A Performance Theory of Order and Constituency*. Cambridge Studies in Linguistics, vol. 73. Cambridge: Cambridge University Press.

(2001). Why are categories adjacent? *Journal of Linguistics* 37: 1–34.

Hawkins, P. R. (2004). Hesitation phenomena and pausing. In B. Bernstein, ed., *Class, Codes and Control*, vol. 2: *Applied Studies Towards a Sociology of Language*. Taylor & Francis (originally published 1973).

Hayes, B. (1982). Extrametricality and English stress. *Linguistic Inquiry* 13: 227–76.

Hegarty, M. (2005). *A Feature-Based Syntax of Functional Categories*. Berlin: De Gruyter.

Henrich, J., Heine, S. J. and Norenzayan, A. (2010). The weirdest people in the world? *Behavioral and Brain Sciences* 33: 61–135.

Henry, A. (1995). *Dialect Variation and Parameter-Setting: A Study of Belfast English and Standard English*. Oxford: Oxford University Press.

Heycock, C. (2013). The syntax of predication. In M. den Dikken, ed., *The Cambridge Handbook of Generative Syntax*, pp. 322–52. Cambridge: Cambridge University Press.

Hill, T. (2015). *Geometry and Faith: A Supplement to the Ninth Bridgewater Treatise – Scholar's Choice Edition*. BiblioLife.

Hiramatsu, K. and Lillo-Martin, D. (1998). Children who judge ungrammatical what they produce. Paper presented at *Boston University Conference on Child Language Development*.

Hoffman, A. (2016). Dogs know when you're praising them: That doesn't mean they understand human speech. *The Smithsonian*, 2 September 2016. www .smithsonianmag.com/science-nature/scientists-say-dogs-understand-human-speech-how-can-we-be-sure-180960336/

Hofmeister, P., Casasanto, L. S. and Sag, I. A. (2013a). Islands in the grammar? Standards of evidence. In J. Sprouse and N. Hornstein, eds, *Experimental Syntax and the Islands Debate*, pp. 42–63. Cambridge: Cambridge University Press.

Hofmeister, P., Jaeger, T. F., Arnon, I., Sag, I. A. and Snider, N. (2013b). The source ambiguity problem: Distinguishing the effects of grammar and processing on acceptability judgments. *Language and Cognitive Processes* 28: 48–87.

Hogenboom, M. (2014). Spectacular real virgin births. *BBC Online*. www.bbc.com/ earth/story/20141219-spectacular-real-virgin-births

Hogg, R. and Denison, D., eds (2006). *A History of the English Language*. Cambridge: Cambridge University Press.

Hopper, P. J. (1987). Emergent grammar. In *Proceedings of the 13th Annual Meeting of the Berkeley Linguistics Society*. Berkeley, CA: Berkeley Linguistics Society.

Hornstein, N. (2012). Why this blog? *Faculty of Language*. http://facultyoflanguage. blogspot.com/2012_09_01_archive.html

Hovdhaugen, E. (1990). *Una et eadem*: Some observations on Roger Bacon's Greek grammar. In G. L. Bursill-Hall, S. Ebbesen and E. F. K. Koerner, eds, *De Ortu Grammaticae: Studies in Medieval Grammar and Linguistic Theory in Memory of Jan Pinborg*. Amsterdam and Philadelphia: John Benjamins.

Huang, C.-T. J. (1984). On the distribution and reference of empty pronouns. *Linguistic Inquiry* 15: 531–44.

Huddleston, R., Pullum, G. et al. (2002). *The Cambridge Grammar of the English Language*. Cambridge: Cambridge University Press.

Hurford, J. R., Heasley, B. and Smith, M. B. (2007). *Semantics: A Coursebook*, second edition. Cambridge: Cambridge University Press.

Ibrahim, M. H. (1973). *Grammatical Gender: Its Origin and Development*. The Hague and Paris: Mouton.

Imai, M., Kita, S., Nagumo, M. and Okada, H. (2008). Sound symbolism facilitates early verb learning. *Cognition* 109: 54–65.

Inagaki, S. (2001). Motion verbs with goal PPs in the L2 acquisition of English and Japanese. *Studies in Second Language Acquisition* 23: 153–70.

Jackendoff, R. (1992). Babe Ruth homered his way into the hearts of America. In T. Stowell and E. Wehrli, eds, *Syntax and the Lexicon*, pp. 155–78. San Diego, CA: Academic Press.

Jacobson, P. and Gibson, E. (2014). Processing of ACD gives no evidence of QR. In *Proceedings of SALT 24*, pp. 156–76.

Jakobson, R. ([1959] 2000). On linguistic aspects of translation. In L. Venuti, ed., *The Translation Studies Reader*, pp. 138–43. London and New York: Routledge.

James, A. (2000). States and sovereignty. In T. Salmon, ed., *Issues in International Relations*, pp. 1–24. Abingdon, UK, and New York: Routledge.

Jawaid, B. and Ahmed, T. (2009). Hindi to Urdu conversion: Beyond simple transliteration. In *Proceedings of the Conference on Language & Technology 2009*. Lahore, Pakistan: National University of Computer and Emerging Sciences.

Jespersen, O. (1949). *A Modern English Grammar on Historical Principles: I-VII*. Heidelberg: Carl Winter.

Johnson, J. S. and Newport, E. L. (1989). Critical period effects in second language learning: The influence of maturational state on the acquisition of English as a second language. *Cognitive Psychology* 21: 60–99.

Johnson, K. (1991). Object positions. *Natural Language & Linguistic Theory* 9: 577–636.

Johnson-Laird, P. N. (1983). *Mental Models: Towards a Cognitive Science of Language, Inference and Consciousness*. Cambridge: Cambridge University Press.

Johnson-Laird, P. N. and Stevenson, R. (1970). Memory for syntax. *Nature* 227 (5256): 412.

Johnston, J. and Slobin, D. I. (1979). The development of locative expressions in English, Italian, Serbo-Croatian, and Turkish. *Journal of Child Language* 16: 531–47.

Jones, S. (1993). *The Language of the Genes: Biology, History and the Evolutionary Future*. London: Harper Collins.

Joos, M. (1957). *Readings in Linguistics: The Development of Descriptive Linguistics in America since 1925*. Washington, DC: American Council of Learned Societies.

Juffs, A. and Harrington, M. (1995). Parsing effects in second language sentence processing: Subject and object asymmetries in *wh*-extraction. *Studies in Second Language Acquisition* 17: 483–516.

(1996). Garden path sentences and error data in second language sentence processing. *Language Learning* 46: 283–326.

Juffs, A. and Rodríguez, G. A. (2015). *Second Language Sentence Processing*. New York and London: Routledge.

Jung, C. G. ([1954] 1981). *Collected Works of C. G. Jung*, vol. 17: *Development of Personality*. Princeton, NJ: Princeton University Press.

Kabuzono, H. (2006). Phonetic and phonological organization of speech. In M. Nakayama, R. Mazuka and Y. Shirai, eds, *The Handbook of East Asian Psycholinguistics*, pp. 191–200. Cambridge: Cambridge University Press.

Kacinik, N. A. (2014). Sticking your neck out and burying the hatchet: What idioms reveal about embodied simulation. *Frontiers in Human Neuroscience* 8: 689.

Kay, J., Lesser, R. and Coltheart, M. (1992). *Psycholinguistic Assessments of Language Processing in Aphasia (Palpa)*. Hove: Lawrence Erlbaum.

Kayne, R. (1994). *The Antisymmetry of Syntax*. Cambridge, MA: MIT Press.

Kayne, R. and Pollock, J.-Y. (2008). Toward an analysis of French hyper-complex inversion. In L. Brugè, A. Cardinaletti, G. Giusti, N. Munaro and C. Poletto, eds, *Functional Heads*. Oxford: Oxford University Press.

Keenan, E. (2003). An historical explanation of some binding theoretic facts in English. In J. Moore and M. Polinsky, eds, *The Nature of Explanation in Linguistic Theory*, pp. 152–89. Stanford, CA: CSLI Publications.

Kellerman, E. and van Hoof, A. (2003). Manual accents. *International Review of Applied Linguistics* 41: 251–69.

Kerswill, P. (1996). Children, adolescents and language change. *Language Variation and Change* 8: 177–202.

Kiefer, F. (1980). Yes-no questions as wh-questions. In J. R. Searle, F. Kiefer and M. Bierwisch, eds, *Speech Act Theory and Pragmatics*, pp. 97–120. Dordrecht, Boston and London: D. Reidel.

Kilbury, J. (2001). German noun inflection revisited. *Journal of Linguistics* 37: 339–53.

Kimberley, A. (2015). On the supposed incompatability of truth-conditional semantics and semantic underdetermination. Conference presentation. https://eastanglia.academia.edu/AdamKimberley

Kiparsky, P. (2013). Towards a null theory of the passive. *Lingua* 125: 7–33.

Kita, S. and Özyürek, A. (2003). What does cross-linguistic variation in semantic coordination of speech and gesture reveal?: Evidence for an interface representation of spatial thinking and speaking. *Journal of Memory and Language* 48: 16–32.

Klein, W. and Perdue, C. (1997). The basic variety (Or: Couldn't natural language be much simpler?). *Second Language Research* 14: 301–47.

Klima, E. (1964). Negation in English. In J. Fodor and J. Katz, eds, *The Structure of Language*. Englewood Cliffs, NJ: Prentice Hall.

Kluender, R. and Kutas, M. (1993). Subjacency as a processing phenomenon. *Language and Cognitive Processes* 8: 573–640.

Knoeferle, P. and Crocker, M. W. (2009). Constituent order and semantic parallelism in online comprehension: Eye-tracking evidence from German *The Quarterly Journal of Experimental Psychology* 62: 2338–71.

Krashen, S. (1977). Some issues relating to the monitor model. In H. D. Brown, C. A. Yorio and R. H. Crymes, eds, *On TESOL '77: Teaching and Learning English as a Second Language: Trends in Research and Practice*. Washington, DC: TESOL.

Krauss, M. (1992). The world's languages in crisis. *Language* 68: 4–10.

Krifka, M., Pelletier, F. J., Carlson, G. N., ter Meulen, A., Chierchia, G. and Link, G. (1995). Genericity: An introduction. In G. N. Carlson and F. J. Pelletier, eds, *The Generic Book*, pp. 1–124. Chicago: University of Chicago Press.

Kripke, S. (1980). *Naming and Necessity*. Cambridge, MA: Harvard University Press.

Kroch, A. S. (1989). Reflexes of grammar in patterns of language Use. *Journal of Language Variation and Change* 1: 199–244.

    (2003). Syntactic Change. In M. Baltin and C. Collins, eds, *Handbook of Contemporary Syntactic Theory*. Malden, MA, and Oxford: Wiley-Blackwell.

Kuhl, P. (2004). Early language acquisition: Cracking the speech code. *Nature Reviews Neuroscience* 5: 831–43.

Kuhl, P. K., Tsao, F.-M. and Liu, H.-M. (2003). Foreign-language experience in infancy: Effects of short-term exposure and social interaction on phonetic learning. *Proceedings of the National Academy of Sciences* 100: 9096–101.

Kuhl, P. K., Williams, K. A., Lacerda, F., Stevens, K. N. and Lindblom, B. (1992). Linguistic experience alters phonetic perception in infants by 6 months of age. *Science* 255: 606–8.

Labov, W. (1981). Resolving the Neogrammarian controversy. *Language* 57: 267–308.

(1994). *Principles of Linguistic Change*, three volumes. Oxford: Blackwell.

Labov, W. and Labov, T. (1978). Learning the syntax of questions. In R. Campbell and P. Smith, eds, *Recent Advances in the Psychology of Language III*, pp. 1–44. New York: Plenum Press.

Ladd, D. R. ([1996] 2008). *Intonational Phonology*, second edition. Cambridge: Cambridge University Press.

Laenzlinger, C. (2005). French adjective ordering: Perspectives on DP-internal movement types. *Lingua* 115: 645–89.

Lakoff, G. ([1965] 1970). On the nature of syntactic irregularity. Dissertation, Indiana University. Published as *Irregularity in Syntax* (1970), New York: Holt, Rinehart and Winston.

(1986). Frame semantic control of the co-ordinate structure constraint. In A. M. Farley, P. T. Farley and K.-E. McCullough, eds, *CLS 22: Papers from the Parasession on Pragmatics and Grammatical Theory*, pp. 152–67. Chicago: Chicago Linguistic Society.

(1987). *Women, Fire and Dangerous Things: What Categories Reveal About the Mind*. Chicago: University of Chicago Press.

Lakoff, G. and Johnson, M. (2003). *Metaphors We Live By*. London: University of Chicago Press.

Land, F. (1974). *The Language of Mathematics*. London: John Murray.

Langacker, R. (1991). *Foundations of Cognitive Grammar*. Stanford, CA: Stanford University Press.

Lardiere, D. (2016). Missing the trees for the forest: Morphology in second language acquisition. *Second Language* 15: 5–28.

Larson, B. (2015). Right node raising and non-grammaticality. *Lingbuzz* 002421. http://ling.auf.net/lingbuzz/002421

Larson, R. K. (1988). On the double object construction. *Linguistic Inquiry* 19: 335–91.

Leopold, W. (1949). *Speech Development of a Bilingual Child*, vol. 4. Evanston, IL: Northwestern University Press.

Lev-Ari, S. and Keysar, B. (2010). Why don't we believe non-native speakers? The influence of accent on credibility. *Journal of Experimental Social Psychology* 46: 1093–6.

Levelt, W. J. M. (1989). *Speaking: From Intention to Articulation*. Cambridge, MA: MIT Press.

Levin, B. and Rappaport Hovav, M. (2007). Reflections on the complementarity of manner and result (handout of a talk on 21 November 2007, Berlin). Manuscript, Stanford University. http://web.stanford.edu/~bclevin/pubs.html

Levinson, S. C. and Evans, N. (2010). Time for a sea-change in linguistics. *Lingua* 120: 2733–58.

Lewis, B. A., Shriberg, L. D., Freebairn, L. A., Hansen, A. J., Stein, C. M., Taylor, H. J. and Iyengar, S. K. (2006). The genetic bases of speech sound disorders: Evidence from spoken and written language. *Journal of Speech, Language and Hearing Research* 49: 1249–312.

Lewis, C. S. ([1960] 2013). *Studies in Words*, third edition. Cambridge: Cambridge University Press.

Lieberman, P. (2015). Review of *The Science of Language: Interviews with James McGilvray (Chomsky)*. *Modern Language Review* 110: 222–4.

Lieven, E., Tomasello, M., Behrens, H. and Speares, J. (2003). Early syntactic creativity: A usage-based approach. *Journal of Child Language* 30: 333–370.

Lightfoot, D. (1991). *How to Set Parameters: Arguments from Language Change.* Cambridge, MA: MIT Press.

    (1992). Why UG needs a learning theory. In C. Jones, eds, *Historical Linguistics*, pp. 191–213. London: Longman.

Long, M. H. (1996). The role of the linguistic environment in second language acquisition. In W. C. Ritchie and T. K. Bhatia, eds, *Handbook of Second Language Acquisition*, pp. 413–68. New York: Academic Press.

Loschky, L. (2008). Comprehensible input and second language acquisition: What is the relationship? *Studies in Second Language Acquisition* 16: 303–23.

Losonsky, M., ed. (1999). *Humboldt: On Language.* Cambridge Texts in the History of Philosophy. Cambridge: Cambridge University Press.

Lyons, J. ([1965] 1996). On competence and performance and related notions. In G. Brown, K. Malmkjaer and J. Williams, eds, *Performance and Competence in Second Language Acquisition*, pp. 9–32. Cambridge: Cambridge University Press.

MacDonald, M.-E. C., Pearlmutter, N. J. and Seidenberg, M. A. (1994). Syntactic ambiguity resolution as lexical ambiguity resolution. In C. Clifton Jr, L. Frazier and K. Rayner, eds, *Perspectives on Sentence Processing*, pp. 123–54. Hillsdale, NJ: Lawrence Erlbaum.

MacWhinney, B. (2000). Connectionism and language learning. In M. Barlow and S. Kemmer, eds, *Usage-Based Models of Language*, pp. 121–50. Stanford, CA: CSLI Publications.

MacWhinney, B. and Bates, E. (1989). *The Cross-Linguistic Study of Sentence Processing.* New York: Cambridge University Press.

MacWhinney, B. and Chang, F. (1995). Connectionism and language learning. In C. A. Nelson, ed., *Basic and Applied Perspectives on Learning, Acquisition and Development.* Mahwah, NJ: Lawrence Erlbaum.

MacWhinney, B. and Leinbach, J. (1991). Implementations are not conceptualizations: Revising the verb learning model. *Cognition* 40: 121–57.

Mameli, M. and Bateson, P. (2006). Innateness and the sciences. *Biology and Philosophy* 21: 155–88.

Marcus, G. F. (2014). The trouble with brain science. *New York Times.* www.nytimes.com/2014/07/12/opinion/the-trouble-with-brain-science.html

Marcus, G. F., Brinkmann, U., Clahsen, H., Wiese, R. and Pinker, S. (1995). German inflection: The exception that proves the rule. *Cognitive Psychology* 29: 189–256.

Marcus, G. F., Pinker, S., Ullman, M., Hollander, M., Rosen, T. J. and Xu, F. (1992). Over-regularization in language acquisition. *Monographs of the Society for Research in Child Development* 57.

Marcus, R. B. (1961). Modalities and intensional languages. *Synthese* 13: 303–22.

Margolis, E. and Laurence, S. (2011). Learning matters: The role of learning in concept acquisition. *Mind & Language* 26: 507–639.

Marr, D., Ullman, S. F. and Poggio, T. A., eds ([1982] 2010). *Vision.* Cambridge, MA: MIT Press.

Marslen-Wilson, W., Tyler, L. K. and Seidenberg, M. (1978). Sentence processing and the clause-boundary. In W. J. M. Levelt and G. Flores d'Arcais, eds, *Studies in the Perception of Language*, pp. 219–46. London: Wiley.

Marslen-Wilson, W., Tyler, L. K., Waksler, R. and Older, L. (1994). Morphology and meaning in the English mental lexicon. *Psychological Review* 101: 3–33.

Martens, M. A., Wilson, S. J. and Reutens, D. C. (2008). Research review: Williams Syndrome: A critical review of the cognitive, behavioral, and neuroanatomical phenotype. *Journal of Child Psychology and Psychiatry* 49: 576–608.

Martin, A., Peperkamp, S. and Dupoux, E. (2014). Learning phonemes with a proto-lexicon. *Cognitive Science* 37: 103–24.

Matsuo, A. (1998). A comparative study of tense and ellipsis. PhD dissertation, Department of Linguistics, University of Connecticut.

Max Planck Society (2016). Language is in the genes. https://www.mpg.de/10751617/simon-fisher-language-research

May, R. (1977). The grammar of quantification. PhD dissertation, Massachusetts Institute of Technology.

(1985). *Logical Form: Its Structure and Derivation*. Cambridge, MA: MIT Press.

McCloskey, J. (1997). A global silencing. *The Poetry Ireland Review* 52: 41–6.

(2001). The morphosyntax of WH-extraction in Irish. *Journal of Linguistics* 37: 67–100.

McDaniel, D., McKee, C. and Cairns, H. S. (1996). *Methods for Assessing Children's Syntax*. Cambridge, MA: MIT Press.

McGilvray, J. ([1999] 2014). *Chomsky: Language, Mind and Politics*. Malden, MA, and Cambridge: Polity Press.

McLaurin, M. A. (2009). *Marines of Montford Point: America's First Black Marines*. Charlotte, NC: University of North Carolina Press.

McLuhan, M. (1964). *Understanding Media: The Extensions of Man*. New York: McGraw-Hill.

Menand, L. (2004). Bad comma. *New Yorker*. www.newyorker.com/magazine/2004/06/28/bad-comma

Mendívil Giró, J. L. (2012). The myth of language diversity. In C. Boeckx, M. Horno Chéliz and J. L. Mendívil Giró, eds, *Language, from a Biological Point of View: Current Issues in Biolinguistics*, pp. 85–134. Newcastle upon Tyne: Cambridge Scholars Publishing.

Merchant, J. (2001). *The Syntax of Silence: Sluicing, Islands, and the Theory of Ellipsis*. Oxford: Oxford University Press.

(2005). Fragments and ellipsis. *Linguistics and Philosophy* 27: 661–738.

Miller, G. A. and Chomsky, N. (1963). Finitary models of language users. In R. D. Luce, R. R. Bush and E. Galanter, eds, *Handbook of Mathematical Psychology*, pp. 419–91. New York: Wiley.

Miller, G. A. and McKean, K. O. (1964). A chronometric study of some relations between sentences. *Quarterly Journal of Experimental Psychology* 16: 297–308.

Millward, C. M. (1989). *A Biography of the English Language*. Fort Worth, TX: Holt, Rinehart and Winston.

Milroy, J. (1998). Children can't speak or write properly anymore. In P. Trudgill and L. Bauer, eds, *Language Myths*, pp. 58–65. London: Penguin.

Milsark, G. L. (1977). Toward an explanation of certain peculiarities of the existential construction in English. *Linguistic Analysis* 3: 1–29.

Miyawaki, K., Strange, W., Verbugge, R., Liberman, A., Jenkins, J. and Fujimura, O. (1975). An effect of linguistic experience: The discrimination of [r] and [l] by native speakers of Japanese and English. *Perception & Psychophysics* 18: 331–40.

Monsell, S. (1987). On the relation between lexical input and output pathways for speech. In A. Allport, D. MacKay, W. Prinz and E. Scheerer, eds, *Language Perception and Production*, pp. 271–311. London: Academic Press.

Moore, T. and Carling, C. (1982). *Understanding language: Towards a post-Chomskyan linguistics*. London: Macmillan.

Morgan, J. (1973). Sentence fragments and the notion 'sentence'. In B. B. Kachru, R. B. Lees, Y. Malkiel, A. Pietrangeli and S. Saporta, eds, *Issues in Linguistics: Papers in Honor of Henry and Renée Kahane*, pp. 719–52. Urbana, IL: University of Illinois Press.

Morgan-Short, K. and Tanner, D. (2014). Event-related potentials. In J. Jegerski and B. van Patten, eds, *Research Methods in Second Language Psycholinguistics*, pp. 127–52. New York and Abingdon, UK: Routledge.

Morris, J. (2012). *Baby Talk*. Harlequin (ebook).doi: 10.1016/j.biopsych.2007.04.006.

Müller, S. (2015). Deriving island constraints with Searle and Grice. *Studia Linguistics* 69 (1): 1–57.

Munafò, M. R., Yalcin, B., Willis-Owen, S. A. and Flint, J. (2007). Association of the dopamine D4 receptor (DRD4) gene and approach-related personality traits: Meta-analysis and new data. *Biological Psychiatry* 63: 197–206.

Neusner, J., ed. (1995). *Judaism in Late Antiquity*, part 1: *The Literary and Archaeological Sources*. Leiden: E. J. Brill.doi: 10.1016/j.biopsych.2007.04.006.

Nevins, A., Pesetsky, D. and Rodriguez, C. (2009). Piraha exceptionality: A reassessment. *Language* 85: 355–404.

Newman, A. J. (2014). Functional magnetic resonance imaging (FMRI). In J. Jegerski and B. van Patten, eds, *Research Methods in Second Language Psycholinguistics*, pp. 153–84. New York and Abingdon, UK: Routledge.

Newman, S. (1946). On the stress system of English. *Word* 2: 171–87.

Newmeyer, F. (1983). *Grammatical Theory: Its Limits and Possibilities*. Chicago: University of Chicago Press.

(1999). *Language Form and Language Function*. Cambridge, MA: MIT Press.

Nichol, J. and Swinney, D. (1989). The role of structure in coreference assignment during sentence comprehension. *Journal of Psycholinguistic Research* 18: 5–20.

Ogura, M. (1993). The development of periphrastic *do* in English: A case of lexical diffusion in syntax. *Diachronica* 10: 51–85.

O'Grady, W. (2003). The radical middle: Nativism without Universal Grammar. In C. J. Doughty and M. H. Long, eds, *The Handbook of Second Language Acquisition*, pp. 43–62. Oxford: Blackwell.

Otake, T., Hatano, G., Cutler, A. and Mehler, J. (1993). Mora or syllable? Speech segmentation in Japanese. *Journal of Memory and Language* 32: 258–78.

Oxford, University of (2016). Charles F. Hockett. www.revolvy.com/main/index .php?s=Charles F. Hockett&uid=1575

Palmer, D. C. (2006). On Chomsky's appraisal of Skinner's *Verbal Behavior*. *The Behavior Analyst* 29: 253–67.

Paradis, M. (2009). *Declarative and Procedural Determinants of Second Languages*. Amsterdam and Philadelphia: John Benjamins.

Parker, D. and Phillips, C. (2016). Negative polarity illusions and the format of hierarchical encodings in memory. *Cognition* 157: 321–39.

Partee, B. (1991). Topic, focus and quantification. In S. Moore and A. Z. Wyner, eds, *Proceedings of SALT 1*, pp. 159–87. Linguistic Society of America.

Patsiurko, N., Campbell, J. L. and Hall, J. A. (2012). Measuring cultural diversity: Ethnic, linguistic and religious fractionalization in the OECD. *Ethnic and Racial Studies* 35: 195–217.

Patterson, K. and Shewell, C. (1987). Speak and spell: Dissociations and word-class effects. In M. Coltheart, G. Sartori and R. Job, eds, *The Cognitive Neuropsychology of Language*, pp. 273–94. London: Lawrence Erlbaum.

Paul, H. (1880). *Prinzipien der Sprachgeschichte* (second edition 1886; third edition 1898). Halle: Max Niemeyer.

Payne, T. E. (1997). *Describing Morphosyntax: A Guide for Field Linguists.* Cambridge: Cambridge University Press.

Peacocke, C. (1986). Explanation in computational psychology: Language, perception and Level 1.5. *Mind & Language* 1: 101–23.

Pepper, J. (1981). *John Pepper's Ulster–English Dictionary*, 1995 edition. Belfast: Appletree Press.

Perez, F. (2016). Nearly 20 years in the making, dictionary awakens Mutsun language. *BenitoLink*. http://goo.gl/3yJgyN

Perovic, A. (2006). Syntactic deficit in Down Syndrome: More evidence for the modular organisation of language. *Lingua* 116: 1616–30.

Pesetsky, D. M. (1995). *Zero Syntax*. Cambridge, MA: MIT Press.
    (2015). Complementizer-trace effects (encyclopaedia article). *Lingbuzz* 002385. http://ling.auf.net/lingbuzz/002385

Pesetsky, D. M. and Torrego, E. (2001). T-to-C movement: Causes and consequences. In M. Kenstowicz, ed., *Ken Hale: A Life in Language*, pp. 355–426. Cambridge, MA: MIT Press.

Philip, W. and de Villiers, J. G. (1992). Monotonicity and the acquisition of weak *wh* islands. In E. Clark, ed., *Proceedings of the 24th Annual Child Language Research Forum*. Stanford, CA: CSLI Publications.

Phillips, C. (1996). Order and structure. PhD dissertation, Massachusetts Institute of Technology.
    (2013). Some arguments and non-arguments for reductionist accounts of syntactic phenomena. *Language and Cognitive Processes* 28: 156–87.

Phillips, C. and Lewis, S. (2013). Derivational order in syntax: Evidence and architectural consequences. *Studies in Linguistics* 6: 11–47.

Phillips, C., Wagers, M. and Lau, E. (2011). Grammatical illusions and selective fallibility in real-time language comprehension. In J. Runner, ed., *Experiments at the Interfaces*, pp. 153–86. Syntax and Semantics, vol. 37. Bingley, UK: Emerald.

Pickering, M. and Barry, G. (1991). Sentence processing without empty categories. *Language and Cognitive Processes* 6 (3): 229–63.

Pienemann, M. (1998). *Language Processing and Second Language Development: Processability Theory.* Amsterdam and Philadelphia: John Benjamins.

Piller, I. (2002). Passing for native: Identity and success in second language learning. *Journal of Sociolinguistics* 6: 179–206.

Pinker, S. (1994). *The Language Instinct*. New York: William Morrow.
    (1998). Words and rules. *Lingua* 106: 219–42.
    (2007). *The Stuff of Thought: Language as a Window into Human Nature*. New York: Viking.

Pinker, S. and Prince, A. (1988). On language and connectionism: Analysis of a parallel distributed processing model of language acquisition. *Cognition* 28: 73–193.

Poeppel, D. (2014). The temporal structure of perceptual experience. Presentation at *Genetics and Neurobiology of Language Conference*, Cold Spring Harbor Laboratory.www.youtube.com/watch?v=lIqO4wz3VCs

Postal, P. M. (1974). *On Raising*. Cambridge, MA: MIT Press.

Potter, M. C. and Lombardi, L. (1990). Regeneration in short-term recall of sentences. *Journal of Memory and Language* 29: 633–54.

Pullum, G. (2010). Creation myths of generative grammar and the mathematics of *Syntactic Structures*. In C. Ebert, G. Jäger and J. Michaelis, eds, *The Mathematics of Language*, pp. 238–54. Berlin: Springer.

Pullum, G. and Scholz, B. (2002). Empirical assessment of stimulus poverty arguments. *The Linguistic Review* 19: 9–50.

Quine, W. v. O. ([1960] 2013). *Word and Object*. Cambridge, MA: MIT Press.

Quirk, R., Greenbaum, S., Leech, G. and Svartvik, J. (1985). *A Comprehensive Grammar of the English Language*. London: Longman.

Radick, G. (2016). The unmaking of a modern synthesis: Noam Chomsky, Charles Hockett and the politics of behaviorism, 1955–1965. *Isis* 107: 49–73.

Rampton, B. (1995). *Crossing: Language and Ethnicity among Adolescents*. London: Longman.

(1999). Styling the other: Introduction. *Journal of Sociolinguistics* 3: 421–7.

Read, C. 2016. *The Lost Boys*. London: The Save the Children Fund.

Recanati, F. (2004). What is said and the semantics/pragmatics distinction. In C. Bianchi, ed., *The Semantics/Pragmatics Distinction*, pp. 45–64. Stanford, CA: CSLI Publications.

Reimer, M. and Michaelson, E. (2016). Reference. *The Stanford Encyclopedia of Philosophy*. http://plato.stanford.edu/archives/sum2016/entries/reference/

Rice, M. L., Smolik, F., Perpich, D., Thompson, T., Rytting, N. and Blossom, M. (2010). Mean length of utterance levels in 6-month intervals for children 3 to 9 years with and without language impairments. *Journal of Speech, Language, and Hearing Research* 53: 333–49.

Richardson, H. (2016). Grammar schools: What are they and why are they controversial? *BBC Online*. www.bbc.com/news/education-34538222

Riddoch, M. J. and Humphreys, G. W. (1987). A case of integrative visual agnosia. *Brain* 110: 1431-62.

Ridley, M. (1999). *Genome: The Autobiography of a Species in 23 Chapters*. London: Fourth Estate.

Riney, T. J., Takagi, N., Ota, K. and Uchida, Y. (2007). The intermediate degree of VOT in Japanese initial voiceless stops. *Journal of Phonetics* 35: 439–43.

Ritter, E. (1987). NSO noun-phrases in a VSO language. In J. McDonough and B. Plunkett, eds, *Proceedings of NELS 17*. Amherst, MA: GLSA Publications.

(1988). A head-movement approach to construct-state noun phrases. *Linguistics* 26: 909–29.

Rivenc, P. (2003). *Apprentissage d'une Langue Étrangère/Seconde*, vol. 3: *La Méthodologie*. Brussels: De Boeck Supérieur.

Rizzi, L. (1997). The fine structure of the left periphery. In L. Haegeman, ed., *Elements of Grammar*, pp. 281–337. Dordrecht: Kluwer.

(2002). Locality and the left periphery. In A. Belletti and L. Rizzi, eds, *The Structure of CP and IP: The Cartography of Syntactic Structures*. Oxford: Oxford University Press.

Rizzi, L. and Roberts, I. (1989). Complex inversion in French. *Probus* 1: 1–30.

Roberts, I. (1985). Agreement parameters and the development of English modal auxiliaries. *Natural Language and Linguistic Theory* 3: 21–58.

(1993). *Verbs and Diachronic Syntax*. Studies in Natural Language and Linguistic Theory, vol. 28. Dordrecht: Kluwer Academic.

(2007). *Diachronic Syntax*. Oxford: Oxford University Press.

Roberts, I. and Roussou, A. (2003). *Syntactic Change: A Minimalist Approach to Grammaticalization*. Cambridge: Cambridge University Press.

Roberts, L., Matsuo, A. and Duffield, N. (2013). Processing VP-ellipsis and VP-anaphora with structurally parallel and non-parallel antecedents: An eye-tracking study. *Language and Cognitive Processes* 28: 29–47.

Robins, R. H. (1989). *General Linguistics*, fourth edition. Longman Linguistics Library. London and New York: Longman.

Robinson, I. (1975). *The New Grammarians' Funeral: A Critique of Noam Chomsky's Linguistics*. Cambridge: Cambridge University Press.

Robson, D. (2014). The mind-bending effects of feeling two hearts. *BBC Online*. www. bbc.com/future/story/20141205-the-man-with-two-hearts

Roeper, T. (1982). Review of *Linguistic Theory and Psycholinguistic Reality* (1981), edited by Halle, Bresnan and Miller. *Language* 58: 467–8.

Roland, D., Elman, J. L. and Ferreira, V. S. (2006). Why is that? Structural prediction and ambiguity resolution in a very large corpus of English sentences. *Cognition* 98: 245–72.

Roseberry, S., Hirsh-Pasek, K., Parish-Morris, J. and Golinkoff, R. M. (2009). Live action: Can young children learn verbs from video? *Child Development* 80: 1360–75.

Ross, J. R. (Haj) (1967). Constraints on variables in syntax. PhD dissertation, Department of Linguistics and Philosophy, Massachusetts Institute of Technology. Published as *Infinite Syntax!* (1986), Norwood, NJ: Ablex.

Ross, J. R. (Haj) (1982). Pronoun deleting processes in German. Paper presented at the *Annual Meeting of the Linguistic Society of America*, San Diego.

Ross, J. R. (Haj) (2015). Why to syntax. Manuscript, University of North Texas.

Ruigendijk, M. E., Baauw, S., Zuckerman, S., Vasic, N., de Lange, J. and Avrutin, S. (2011). A cross-linguistic study on the interpretation of pronouns by children and agrammatic speakers: Evidence from Dutch, Spanish and Italian. In E. Gibson and N. J. Pearlmutter, eds, *The Processing and Acquisition of Reference*. Cambridge, MA, and London: MIT Press.

Russell, B. ([1911] 1917). Knowledge by acquaintance and knowledge by description. *Proceedings of the Aristotelian Society* 11: 108–128. Republished in *Mysticism and Logic* (1917), London: George Allen and Unwin.

(1912). *The Problems of Philosophy*. London: Williams and Norgate.

Sabbagh, J. (2007). Ordering and linearizing rightward movement. *Natural Language & Linguistic Theory* 25: 349–401.

Saberi, K. and Perrott, D. R. (1999). Cognitive restoration of reversed speech. *Nature* 398 (6730): 760–760.

Sabourin, L. (2003). Grammatical gender and second language processing: An ERP study. PhD dissertation, Department of Linguistics, Rijksuniversiteit Groningen.

Sachs, J. D. S. (1967). Recognition memory for syntactic and semantic aspects of connected discourse. *Perception & Psychophysics* 2: 437–42.

Sachs, O. (2007). *Musicophilia: Tales of Music and the Brain*. New York: First Vintage Books.

Sag, I. (1976). Deletion and logical form. PhD dissertation, Massachusetts Institute of Technology.

Salzmann, M., Häusler, J., Bader, M. and Bayer, J. (2013). *That*-trace effects without traces. An experimental investigation. In S. Keine, ed., *Proceedings of the 42nd Annual Meeting of the North East Linguistic Society*, pp. 149–62. Amherst, MA: GLSA Publications.

Sampson, G. (1980). *Schools of Linguistics: Competition and Evolution*. London: Hutchison.

   (2014). Minds in uniform: How generative grammar regiments culture, and why it shouldn't. In G. Sampson and A. Babarczy, eds, *Grammar without Grammaticality: Growth and Limits of Grammatical Precision*. Berlin and Boston: De Gruyter.

   (2015). Two ideas of creativity. *Lingbuzz* 002619. http://ling.auf.net/lingbuzz/002619

Sanford, A. J. and Sturt, P. (2012). Depth of processing in language comprehension: Not noticing the evidence. *Trends in Cognitive Sciences* 6: 382–6.

Sapir, E. ([1907] 2008). The problem of an international auxiliary language. In P. Swiggers, ed., *The Collected Works of Edward Sapir*, vol. 1. Berlin and New York: Mouton de Gruyter.

   (1921). *Language: An Introduction to the Study of Speech*. New York: Harcourt, Brace and Company.

Saxton, M. (2010). *Child Language: Acquisition and Development*. London: SAGE Publications.

Schlinger, H. D. (2008). The long good-bye: Why B. F. Skinner's *Verbal Behavior* is alive and well on the 50th anniversary of its publication. *The Psychological Record* 58: 329–37.

Schmid, M. (2013). *Language Attrition*. Cambridge: Cambridge University Press.

   (2016). The best age to learn a second language. *Independent*. www.independent.co.uk/news/education/the-best-age-to-learn-a-second-language-a6860886.html

Schütze, C. T. (1996). *The Empirical Base of Linguistics*. Chicago: University of Chicago Press.

Schwartz, B. and Sprouse, R. (1996). L2 cognitive states and the Full Transfer/Full Access model. *Second Language Research* 12: 40–72.

Schwartz, B. and Vikner, S. (1996). The verb always leaves IP in V2 clauses. In A. Belletti and L. Rizzi, eds, *Parameters and Functional Heads*, pp. 11–63. Oxford: Oxford University Press.

Searle, J. R. (1975). Indirect speech acts. In P. Cole and J. L. Morgan, eds, *Syntax and Semantics*, pp. 59–82. New York: Academic Press.

   (1983). *Intentionality*. Cambridge: Cambridge University Press.

Segel, E. and Boroditsky, L. (2011). Grammar in art. *Frontiers in Psychology* 1. doi:10.3389/fpsyg.2010.00244

Seidenberg, M. S. and MacDonald, M. C. (1999). A probabilistic constraints approach to language acquisition and processing. *Cognitive Science* 23: 569–88.

Seliger, H. W. and Vago, R. M., eds (1991). *First Language Attrition*. Cambridge: Cambridge University Press.

Sick, B. (2004). *Der Dativ ist dem Genitiv sein Tod: Ein Wegweiser durch den Irrgarten der Deutschen Sprache*. Cologne: Kiepenheuer and Witsch.

Sidtis, D. V. L. and Bridges, K. A. (2013). Formulaic language in Alzheimer's disease. *Aphasiology* 27: 799–810.

Sidtis, D. V. L., Kougentakis, K. M., Cameron, K., Falconer, C. and Sidtis, J. J. (2012). 'Down with _____': The linguistic schema as intermediary between formulaic and novel expressions. *Yearbook of Phraseology* 3: 87–108.

Siegal, M. (2008). *Marvelous Minds: The Discovery of What Children Know.* Oxford: Oxford University Press.

Slobin, D. I. (2003). Language and thought online: Cognitive consequences of linguistic relativity. In D. Gentner and S. Goldin-Meadow, eds, *Language in Mind: Advances in the Study of Language and Thought*, pp. 157–92. Cambridge, MA: MIT Press.

Smith, N. V. (1973). *The Acquisition of Phonology: A Case Study.* Cambridge: Cambridge University Press.

Snedeker, J. and Trueswell, J. (2003). Using prosody to avoid ambiguity: Effects of speaker awareness and referential context. *Journal of Memory and Language* 48: 103–30.

Soames, S. (1985). Semantics and psychology. In J. Katz, ed., *The Philosophy of Linguistics.* Oxford: Oxford University Press.

Sobin, N. (1987). The variable status of comp-trace phenomena. *Natural Language & Linguistic Theory* 5: 33–60.

  (2002). The comp-trace effect, the adverb effect and minimal CP. *Journal of Linguistics* 38: 527–60.

Solan, L. (1983). *Pronominal Reference: Child Language and the Theory of Grammar.* Dordrecht: Reidel.

Sorace, A. (2000). Gradients in auxiliary selection with intransitive verbs. *Language* 76: 859–90.

  (2004). Native language attrition and developmental instability at the syntax–discourse interface: Data, interpretations and methods. *Bilingualism: Language and Cognition* 7 (2): 143–5.

Sorensen, R. (2012). Veridical idealizations. In M. Frappier, L. Meynell and J. R. Brown, eds, *Thought Experiments in Science, Philosophy and the Arts*, pp. 30–52. New York and Oxford: Routledge.

Spelke, E. and Hespos, S. (2002). Conceptual development in infancy: The case of containment. In N. Stein, P. Bauer and M. Rabinowitz, eds, *Representation, Memory and Development: Essays in Honor of Jean Mandler*, pp. 223–46. Mahwah, NJ: Lawrence Erlbaum.

Spelke, E. and Kinzler, K. (2007). Core knowledge. *Developmental Science* 10: 86–96.

Spinelli, E., Meunier, F. and Seigneuric, A. (2006). Spoken word recognition with gender-marked context. *The Mental Lexicon* 1: 277–97.

Spivey, M. J., McRae, K. and Joanisse, M. F., eds (2012). *The Cambridge Handbook of Psycholinguistics.* Cambridge: Cambridge University Press.

Sportiche, D. (1995). French predicate clitics and clause structure. In A. Cardinaletti and M. T. Guasti, eds, *Small Clauses.* San Diego, CA: Academic Press. Reprinted in Sportiche (1998).

Sportiche, D. (1998). *Partitions and Atoms of Clause Structure: Subjects, Agreement, Case and Clitics.* London: Routledge.

Sproat, R. and Shih, C. (1991). The crosslinguistic distribution of adjective ordering restrictions. In C. Georgopoulos and R. Ishihara, eds, *Interdisciplinary Approaches to Language: Essays in Honor of S.-Y. Kuroda*, pp. 565–92. Dordrecht: Kluwer.

Sprouse, J. and Almeida, D. (2012). Assessing the reliability of textbook data in syntax: Adger's *Core Syntax*. *Journal of Linguistics* 48 (3): 609–652.

Sprouse, J., Wagers, M. and Phillips, C. (2012). A test of the relation between working-memory capacity and syntactic island effects. *Language* 88: 82–123.

Steiner, G. (1961). The retreat from the word. *Kenyon Review* 23: 187–216.

(1976). *After Babel: Aspects of Language and Translation*. Oxford: Oxford University Press.

(1978). *On Difficulty, and Other Essays*. Oxford: Oxford University Press.

(1989). *Real Presences: A Secondary City*. London: University of Chicago Press/ Faber & Faber.

Steinhauer, K. and Drury, J. E. (2012). On the early left-anterior negativity (ELAN) in syntax studies. *Brain and Language* 120: 135–62.

Stemberger, J. P. and MacWhinney, B. (1988). Are inflected forms stored in the lexicon. In M. Hammond and M. Noonan, eds, *Theoretical Morphology: Approaches in Modern Linguistics*, pp. 101–16. San Diego, CA: Academic Press.

Stern, C. and Stern, W. (1907). *Die Kindersprache [Children's Language]*. Reprinted by Kessinger Publishing LLC (2010).

Stone, T. and Davies, M. K. (2012). Theoretical issues in cognitive psychology. In N. Braisby and A. Gellatly, eds, *Cognitive Psychology*, pp. 639–79. Oxford: Oxford University Press.

Stowe, L. (1986). Evidence for online gap location. *Language and cognitive processes* 1: 227–45.

Street, J. and Dabrowska, E. (2014). Lexically specific knowledge and individual differences in adult native speakers' processing of the English passive. *Applied Psycholinguistics* 35: 97–118.

Sussman, R. S. and Sedivy, J. C. (2003). The time-course of processing syntactic dependencies: Evidence from eye movements. *Language and Cognitive Processes* 18: 143–61.

Sutton, M., Lukyanenko, C. and Lidz, J. (2011). The onset of Principle C at 30 months: The role of vocabulary, syntactic development, and processing efficiency. In N. Danis, K. Mesh and H. Sung, eds, *Proceedings of the 35th Boston University Conference on Language Development*, pp. 577–98. Somerville, MA: Cascadilla Press.

Swain, M. (1985). Communicative competence: Some roles of comprehensible input and comprehensible output in its development. In S. Gass and C. Madden, eds, *Input in Second Language Acquisition*, pp. 235–53. Rowley, MA: Newberry House.

Sweet, H. (1899). *The Practical Study of Languages*. London: Dent.

Syed, M. (2011). *Bounce: The Myth of Talent and the Power of Practice*. London: Fourth Estate.

Szabolcsi, A. and Zwarts, F. (1993). Weak islands and an algebraic semantics for scope taking. *Natural Language Semantics* 1 (3): 235–84.

Talmy, L. (1985). Lexicalization patterns: Semantic structure in lexical forms. In T. Shopen, ed., *Language Typology and Syntactic Description*, vol. 3: *Grammatical Categories and the Lexicon*, pp. 57–149. New York: Cambridge University Press.

(2000). *Toward a Cognitive Semantics: Typology and Process in Concept Structuring*, vol. 2. Cambridge, MA: MIT Press.

Tchernichovski, O. and Marcus, G. (2014). Vocal learning beyond imitation: Mechanisms of adaptive vocal development in songbirds and human infants. *Current Opinion in Neurobiology* 28: 42–7.

Teodorescu, A. (2006). Adjective ordering restrictions revisited. In D. Baumer, D. Montero and S. Scanlon, eds, *Proceedings of the 25th West Coast Conference on Linguistics*, pp. 399–407. Somerville, MA: Cascadilla Press.

Theakston, A. L. (2004). The role of entrenchment in children's and adults' performance on grammaticality judgment tasks. *Cognitive Development* 19: 15–34.

Thomas, E. (2010). *Sociophonetics: An Introduction*. London: Palgrave.

Thompson, E., Palacios, A. and Varela, F. J. (2002). Ways of coloring: Comparative color vision as a case study for cognitive science. In A. Noë and E. Thompson, eds, *Vision and Mind: Selected Readings in the Philosophy of Perception*. Cambridge, MA: MIT Press.

Thornton, R. (1994). Why continuity? In A. Brugos, L. Micciulla and C. Smith, eds, *Proceedings of the 28th Boston University Conference on Language Development*, pp. 620–32. Somerville, MA: Cascadilla Press.

Tillyard, E. M. (2011). *The Elizabethan World Picture*. London: Random House. (Original edition 1959.)

Tomasello, M. (1992). *First Verbs: A Case Study of Early Grammatical Development*. Cambridge: Cambridge University Press.

Travis, L. (1984). Parameters and effects of word order variation. PhD dissertation, Massachusetts Institute of Technology.

(1991). Parameters of phrase structure and verb-second phenomena. In R. Freidin, ed., *Principles and Parameters in Comparative Grammar*, pp. 339–364. Cambridge, MA: MIT Press.

Trudgill, P. (2001). Received Pronunciation: Sociolinguistic aspects. *Studia Anglica Posnaniensia* 36: 3–13.

(2008). The historical sociolinguistics of elite accent change: On why RP is not disappearing. *Studia Anglica Posnaniensia* 44: 3–11.

Truss, L. (2003). *Eats, Shoots and Leaves*. London: Profile Books.

Ullman, M. T. (2001a). The declarative/procedural model of the lexicon and grammar. *Journal of Psycholinguistic Research* 30: 37–69.

(2001b). The neural basis of lexicon and grammar in first and second language: The declarative/procedural model. *Bilingualism: Language and Cognition* 4: 105–22.

(2004). Contributions of memory circuits to language: The declarative/procedural model. *Cognition* 931: 231–70.

Ullman, M. T. and Pierpont, E. I. (2005). Specific language impairment is not specific to language: The procedural deficit hypothesis. *Cortex* 41: 399–433.

van Urk, C. and Richards, N. (2013). Two components of long-distance extraction: Successive cyclicity in Dinka. *Lingbuzz* 001766. http://ling.auf.net/lingbuzz/001766

Van Valin, R. D. and La Polla, J. R. (1997). *Syntax: Structure, Meaning and Function*. Cambridge: Cambridge University Press.

Vardon-Smith, G. M. (2014). Safety and security: Staying safe in a humanitarian conflict. In J. Ryan et al., eds, *Conflict and Catastrophe Medicine: A Practical Guide*, pp. 341–360. London: Springer.

Varga, E. (2005). Lexical V-to-I raising in Late Modern English. *GG@G (Generative Grammar in Geneva)* 4: 261–85.

Vargha-Khadem, F., Watkins, K., Alcock, K., Fletcher, P. and Passingham, R. (1995). Praxic and nonverbal cognitive deficits in a large family with a genetically transmitted speech and language disorder. *Proceedings of the National Academy of Sciences* 92: 930–3.

Vidal, J. (2014). Why we are losing a world of languages. *The Guardian.* www.theguardian.com/environment/2014/jun/08/why-we-are-losing-a-world-of-languages

Vitevich, M. S. (1997). The neighborhood characteristics of malapropisms. *Language and Speech* 40: 211–28.

de Vries, M. (2009). On multidominance and linearization. *Biolinguistics* 3: 344–403.

Vulanović, R. (2010). The rise and fall of periphrastic *do* in affirmative declaratives. *Journal of Quantitative Linguistics* 12: 1–31.

Walker, J. (2012). *Variation in Linguistic Systems*. London: Routledge.

Wang, W. S.-Y. (1969). Competing changes as a cause of residue. *Language* 45: 9–25.

Warner, A. R. (2005). Why *do* dove: Evidence for register variation in Early Modern English negatives. *Language Variation and Change* 17: 257–80.

Warner, N., Butler, L. and Geary, Q. (2016). *Mutsun–English English–Mutsun Dictionary: mutsun-inkiS inkiS-mutsun riica pappel.* Language Documentation & Conservation Special Publication no. 11. Honolulu: University of Hawai'i Press. http://hdl.handle.net/10125/24679

Warren, P. (2013). *Introducing Psycholinguistics*. Cambridge: Cambridge University Press.

Wasow, T. (2015). Ambiguity avoidance is overrated. In S. Winckler, ed., *Ambiguity: Language and Communication*, pp. 29–47. Berlin: De Gruyter.

Weijerman, M. E. and de Winter, J. P. (2010). Clinical practice: The care of children with Down Syndrome. *European Journal of Pediatrics* 169: 1445–52.

Wellman, H. M., Cross, D. and Watson, J. (2001). Meta-analysis of theory-of-mind development: The truth about false belief. *Child Development* 72: 655–84.

Werker, J. and Lalonde, C. E. (1988). Cross-language speech perception: Initial capabilities and developmental change. *Developmental Psychology* 24: 672–83.

Werker, J. and Tees, R. C. (1984). Cross-language speech perception: Evidence for perceptual reorganization during the first year of life. *Infant Behavior and Development* 7: 49–63.

Wexler, K. (1994). Optional infinitives, head movement and the economy of derivations. In D. Lightfoot and N. Hornstein, eds, *Verb Movement*, pp. 305–50. Cambridge: Cambridge University Press.

(1998). Very early parameter-setting and the unique checking constraint: A new explanation of the optional infinitive stage. *Lingua* 106: 23–79.

Wexler, P. (1990). *The Schizoid Nature of Modern Hebrew: A Slavic Language in Search of a Semitic Past*. Mediterranean Language and Culture Monograph Series, vol. 4. Wiesbaden: Otto Harrassowitz.

Whaley, L. J. (1998). *Introduction to Typology: The Unity and Diversity of Languages*. Thousand Oaks, CA: SAGE Publications.

White, L. (1987). Against comprehensible input: The input hypothesis and the development of second-language competence. *Applied Linguistics* 8: 95–110.

(1996). Universal Grammar and second language acquisition: Current trends and new directions. In W. Ritchie and T. Bhatia, eds, *Handbook of Language Acquisition*. New York: Academic Press.

(2003). *Second Language Acquisition and Universal Grammar.* Cambridge: Cambridge University Press.

Wiggins, G. (2013). Computer models of music cognition. In P. Rebuschat, ed., *Language and Music as Cognitive Systems*, pp. 169–88. Oxford: Oxford University Press.

Wilshire, C. E. (2008). Cognitive neuropsychological approaches to word production in aphasia: Beyond boxes and arrows. *Aphasiology* 22: 1019–53.

Winer, G. A., Cottrell, J. E., Gregg, V., Fournier, J. S. and Bica, L. A. (2002). Fundamentally misunderstanding visual perception: Adults' belief in visual emissions. *American Psychologist* 57: 417–24.

Winograd, T. (1983). *Language as a Cognitive Process*, vol. I: *Syntax.* Reading, MA: Addison-Wesley.

de Winter, J. C. F. and Dodou, D. (2010). Five-point Likert items: T-Test versus Mann–Whitney–Wilcoxon. *Practical Assessment, Research and Evaluation* 15 (11): 1–7.

Wundt, W. (1874). *Grundzüge der Physiologischen Psychologie [Principles of Physiological Psychology].* Leipzig: Engelmann.

Xia, L., Murray, A., Zheng, D., Liu, F., Ye, X. and Ning, G. (2012). Cardiovascular system modeling (editorial). *Computational and Mathematical Methods in Medicine* 2012: 583172.

Yngve, V. H. (1960). A model and a hypothesis for language structure. *Proceedings of the American Philosophical Society* 104: 444–66.

(1986). *Linguistics as a Science.* Bloomington, IN: Indiana University Press.

Zhang, Y., Kuhl, P. K., Imada, T., Kotani, M. and Mohkura, Y. (2005). Effects of language experience: Neural commitment to language-specific auditory patterns *Neuroimage* 26: 703–20.

Zubizarreta, M. L. (1998). *Prosody, Focus and Word Order.* Cambridge, MA: MIT Press.

Zukav, G. (2001). *The Dancing Wu Li Masters: An Overview of the New Physics.* New York: Perennial Classics.

Zwicky, A. M. (1978/79). Classical malapropisms. *Language Sciences* 1: 339–49.

Index